PLANNING

FOR

SOCIAL WELFARE:

Issues,
Models,
and Tasks

PLANNING

FOR

SOCIAL WELFARE:
Issues,
Models,
and Tasks

NEIL GILBERT
University of California at Berkeley

HARRY SPECHT
University of California at Berkeley

Prentice-Hall, Inc., Englewood Cliffs, New Jersey 07632

Library of Congress Cataloging in Publication Data

Main entry under title:

Planning for social welfare.
    Includes bibliographical references and index.
    1. Social policy—Addresses, essays, lectures.
2. Public welfare—Addresses, essays, lectures.
3. Community organization—Addresses, essays, lectures.
I. Gilbert, Neil II. Specht, Harry.
HV40.P58   361.2   76-56130
ISBN 0-13-679555-2

© 1977 by Prentice-Hall, Inc., Englewood Cliffs, N.J. 07632

Printed in the United States of America

10 9 8 7 6 5 4

PRENTICE-HALL INTERNATIONAL, INC., *London*
PRENTICE-HALL OF AUSTRALIA PTY. LIMITED, *Sydney*
PRENTICE-HALL OF CANADA, LTD., *Toronto*
PRENTICE-HALL OF INDIA PRIVATE LIMITED, *New Delhi*
PRENTICE-HALL OF JAPAN, INC., *Tokyo*
PRENTICE-HALL OF SOUTHEAST ASIA PTE. LTD., *Singapore*
WHITEHALL BOOKS LIMITED, *Wellington, New Zealand*

FOR

ARTHUR AND GERTRUDE
CHARLES AND SARA
JOSEPH AND KATHRYN

Contents

Acknowledgments

During the preparation of this book a host of friends and colleagues provided us with encouragement and advice. A book of readings is, after all, the product of many labors, primary among which are those of its contributors—to whom we owe a special debt for making this book possible. We are also indebted to Ed Stanford, of Prentice-Hall, Inc., for his friendly support and gentle persistence in guiding this project through to publication.

Richard S. Bolan of Boston College School of Social Work, David Hardcastle of the University of Kansas School of Social Work, Alfred J. Kahn of Columbia University School of Social Work, and Robert Perlman of the Florence Heller Graduate School for Advanced Studies in Social Welfare, Brandeis University, reviewed an early draft of our ideas for this book. Their thoughtful criticisms and suggestions are gratefully acknowledged.

Peter Ching-yung Lee provided cheerful and diligent assistance as our bibliographer, file manager, and locator of lost authors. Marcy McGaugh, our typist on this and other ventures, once again displayed her almost magical talents for transforming scribbled tablets into neat and orderly manuscripts. On the home front, our families persevered in good spirits.

Finally we would like to take this opportunity to acknowledge our appreciation of Dean Milton Chernin who, after 30 years in office, will be retiring from the Deanship in the year that this volume is published. During his tenure Dean Chernin built and led the School of Social Welfare at the University of California, Berkeley with great skill and dedication. We have benefited from his administrative dexterity and enjoyed the personal encouragement he has given to us as teachers and scholars.

NEIL GILBERT
HARRY SPECHT

School of Social Welfare
University of California, Berkeley

Introduction

Planning is the conscious attempt to solve problems and control the course of future events by foresight, systematic thinking, investigation, and the exercise of value preferences in choosing among alternative lines of action. According to this definition almost everybody engages in some form of planning, and there are numerous settings and specific ends to which the act of planning may be applied. This book is about the kinds of planning conducted by professionals through public and publicly sanctioned voluntary organizations in the interests of community well-being. It is planning not for private profit and individual advancement but for the public good.

There is a wide range of opinion about what constitutes the "public good"; at one extreme it has been expressed as "What is good for General Motors is good for the country," a conception of the public good that is somewhat removed from the perspective of this book. At the other extreme, communalists believe that the "public good" is reducible to a concrete plan for the entire society that will beat a tune to which all can march together. This conception requires one to adopt the view that "each man's joy is joy to me; each man's dream is my own"—an uncomplicated and appealing sentiment. But planning for social welfare must be based on a conception of the public good that allows for greater complexity in social relationships and more contradictions in social values. Urban American society is composed of racial, religious, ethnic, educational, occupational, financial, age, and other social categories that form the bases for group interests. It would surely be a pleasanter and more gentle world if groups like General Motors were able to plan according to their lights without interfering with the interests of others. And while it may lack a certain excitement, the conception of society as a harmony of human interests is certainly inviting. As Myrdal observes, "We want to believe that what we hold to be desirable for society is desirable for all its members." [1] If this were actually the case, instances of social conflict would dwindle to an insignificant number. However, when many disparate groups plan to maximize their welfare in the complex and highly interdependent communities of modern society, their efforts frequently intrude upon others holding alternative views of what constitutes a good life and who deserves its fruits. Hence, decisions on housing, transportation, building, communal facilities, and so forth are usually hot issues on the community agenda. For example, people in business may want transportation and parking facilities that will enhance potential for trade; residents will be concerned about space, quiet, and safety; environmentalists undoubtedly will opt to preserve things as they are; religious and ethnic groups will want either separate or integrated

[1] Gunnar Myrdal, *Value in Social Theory*, ed. Paul Streeten (London: Routledge and Kegan Paul, 1958), p. 137.

1

facilities as the case may be. Under these circumstances there is an obvious need for collective intervention and some regulation of individual and group interests, not only to restrain the "unsocial" planning that may occur, but also to structure, moderate, and direct the decision-making process. It is in this context that the professional planner is called upon to help define the nature of the problem, survey the resources needed for alternative solutions, consider the value preferences attached to these alternatives, develop programs, and assess the extent to which program results match expectations.

PROFESSIONAL PLANNERS

Professional planners are employed in diverse functional areas. Indeed it would be hard to find any area of community decision making that does not have a planning specialization associated with it. Thus there are transportation planners, water resources planners, new town planners, health and hospital planners, and social welfare planners, to name a few.

This wide range of functions was formally recognized by one of the major organizations of professional planners in the 1966 *Report* of the American Institute of Planners Committee on Restatement of Institute Purposes.[2] The committee rejected a conception of the profession limited to city land-use planning and physical design. The scope of planning, in the committee's view, should include social and economic concerns:

While, in the past, planners have been primarily engaged in the preparation of plans for the physical development of urban areas, there is a definite trend toward involvement of increasing numbers of planners in planning programs for larger areal units (counties, regions, states).

There is a clear trend toward emergence of comprehensive planning which includes social and economic development as activities integral with planning for the physical development of areas. A significant number of Institute members are engaged in these activities.

Relatively speaking, the number of individuals practicing the full range of the planning process is declining. Increasing numbers of those engaged in the practice of planning are becoming specialists in various areas of planning work such as: economic studies, transportation planning, or urban renewal; municipal, state or regional jurisdictions; and physical, social or economic development.[3]

The committee's view of the scope of the profession can be described

---

[2] American Institute of Planners, *Report of the Committee on Restatement of Institute Purposes* (Washington, D.C:. American Institute of Planners, 1966). The American Institute of Planners (AIP) is one of two major national organizations of professional planners; the American Society of Planning Officials (ASPO) is the other.

[3] *Ibid.*

along three dimensions as depicted in Figure 1.[4] The first is a process dimension. Here, the sequential phases of the planning process are described in a varying number of steps.[5] The steps themselves may provide bases for specialization within the profession. For example, some planners deal primarily with analytic tasks such as problem analysis and evaluation; others deal with administrative tasks like program development and implementation. The second dimension has to do with geographic scope, and here too, the different geographic units described may be perceived as practice specializations. The third dimension is functional area. The three broad categories of functional specializations listed in Figure 1 can be further subdivided.[6] For example, social planning might have subspecializations like social welfare, education, and public health.

The wide-ranging and open-ended character of the dimensions described in Figure 1 suggests that the boundaries of the planning profession are not distinct. They have been expanding continuously during this century. The majority of the members of the American Institute of Planners (AIP) and American Society of Planning Officials (ASPO) who take the label "planner" as their primary professional identification—are associated with city and regional planning; by and large most of the functions they carry out are related to physical design and locational decisions. There are many other professionals engaged in planning who are not known as "planners," but by a professional title commonly used in their functional field. Planners in social welfare, for example, are likely to be known as "social workers" because that is consonant with their educational degrees and agency positions; health planners, similarly, may carry titles that are in line with their educational and professional credentials in medicine and public health.

The boundaries of professional planning have expanded with the growth of urban communities and the increasing public responsibility for community welfare. Planning has its roots in city planning. The profession began as a social reform movement in the latter part of the nineteenth

4 Figure 1 is adapted from Louis B. Wetmore, "Preparing the Profession For Its Changing Role," *Urban Planning in Transition,* Ernest Erber, Ed. (New York: Grossman Publishers, 1970), p. 236.
5 We will discuss various approaches to the conceptualiaztion of process in Part I.
6 We should note that these broad functional specializations often overlap. Physical planning, such as for highway corridor placement, generally has social consequences. And the line between economic and social planning is frequently a matter of debate. For discussion of these issues, see Margaret S. Gordon, *The Economics of Welfare Policies* (New York: Columbia University Press, 1963); Alfred J. Kahn, *Theory and Practice of Social Planning* (New York: Russell Sage Foundation, 1969), pp. 1–27; Marshall Kaplan, Gans, and Kahn, *Social Characteristics of Neighborhoods as Indicators of the Effects of Highway Improvements* (Washington, D.C.: U.S. Department of Transportation, 1972); and the reports by Goffredo Zappa and R. Khafisov, "Concepts of Social Planning: Social Planning and Economic Planning, Similarities and Differences," in *The Problems and Methods of Social Planning,* Report of the Expert Group (Dubrovnik: United Nations, 1963), pp. 21–37.

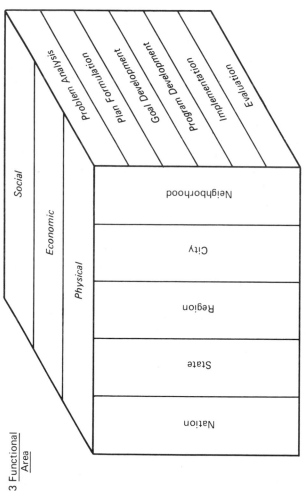

FIGURE 1. The Dimension of Process, Geographic Scope, and Functional Area in Planning.

century; at first it was concerned mostly with land-use control and keeping urban development free of politics. The spirit of the movement was essentially rationalistic and utopian; the thrust was toward good government that would utilize science and expertise to design the City Beautiful.[7] Physical planning became an integral part of urban development. By 1964 over 90 percent of the cities with a population in excess of 10,000 had a public planning agency.[8]

Proposals and experiments to combine physical and social planning were introduced in the 1920s through the efforts of the Regional Planning Association of America, and were backed by the talents of men such as Lewis Mumford and Clarence Stein. However, these efforts did not alter the planning profession's overriding concern with physical development.[9] The major stimuli for economic and social planning in the United States were to develop later during the New Deal administration, World War II, and the Kennedy and Johnson administrations. As the realm of public responsibility for planning extended from city design, to economic programs, to social and ecological concerns, so have the parameters of the profession enlarged to include professionals trained in a wide range of disciplines to deal with a variety of institutional concerns.

These trends are reflected in the growth and current membership interests of the major organizations of planning professionals. Summarizing several studies of these organizations, Kaufman notes that in 1974 the American Institute of Planners had 10,000 members and the American Society of Planning Officials 11,000, compared to memberships of 1,000 and 1,700 respectively twenty years earlier.[10] Fewer than twenty universities offered masters degrees in planning in 1954 compared to over sixty in 1974. Kaufman estimates that in 1974 there were approximately 11,750 governmental planning bodies in the United States and approximately one-quarter of them had professional planning staffs.[11]

Kaufman notes, too, that over the last fifteen years planning professionals' interests in social service and social welfare have increased consid-

---

7 For details on these historical developments see Kahn, *Theory and Practice of Social Planning*, pp. 23–24; Melvin Webber, "Comprehensive Planning and Social Responsibility," in *Urban Planning and Social Policy*, Bernard J. Frieden and Robert Morris, eds. (New York: Basic Books, Inc., 1968), pp. 9–10; William Alonso, "Critics, Planners, and Urban Renewal," *Urban Renewal: The Record and the Controversy* (Cambridge, Mass.: The MIT Press, 1966), pp. 437–44; and Donald A. Schon and Thomas E. Nutt, "Endemic Turbulence: The Future for Planning Education," in *Planning in America: Learning from Turbulence*, David R. Godschalk, ed. (Washington, D.C.: American Institute of Planners, 1974), pp. 181–86.

8 Francine F. Rabinovitz, *City Politics and Planning* (New York: Atherton Press, 1969), p. 3.

9 For an historical account of these efforts, see Roy Lubove, *Community Planning in the 1920's: The Contribution of the Regional Planning Association of America* (Pittsburgh: University of Pittsburgh Press, 1963).

10 Jerome L. Kaufman, "Contemporary Planning Practice: State of the Art," in *Planning in America: Learning from Turbulence*, Godschalk, ed., pp. 113–14.

11 *Ibid.*, p. 111.

erably. However, the studies he cities also indicate that actually only a small percentage of professional planners are interested in work in these areas. For example, a 1973 study of ASPO membership revealed that land-use planning and environmental design were still the primary areas of interest to most planners, even to those under age twenty-five, although more planners in this age group were interested in social concerns compared to older planners.[12]

This is not to say that planning is highly restricted in areas such as social services and social welfare; rather, it suggests that much of the planning in these fields is done by social welfare practitioners who are not identified with the planning profession and are not enrolled in AIP or ASPO. Further, these findings suggest that there is considerable room in professional planning for those interested in social welfare.

SOCIAL WELFARE PLANNING [13]

Historically, planning functions in social work and social welfare have been subsumed under the practice heading of "community organization." The social work literature on "community organization" has usually emphasized the sociopolitical aspects of the planning process. "Social welfare planning," the term we will use here, is of recent vintage; only in the last ten years has social welfare planning begun to extend and strengthen its repertoire of technical skills, particularly in such areas as needs assessment and evaluative research, to complement the sociopolitical skills of community organizing. Interestingly, during this same period, professional planning, as described in the previous section, has become more attentive to the sociopolitical aspects of planning.

Social welfare planning originated from several practical programs that were generated by two nineteenth-century social movements: the Charity Organization Societies and the settlements. The Charity Organization Society movement, which began in the 1880s, was an early attempt to achieve some degree of rational order in social welfare, and it immediately preceded initial efforts at social welfare planning. The organizers of the Charity Organization Society believed it to be a solution to the chaos of indiscriminate giving of charitable funds, fraud, duplication, and other alleged evils of benevolent charity.

The reformers associated with the settlement houses, another important social movement of the era, based many of their programs on social action to promote social legislation aimed at relieving distress among the working

[12] *Ibid.*, pp. 119–22.
[13] The discussion under the next three headings is based on a summary and revision of material in Neil Gilbert and Harry Specht, "Social Planning and Community Organization," *Encyclopedia of Social Work,* John B. Turner, ed. (New York: National Association of Social Workers, 1977).

classes. These settlement reformers (e.g., Jane Addams, Lillian Wald, and Florence Kelly) engaged in political action to achieve change through social legislation. Workmen's compensation laws, the White House Conference on Children, child labor laws, the establishment of the Children's Bureau, and some of the social experiments of the New Deal can be attributed in part to the actions and spirit of the settlement movement.

Community welfare councils and councils of social agencies were first organized in 1908. Continuing in the efforts begun by the Charity Organization Society movement, they pressed for efficiency, centralization, high standards of service, and specialization within the voluntary social welfare field, and for effective leadership in joint planning. These goals have persisted in community councils up to the present. The term "community organization," first used by American sociologists and adult educators before World War I, was adopted by practitioners in these agencies.

World War I gave great impetus to the proliferation of "war chests," which were centralized fund-raising agencies to achieve efficient use of funds and to coordinate services. These organizations heralded what was to become the community chests and council of social agencies movement, the first large-scale attempt at overall community planning and control of welfare funds.

In these first decades of the twentieth century, the primary function of social welfare planning practice was to allocate funds among social welfare agencies. In the 1930s, with the shift of welfare responsibilities from voluntary agencies to the newly established public welfare bureaucracies, and from local to state and federal agencies, social welfare planning efforts, along with all the rest of private philanthropy, focussed on the community problems that were left to voluntary action: counseling and guidance, health, recreation and group services, and adult education. The composition and structure of social welfare planning agencies reflected these concerns; the agencies drew their leadership from local elites, philanthropists, and professionals in private agencies. In this period the reform tradition of social work was overshadowed by the preeminent social casework practice, which had become markedly influenced by psychoanalytic concepts.

There were, in these early years, several large-scale attempts at community improvement and social change outside of the health and welfare councils. In 1917, for example, the short-lived Cincinnati Social Unit Project demonstrated that residents of neighborhoods could be organized to plan and operate their own social service programs and serve as a political force for change.[14] Another effort, the Chicago Area Project, begun

14 Sidney Dillick, *Community Organization for Neighborhood Development: Past and Present* (New York: William Morrow and Co., 1953); and Anatole Shaffer, "The Cincinnati Social Unit Experiment: 1917–1919," *Social Service Review*, 45:2 (June 1971), 159–72.

in 1934 by the State of Illinois, was an innovative program to help residents of slum areas organize to prevent juvenile delinquency.[15] The organization of the Back of the Yards movement in Chicago by Saul Alinsky in the early 1940s, which is reported in his book, *Reveille for Radicals,* was another significant landmark in the development of sociopolitical aspects of planning.[16]

By the end of the 1950s there were over 2,000 community chests and health and welfare councils operating in the United States and Canada; these agencies were responsible for dispersing approximately a half billion dollars of voluntary funds.[17] This, of course, represented only a part of the total of voluntary welfare activity. And by that time federal and state involvement in health and welfare programs had soared to astronomical proportions. By 1960, the federal government alone was spending close to twenty-five billion dollars on social welfare compared to less than one billion dollars in 1929.[18]

As the institution of social welfare grew larger, social work became a distinct profession having major responsibility for management and planning. Social welfare planning was concerned not only with allocating funds within the voluntary social welfare field, but also with assessing the need for services and coordinating efforts among a wide variety of social-service providers in public and private agencies, at local, state, and federal levels, and in different areas such as family services, group work, and public assistance. As social work became a large and complex business, the management of external relations of social service agencies became an increasingly important professional activity.

The civil rights movement of the late 1950s and early 1960s and major federal programs in housing, urban renewal, and the War on Poverty dramatically broadened the field of social welfare planning. Many people concerned with social welfare had come to believe that the New Deal programs had failed to cope effectively with poverty, dependency, ghettoes, discrimination, and unemployment.

Several new ways of organizing to enlist community support in carrying out change developed in this period. The 1954 amendments to the Housing Act of 1949, for example, required citizen participation in the preparation of "workable programs." At the time, physical planners considered this innovation to be a major stumbling block to the implementation of their objectives. Until then, city planning had been more concerned with short-

15 Solomon Kobrin, "The Chicago Area Project—A 25-Year Assessment," *Annals of the American Academy of Political and Social Science,* 322 (March 1959), 19–29.
16 Saul D. Alinksy, *Reveille for Radicals* (Chicago: University of Chicago Press, 1946).
17 United Way of America, *1974–75 Annual Report* (Washington, D.C.: United Way of America, 1975).
18 Alfred M. Skolnick and Sophie R. Dales, "Social Welfare Expenditures, Fiscal Year 1974," *Social Security Bulletin,* 38:1 (January 1975), 3–18.

run, locational urban problems that involved land use and industrial interests and with long-range formulation of a comprehensive master plan. The "social" goals of planning were frequently dictated by economic and political interests, and the function of the social welfare planner was perceived to be that of making goals more palatable to an ever more resistant community. Human relations personnel—intergroup relations workers, social workers, and psychologists—were sometimes included as an afterthought to deal with the "social components" of planning. Some other significant programs of that period were the comprehensive planning models supported by the President's Committee on Juvenile Delinquency and the "gray area" projects of the Ford Foundation, the Community Action Programs of the Office of Economic Opportunity, and grassroots and self-help programs. In many of these attempts at social welfare planning, city planners, community organizers, and the personnel of social welfare agencies were brought together to undertake joint planning of programs in close cooperation with grassroots citizens' groups. Title II of the Demonstration Cities and Metropolitan Development Act of 1966, which established the Model Cities Program, extended some of these newer ideas in citizen participation, coordination, and planning to model neighborhoods.

However, the emphasis on grassroots groups was short-lived, and in the late 1960s and early 1970s the focus of social welfare planning shifted. The Community Action Programs of the War on Poverty had emphasized the value of citizen participation. But the 1966 legislation establishing the Model Cities Program called for a rapprochement between grassroots groups and established political leadership; it stated unequivocally that local implementation must be controlled by the local governing body of the city or county. Although the Model Cities Program had been conceived in the spirit of the community action program, this difference in legislative goals was to become more pronounced. By 1970 there had been a major shift of planning authority and resources away from neighborhoods and resident organizations to the chief executive of the city.[19]

As the precursor of federal revenue sharing, the Model Cities Program was the first attempt to disperse power from the federal to the local level and to centralize it at the local level. The costs and benefits of these changes are still not evident.

One trend, however, is obvious. Revenue-sharing programs will compel state and city governments to assume primary decision-making responsibility for setting priorities and allocating federal block grants among competing needs and interests. That will require a far greater generalized planning capacity at the local level than currently exists in most places.

19 Neil Gilbert, Armin Rosenkranz, and Harry Specht, "Dialectics of Social Planning," *Social Work*, 18:2 (March 1973), 78–86.

In the next decade, the shape of social welfare planning practice will be influenced substantially by the ways local governments respond to this need for increased planning capacity.

THE RELATIONSHIP OF SOCIAL WELFARE PLANNING
TO OTHER SOCIAL WORK METHODS

From a methodological point of view social welfare planners seem to have more in common with professionals in other fields who are engaged in planning and organizing, such as trade unionists, politicians, and city and regional planners than they do with social workers who provide direct services to individuals, families, and small groups. This difference in methodologies has been a source of great strain in the social work profession for decades; for if these methodologies are so different, one might ask, what unites social work practitioners in one profession?

Before the 1960s, most writings on social welfare planning came under the rubric of "community organization" and were influenced by efforts to identify this practice with the profession as defined by the traditional parameters of social casework and social group work. The task of reconciliation between social welfare planning practice and the prevailing images of professional social workers was complicated by the diverse views held concerning the appropriate range of activities encompassed by, and the central purpose of, planning and organizing in social welfare settings.[20] When formulated rather narrowly as "intergroup work," the range of community organization activities was most analogous to the post-World War II mainstream of social work practice. The "intergroup" concept of practice was given primacy by Newstetter, to whom "the community" was, essentially, an association of interacting groups. According to Newstetter, the community organization worker aims to achieve mutually satisfactory relationships among the groups.[21] The important feature of this concept is that intergroup activities are an extension of social group work and, as such, represent the social work practice of community organization, which was only marginally related to social welfare planning.

An alternative view, expressed by Arthur Dunham, among others, defined more broadly the practice of social work and the place of social welfare planning and organizing activities within the profession. Dunham thought that social work practice should encompass all relevant social

---

[20] For a more detailed discussion of these historical developments, see Meyer Schwartz, "Community Organization," in Harry L. Lurie, ed., *Encyclopedia of Social Work* (New York: National Association of Social Workers, 1965), pp. 177–90.

[21] Wilber I. Newstetter, "The Social Inter-Group Work Process: How Does It Differ from Social Group Work Process?" in *Community Organization: Its Nature and Setting,* Donald S. Howard, ed. (New York: National Association of Social Workers, 1947), pp. 19–28.

agency work; it would include, therefore, the major professional functions required to maintain social work agencies such as planning, administration, and coordination, as well as direct-service activities.[22] While Dunham did not reject the intergroup work process, he did give equal attention to the *technical* orientation of social welfare planning. This wider view of the range of practice activities was a more accurate and more inclusive representation of the work in which the social welfare organizer-planner was actually engaged; it was also a more difficult formulation of practice to reconcile neatly with the prevailing views of social work than the intergroup work conception.

As there were different views of the appropriate range of activities, so there were different ideas about the central purpose of social welfare planning. The central purpose of the practice varied according to two general objectives: (1) integration/capacity building, and (2) program development/social reform. Integration/capacity-building objectives fit comfortably with a *process orientation* to practice, and they rely heavily on the intergroup work conception of method. Program development/social reform objectives are supported by a *technical orientation* to practice, which relies on analytic concepts useful for program evaluation, and policy and organizational analysis.

Most writers of the period between 1939 and 1960 take into account both sets of objectives but emphasize one or the other. The Lane Report of 1939 was a landmark document that stressed program development and reformist goals as the primary objectives of practice. In that report, integration/capacity-building objectives were considered to be secondary.[23] This position was supported by Dunham and others.

In contrast, Pray and Newstetter, writing in 1947, gave primary emphasis to integration/capacity-building objectives. Murray Ross, author of a 1955 definitive text on practice, reinforced Pray and Newstetter. Ross defined community organization as a problem-solving process by which

a community identifies its needs or objectives, orders (or ranks) these needs or objectives, finds the resources (internal or external) to deal with these needs . . . takes action in respect to them and in so doing extends and develops cooperative and collaborative attitudes and practices in the community.[24]

For Ross, the most important aspect of this process is the integration/capacity-building objectives, as noted in the final phrase of his definition.

The 1960s marked a turning point in efforts to define the boundaries

22 Arthur Dunham, "What Is the Job of the Community Organization Worker?" *Proceedings of the National Conference of Social Work* (New York: Columbia University Press, 1948), pp. 162–72.

23 Robert Lane, "The Field of Community Organization," *Proceedings of the National Conference of Social Work* (New York: Columbia University Press, 1939), pp. 456–73.

24 Murray Ross, *Community Organization: Theory and Principles* (New York: Harper and Brothers, 1955), p. 39.

of planning and organizing activities in social work. The first important signal for the change came from the generic definition of social work issued by the National Association of Social Workers (NASW) Commission on Practice.[25] Following the broad framework set forth by the commission, the NASW Committee on Community Organization formulated a working definition of practice. Their report, published in 1962, notes that "the practice of community organization is rooted in the values traditionally associated with the practice of social work." [26] In this view, the values, sources of sanction, and knowledge for social welfare planning coincide with those traditionally associated with social work. And the purpose of social welfare planning was said to include, equally both integration/capacity-building and program development/social reform objectives. Thus, the working definition of the Committee on Community Organization put to rest the issues of how, and to what extent, social welfare planning fit into the social work profession.

Taking an expansive view of social welfare planning, the 1962 definition implicitly recognized its wide diversity. That diversity is, perhaps, best captured in Jack Rothman's typology of three models of practice.[27] This work is a cogent summation of the essential characteristics of three basic orientations toward practice: *locality development, social planning,* and *social action. Locality development* emphasizes integration/capacity-building objectives and is typically employed in community development projects and settlement house-sponsored neighborhood self-help programs. The *social planning* approach emphasizes program development objectives through the use of technical problem-solving methods; it is practiced most frequently in health and welfare councils and government planning agencies. *Social action* stresses reformist objectives in behalf of disadvantaged segments of the community; this is the practice orientation of choice for organizations such as civil rights groups, Saul Alinsky's Industrial Areas Foundation projects, and activist community action agencies. These orientations had been identified and given various positions of prominence throughout the debate over the boundaries of social welfare planning dating back to the 1939 Lane Report.

There is one other noteworthy boundaries issue in social welfare planning that has appeared in recent years. This is the question of how wide ranging the boundaries of social welfare planning *ought* to become. Many social welfare planners are employed by organizations such as intergovernmental planning bodies, housing agencies, legislative bodies, and city

[25] NASW Commission on Practice, "Working Definition of Social Work Practice," *Social Work,* 3:2 (April 1958), 5.

[26] NASW Committee on Community Organization, *Defining Community Organization Practice* (New York: National Association of Social Workers, 1962), p. 7 (mimeographed).

[27] Jack Rothman, "Three Models of Community Organization Practice," *Social Work Practice, 1968* (New York: Columbia University Press, 1968), pp. 16–47.

planning agencies. These work environments present social welfare planners with opportunities to extend the boundaries of their practice to include economic development and the planning of health and medical care systems. Just as psychiatric social workers of an earlier time were tempted to identify themselves with the prestigious physicians in their field of practice, so social welfare planners compete with and wish to achieve the social and professional recognition of their colleagues in other professions.

An issue that arises from this situation is the extent to which the social work profession should and can maintain some degree of precision in its conception of the practice of social welfare planning. That is, to what extent should the profession's claim to expertise and authority be for planning *in social work and social welfare,* and to what extent for social planning *in general?* There is another side to this issue—namely, to what extent is the expertise of city planners, public policy makers, and public health professionals applicable to social work and social welfare? These issues are likely to become more prominent as methodological developments in social welfare planning converge with those of other planners.

EDUCATION FOR SOCIAL WELFARE PLANNING

The training of social welfare planners in schools of social work over the last decade has become much more diverse and technically sophisticated; it has grown dramatically in size, as well. The diversity in social welfare planning education was encouraged by the great ferment and change that has stirred the social work profession since the 1960s. The profession's orientation towards practice was profoundly affected by: (1) the civil rights movement, which was part of a general revolution in human relations; (2) by the evolution of national programs, such as the War on Poverty and Model Cities, that were directed at producing community change; and (3) by the growing concern at the start of the 1970s with questions of institutional inequality.[28] Schools of social work responded by experimenting with and reorganizing their curricula to address these developments. Many training programs that were based on the traditional casework-group-work-community organization trinity gave way to new curricula patterns, some of which emphasized the training of social work "generalists" versed in casework as well as methods of social welfare planning. Other programs focused on training for the direct and indirect services, or clinical and social change tracks.[29] Social work programs for training in social welfare

[28] For a more thorough analysis of the impact of these changes on practice, see Alfred J. Kahn, "Do Social Services Have a Future in New York City?" *City Almanac,* 5 (February 1971).

[29] These various curriculum models are reviewed in Neil Gilbert and Harry Specht, "The Incomplete Profession," *Social Work,* 19:6 (November 1974), 665–74.

planning are now listed under such headings as: Organization, Planning and Administration; Community Planning; and Social Policy and Community Service.

The growth in the number of such programs reflects, in part, the rapid increase in the total number of social work students at the Masters level, which almost doubled to approximately 13,000 students between 1965 and 1970. During that period the proportion of social work students in social welfare planning-community organization concentrations rose from 1 percent to almost 10 percent of total enrollments, and many others were receiving some social welfare planning-community organization training in generalist programs.[30]

There have been many qualitative changes in the training of social welfare planners over the last decade. The incorporation of social science theory has begun to yield propositions for course material that bear on practice issues. The teaching of social welfare policy has developed more analytic focus, examining the basic elements of program design rather than offering a series of program descriptions. And courses dealing with the economics of social welfare are increasingly becoming a part of the social welfare planning curriculum. Among the most significant developments is the introduction of computer technology and advanced research methods in many training programs. Overall, the most recent developments in training for social welfare planning address the analytic tasks in the problem-solving process. This trend complements the strong focus on preparation for handling interactional tasks, involving group dynamics and interpersonal relations, which traditionally had characterized social work training for social welfare planning.[31]

PLAN OF THIS BOOK

This book was planned to serve a number of objectives in the education of social welfare planners. The first, and most general, is to highlight planning perspectives through a framework that provides the beginning student with a coherent approach to the literature. To that end we have organized the readings to underline some important areas of philosophical debate, theoretical models, and two basic sets of practical tasks.

Part I of the book deals with the philosophical issues that planners of all

---

[30] Arnulf M. Pins, "Changes in Social Work Education and Their Implications for Practice," in *The Emergence of Social Welfare and Social Work*, Neil Gilbert and Harry Specht, eds. (Itasca, Ill.: F. E. Peacock, 1976).

[31] For a detailed description of one proposed curriculum for social welfare planning, see Frederick L. Ahearn, Jr., Richard S. Bolan, and Edmund M. Burke, "A Social Action Approach for Planning Education in Social Work," *Journal of Education for Social Work,* 11:3 (Fall 1975).

breeds confront: freedom vs. control; centralization vs. decentralization; direction by experts vs. citizen participation. These issues are discussed by authors such as Wootton, Hayek, and Banfield (Readings 1, 2, and 3). In Part II alternative models of the planning process are examined in light of the philosophical issues. While the models represent somewhat different conceptions of planning, the reader will find that theoreticians such as Kahn, Etzioni, and Lindblom (Readings 5, 6, and 7) have many common understandings of the complexities and contradictions that the planner confronts. Differences occur mainly in the relative emphasis given to one or another aspect and the authors' views on the epistemological boundaries of planning, which Rittel and Webber explore in depth (Reading 10). The papers in Part III deal with the sociopolitical tasks of the planner. And, finally, Part IV focuses upon the technical aspects of planning. In Parts III and IV, authors such as Bolan, Davidoff, and Warren (Readings 12, 14, and 15) provide insights into the scope and quality of the planner's social interactions, while the range of practical techniques that planners use is illustrated in papers by Thayer, Molnar and Kammerud, and Bennet and Weisinger (Readings 21, 23, and 26).

The second objective that guided our selection of readings is to introduce students to writings in the planning field that have particular salience to the institution of social welfare. The reason for this focus is that despite the major and enduring philosophical questions that confront *all* planners, and the practical skills that planners learn from their day-to-day efforts at problem solving, there are differences in institutional emphases in planning. Social welfare planners, water-resource planners, and transportation planners, for example, obviously must have an extensive knowledge about the areas in which they work; and for this knowledge they must draw upon different disciplines and practices. Water-resource planners must know a good deal about geography and geology; social welfare planners require knowledge about human growth and development and community relations. The best-laid plans of water-resource planners will interfere sometimes with the social-developmental needs of communities, and frequently the plans of social welfare planners will affect and be affected by the geography of an area. However, the fact that everything in this world is related to everything else does not argue against the need for professionals to develop expertise, to know about *some* institutional area in depth. (It is, though, an argument for *generalist* and *comprehensive* planning, a point that we shall discuss below.) Following that premise, the majority of papers we have selected for this volume use examples or discuss substantive variables that are directly relevant to social welfare planning. For example, authors such as Kahn, Davidoff, and Warren address problems that are especially meaningful for the contexts in which social welfare planners work: Kahn (Reading 5) writes about *social* planning; Davidoff (Reading 14) discusses the planner's practice in regard to the *social and political* characteristics of groups; Warren (Reading 15) develops useful propositions for analyzing relationships among the *human-services* decision-making organizations of a community. Similarly Gilbert (Reading 13), Connery *et al.* (Reading 16), and Thayer (Reading 21) deal with case examples drawn from social welfare programs.

Other questions that were important in our selection of readings are comprehensiveness and centralization in planning. Centralization refers to both the scope of planning (e.g., national vs. local) and to the distribution of power among the units in any system regardless of its scope. Questions about the distribution of power are discussed in Arnstein (Reading 18); Brager and Specht (Reading 17); Warren (Reading 15); and Aiken and Alford (Reading 11). In regard to questions of scope, we have tended to favor articles that are geared to local instead of national planning because the majority of social welfare planners deal with specific local programs.[32]

The related issue of comprehensiveness is more subtle. Students, in beginning their study of planning, often express some impatience with the notion of planning only a single program. Many prefer comprehensive planning rather than the piecemeal incrementalism that comes from planning more specific programs. We sympathize with the impatience because, in the real world, social, physical, and economic problems are interrelated. How can you plan a tutoring program for children if they are hungry? How can you plan a school lunch program when you leave children in homes that are overwhelmed by physical and nutritional poverty? How can you plan family income-maintenance programs when there is a scarcity of resources in housing and medical care?

The answers to these compassionate questions do not lie in planning alone. These questions raise further questions about the values of our society and the ways these values reveal themselves in all our political and social institutions. These are problems not only for planners but for *all* citizens, and the appropriate responses to them must come from a wide range of social and political collectivities. Planners are only one set of actors in the sociopolitical processes through which decisions are made about such questions.

However, any society that undertakes to solve its problems will require that choices be made and specific programs be planned. Whether it is a highly individualistic and competitive society like ours, or a highly collectivist and communalist society like some of the socialist and communist countries, planning must concern specific programs. The planner must be able to help articulate the specific ways in which the goals of society

[32] For a discussion of the different aspects of national planning, see Robert Mayer, Robert Moroney, and Robert Morris, eds., *Centrally Planned Change: A Reexamination of Theory and Experience* (Urbana: University of Illinois Press, 1974).

(whether comprehensive or fragmented) can be implemented. And the planner who brings sufficient competence to the enterprise helps a community understand the real needs of its people, the reasonable expectations they may hold for specific programs, and the exact requirements of meeting social needs. The final objective of this book is to provide the initial intellectual groundwork for developing that competence.

To Plan
or Not to Plan

part I

A group of residents met with the staff of their local human resource planning agency to discuss the agency's proposal for a community mental health outpatient facility on city-owned property in their neighborhood. The planning staff presented a series of alternatives for the physical design of the facility and the services to be offered therein. The citizens listened politely.

After the presentation the audience was asked for their opinions. The president of the local PTA rose to inquire, "I can understand that these people released from mental hospitals need a half-way house type facility to ease their reintegration into the community. But why should that facility be in our neighborhood and by what right does the planning department present us with a scheme so clearly damaging to the interests of our community?"

With a benevolent nod, the senior planner replied, "I realize your concerns, but surely you can see that it is in the public interest that we create a humane community-based program to help rehabilitate these unfortunate people. . . ."

"Quite so," interrupted the citizen, "but the plans you presented tonight are not in the interests of this public," as she waved her arm over the crowd, eliciting a clamorous assent.

Most students of social planning should be familiar with the problem of how to interpret the "public interest." This is a basic philosophical issue that separates those who support centralized, comprehensive social planning from those who favor decentralized, fragmented planning; and it further separates both of these groups from those who oppose any kind of collective intervention for the sake of the commonweal.

Those who are philosophically opposed to central broadscope social planning argue that the "public interest," or "common welfare," is a fiction that is meaningful only at a high level of abstraction. That is, for example, people may agree in general that social planning to eliminate poverty is in the public interest and that it will benefit all of society. Yet, when the abstract goal of eliminating poverty is translated into specific actions (e.g., redistributing income vs. increasing public spending vs. providing social services for the poor) the widespread agreement on ends quickly vanishes.

A classic representation of this diffident conception of the public interest and its implications for social planning are developed by Friedrich A. Hayek in "Planning and Democracy," Reading 1. The paper is an excerpt from Hayek's book, *The Road to Serfdom* (so named because Hayek believes that social planning, centrally organized and broad in scope, must eventually result in a form of mass servitude).

Hayek's argument has not gone unchallenged. The gauntlet has been taken up by Barbara Wootton, among others. One of the most articulate and persuasive advocates of social planning, Wootton explains in Reading 2, "Political Freedom," that the validity of Hayek's view of the common welfare depends on the actual extent of genuine agreement on what is thought to be good for society. Wootton challenges Hayek's belief that there are virtually no meaningful areas of agreement. She points out that some social objectives such as full employment and guaranteed minimal levels of nutrition have enjoyed broad support from the entire spectrum of English political groups. While political parties have their differences, none condones hunger or unemployment. "Either there is now general agreement that these are elements in the common evil," says Wootton, "or somebody is telling a crashing load of lies." [1] Still, she does recognize that those who agree on ends may disagree on means, and that theoretical distinctions between ends and means often dissolve in the cauldron of hot, practical issues.

Hayek and Wootton disagree on the fundamental nature of the public interest. Their writings illustrate how the public interest may be defined, broadly speaking, in terms of either *individualistic* or *unitary* conceptions. According to the *individualistic* view, there is no such thing as a unitary public interest or common welfare. Rather, there are different publics with different interests, which makes the justification of social planning on the basis of shared interests and mutual benefit a rather tenuous matter. From this perspective the public interest is at best a momentary compromise that arises from the interplay of competing interests. It changes as new groups and individuals are able to influence the planning process. The *unitary* view of the public interest as expressed by Wootton holds that there are communal interests shared by the vast majority. These interests are common ends that are more valuable in defining the public interest than the unshared ends of individuals and groups.

Another variation of the unitary conception of the public interest is derived from viewing the community as a "public body," a social organism whose well-being transcends the specific preferences and interests of individuals. From this viewpoint the community has certain anthropomorphic

---

[1] Barbara Wootton, *Freedom Under Planning* (Chapel Hill: University of North Carolina Press, 1945), p. 145.

needs that must be satisfied if the organism is to remain healthy: its arteries must be able to maintain a system of transport that brings in and sends out material and conceptual products; it must have a financial base to sustain itself; medicine, psychotherapy, sanitation, and other helping services must be available to mend, clean, and nurture it. The public interest, perceived in this way, can only be determined by experts who are trained in the art and science of planning to diagnose these needs and prescribe appropriately.

These unitary and individualistic conceptions of the public interest are discussed by Edward Banfield in "The Public Interest," Reading 3. He describes the "communal" and "organismic" views as contrasting types of unitary conceptions. Banfield notes that individualistic conceptions vary in terms of the degree of compromise they are willing to grant among competing interests. These different views of the public interest are not merely concepts upon which scholars ruminate; they are powerful ideas that influence the course of action in social planning. Banfield observes:

A somewhat different decision-making mechanism is implied by each of these conceptions of the public interest. A unitary conception implies a cooperative choice process, i.e., one in which the outcome or settlement is derived from a single set of ends. Any individualistic conception, on the other hand, implies a mechanism through which competing ends are compromised.[2]

Claims to serving the public interest lend an abstract justification and legitimacy to the social planning enterprise.

A closely related and more concrete sanction for social planning is acquired from the sources of authority to which the planner is responsible. In Reading 4, "Social Planning: The Search for Legitimacy," Martin Rein identifies the following sources of authority upon which planners rely to legitimate their intervention: bureaucratic position; consumer preference; expertise; and professional values. *Bureaucratic position* refers to situations where the planner is an employee in a public or private bureaucracy and "secures his authority from the director of a planning organization whose head is appointed by elected representatives who in turn secure their authority from voting citizens."[3] Here the source of authority supports a unitary-communal view of the public interest. That is, planners are accountable to elected political leaders who (theoretically at least) represent the agreed-upon policies of the community.[4] The sanction derived from the planner's *values and expertise* is rooted in his training in and account-

2 Martin Meyerson and Edward Banfield, *Politics, Planning, and the Public Interest* (New York: The Free Press, 1955), p. 327.

3 Martin Rein, "Social Planning: The Search for Legitimacy," *Journal of the American Institute of Planners*, 35:4 (July 1969), 234.

4 For additional discussion of this general topic, see Edmund M. Burke, "The Search for Authority in Planning," *Social Service Review*, 41:3 (September 1967), 250–60.

ability to a profession. As Greenwood has observed, one of the distinguishing attributes of a profession is the sanction it receives from the community to perform special services over which the profession has a monopoly.[5] This source of authority girds a unitary-organismic view of the public interest. Diagnosing the community's interests requires the special knowledge, objectivity, and values that are acquired through professional training. The sanction of *consumer preference* operates when the planner identifies with a specific client group and helps them express their views and values as they participate in the planning process. An individualistic conception of the public interest is sustained by this source of authority which presumes that there will be different groups competing to influence the community plan.

These sources of authority and corresponding notions of the public interest suggest planning processes that emphasize alternative planner roles and different arrangements among planners, political and administrative leaders, and consumer publics. In Table 1 we summarize the logically

TABLE 1. CONCEPTIONS OF THE PUBLIC INTEREST, SOURCES OF AUTHORITY,
AND PLANNER ROLES

Public Interest	Source of Authority	Planner Roles
Unitary-Organismic	Professional values and expertise	Technocrat—accountable primarily to the profession and operating with a view of the public interest derived from special skills and knowledge.
Unitary-Communal	Bureaucratic hierarchy and political leadership	Bureaucrat—accountable primarily to political and administrative leaders and operating with a view of the public interest derived from common ends as interpreted by elected representatives of the people.
Individualistic	Consumer preference	Advocate—accountable primarily to the consumer group that purchases his services and operating with a view of the public interest derived from consumer group preferences.

consistent relationships among these three sets of variables: conceptions of the public interest, sources of authority, and planning roles.

Reality is not quite as static or neatly pigeonholed as the relationships in Table 1 might suggest. While these planner roles simplify reality, it is nevertheless useful for heuristic purposes to extract these modal types from the range of possibilities. Planners often perform more than one role simultaneously, draw their authority from a variety of sources, and hold alternative and perhaps contradictory views about what constitutes the

[5] Ernest Greenwood, "Attributes of a Profession," *Social Work*, 2:3 (July 1957).

public interest at different points in the planning process and according to the different problems dealt with.[6]

We entitled this section "To Plan or Not to Plan," not to express our uncertainty but, rather, to act the devil's advocate. The unsettled issue is not whether to engage in social welfare planning but how to do it. A good deal of current debate on social planning may be reduced to the following basic question: to what extent is the process envisioned as a rational problem-solving endeavor amenable to technical expertise that can yield the "best" solution for the common good in light of all theoretically possible alternatives, and to what extent is it primarily a matter of exchange and compromise that yields the "most feasible" solution given the political constraints of a wide range of competing interests? Practically, the issue involves the extent to which the activities of the technocrat, bureaucrat, and advocate are more or less appropriate as functional guides to the planner in the social welfare planning process. In a broader context this issue is reflected in models of how planning is and ought to be done, which is the subject of the papers in Part II.

[6] For an excellent analysis of the complexities and some variations in these planning relationships, see Francine F. Rabinovitz, *City Politics and Planning* (New York: Atherton Press, 1969), pp. 79–117.

1   Not to Plan

PLANNING AND DEMOCRACY

Friedrich A. Hayek

The common features of all collectivist systems may be described, in a phrase ever dear to socialists of all schools, as the deliberate organization of the labors of society for a definite social goal. That our present society lacks such "conscious" direction toward a single aim, that its activities are guided by the whims and fancies of irresponsible individuals, has always been one of the main complaints of its socialist critics.

In many ways this puts the basic issue very clearly. And it directs us at once to the point where the conflict arises between individual freedom and collectivism. The various kinds of collectivism, communism, fascism, etc., differ among themselves in the nature of the goal toward which they want to direct the efforts of society. But they all differ from liberalism and individualism in wanting to organize the whole of society and all its resources for this unitary end and in refusing to recognize autonomous spheres in which the ends of the individuals are supreme. In short, they are totalitarian

Reprinted with permission of author and publisher from: Friedrich A. Hayek, *The Road to Serfdom* (Chicago: University of Chicago Press, 1944), pp. 56–71.

in the true sense of this new word which we have adopted to describe the unexpected but nevertheless inseparable manifestations of what in theory we call collectivism.

The "social goal," or "common purpose," for which society is to be organized is usually vaguely described as the "common good," the "general welfare," or the "general interest." It does not need much reflection to see that these terms have no sufficiently definite meaning to determine a particular course of action. The welfare and the happiness of millions cannot be measured on a single scale of less and more. The welfare of a people, like the happiness of a man, depends on a great many things that can be provided in an infinite variety of combinations. It cannot be adequately expressed as a single end, but only as a hierarchy of ends, a comprehensive scale of values in which every need of every person is given its place. To direct all our activities according to a single plan presupposes that every one of our needs is given its rank in an order of values which must be complete enough to make it possible to decide among all the different courses which the planner has to choose. It presupposes, in short, the existence of a complete ethical code in which all the different human values are allotted their due place.

The conception of a complete ethical code is unfamiliar, and it requires some effort of imagination to see what it involves. We are not in the habit of thinking of moral codes as more or less complete. The fact that we are constantly choosing between different values without a social code prescribing how we ought to choose does not surprise us and does not suggest to us that our moral code is incomplete. In our society there is neither occasion nor reason why people should develop common views about what should be done in such situations. But where all the means to be used are the property of society and are to be used in the name of society according to a unitary plan, a "social" view about what ought to be done must guide all decisions. In such a world we should soon find that our moral code is full of gaps.

We are not concerned here with the question whether it would be desirable to have such a complete ethical code. It may merely be pointed out that up to the present the growth of civilization has been accompanied by a steady diminution of the sphere in which individual actions are bound by fixed rules. The rules of which our common moral code consists have progressively become fewer and more general in character. From the primitive man, who was bound by an elaborate ritual in almost every one of his daily activities, who was limited by innumerable taboos, and who could scarcely conceive of doing things in a way different from his fellows, morals have more and more tended to become merely limits circumscribing the sphere within which the individual could behave as he liked. The adoption of a common ethical code comprehensive enough to determine a unitary economic plan would mean a complete reversal of this tendency.

The essential point for us is that no such complete ethical code exists. The attempt to direct all economic activity according to a single plan would raise innumerable questions to which the answer could be provided only by a moral rule, but to which existing morals have no answer and where there exists no agreed view on what ought to be done. People will have either no definite views or conflicting views on such questions, because in the free society in which we have lived there has been no occasion to think about them and still less to form common opinions about them.

Not only do we not possess such an all-inclusive scale of values: it would be impossible for any mind to comprehend the infinite variety of different needs of different people which compete for the available resources and to attach a definite weight to each. For our problem it is of minor importance whether the ends for which any person cares comprehend only his own individual needs, or whether they include the needs of his closer or even those of his more distant fellows—that is, whether he is egoistic or altruistic in the ordinary senses of these words. The point which is so important is the basic fact that it is impossible for any man to survey more than a limited field, to be aware of the urgency of more than a limited number of needs. Whether his interests center round his own physical needs, or whether he takes a warm interest in the welfare of every human being he knows, the ends about which he can be concerned will always be only an infinitesimal fraction of the needs of all men.

This is the fundamental fact on which the whole philosophy of individualism is based. It does not assume, as is often asserted, that man is egoistic or selfish or ought to be. It merely starts from the indisputable fact that the limits of our powers of imagination make it impossible to include in our scale of values more than a sector of the needs of the whole society, and that, since, strictly speaking, scales of value can exist only in individual minds, nothing but partial scales of values exist —scales which are inevitably different and often inconsistent with each other. From this the individualist concludes that the individuals should be allowed, within defined limits, to follow their own values and preferences rather than somebody else's; that within these spheres the individual's system of ends should be supreme and not subject to any dictation by others. It is this recognition of the individual as the ultimate judge of his ends, the belief that as far as possible his own views ought to govern his actions, that forms the essence of the individualist position.

This view does not, of course, exclude the recognition of social ends, or rather of a coincidence of individual ends which makes it advisable for men to combine for their pursuit. But it limits such common action to the instances where individual views coincide; what are called

"social ends" are for it merely identical ends of many individuals—or ends to the achievement of which individuals are willing to contribute in return for the assistance they receive in the satisfaction of their own desires. Common action is thus limited to the fields where people agree on common ends. Very frequently these common ends will not be ultimate ends to the individuals but means which different persons can use for different purposes. In fact, people are most likely to agree on common action where the common end is not an ultimate end to them but a means capable of serving a great variety of purposes.

When individuals combine in a joint effort to realize ends they have in common, the organizations, like the state, that they form for this purpose are given their own system of ends and their own means. But any organization thus formed remains one "person" among others, in the case of the state much more powerful than any of the others, it is true, yet still with its separate and limited sphere in which alone its ends are supreme. The limits of this sphere are determined by the extent to which the individuals agree on particular ends; and the probability that they will agree on a particular course of action necessarily decreases as the scope of such action extends. There are certain functions of the state on the exercise of which there will be practical unanimity among its citizens; there will be others on which there will be agreement of a substantial majority; and so on, until we come to fields where, although each individual might wish the state to act in some way, there will be almost as many views about what the government should do as there are different people.

We can rely on voluntary agreement to guide the action of the state only so long as it is confined to spheres where agreement exists. But not only when the state undertakes direct control in fields where there is no such agreement is it bound to suppress individual freedom. We can unfortunately not indefinitely extend the sphere of common action and still leave the individual free in his own sphere. Once the communal sector, in which the state controls all the means, exceeds a certain proportion of the whole, the effects of its actions dominate the whole system. Although the state controls of its decisions on the remaining part directly the use of only a large part of the available resources the effects of the economic system become so great that indirectly it controls almost everything. Where, as was, for example, true in Germany as early as 1928, the central and local authorities directly control the use of more than half the national income (according to an official German estimate then, 53 per cent), they control indirectly almost the whole economic life of the nation. There is, then, scarcely an individual end which is not dependent for its achievement on the action of the state, and the "social scale of values" which guides the state's action must embrace practically all individual ends.

It is not difficult to see what must be the consequences when democracy embarks upon a course of planning which in its execution requires more agreement than in fact exists. The people may have agreed on adopting a system of directed economy because they have been convinced that it will produce great prosperity. In the discussions leading to the decision, the goal of planning will have been described by some such term as "common welfare," which only conceals the absence of real agreement on the ends of planning. Agreement will in fact exist only on the mechanism to be used. But it is a mechanism which can be used only for a common end; and the question of the precise goal toward which all activity is to be directed will arise as soon as the executive power has to translate the demand for a single plan into a particular plan. Then it will appear that the agreement on the desirability of planning is not supported by agreement on the ends the plan is to serve. The effect of the people's agreeing that there must be central planning, without agreeing on the ends, will be rather as if a group of people were to commit themselves to take a journey together without agreeing where they want to go: with the result that they may all have to make a journey which most of them do not want at all. That planning creates a situation in which it is necessary for us to agree on a much larger number of topics than we have been used to, and that in a planned system we cannot confine collective action to the tasks on which we can agree but are forced to produce agreement on everything in order that any action can be taken at all, is one of the features which contributes more than most to determining the character of a planned system.

It may be the unanimously expressed will of the people that its parliament should prepare a comprehensive economic plan, yet neither the people nor its representatives need therefore be able to agree on any particular plan. The inability of democratic assemblies to carry out what seems to be a clear mandate of the people will inevitably cause dissatisfaction with democratic institutions. Parliaments come to be regarded as ineffective "talking shops," unable or incompetent to carry out the tasks for which they have been chosen. The conviction grows that if efficient planning is to be done, the direction must be "taken out of politics" and placed in the hands of experts—permanent officials or independent autonomous bodies.

The difficulty is well known to socialists. It will soon be half a century since the Webbs began to complain of "the increased incapacity of the House of Commons to cope with its work." [1] More recently, Professor Laski has elaborated the argument:

"It is common ground that the present parliamentary machine is quite unsuited to pass rapidly a great body of complicated legislation. The National Government, indeed, has in substance admitted this by implementing its economy and tariff measures not by detailed debate in the House of Commons but by a wholesale system of delegated legislation. A Labour Government would, I presume, build upon the amplitude of this precedent. It would confine the House of Commons to the two functions it can properly perform: the ventilation of grievances and the discussion of general principles of its measures. Its Bills would take the form of general formulae conferring wide powers on the appropriate government departments; and those powers would be exercised by Order

in Council which could, if desired, be attacked in the House by means of a vote of no confidence. The necessity and value of delegated legislation has recently been strongly reaffirmed by the Donoughmore Committee; and its extension is inevitable if the process of socialisation is not to be wrecked by the normal methods of obstruction which existing parliamentary procedure sanctions."

And to make it quite clear that a socialist government must not allow itself to be too much fettered by democratic procedure, Professor Laski at the end of the same article raised the question "whether in a period of transition to Socialism, a Labour Government can risk the overthrow of its measures as a result of the next general election"—and left it significantly unanswered. [2]

It is important clearly to see the causes of this admitted ineffective-

---

[1] Sidney and Beatrice Webb, *Industrial Democracy* (1897), p. 800 n.

[2] H. J. Laski, "Labour and the Constitution," *New Statesman and Nation*, No. 81 (new ser.), September 10, 1932, p. 277. In a book (*Democracy in Crisis* [1933], particularly p. 87) in which Professor Laski later elaborated these ideas, his determination that parliamentary democracy must not be allowed to form an obstacle to the realization of socialism is even more plainly expressed: not only would a socialist government "take vast powers and legislate under them by ordinance and decree" and "suspend the classic formulae of normal opposition" but the "continuance of parliamentary government would depend on its [i.e., the Labour government's] possession of guarantees from the Conservative Party that its work of transformation would not be disrupted by repeal in the event of its defeat at the polls"!

As Professor Laski invokes the authority of the Donoughmore Committee, it may be worth recalling that Professor Laski was a member of that committee and presumably one of the authors of its report.

ness of parliaments when it comes to a detailed administration of the economic affairs of a nation. The fault is neither with the individual representatives nor with parliamentary institutions as such but with the contradictions inherent in the task with which they are charged. They are not asked to act where they can agree, but to produce agreement on everything—the whole direction of the resources of the nation. For such a task the system of majority decision is, however, not suited. Majorities will be found where it is a choice between limited alternatives; but it is a superstition to believe that there must be a majority view on everything. There is no reason why there should be a majority in favor of any one of the different possible courses of positive action if their number is legion. Every member of the legislative assembly might prefer some particular plan for the direction of economic activity to no plan, yet no one plan may appear preferable to a majority to no plan at all.

Nor can a coherent plan be achieved by breaking it up into parts and voting on particular issues. A democratic assembly voting and amending a comprehensive economic plan clause by clause, as it deliberates on an ordinary bill, makes nonsense. An economic plan, to deserve the name, must have a unitary conception. Even if a parliament could, proceeding step by step, agree on some scheme, it would certainly in the end satisfy nobody. A complex whole in which all the parts must be most carefully adjusted to each other cannot be achieved through a compromise between conflicting views. To draw up an economic plan in this fashion is even less possible than, for example, successfully to plan a military campaign by democratic procedure. As in strategy it would become inevitable to delegate the task to the experts.

Yet the difference is that, while the general who is put in charge of a campaign is given a single end to which, for the duration of the campaign, all the means under his control have to be exclusively devoted, there can be no such single goal given to the economic planner, and no similar limitation of the means imposed upon him. The general has not got to balance different independent aims against each other; there is for him only one supreme goal. But the ends of an economic plan, or of any part of it, cannot be defined apart from the particular plan. It is the essence of the economic problem that the making of an economic plan involves the choice between conflicting or competing ends—different needs of different people. But which ends do so conflict, which will have to be sacrificed if we want to achieve certain others, in short, which are the alternatives between which we must choose, can only be known to those who know all the facts; and only they, the experts, are in a position to decide which of the different ends are to be given preference. It is inevitable that they should impose their scale of preferences on the community for which they plan.

This is not always clearly recognized, and delegation is usually justified by the technical character of the task. But this does not mean that only the technical detail is delegated, or even that the inability of parliaments to understand the technical detail is the root of the difficulty.[3] Alterations in the structure of civil law are no less technical and no more difficult to appreciate in all their implications; yet nobody has yet seriously suggested that legisla-

[3] It is instructive in this connection briefly to refer to the government document in which in recent years these problems have been discussed. As long as thirteen years ago, that is before England finally abandoned economic liberalism, the process of delegating legislative powers had already been carried to a point where it was felt necessary to appoint a committee to investigate "what safeguards are desirable or necessary to secure the sovereignty of Law." In its report the Donoughmore Committee (*Report of the [Lord Chancellor's] Committee in Ministers' Powers*, Cmd. 4060 [1932]) showed that even at that date Parliament had resorted "to the practice of wholesale and indiscriminate delegation" but regarded this (it was before we had really glanced into the totalitarian abyss!) as an inevitably and relatively innocuous development. And it is probably true that delegation as such need not be a danger to freedom. The interesting point is why delegation had become necessary on such a scale. First place among the causes enumerated in the report is given to the fact that "Parliament nowadays passes so many laws every year" and that "much of the detail is so technical as to be unsuitable for Parliamentary discussion." But if this were all there would be no reason why the detail should not be worked out *before* rather than after Parliament passes a law. What is probably in many cases a much more important reason why, "if Parliament were not willing to delegate law-making power, Parliament would be unable to pass the kind and quantity of legislation which public opinion requires" is innocently revealed in the little sentence that "many of the laws affect people's lives so closely that elasticity is essential"! What does this mean if not conferment of arbitrary power—power limited by no fixed principles and which in the opinion of Parliament cannot be limited by definite and unambiguous rules?

tion there should be delegated to a body of experts. The fact is that in these fields legislation does not go beyond general rules on which true majority agreement can be achieved, while in the direction of economic activity the interests to be reconciled are so divergent that no true agreement is likely to be reached in a democratic assembly.

It should be recognized, however, that it is not the delegation of law-making power as such which is so objectionable. To oppose delegation as such is to oppose a symptom instead of the cause and, as it may be a necessary result of other causes, to weaken the case. So long as the power that is delegated is merely the power to make general rules, there may be very good reasons why such rules should be laid down by local rather than by the central authority. The objectionable feature is that delegation is so often resorted to because the matter in hand cannot be regulated by general rules but only by the exercise of discretion in the decision of particular cases. In these instances delegation means that some authority is given power to make with the force of law what to all intents and purposes are arbitrary decisions (usually described as "judging the case on its merits").

The delegation of particular technical tasks to separate bodies, while a regular feature, is yet only the first step in the process whereby a democracy which embarks on planning progressively relinquishes its powers. The expedient of delegation cannot really remove the causes which make all the advocates of comprehensive planning so impatient with the impotence of democracy. The delegation of particular powers to separate agencies creates a new obstacle to the achievement of a single co-ordinated plan. Even if, by this expedient, a democracy should succeed in planning every sector of economic activity, it would still have to face the problem of integrating these separate plans into a unitary whole. Many separate plans do not make a planned whole—in fact, as the planners ought to be the first to admit, they may be worse than no plan. But the democratic legislature will long hesitate to relinquish the decisions on really vital issues, and so long as it does so it makes it impossible for anyone else to provide the comprehensive plan. Yet agreement that planning is necessary, together with the inability of democratic assemblies to produce a plan, will evoke stronger and stronger demands that the government or some single individual should be given powers to act on their own responsibility. The belief is becoming more and more widespread that, if things are to get done, the responsible authorities must be freed from the fetters of democratic procedure.

The cry for an economic dictator is a characteristic stage in the movement toward planning. It is now several years since one of the most acute of foreign students of England, the late Élie Halévy, suggested that, "if you take a composite photograph of Lord Eustace Percy, Sir Oswald Mosley, and Sir Stafford Cripps, I think you would find this common feature —you would find them all agreeing to say: 'We are living in economic chaos and we cannot get out of it except under some kind of dictatorial leadership.' " [4] The number

of influential public men whose inclusion would not materially alter the features of the "composite photograph" has since grown considerably.

In Germany, even before Hitler came into power, the movement had already progressed much further. It is important to remember that, for some time before 1933, Germany had reached a stage in which it had, in effect, had to be governed dictatorially. Nobody could then doubt that for the time being democracy had broken down and that sincere democrats like Brüning were no more able to govern democratically than Schleicher or von Papen. Hitler did not have to destroy democracy; he merely took advantage of the decay of democracy and at the critical moment obtained the support of many to whom, though they detested Hitler, he yet seemed the only man strong enough to get things done.

The argument by which the planners usually try to reconcile us with this development is that, so long as democracy retains ultimate control, the essentials of democracy are not affected. Thus Karl Mannheim writes:

"The only [sic] way in which a planned society differs from that of the nineteenth century is that more and more spheres of social life, and ultimately each and all of them, are subjected to state control. But if a few controls can be held in check by parliamentary sovereignty, so can many. . . . In a democratic state sovereignty can be boundlessly strengthened by plenary powers without renouncing democratic control." [5]

This belief overlooks a vital dis-

[4] "Socialism and the Problems of Democratic Parliamentarism," *International Affairs*, XIII, 501.

[5] *Man and Society in an Age of Reconstruction* (1940), p. 340.

tinction. Parliament can, of course, control the execution of tasks where it can give definite directions, where it has first agreed on the aim and merely delegates the working-out of the detail. The situation is entirely different when the reason for the delegation is that there is no real agreement on the ends, when the body charged with the planning has to choose between ends of whose conflict parliament is not even aware, and when the most that can be done is to present to it a plan which has to be accepted or rejected as a whole. There may and probably will be criticism; but as no majority can agree on an alternative plan, and the parts objected to can almost always be represented as essential parts of the whole, it will remain quite ineffective. Parliamentary discussion may be retained as a useful safety valve and even more as a convenient medium through which the official answers to complaints are disseminated. It may even prevent some flagrant abuses and successfully insist on particular shortcomings being remedied. But it cannot direct. It will at best be reduced to choosing the persons who are to have practically absolute power. The whole system will tend toward that plebiscitarian dictatorship in which the head of the government is from time to time confirmed in his position by popular vote, but where he has all the powers at his command to make certain that the vote will go in the direction he desires.

It is the price of democracy that the possibilities of conscious control are restricted to the fields where true agreement exists and that in some fields things must be left to chance. But in a society which for its functioning depends on central planning this control cannot be made dependent on a majority's being able to agree; it will often be necessary that the will of a small minority be imposed upon the people, because this minority will be the largest group able to agree among themselves on the question at issue. Democratic government has worked successfully where, and so long as, the functions of government were, by a widely accepted creed, restricted by free discussion; and it is the great merit of the liberal creed that it reduced the range of subjects on which agreement was necessary to one on which it was likely to exist in a society of free men. It is now often said that democracy will not tolerate "capitalism." If "capitalism" means here a competitive system based on free disposal over private property, it is far more important to realize that only within this system is democracy possible. When it becomes dominated by a collectivist creed, democracy will inevitably destroy itself.

We have no intention, however, of making a fetish of democracy. It may well be true that our generation talks and thinks too much of democracy and too little of the values which it serves. It cannot be said of democracy, as Lord Acton truly said of liberty, that it "is not a means to a higher political end. It is itself the highest political end. It is not for the sake of a good public administration that it is required, but for the security in the pursuit of the highest objects of civil society, and of private life." Democracy is essentially a means, a utilitarian device for safeguarding internal peace and individual freedom. As such it is by no means infallible or certain. Nor must we forget that there has often been much more culture and spiritual freedom under an autocratic rule than under some democracies— and it is at least conceivable that under the government of a very homogeneous and doctrinaire majority democratic government might be as oppressive as the worst dictatorship. Our point, however, is not that dictatorship must inevitably extirpate freedom but rather that planning leads to dictatorship because dictatorship is the most effective instrument of coercion and the enforcement of ideals and, as such, essential if central planning on a large scale is to be possible. The clash between planning and democracy arises simply from the fact that the latter is an obstacle to the suppression of freedom which the direction of economic activity requires. But in so far as democracy ceases to be a guaranty of individual freedom, it may well persist in some form under a totalitarian regime. A true "dictatorship of the proletariat," even if democratic in form, if it undertook centrally to direct the economic system, would probably destroy personal freedom as completely as any autocracy has ever done.

The fashionable concentration on democracy as the main value threatened is not without danger. It is largely responsible for the misleading and unfounded belief that, so long as the ultimate source of power is the will of the majority, the power cannot be arbitrary. The false assurance which many people derive from this belief is an important cause of the general unawareness of the dangers which we face. There is no justification for the belief that, so long as power is conferred by democratic procedure, it cannot be arbitrary; the contrast suggested by this statement is altogether false: it is not the source but the limitation of power which prevents it from being arbitrary. Democratic control *may* prevent power from becoming arbitrary, but it does not do so by its mere existence. If democracy resolves on a task which necessarily involves the use of power which cannot be guided by fixed rules, it must become arbitrary power.

2   To Plan

POLITICAL FREEDOM

BARBARA WOOTTON

The essential political freedoms are the right freely to express criticism of the Government and its works; the right to form opposition political parties; the right to replace one Government and legislature by another, without resort to force. All the constitutions that are generally classified as democratic secure these rights by one device or another. They differ in the particular mechanics used, as also in the generosity with which they accord these rights to all, or restrict them to a limited class of, citizens. Ultimately, all democratic Governments derive their mandate from some kind of popular vote, though there is, of course, no common rule as to who may exercise this franchise. Such matters, however, as the age of enfranchisement, the disfranchisement of women or of persons owning less than a certain amount of property, or even of persons holding particular opinions, such as conscientious objectors, are, for all their importance, nevertheless secondary to the fundamental question whether there is, or is not, freedom of political agitation, and

Reprinted with permission of author and publisher from: Barbara Wootton, *Freedom Under Planning* (Chapel Hill, N.C.: University of North Carolina Press, 1945), pp. 130–57.

freedom to replace one Government by another otherwise than by force. So long as these freedoms are secured, they can be used to widen and democratize a limited suffrage. Without them we are all equally powerless.

The obverse of these freedoms is that the tenure of every democratic Government and legislature is necessarily insecure. The degree of insecurity varies under different constitutions. In this country it reaches a maximum, in that any Government is liable to defeat in the House at any time, is expected to resign if defeated on any issue of consequence, and has the right, on defeat, to dissolve Parliament and appeal to the country. In the absence of any such interim dissolution the maximum peace-time life of any British House of Commons is five years. Other Constitutions, like the American, provide a definite term for the legislature or executive or both, without any provision for interim renewal; or achieve continuity by providing that a proportion of the members of one House of the legislature, as in the American Senate, should retire (unless re-elected) at fixed intervals. The long and the short of it is that under the pre-war constitutions of the world the members of democratic governments and democratically elected chambers could not normally expect a life of *more than* five years, and were often liable to, and actually suffered, sudden political death, at much shorter intervals.

The dilemma that we have to resolve here is that economic planning demands continuity, and political freedom appears to imply instability. Nothing can alter the fact that we cannot both make effective long-term plans, and continually exercise the right to change our minds about anything at any time.

There can be little doubt that insistence on this right has, in the literal sense, made short work of attempts at planning in this country in the past. The most egregious example is perhaps that of housing policy in the nineteen-twenties. . . .

It cannot, however, pass the wit of man or woman to devise means whereby some continuity could be given to those Acts of government which form an integral part of a long-term plan. In fact this has indeed sometimes been done. The modern practice of establishing by Act of Parliament permanent, or near-permanent, Boards or Commissions, with a definite job to do, is an effective way of circumventing the effects of political crises and the changeableness of Parliaments and their electors. London Transport, the Central Electricity Board, and the B.B.C. are familiar examples of such independent Boards. The details of the constitution and powers vary from one case to another, but certain principles are common to all. In particular, in every case the Board is itself created by Parliament, normally by statute, though the constitution of the B.B.C. is embodied, as befits the dignity of that corporation, in a Royal Charter. Further, the instrument which establishes each of these Boards defines both its constitution (that is, such matters as the method of appointment and term of office of the members of the Board itself, who are in effect the governing body of the whole enterprise), and the job which it has to do. There is also always provision for periodical review, on some Parliamentary occasion, of the work of every such Board. In the case of the B.B.C. a full-dress debate is devoted to this inquest, which takes place at intervals of several years on the occasion of the renewal of the charter: in other cases the matter is less dramatically staged, and is, as a rule, annually dealt with under the vote for the Government department most closely concerned with the work of the Board in question.

There can be no doubt that the establishment of these Boards has in fact resulted in real continuity. We have only to contrast the history of housing with, say, the history of the unification and development of wholesale electricity production by the Central Electricity Board, or with the eleven years' work of the London Passenger Transport Board, to see how true this is. If the business of house-building had been entrusted to such a permanent corporation, it would certainly not have been blown about as it was by the changing currents of the political atmosphere; even though it remains true, that what Parliament has done, Parliament, under our constitution, can also undo. The Act or instrument establishing any of these Boards *could* constitutionally be revoked or modified, at any time; just as every local authority in the country could, for that matter, be legislated out of existence at any time. Nevertheless it is a *fact* that although one Parliament may be ready and eager to reverse the *policies* of another (and may indeed have been elected with that very end in view), there is in practice far greater reluctance to wind up an independent going concern, which is charged with a specific task, even though this may have been established by a Government of a different political complexion. This is one of the intangibles which, in the real world of conventions, common sense and tradition, so often prove decisive.

It is clear that large programs of planned production might be carried through by extended use of such Boards. Sir John Orr, for instance, has suggested [1] the establishment of a National Food Board, charged with the duty of bringing a sufficient diet within reach of everybody's pocket. The same kind of model could be used to organize the production of any goods to which a considered plan had assigned priority.

Like every form of organization, these Boards have their own peculiar vices and virtues, which have been fully and admirably discussed elsewhere.[2] Some are better organized than others, some have better systems of staff recruitment and promotion, while in some the method and tenure of appointment of the responsible heads is more straightforward than it is in others. If the scope and number of such Boards is to be increased, these are all matters for careful consideration, in which the

worst need to be leveled up at least to the standard of the best. These issues are not, however, primary for our purpose of combining political freedom with the continuity necessary for purposeful planning. . . .

The real question is then: is there a will? The most powerful of all criticism of long-term planning comes from those who suggest that the reason for continual changes of mind is the lack of any common agreement to give shape and direction to our plans. Since a plan without a purpose is a contradiction in terms, no group can make an effective plan unless there is some purpose upon which the members of that group are agreed, and which the plan is accordingly intended to fulfill. Professor Hayek has argued that, in modern political units, no such common agreement is possible. In his view, there is, for instance, no agreement, and no possibility of agreement, among English people as to the kind of economic pattern that they would wish to see in this country. Any conscious attempt to shape our economic life in a particular way—to foster this industry in preference to that—simply reflects the victory of one sectional interest over another. It follows that only a tyrannical Government will attempt to sponsor any kind of economic design or plan. Indeed, planning and tyranny are, in his view, so far synonymous that the only innocent laws are those which are so general in character that their impact on particular groups or individuals cannot even be foreseen. In this context Professor Hayek draws a contrast between "laying down a Rule of the Road, as in the Highway Code, and ordering

[1] In his *Fighting for What?*
[2] See, for instance, *Public Enterprise*, ed. Robson.

people where they are to go." [3] The effect of the Highway Code on individuals is unforseeable in the sense that the rule that all must drive on the left permits no inference as to what particular persons will be found driving in a particular place at a particular time. On this account, it is argued, the Highway Code benefits all at the expense of none. A public decision, on the other hand, as to the number of pigs to be reared not only permits, but demands, inferences as to the position of pigbreeders after the decision has been put into effect. Its whole purpose is to enrich or impoverish the pigbreeders, or to compel them to breed, or not to breed, such and such pigs: if the particular effects could not be in some degree foreseen, the regulation would not be worth making.

Since the area of genuine agreement is thus limited (the argument runs), the planner is driven to resort to improper devices for concealing disagreement, or for creating the appearance of an agreement which has no real existence. Among such devices Professor Hayek particularly mentions the practice of delegated legislation—not only in the form in which particular tasks are entrusted to Boards and Corporations, such as we have mentioned, but also in the many instances in which Ministers have power to fill in the details of legislation by Statutory Rules and Orders. Parliamentary discussion and control would reveal disagreement; the planner therefore by-passes Parliament by throwing the onus of unpalatable decisions on to Ministers and officials whose actions cannot be

defeated by a critical Opposition. Moreover, as soon as Government passes beyond formal rules "providing opportunities for unknown people to make whatever use of them they like" [4] to actual choice between the needs of different people, the volume of decisions to be made becomes enormously multiplied, and Parliament gets pushed out by sheer inability to manage the weight of its task. Finally, in order to cover all this up, attempts are made to manufacture the appearance of agreement by dishonest propaganda, and eventually by the forcible suppression of any dissident opinions, so that the will of a few is passed off as the will of the majority, if not of all. Planning thus leads to the eventual abolition of all political, as well as of a good slice of cultural and civil freedom.

This is an extraordinarily depressing and pessimistic doctrine. Its validity all turns on this question of the limits of *genuine* agreement. Professor Hayek's contention that agreement stops when we pass from formal rules with unforeseen effects, to specific rules with foreseen and intended effect upon individuals is, of course, part and parcel of his denial of the possibility of planning for indeterminate cultural ends. [5] It presumes an utterly skeptical attitude as to the common good. Here we have a curious illustration of extremes meeting. On the one hand is the cheerful assumption of the writers whom Professor Hayek quotes. To them the common good appears so obvious that not a word

[3] *The Road to Serfdom*, p. 74.

[4] *The Road to Serfdom*, p. 73.
[5] On which, see the argument of pp. 23–33 of this book [*Freedom Under Planning*— ED.]

is given to its definition, or to explaining how it is to be interpreted into practical policies: to Professor Hayek, on the other hand, definition is equally superfluous since no common good exists at all.

Now, if the common good means only the literal, direct, personal, advantage of every individual, it is true that there are, in time of peace, few, if any, concrete policies or plans by which that good can truthfully be said to be promoted. This is the fact which is too glibly passed over by the uncritical advocates of "planning for the common good." In this sense, but only in this, Professor Hayek is right in his denial that, for practical purposes, any common good exists at all. Such elementary social objectives, for instance, as the prevention of unemployment or of under-nourishment are pretty sure to demand personal sacrifice from some sections of the community. Unemployment has its attractions to an employer picking and choosing in an overstocked labor market; and effective nutrition policies are likely, at least in the beginning, to involve taxation which somebody must pay. In time of war, it may perhaps be said that effective measures of defense are directly advantageous to everybody without exception (though even then, these measures cost some people a great deal more than others). There is, I suggest, no parallel in time of peace.

To show that no plan or policy is likely to redound to the personal advantage of every citizen is, however, in no way to prove either that no policies or plans can commend themselves as desirable to those who do not personally stand to gain, and may actually lose by them; or that

the only "goods" in the world are those which can be literally bought and sold. It is, happily, a fact that opinions are not always entirely determined by the direct economic advantage of those who hold them; and it is also a fact that people do have definite preferences about such unsalable values as the kind of social pattern which they find desirable. Just because these values are unsalable, however, the ballot-box of the market place . . . must fail to count them. For by its very nature, the market is incapable of registering preferences which cannot be reflected in the consumers' demand for particular articles. One can buy a theater ticket, and so register a preference for a particular play; but, as we have seen, no one can *buy* full employment, however much he wants it. And what is true of full employment is true of all other essentially social values: that is, of all preference for one kind of social picture rather than another. The fanatical admirers of the market are, however, reduced to saying, at least by implication, that since these social values cannot be measured by so perfect an instrument as the market, they cannot be values at all.

This last assumption is ridiculous. A man may desire to live in a world where everybody (not only he himself) has enough work and enough to eat, just as keenly as he wants to see *Chu Chin Chow*, even if no objective machinery has been invented by which the relative strength of his two desires can be quantitatively measured. Different people may feel the attraction of a world where everyone has enough to eat and enough work, with different degrees of intensity, even though these degrees cannot be compared as the value of one man's purchases in a shop can be compared with the value of his neighbor's. That which cannot be mathematically measured (at any rate in the present state of the science of social measurement) does not, on that account, cease to exist, or even to matter. Social elements in the common good, such as full employment and full nutrition, are real enough. But in a complex society, where, as we have seen, every social policy is bound to tread on somebody's toes or touch somebody's pocket, they can only be defined in terms of common agreement, not of common interest; and they can only be promoted by deliberate planning, and not by any commercial market. The common good is, in fact, anything which is commonly thought to be good.

In interpreting this principle in practice, it is important not to slip into the prevalent and dangerous error of identifying the common good with the social objectives of one's own particular sect or party, and of ascribing the rejection of these by others as necessarily due to their stupid or selfish disregard of the general welfare. . . . The critical question is simply: are we, or are we not, so deeply divided that there are no genuinely agreed social objectives which could be embodied in a long-term plan?

The most convincing evidence that the British people are not, and were not even in the inter-war period, so deeply divided as this, is the large measure of agreement between the professed objectives of all political parties. At the least they all now offer, with Mr. Churchill, food, work, a home to every citizen. The

differences appear in what more is offered over and above this minimum, and in the parties' several opinions about methods. Traditionally (at the time of writing it is too soon to be specific about post-war election programs) the Labour Party wants much nationalizing and much education, whilst the Conservatives are more concerned with strong defenses and the remission of taxes upon business firms. But no party upholds or condones hunger, slum living, or unemployment. Either there is now general agreement that these are elements in the common evil, or somebody is telling a crashing load of lies. . . .

Much of the present confusion of English politics probably arises from a conscious or unconscious hangover of this doctrine that each political party must be tied up with the cause of a definite economic interest, which is itself coincident with a definite group of individuals. The decay of enthusiasm for the established political parties is, in part at least, due to the fact that the traditional battle-cries no longer make sense in a world in which so many people are, so to speak, fighting on several sides at once. Yet the malcontents with the old parties are far too miscellaneous to shape themselves into a new party with a clear class basis.

If we could shake off this hangover, we might develop political attitudes in which the limits of agreement and difference would become much clearer. At present all the emphasis is on points of difference. In political controversy it is generally customary (especially under a constitution as unstable as ours) for opposing parties to attack the *whole* of each other's program. The effect of this tradition is felt, I think, at all political levels. . . .

Some modification of this attitude will, I think, be necessary if democratic governments are to undertake extensive economic planning. As we have seen, planning is possible without sacrifice of political freedom only if the limits of any plan which is to be exempt from continual disturbance fall within the boundaries of genuine agreement on the purposes which the plan is to achieve. This brings to the front the new task of determining where those limits lie. It is not, as Professor Hayek asserts, a case of *manufacturing* agreement for the sake of action. It is a case of *discovering* agreement prior to action. This is the technique in which democracy is so little practiced. . . .

It is, of course, easy to argue that, since in fact governments of different political complexions do cheerfully reverse each other's policies when steps have not been taken (as for example with the B.B.C.) to put these beyond the range of continued Parliamentary interference, opposing parties really agree only when they are more or less compelled to do so. In this context the example of the continual changes of housing policy, . . . may be used as superficial evidence that no common opinion on housing policy ever existed. It will be said that if the job of housebuilding had been handed over to a non-Parliamentary Board this could only have meant the successful suppression of one opinion on the subject by another. Had there, in fact, been substantial agreement on the whole subject, all the chopping and changing about expressed in the successive Acts would never have happened.

This is a specious argument. Yet it does not necessarily follow that, because successive Parliaments change their minds and their policies, there is in fact no continuity of opinion between them. Here we have to give weight to that emphasis on differences rather than on agreements which, as has already been suggested, is so deeply characteristic of our whole political makeup. Good party capital is made not only by doing things differently from the Opposition, but by doing as many things as much differently as possible. And this emphasis on differences is powerfully reinforced in Parliament by the fact that its successful use can shorten the road to power. The way to throw a Government out before its full course has run, and so perhaps to get your own Party into power in its place, is to defeat that Government in the House of Commons. For this purpose it does not greatly matter what the defeat is about. The subsequent general election campaign will, as a rule, range over issues much wider than the particular topic which led to the Government's resignation. Opposition parties, therefore, with their eye on early prospects of power, are naturally on the watch to seize any and every point on which there is a chance that they may carry a majority against the Government in office. It is the fact of a Government's defeat, much more than the matter upon which it has been defeated, which in these circumstances becomes of first importance.

So long as political *tactics* demand that every disagreement should be exploited and magnified, and every agreement minimized or kept dark, so long in fact as the Opposition's attitude is of the old fashioned "Go-and-see-what-the-Government's-doing-and-tell-it-not-to" type, so long must it be impossible fairly to judge the extent of common opinion: and so long shall we be more disposed to under-estimate, than to exaggerate, the measure to which we are agreed. If, however, any serious attempt at continuous planning within, but not beyond, the limits of the area of common agreement is to be made, some method must be found of determining when that area ends. We must not lay ourselves open to Professor Hayek's charges of simulating or manufacturing agreement.

I have said above that common agreement does not mean majority agreement. This opens the door to slippery mathematical arguments. If a bare majority is not enough, how much more is necessary? Does a three-quarters or four-fifths majority constitute "general agreement?" Or must we reserve this expression for cases in which complete unanimity obtains, and no single objector can be found? Here, surely, the practical test must lie, not so much in a mere matter of numbers, as in the opinion of organized political parties. In a political democracy, common agreement exists on those policies or objectives which every political party will accept. Planning on the basis of such agreement is therefore only possible, if the parties are themselves willing jointly to define the purposes which they have in common. This means a new kind of inter-party conference—or inter-party-leader conference—using the unfamiliar technique of searching for agreement, instead of magnifying differences. The purpose of such explorations must be strictly to define, not to belittle or to exaggerate, agreement. At any given moment agreement and disagreement are facts. Conferences to distinguish the controversial from the non-controversial should, therefore, be strictly fact-finding. It is just as important that controversy should rage unchecked about matters which are genuinely in dispute, as that it should not be artificially inflamed, for tactical reasons, where differences are microscopic or imaginary. . . .

We may now sum up what all this means in terms of political freedom and political controversy. Nothing that has been suggested here touches the essential political freedom—the right at any time to remove by constitutional process and not by force the persons holding supreme political power, and to put others in their place. Nothing that has been said touches the freedom to criticize openly the actions of the Government in power, and to agitate publicly for different policies, or for a different Government. As long as these liberties are secure, there is no totalitarianism, no dictatorship. These are the political freedoms which are lacking in all totalitarian states. Even in the U.S.S.R. no alternative government to that of M. Stalin can be constitutionally offered to the electors: not at intervals of five or ten years, much less by a defeat in the Supreme Soviet at any time. Perhaps nobody wants, or ever has wanted, to suggest such an alternative? To that question there can be no answer, so long as no constitutional channel exists through which an opposition could make its voice heard. And in these conditions there can be no answer to the charge that political agreement is manufactured or simulated.

What I have suggested is, on the

contrary, that agreement should be *discovered;* and that, where and in so far as it obtains, so far and no further, should economic and political programs be placed out of reach of the unstable gusts of Parliamentary democracy. Governments will come and go, answerable still to Parliament, and through Parliament to the electorate beyond. The only difference is that when they go, that part of their work which has the electorate's approval will be protected from the risk of being swept away along with that which is distasteful. This means, I think, some quite unspectacular changes in Parliamentary procedure; and a more considerable change in political attitudes. It means that politicians must have the courage to admit agreement.

What the extent of common agreement in contemporary England may turn out to be (war objectives apart) no one can say: for, with our continual emphasis on differences, no one has ever tried to find out. In practice some of the most difficult issues are likely to arise where there is agreement on ends, but disagreement about the methods by which those ends are to be reached. More people, for instance, are convinced that unemployment must be prevented, than are of one mind as to the right way to prevent it. In social affairs the line between ends and means is not at all clearly drawn: it is indeed by no means easy to draw. Practical politicians appear to trouble very little about the distinction, with the result that attachment to a particular method becomes as passionate as devotion to the objective which that method is intended to promote. For instance: in housing policy what matters is that good, convenient houses should be expeditiously and economically built where they are wanted. The question whether those houses should be built directly by municipalities or through contractors, or in some other way, is a question of method. The first consideration in choice of method must always be the measure in which this or that way of tackling a job will get the job done: and that is (after the event, anyhow) a question of fact. The contractor-versus-municipality issue turns, therefore, primarily on the question—in which the appeal must lie to experience—which of the two will actually show the best performance in the economical and expeditious building of houses where they are wanted. There may well, of course, be no general answer to this question, but different answers in different social and economic environments.

3   *Planning in Whose Interest?*

THE PUBLIC INTEREST

EDWARD BANFIELD

A decision is said to serve special interests if it furthers the ends of some part of the public at the expense of the ends of the larger public. It is said to be in the *public interest* if it serves the ends of the whole public rather than those of some sector of the public.

Within this very general framework, a variety of conceptions are held of the logical structure of the public interest—varying conceptions which significantly influence the kinds of political and planning decisions made. The differences among the views as to the nature of the public interest seem to turn on what is meant by "the ends of the whole public." We will distinguish five differing conceptions:

A. *Unitary Conceptions.* The "whole" may be conceived as a single set of ends which pertain equally to all members of the public. Two contrasting unitary conceptions may be distinguished:

1. *Organismic.* According to this conception, the plurality is an entity or body politic which entertains ends in a corporate capacity; these ends

may be different from those entertained by any of the individuals who comprise the public. A person who thinks of Chicago as a "social organism" having certain ends, such as the viability of the organism, which should have precedence over the ends of individuals entertains this conception of the public interest.

2. *Communalist.* According to this conception, the ends which the plurality entertains "as a whole" are ends which its individual members universally or almost universally share: they are in this sense "common." [1] Ends which many people share are, according to the communalist conception, more valuable than others simply by virtue of being shared. Thus, the communalist attaches more weight to common ends than to unshared ones even though the individuals who entertain the ends may themselves attach more weight to the unshared ones. Thus, for example, a person who takes this

Reprinted with permission of authors and publisher from: Martin Meyerson and Edward Banfield, *Politics, Planning, and Public Interest* (New York: The Free Press, 1955), pp. 322–29.

[1] "The public interest," Professor Schattschneider has written, "may be described as the aggregate of common interests, including the common interest in seeing that there is fair play among private interests." E. E. Schattschneider, "Political Parties and the Public Interest," *Annals of the American Academy of Political and Social Science*, Volume No. 280, March 1952, p. 23.

view of the public interest would maintain that the end of "providing decent housing for all" (presumably a common or at least a widely shared end) should take precedence over such ends as "to maintain property values in Fernwood," "to retain a slum structure from which Messrs. A and B make large profits," and "to prevent Negroes from moving into our block" (all presumably ends that are not common or widely shared).

In the nature of the case, of course, common ends are likely to be very general or vague in their formulation. The communalist tends to feel that a concrete proposal (e.g., to build a certain project in a certain place) should be evaluated in terms of the general (common) end (e.g., "to improve the housing of low-income people") rather than in terms of the more particularized (and less widely shared) ends which become relevant in the concrete case (e.g., to avoid the destruction of some units of good housing in this particular neighborhood).

B. *Individualistic Conceptions.* According to these conceptions, the ends of the plurality do not comprise a single system, either one which pertains to the plurality as an entity or one which is common to individuals. The relevant ends are those of individuals, whether shared or unshared. The ends of the plurality "as a whole" are simply the aggregate of ends entertained by individuals, and that decision is in the public interest which is consistent

with as large a part of the "whole" as possible.[2] This view implies the possibility of making meaningful comparisons not only as to the amount of satisfaction to be had from various classes of ends but also as to the worth of that satisfaction.

Three sub-types may be distinguished:

1. *Utilitarian.* The distinguishing feature of this conception is that the ends of the individual, as selected and ordered by himself, are taken as the relevant quantity: the public interest is "the greatest happiness of the greatest number" of those who constitute the public. According to this view, if there are common ends, there is no reason to attach special value to them simply because they are common; the relevant ends are whatever ends the individual happens to have uppermost —his utility—be they idiosyncratic, widely shared, or common.

According to this conception, one discovers whether or not a decision is in the public interest by identifying all of the gains and losses in utility that are likely to be caused by it and, treating everyone's utility as of equal worth (for to do otherwise would be to introduce a standard other than the utilitarian one), by estimating whether or not there has been a gain in the "total utility" or, to put it more properly, whether or not the magnitude of the gains

---

2 "The interest of the community," Jeremy Bentham wrote, "is one of the most general expression that can occur in phraseology of morals: no wonder that the meaning of it is often lost. When it has a meaning, it is this. The community is a fictitious *body*, composed of the individual persons who are considered as constituting as it were its *members*. The interest of the community then is—what? The sum of the interests of the various members who compose it." *Principles of Morals and Legislation*, Clarendon Press, Oxford, 1876 reprint, p. 3.

in utility is greater than that of the losses.[3]

Thus, according to this view, the dissatisfaction a pillbox dweller feels from having what he considers an unsightly project located near him and the dissatisfaction of a white property owner at having Negroes move into his neighborhood are as worthy of being taken into account (since one man's utility is as good as another's and since utility is the indiscriminate satisfaction of ends) as the dissatisfaction of a Negro at having to live in a slum or of a civic booster at having to admit that his city contains vast slums. To determine the public interest, the loss of satisfaction of the pillbox dweller and of the white property owner must somehow be measured against the gain in satisfaction to the Negro and the booster.

2. *Quasi-Utilitarian.* According to this conception, the utility of the individual is the relevant quantity, but a greater value is attached to

some men's utility than to others: i.e., along with utility, a second standard is introduced. Thus, the ends of the "whole" are whatever ends the individuals who comprise it may happen to have uppermost, but with those of some individuals being given more weight than those of others. Thus, for example, one decision-maker might attach more weight to the utility of white property owners than to that of Negroes while another might make the opposite valuation; both decision-makers, however, would have the same conception of the logical structure of the public interest.

3. *Qualified Individualistic.* According to this conception, the ends of the "whole" are the aggregate of those selected by individuals, but only of those selected by them *from among certain classes of ends* that are deemed appropriate. In other words, in considering the ends of the plurality the person who employs this conception of the public interest excludes from account altogether certain classes of ends which he deems inappropriate or irrelevant.

Various principles may be employed to include or to exclude certain classes of ends. Perhaps the most familiar pattern in our society admits into account ends which: (a) are community-regarding rather than self-regarding; (b) are stable rather than transitory; (c) are general rather than particular in reference; (d) pertain to the role of citizen rather than to some private role; (e) are common or statistically frequent rather than idiosyncratic or infrequent; (f) are logically or morally justified rather than (as with mere whims) expressively justified or not justified

---

[3] Whether or not inter-personal comparisons of utilities can meaningfully be made has been the subject of elaborate discussion among welfare economists. See Charles Kennedy, "Concerning Utility," *Economica,* February 1954. Kennedy concludes that we cannot speak of "greater or less total utility" or of "maximizing the utility of the community" (p. 18), but that "the difference between any pair of magnitudes of utility—which, for one interpretation of utility, may be identified as a 'preference'—is a quantity of a kind to which a special type of addition and subtraction can be applied." (p. 15). Thus, the difference between the magnitude of a Negro's happiness before and after the elimination of segregation may be similarly compared. But the happiness of the whites and of the Negroes cannot be added or subtracted to yield a "total utility."

at all.[4] Thus, for example, an official trying to decide whether to locate a housing project in a particular neighborhood may ignore the arguments of all those persons who view the question not from the standpoint of citizens concerned with the welfare of the city as a whole but from the standpoint of some private and personal interest.

It will be seen that since either the same or different decision-makers employ opposed conceptions of the public interest, the question of which conception is to be regarded as *the* public interest, either in a specific situation, or in general, may itself become a matter of controversy. Moreover, given agreement on any one conception of the formal nature of the public interest, there may be controversy as to its concrete content. Indeed, the agreed upon conception may imply equally any one of a wide range of outcomes.

A somewhat different decision-making mechanism is implied by each of these conceptions of the public interest. A unitary conception implies a cooperative choice process, i.e., one in which the outcome or settlement is derived from a single set of ends. Any individualistic conception, on the other hand, implies a mechanism through which competing ends are compromised.

Thus, a unitary conception implies central decision-makers who are specially well qualified to know the ends of the body politic or the common ends, who can perform the largely technical function of adapting means most efficiently for the attainment of these ends, and who have power to assert the unitary interest of the "whole" over any competing lesser interests. The decision-maker whose task it is to spell out the implications for action of the body politic or of the *ethos* ought, of course, to be free to take account of the "real" rather than the "apparent" interest of the members of the society and to ignore their preferences in the immediate situation if these are inconsistent with the most general and fundamental ends of the society.[5]

A mechanism which is to assert an individualistic conception of the public interest, on the other hand, must select from among or must compromise individual interests in such a way as to create the greatest

---

[4] Thus, for example, J. S. Mill observes that electors will often "have two sets of preferences—those on private and those on public grounds." Private preferences, however, ought to be altogether excluded from account: the elector's vote "has no more to do with his personal wishes than the verdict of a juryman." [J. S. Mill *Utilitarianism, Liberty and Representative Government*, J. M. Dent, London, 1910] pp. 306 and 299. Mill will also give more weight to one's "real ultimate interest" than to his "immediate and apparent interest" (p. 251) and to "higher motives and more comprehensive and distant views." (p. 256.)

A classification of types of ends which may be useful in analyzing such conceptions has been worked out by E. A. Shils and E. C. Banfield in an unpublished paper, "Individual Ends and the Structure of Social Choice."

[5] "Parliament," Edmund Burke said, "is not a *congress* of ambassadors from different and hostile interests, which interests each must maintain as an agent advocate, against other agents and advocates, but Parliament is a *deliberative* assembly of one nation, with *one* interest, that of the whole; where not local purposes, not local prejudices ought to guide, but the general good. . . ." Quoted by C. J. Friedrich, *Constitutional Government and Politics*, Harper, New York, 1937, p. 230.

"total" of end-satisfaction. The utilitarian and quasi-utilitarian conceptions are most nearly realized in a free market (assuming in the one case that the income distribution is such as to give everyone's utility the same weight and in the other case that it gives more weight to the utility of some than of others), for in a market each individual expresses whatever ends he has uppermost (within the range of expression allowed by the market) and the ends expressed are brought into an equilibrium which is the mutually most satisfactory compromise among them. The utilitarian conceptions of the public interest may also be asserted through mechanisms other than the market, of course, but non-market (i.e., political or administrative) mechanisms, if they are to serve the utilitarian conception of the public interest, must perform compromising and equilibrating functions analagous to those performed by the market.[6] To the extent that legislators or other representatives are able to perform the functions of the market, i.e., to arrange that compromise which is mutually most satisfactory in terms of the preferences of the constituents as ordered by the constituents themselves, they function as a utilitarian choice mechanism.

Non-market mechanisms intended to exemplify this conception of the public interest must make use of representatives, but they should employ representatives who represent the smallest possible number of constituents (the more numerous the constituents, the more the representatives must make selections among the ends to be served), and the representatives should be under the necessity of acting only as their constituents specifically instruct (for otherwise the constituents' preferences would be imperfectly represented).

The qualified individualist conception of the public interest implies a mechanism which takes into account the appropriate classes of ends and excludes from account those which are not appropriate. The market will not do this, of course: it makes no distinction between self-regarding ends and community-regarding ones, for example. What is indicated is a political process in which an equilibrium is reached among those ends which are appropriate. A representative process in which the representative gives more weight to his constituents' "real ultimate interest" than to their "immediate and apparent interest" and special weight to "higher motives and more comprehensive and distant views" is implied.[7] This is likely to be a system in which the repre-

[6] Of liberalism Professor Knight has written, ". . . the end of action is whatever the individual wants and strives to do, or to get, or to be. . . ." "Thus ideally all political decisions in a liberal state represent the best possible compromise between the (more or less conflicting) interests of individuals—a composite, or center of gravity, or 'equilibrium of forces,' force being the form under which interests are conceived as operating." *Freedom and Reform*, Harper, New York, 1947, pp. 53 and 78.

[7] The quoted phrases are from J. S. Mill, *op. cit.* pp. 251 and 256. The structure of the choice process ought to be such as to encourage the representative to make the appropriate selection from among his constituents' ends. He should, for example, "have such a term of office to look forward to as will enable him to be judged, not by a single act, but by his course of action." *Ibid*, p. 313.

sentative can be called to account only infrequently and then by a relatively large constituency, an arrangement which permits him to ignore all inappropriate ends and to bring into equilibrium with others only those ends which, by the standards deemed relevant, ought to be taken into account in determining the greatest satisfaction "of the whole."

An institution may function as a mechanism which asserts at the same time different, and perhaps logically opposed, conceptions of the structure of the public interest. The members of a citizen board, for example, may endeavor to explicate the meaning of some very general ends which pertain to the body politic or *ethos* while at the same time—and perhaps inconsistently—seeking to find that compromise among the ends of individuals which will represent the greatest "total" satisfaction. Thus, the outcome of a process in which various conceptions of the public interest are asserted is likely to be an amalgam.

Since the nature of the choice mechanism employed determines in part of the content of the public interest, the question of which conception of the structure of the public interest is appropriate, in particular circumstances or in general, is suitably discussed in terms of which *mechanism* of choice is preferable—or whether, for example, representatives should have long terms or short, large constituencies or small, or whether the market or another mechanism should be employed.

4   Planning by What Authority?

SOCIAL PLANNING:
THE SEARCH FOR LEGITIMACY

Martin Rein

All planning must in some fashion resolve the problem of legitimacy— what authority justifies its intervention. This is particularly true for those types of social reform and city planning that share a common ideological commitment to introduce *social innovation*—new programs and new ideas that will reduce or eliminate social problems.

What makes the intervention of the reformer and planner meaningful and desirable? How is the need for innovative intervention justified and support for it secured? The problem of legitimacy is especially acute in American democratic society because the reformer-planner has only limited power to implement his objectives. Lacking power, "the ability to control external and internal environments and/or to counteract the consequences of imperfect control,"[1] he needs, therefore, to win cooperation to achieve his aims. He must collect and harness fragmented power in order to bring about planned change.

Some planning organizations hope to bypass this dilemma by repudiating the mandate to innovate or to promote planned change. They define their mission as providing only a forum to help others reach agreement through the intervention of "enablers" rather than "planners."[2] In contrast, organizations promoting planned change must seek the authority to impose limits on the freedom of other organizations. They attempt to subordinate interests or change functions and purposes of some organizations in order to promote that elusive ideal we call the public interest. Yet, as soon as such

Reprinted with permission of author and publisher from: Martin Rein, "Social Planning: The Search for Legitimacy," *Journal of the American Institute of Planners*, 35: 4 (July 1969), 233–44. Author's Note: The author wishes to thank Peter Marris, Thomas Reiner, Bernard Frieden, and Melvin Webber for critical reactions to earlier versions of this paper.

1 David A. Armstrong, "Some Notes on the Concept of Planning" (Tavistock Institute of Human Relations, London, July 1964), p. 8. (Mimeographed.)
2 For an analysis of the dilemma that such organizations confront when they seek to promote change, or when they fail to embrace all relevant community interests in their forum, see Martin Rein and Robert Morris, "Goals, Structures and Strategies of Planned Change," in *Social Work Practice, 1962* (New York: Columbia University Press, 1962).

organizations are powerful enough to be effective, they are also strong enough to abuse their power. Efforts must then be developed to contain their power. In a democratic society, great restraints are placed on the centralization of power, while greater freedom is given to individual units. Still, when injustices exist, some centralized power is needed to correct them. How to reconcile the clashing demands between the resources needed to check social abuse and the power needed to reduce human suffering, with their reduction in the freedom of action of others which such action requires, is a great challenge to democratic societies. The search for legitimacy is an effort to resolve this dilemma.

CITY PLANNING SOURCES OF AUTHORITY

A review of the experience of city planners in the United States suggests that they have relied on four different sources of authority to justify and legitimate their intervention. These might be called the authorities of *expertise, bureaucratic position, consumer preferences,* and *professional values.*

THE AUTHORITY OF EXPERTISE

This approach is based on the assumption that planners have command of a technical-scientific body of knowledge that enables them to challenge irrationality in the political process of city government, which has produced decisions based on "opportunistic bargaining among vested political economic interests

of great strength."[3] The early planning movement was based on a doctrine which said that what planners needed was great formal powers, independent of the political process, which would enable them to act as an autonomous "fourth power" in city government.[4] In 1934, the first City Planning Commission of New York City was comprised of a majority of members who "were committed to the premise that the Commission should be an institution of experts with an authoritative voice in the decisions of city government, yet be itself aloof and protected, without the necessity of bargaining with and making concessions to the 'politicians' and special interests."[5] Experience soon suggested that political autonomy leads to isolation and independence leads to impotence. Authority that is depoliticized, that is independent from the political process and based on technical-scientific rationality, offers only the authority to propose, rather than the power to achieve.[6] Not surprisingly, the need for new sources of authority was soon recognized.

[3] Wallace S. Sayre and Herbert Kaufman, *Governing New York City: Politics in the Metropolis* (New York: Russell Sage Foundation, 1960), p. 372.
[4] This argument was again set forth when a group of planners was asked to advise on the development of planning in Puerto Rico. See Rexford Gray Tugwell, "The Place of Planning in Society," a series of seven lectures on the place of planning in society with special reference to Puerto Rico (Technical Paper No. 7, San Juan Puerto Rico Planning Board, 1954).
[5] Sayre and Kauman, *Governing New York City,* pp. 372–73.
[6] See Robert C. Fried, "Professionalism and Politics in Roman Planning," *Journal of the American Institute of Planners,* XXXV, No. 3 (May 1969), 150–59.

THE AUTHORITY
OF BUREAUCRACY

During the 1940s, public administrators debated the possibility of separating politics and administration.[7] This debate centered around the issue of whether every administrative act also entailed a political consequence that obviated the purely technological solution. If politics cannot be separated from administration, then the planner secures his authority from politicians rather than technology. However, the more incomplete the control over the administrative process, the wider the influence of the professional, thus the planner's role in developing policy is ambiguous. According to this interpretation, the difficulty with the concept of planning as a "fourth power" was that the claims of the planners conflicted with those of the politicians.

In a recent analysis of this debate, Beckman took the position that this conflict of identity between the planner and the politician "can best be resolved . . . if he (the planner) is willing to accept the vital but more limited role that our system assigned to the public employee."[8] Beckman

urges the planner to assist and serve the policy-maker since the planner's "influence on public policy is achieved within the bureaucracy through competence. Planners and other staff advisers have influence only as they can persuade their political superiors . . . it must be remembered that in our system of government politics subordinates the public employee, grants responsibility and power to the politician, invests open authority in the voter."[9]

The planner who repudiates a decision of his superiors can try to persuade them to accept his opinion or he can resign in indignation. But in his role as an employee, the planner secures his authority from the director of a planning organization whose head is appointed by elected representatives who in turn secure their authority from voting citizens.

The theory about the relationship between the planner as a bureaucrat and the politician as the representative of the electorate often disintegrates in practice. The scope and complexity of public bureaucracies make them increasingly independent of review by elected officials. They control the information by which their competence can be challenged, and they outlast the politicians whose policies they execute. Moreover, elected officials serve the interests of certain groups better than the interests of others or of some hypothesized overall public interest.

[7] For opposing arguments, see Carl Friedrich, *Constitutional Government and Democracy* (Boston: Ginn and Company, 1946); and Herman Finer, *Theory and Practice of Modern Government* (Rev. ed., New York: Henry Holt and Company, 1949), pp. 871–85. For a useful summary of the debate, see, Glendon Schubert, *The Public Interest* (Glencoe, Illinois: The Free Press, 1960), pp. 120–21.

[8] Norman Beckman, "The Planner as a Bureaucrat," *Journal of the American Institute of Planners*, XXX, No. 4 (November 1964), p. 324. See also Alan Altshuler, *The City Planning Process: A Political Analysis* (New York: Cornell University Press, 1965).

[9] *Ibid.*, pp. 326–27. Altshuler argues that since "political officials seldom give planners any clear instructions to guide the value-choice aspects of their work, much discretion remains with the experts." He thus appears to reject Beckman's formulation of the planner's role as bureaucrat. Mr. Altshuler's comments apply to any bureaucrat in the strict Weberian sense of the term.

In theory an aggrieved citizen can protest directly to his representative against any intrusion of his rights or neglect of his needs. In practice, in a democracy, the needs and preferences of unpopular, unwanted, and powerless groups are neglected. Politicians are committed to political survival. They respond to the preferences of the constituencies that elect them rather than the needs of the inarticulate and hence unrepresented groups.

THE AUTHORITY
OF CONSUMERS

In the 1950s, the critique against the planner as a bureaucrat began to emerge in Herbert Gans', John Dyckman's, and Martin Meyerson's studies of recreation, education, and health care facilities. They came to recognize that planning which was responsive to professional discretion and to political leadership might in the process forsake the preferences, needs, and desires of the consuming population. What they seemed to be calling for was a new technology which could develop new standards by feeding new information into the planning process—namely data derived from social scientific inquiries about the preferences of present and potential service users. Gans, Dyckman, and Meyerson wrote that planning must be responsive to the consumer market. Explicit criteria as to how to establish procedures to resolve differences among the clashing preferences of different income or age groupings or to resolve conflicts that might arise when consumer preferences clashed with the policies of planners, the established

bureaucracy, or elected officials were not developed.[10]

Rapkin, Winnick, and Blank in their monograph on Housing Market Analysis developed a similar position, holding that the criteria for developing public policy should rest on the choices of users as these are identified through the mechanism of the market.[11] Turning to the ultimate consumer as the source of legitimacy for planning opened important ideological questions concerning the limits and possibilities of exploiting the market as a mechanism for assessing consumer choices. Davidoff and Reiner extended the general argument—"It is not for the planner to make the final decision transforming values into policy commitments. His role is to identify distribution of values among people, and how values are weighed against each other." [12]

By 1960, new forces emerged in the political process which gave currency and acceptability to the idea of consumer advocacy. A new body of literature and experience developed which sought to derive the legitimacy of the planner from the preferences of consumers, especially those who are politically inarticulate. Some planners were urging that a new source of legitimacy be

10 Though they taught together and wrote a great deal on this theme, these scholars have not yet written up their work in a single report.

11 Chester Rapkin, Louis Winnick, and David Blank, *Housing Market Analyses: A Study of Theory and Method*, a report from the Institute for Urban Land Use and Housing Studies for the Housing and Home Finance Agency, 1952.

12 Paul Davidoff and Thomas A. Reiner, "A Choice Theory of Planning," *Journal of the American Institute of Planners*, XXVIII, No. 2 (May 1962), 108.

found with the planner acting as a more direct advocate of the values, preferences, and needs of consumer groups—planning should derive its legitimacy from the needs of the people to be serviced. The planner could then offer his skills to a user-bureaucracy as contrasted with the supplier-bureaucracy to which planners presently offer their services.

These ideas found expression in the theory of advocacy planning which asserts that planners can derive their legitimacy from the clients to be served. Advocacy implies argument and contention on behalf of a point of view or of a specific proposal. Paul Davidoff in his influential article, "Advocacy and Pluralism in Planning," makes this position explicit when he urges that "the advocate planner would be responsible to his client and would seek to express his clients' views." [13]

All of these writers accepted the position that planners derive their legitimacy from the preferences, choices, and needs of the users, consumers, and clients who are affected by planning decisions. But they differ on this position's implications for action. A point of view oriented to clients can lead to social surveys of consumer choices, or to faith in the market as the ultimate mechanism for the expressions of choice, or to the defense of consumer rights within an adversary rather than a market framework. Each position has its difficulties. The preferences of all individuals as revealed from survey rankings of values cannot be aggregated into collective preferences without violating the choices

of some individuals (following the famous Arrow paradox). Planning originated as an effort to supplement or supersede the market when it failed to meet individual needs or solve the problem of externalities. Faith in market freedom and choice for users did not contribute substantially to resolving these issues of public policy, and as we have begun to experiment with advocacy, intractable problems have emerged. . . .

THE AUTHORITY OF PROFESSIONAL VALUES

Another source of legitimacy rests on the professional values to which the planner is committed as well as the technical competence he claims. According to this formulation, city planning is a value-laden profession, and these values offer a course of authority—a sanction to plan. There is surely an uneasy nestling together of expertise and ideology, and a general reluctance to act on the authority of the latter is evident. Nevertheless, as the impossibility of separating values and technology is accepted, action based on values is taken. One form is the creation of a competing professional association committed to implementing different values. "It appears that the profession is being split into progressive and conservative wings: the former calling for social planning to reduce racial and economic inequalities, and the latter defending traditional physical planning and the legitimacy of the middle-class values." [14]

[13] Paul Davidoff, "Advocacy and Pluralism in Planning," *Journal of the American Institute of Planners*, XXXI (November 1965), 331–38.

[14] Herbert Gans, "Social Planning: Regional and Urban Planning," in *International Encyclopedia of the Social Sciences* (New York: The Macmillan Company and The Free Press, 1968), p. 131.

Increasingly planners are enjoined to act as insurgents within the bureaucracies where they are employed and to seek change in the policies and purposes of the bureaucracy according to the declared value assumptions. These values are procedural as well as substantive. Decision rules, such as involvement of those affected by decisions, illustrate the former, and goals, such as racially and economically integrated communities or reduction of inequalities illustrate the latter.

Public opinion and official policies of the bureaucracy may be hostile to these values. The planner who acts as a rebel within his bureaucracy challenges its established procedures and policies. A declaration of open warfare forces the bureaucrat to resign on principle. As an outsider he may elect to infiltrate in his role as consultant or researcher. Many private consultant firms and individual planners are committed to promoting their professional values as well as their technology. The bureaucrat may elect to stay and wage guerilla warfare, choosing points where the system is internally vulnerable, or he may develop coalitions with external groups to create internal change. He may lie dormant for years when levers for change are absent. Yet, every bureaucracy has insurgents who are ready to act as guerilla-reformers to shake up the bureaucracy.[15] . . .

[15] In the planning field, there has been at least one effort to create a loose coalition of insurgents who are seeking to change the policies of their own and other programs. Leonard Duhl calls this coalition a "floating crap game." The analogy is misleading though because the players are not in competition with each other but rather seek to support each other in their

This source of legitimacy poses awkward issues concerning the boundaries between professional and personal values, ethics of means and ends to be adopted, and procedures of professional accountability to judge when ethics have surrendered to expediency. But despite these and other difficulties, planners who repudiate the position that values and technology are separable are experimenting with this source of legitimacy.

STRATEGIES OF LEGITIMACY

Even this condensed review of the history of physical planning makes it evident that city planners have sought different sources of legitimacy: as scientific experts, independent of the political process; as agents of elected political representatives and the bureaucracies which are accountable to them; as translators and advocates of the preferences of user-groups; and finally, as implementors of professional values. Each source of legitimacy has its characteristic difficulties, as this brief review of the experience of physical planners as expert, bureaucrat, advocate, and insurgent has suggested.

But why must planners be forced to choose among these alternative sources of legitimacy? The position of planning could be substantially strengthened if it could simultaneously call upon professional technology, values, and standards, established political power, and the needs and wishes of client groups as sources of legitimacy. However, if

common mission. Professional associations, such as Planners for Equal Opportunity (PEO), may also serve as reference groups.

these sources of legitimacy conflict when pursued together—and they nearly always do—then the planner must choose among them.

A review of the experience of what Reston called the "new breed of anti-poverty planners" helps to illuminate the problems which arise in adapting each source of legitimacy and in pursuing multiple sources of legitimacy which are in conflict. Federal legislation, such as the Juvenile Delinquency and Youth Offences Control Act of 1961 and the Economic Opportunity Act of 1964, provided the resources which made this form of social planning possible. More recently, through legislation made possible by the Demonstration Cities and Metropolitan Development Act of 1966, the style of planning has been extended to cope with problems of deterioration in the urban environment. The search conducted by these social planners and reformers for a relevant form of legitimacy is strikingly parallel to the search for legitimacy among city planners.

The city planner and this type of social planner share much in common. They both spend a great deal of their energies writing proposals in an effort to secure federal and state funds; they are both concerned with developing specific programs to implement ambiguous and ill-defined social objectives; they are both committed to drawing up both long-range and short-range plans; both are in principle committed to introduction of new ideas and to generation of social innovations that can lay the foundation for further experimentation; and finally, both hope to have the plans they developed implemented administratively. But, in the context of this paper, the

important common ground they share is the search for legitimacy. How can their intervention be justified?

In the remainder of this paper three strategies are examined from the perspective of how they contribute to resolving the problem of legitimation of reform.[16] They are *elite consensus, rational analysis,* and *citizen participation.* Each strategy is crucial. None is sufficient by itself, for each has inherent limitations, but the efforts to pursue more than one strategy at a time often lead to conflict and contradiction. Thus in the effort to resolve one dilemma another is created.

THE CONSENSUS OF ELITES

One way of justifying intervention is to have it endorsed and supported by the leadership of the major institutions in the community. This strategy acknowledges the power of established institutions. One version seeks to influence power by boring from within, by co-opting the institutions to serve its purposes. The endorsement by established power legitimates the efforts of reform and change.

At one time in the social services this power of change was vested in the coalition of *voluntary* institutions that represented the elite of the community leaders.

Welfare services and planning became recognizably controlled by an essentially

16 The claim to a source of legitimacy must be only illusory. Hence we need to pay attention to inauthentic claims to legitimacy. Under special circumstances, myths can be very important in convincing others that the claim should be heeded. This article does not systematically explore this important issue.

elite leadership in each community. . . . Associated with the socially elite were an economic elite. . . . These economic sinews became the foundation for the support of much of social welfare. It was only later recognized that this elite leadership was primarily white and Protestant, representing the early stratification of American society.[17]

These early economic and social elites often rejected the role of government in welfare, substituting voluntary health and welfare councils. They held an elitist view of democracy, assuming that they were best able to comprehend, to represent, and to protect the interests of the "total community."

Today, because of the changing role of government and the development of new centers of power, such voluntary bodies can no longer provide an adequate base for legitimate change. Consequently, planners have had to seek the participation of city government by forming a coalition of departments such as welfare, recreation, police, and the like, or a coalition of units of government such as the city, the county, the school boards, and the state. Legitimacy depends on bringing together a broad range of groups representing old and new sources of power—influential leaders, established organizational interests, and government.

A new factor is national influence on local action. In a penetrating analysis of the relationship between sociology and the welfare state, Gouldner calls attention to "the manner in which social reform in the United States has changed in character. What is new is not the 'plight

[17] Robert Morris and Martin Rein, "Emerging Patterns in Community Planning," in *Social Work Practice, 1963* (New York: Columbia University Press, 1963), p. 156.

of the cities,' however increasing their deterioration, but rather . . . the locus of reform initiatives and resources is increasingly found on the level of national politics and foundations, rather than in the political vitality, the economic resources, or the zealous initiatives of elites with local roots." [18]

A broad-based representative organizational structure that serves to legitimate reform may likely conflict with its very purpose—the search for innovation and change.[19] The greater the diversity of institutional interest that is embraced within such a planning structure, the greater can

[18] Alvin W. Gouldner, "The Sociologist as Partisan: Sociology and the Welfare State," *The American Sociologist,* III, No. 2 (May 1968), 109.

[19] The use of the terms innovation and change may require some explanation. I find useful the distinction developed by Lake in his review of theories and research about social change. He states, "there is no clear distinction in the literature reviewed between a *strategy* of innovation and a *theory* of change. . . . When concepts are tied in with tactics of inducing those concepts (about change) and when time phasing activities are suggested, then the theories become strategies of innovation . . . a theory of change . . . is not accompanied by a program for inducing change." Dale G. Lake, "Concepts of Change and Innovation in 1966," *Journal of Applied Behavioral Science,* IV, No. 1 (1968), 4–5. Kahn and his colleagues treat innovation as the procedures, roles, and activities that enable an organization to depart from fixed rules in the face of changing circumstances. For their discussion of innovative roles within an organization, see Robert Kahn *et al., Organizational Stress: Studies in Role Conflict and Ambiguity* (New York: John Wiley and Sons, 1964), chap. 7.

This paper is concerned with the effort of some organizations to induce innovation in other organizations. This process I define as planned change or social reform.

be the claim for legitimacy, since it can be claimed that most of the total community is represented. But as legitimacy is strengthened, innovation will probably be forsaken in favor of maintaining a consensus on which these divergent interests can agree. These new planning structures are continually beset with internal insurrection. In practice the commitment to shared goals seems less compelling than the preservation of organizational autonomy. Involvement of community leaders does little to resolve the problems of jurisdictional conflict; indeed, it may only aggravate the task. Voluntary planning bodies and the elite community leaders who represent them want more influence than they receive as only members (rather than convenors) of the coalition. Whereas they once enjoyed preeminence in the area of planning, they have now been cast aside and relegated to a secondary role by this new, more widely representative structure. Consequently, much of the energy of the planning organization is directed away from promoting innovation and change and toward solving the more intractable problems of sheer survival—maintenance of the coalition.[20]

20 For further evidence on the conflict between innovation and broad-based organizations in voluntary social welfare organizations and in health and welfare councils, see Martin Rein, "Organization for Change," *Social Work*, IX, No. 2 (April 1964), 32–41; and Martin Rein and Robert Morris, "Goals, Structures and Strategies for Community Change," pp. 32–41. For a review of the literature of international organizations that reaches a similar conclusion, see Richard E. Walton, "Two Strategies of Social Change and their Dilemmas," *Journal of Applied Behavioral Science*, I, No. 2 (April/May/June 1965), 167–79.

The national reformers who made available the funds for these local planning organizations recognized this dilemma, but hoped that it could be solved. Essentially, their strategy rested on two related assumptions: that a marginal increase in funds can stimulate change, and that the involvement of voluntary and public bureaucracies is a necessary precondition for change. They hoped the power of federal money—small outlays with the anticipation of larger amounts of funds—and the process of participation would lead to change. They assumed that financially starved institutions would be willing to make changes in their operation in order to secure available and needed funds. Local reformers operating from these local planning organizations would play a central role in this process, for they could serve as interpreters of the institutional changes that would be required if funds were to be forthcoming. The professional reformer, enjoying a monopoly of knowledge and special access to nonlocal funders, could assert a substantial amount of influence on the direction in which the local coalition of elites would develop in order to obtain the wanted funds. *The fundamental premise in these negotiations was that because funds were so desperately needed by local institutions, they would be willing to participate in self-reform in order to secure them.* That the institutions might both obtain the funds from established and new sources and resist change was a contingency to which local and national planners seemed to have given little attention.

This second assumption rested on the faith that the process of involvement and participation might lead to self-education and the acceptance of the need to change. The implicit theory of bureaucracy on which this belief rests is that the sources of organizational rigidity are largely ignorance and faulty communication. If a context were provided in which institutional representatives could more freely communicate with one another, the validity of the need for change would more readily be recognized and accepted. Such a theory is, however, incomplete, for it ignores the existence of the more fundamental conflict of values and interests among institutions that more open communication might serve to exacerbate rather than to alleviate. The insistence upon participation of power in self-reform appeals to common sense yet it rests on inadequate assumptions about how institutions perform. In practice, organizations often agreed or participated to protect their interests rather than to promote the more illusive common goals on which the concept of the public interest rests. Thus agreement on a new form that committed organizations to involvement in a process did not equally commit them to accept changes in their policy and programs. The latent conflict was only postponed. When it emerged, the coalition of autonomous participants was in danger of falling part. As a result of these challenges, compromises were made to assure survival, and in the process innovation was sacrificed to achieve consensus.

Much as a representative structure may reduce innovation, participation by institutions in their own reform may lead to continuity of established policy. The funds made available by planners were simply not large enough to finance major reforms in these institutions. But even if sufficient funds were available, it is hard to see how planners could conceivably hope to initiate major structural changes unless the changes were in conformity with the institutions' prevailing interpretation of their functions and reflected directions the institutions were already prepared to take. Under these conditions it is the planners who have been co-opted by the institutions. *Involvement, although it facilitates legitimation, impedes innovation.*

An alternative to the theory that institutions change with self-education is derived from the assumption that institutions must be challenged, for they will not change of their own accord. The public health movement, which was promoted largely by lay groups, arose (with the support of some professionals) above the vigorous opposition of physicians; similarly, the Charity Organization Society (the mainstay and bulwark behind social casework before the depression) was opposed to pensions for widows and the aged in the early part of the century; and the Charity School opposed public education. According to this view, reform cannot depend solely upon the willing cooperation of the institutions to be reformed.

While it is useless to ignore the realities of established institutional power, a program of planned change runs the dire risk of losing its sense of purpose if it relies only on established leadership. Increasingly, planners find that the more they work with established institutions, the more compromises they have to make, the more difficult it becomes to ensure that funds are spent for innovation rather than for expansion of the status quo. This frustration has led to a tendency to bypass major service institutions. For example, we find in education the development of preschool programs, afterschool programs, summer school programs, tutorial programs which consistently circumvent the heart of the school's mission—everyday teaching—and create instead a whole series of special remedial programs. Remediation becomes a kind of index of the failure to achieve more basic structural change. It represents response to the more frustrating task of directly influencing the essential functions of the institution itself. Institutional resistance leads to program proliferation. . . .

THE POWER OF KNOWLEDGE

Another way of legitimizing planned change is to offer reforms as rational, coherent, intellectual solutions to the problems that are being dealt with. This tends to be the approach favored by academia and professional consultants. Knowledge in the rationalistic-scientific tradition in general and knowledge derived from empirical research in particular can provide a basis for legitimacy because, presumably, it can yield valid solutions. These, in turn, depend on a value-free social science capable of objectively probing the etiology of social problems and presenting programs for action based upon fact rather than upon institutional or other value biases. The analysis of social problems and the remedies proposed for reducing or eliminating them are viewed as technical rather than ideological issues. For example, the President's Committee on Juvenile Delinquency

was especially committed to the importance of rational analysis as the basis for planning and program development. As a condition for receiving funds, national reformers required that communities attempt to conceptualize the problems of delinquency, poverty, or physical and social decay in the light of relevant data and social theory.

Reform stakes out a claim for legitimacy when it is based, not upon political consensus or ideological bias, but primarily upon the hard dispassionate facts provided by a rigorous social science analysis. Proponents of this position believe that science can and should "supersede moral and ideological speculation." Earlier, this position was expressed by those committed to the idea of policy sciences (1940s) and the end of ideology thesis (1950s).[21] Consistent with this philosophy, the President's Committee promoted the ideals that not only are social plans to be based on a thorough, objective appraisal of the social problem, but the efforts at solution themselves are to be rigorously evaluated. With ruthless disregard for bureaucratic interests, those programs judged to be successful would be continued, whereas those falling short of the objective standards would be rejected and discontinued. Change is to be based not upon fads and vested interests but upon the evidence provided by evaluative research of program outputs. Science, rather than elitism, justifies intervention.

This strategy of reform has its own inherent contradictions. Perhaps not

21 For a thoughtful review of these issues, see T. S. Simey, *Social Science and Social Purposes* (London: Constable and Co., Ltd., 1968), p. 138.

in the long run since researchers can always justify their activities as ultimately contributing to truth and knowledge; but in the short run, it does indeed involve conflict, for gathering information is not without its costs. Consider the difficulty that many planning organizations have encountered in their efforts to study the conditions and problems of the Negro urban ghetto. Research, as one angry account has put it, can serve as "transparent dodges for the postponement of action, that those involved in the charade of research into the problems of disadvantaged youth are willing or inadvertent accessories to those who seem to perpetuate the clear and present injustices." [22] A disillusioned Negro community wants authentic action, not rhetoric, promises, or studies.

Although these resentments may not be altogether rational, they are surely understandable, particularly when we recognize that the preliminary research and analysis of so many of the community action programs became extremely esoteric, and in many cases never really issued any pragmatic proposals. Indeed, it is often difficult to find coherence among the social theory, the facts presented, and the programs that are developed to reduce the problem. This widespread disjunction between programs of reform and research and theoretical insights represents an important limitation of the contribution of research and theory to the reduction of social problems. Much of the research growing out of these planning efforts has not yielded new knowledge about the poor, nor has it yielded especially new insights into our understanding of delinquency, nor has it led to the kinds of new programs that need to be developed to tackle these problems. From these experiences it would appear that the contribution of value-free social science information to the development of social policy has been greatly oversold.

The rigorous testing of experimental action programs has also encountered fundamental obstacles. The most difficult problem the researcher found was explication of the social objectives for which the intervention was introduced. This was especially true for programs with broad, multiple, and partially conflicting goals directed at expanding opportunity or promoting organizational change. There were administrative as well as conceptual problems. It is difficult to include in most experimental social action programs the rigid controls that are necessary to provide the kind of clear-cut findings upon which it is possible to accept or reject particular techniques of intervention.

When this rationale of reform calls for comprehensive action involving many interrelated programs, committed to broad and diffuse goals, a difficult research task becomes even more discouragingly complex. The demands of action are such that planners need to be somewhat opportunistic, flexibly adapting to shifting political coalitions that substantially alter the content on which their comprehensive program rests. But when the input variables are subject to significant change, the

22 Harlem Youth Opportunities Unlimited, *Youth in the Ghetto: A Study of the Consequences of Powerlessness and a Blueprint for Change* (New York: Har-YOU, 1964), pp. 2–3.

research task becomes even more tangled. As the limitations of the research design grow more apparent, it becomes hard to know what caused the measured outcomes. As a result, the interpretation to be drawn from the findings is open to serious question. Staunch supporters of particular programs are more likely to reject the research methodology and repudiate the criteria of evaluation, rather than accept the implications of negative findings that most evaluative research tends to yield.[23]

A strategy that relies upon the power of knowledge has other inherent limitations as well, for it can also conflict with other strategies of change. Research requires a degree of autonomy if it is to follow a problem, not yielding to political expediency and feasibility. But the ruthless pursuit of a problem, without regard to the question of implementation, may lead to a solution that, while it is rational, is not politically relevant. This, of course, is the fundamental dilemma of all rational planning, the attempt to reconcile the conflicting requirements of rationality and feasibility. Planning that disregards the question of implementation languishes as an academic irrelevancy; it may be right but not relevant, correct but not useful. While planning and research require

close integration, they make competing claims for resources. Enterprising researchers have been able to secure a very substantial portion of total budgets available to planning agencies, while unwary planners are left with reduced resources to carry out their tasks. Irrelevancy can arise not only in the competition for resources, but in the conflicting value biases of the researcher and reformer—the different emphases they give to knowledge and action. Research can become preoccupied with a spurious rigor, leading to a kind of dustbowl empiricism that provides data overload. Without theory to guide in sorting the findings we have a situation where answers (data) are in search of questions. Bewildered planners are left with a maze of tables and data that yield no immediately coherent themes and that provide little information from which implications can be drawn. Reformers often hope that researchers will guide the development of planning policy by conducting studies that will help confirm or reject the basic underlying rationale of the organizations. Yet to develop new programs requires social inventiveness, rarely a product of formal research.

Even more than being a costly irrelevance, research can subvert the reformers' goals. The experience of the delinquency prevention programs offers an interesting example. The national reformers sought programs that would test the assumption that social institutions throw up barriers and block access to achievement—a process that contributes to increased disengagement and deviancy on the part of the rejected

23 See, for example, Melvin Herman, "Problems of Evaluation," *The American Child*, XLVII, No. 2 (March 1965), 5–10; and U.S. Congress, Senate Subcommittee on Employment, Manpower and Poverty of the Committee on Labor and Public Welfare, *Hearings on S. 1545, Part 10* (Comments on Sar Levitan, "Work Experience and Training," staff paper), 90th Cong., 1st Sess., 1968, pp. 3072–81.

populations. Yet the methodological bias of researchers led the reformers away from their original commitment to institutional change and toward a redefinition of the problem in terms of individual rehabilitation. Thus, social scientists sometimes act to reinforce those pressures on planning organizations that prevent focus on community institutions as prime targets of change. Researchers usually favor the more rigorous, traditional, and tested approaches of their disciplines, such as surveys of individual attitudes, self-perceptions, and role models. The indices they have developed to measure the impact of demonstration programs have occasionally been behavioral but more often attitudinal. They have, by and large, avoided indices that would measure institutional change in favor of a more individualistic approach.

Research may conflict not only with the purposes of reform, but also with the search for elite consensus. Organizational studies that lead to the documentation of bureaucratic rigidities and social injustice may conflict with efforts to promote cooperation and secure consensus among institutions that are being researched. If research relentlessly pursues data on the operation of the bureaucracy, it will uncover findings that could become a source of embarrassment to cooperating institutions. Indeed, where such information is available, it is extremely awkward to know exactly what to do with it. If the information becomes public knowledge, it would only antagonize the institutions whose cooperation is so desperately sought. Yet, maintaining secrets is always

hazardous. This may account, in part, for the fact that planners have rarely insisted that researchers study institutional performance.

Finally, research may not be able to answer the problems posed by the reformer. Consider briefly one such question that local, gradual, and comprehensive programs must confront. The hub of a comprehensive social welfare program can be developed around many institutions— the outreach school, the welfare department, the mental hygiene clinic, and employment centers. Some of the traditional voluntary services— settlement houses and welfare councils—are no longer regarded as adequate focal institutions for the coordination of local service programs. But do we have any factual data that can guide us in the selection of one or another of these institutions as the appropriate focus for a comprehensive community program? Should social programs center around health, housing, employment, education, reducing dependency? If all of these are legitimate, must we then abandon the search for a truly comprehensive program and settle for the present muddle of coordination, saturation, and concerted services?

Just as a broadly representative planning structure can subvert innovation in order to preserve the frail coalition of conflicting interests, so too can researchers subvert the reformers' mission if they become preoccupied with methodology and use their studies to promote their professional identities rather than the interests of the action program. The concern for rigor and professional identity may lead to neglect of relevant action problems. The concern for knowledge without explicit, carefully developed social purposes contributes to narrow technicism.

THE POWER OF THE PEOPLE

Reformers can also claim legitimacy if their programs are endorsed, supported, and created by the recipients of the service. Such an approach has the advantage of avoiding the arrogant assumption that the technical expert or the elitist best knows the needs of the poor. It avoids the onerous charge of welfare colonialism or paternalism, wherein one group in society provides services on behalf of another. Recipients of the service are defined as politically articulate consumers, as citizens rather than as clients in need of therapy and care. Democracy is, after all, not only the search for elite consensus but also the mobilization of interest groups, each striving to pursue its own aims in the context of a pluralistic society. The American democratic system, according to this view, depends on rectifying "the basic imbalance between elites and non-elites by modifying the power differential between them." [24] It attempts to carry out this strategy by providing disadvantaged groups with more powerful instruments for articulating their demands and preferences. It helps them to organize protests in which their moral claim to justice and equal treatment can find expression. In addition to collective action it places before the poor the machinery of law through which they can

act as plaintiffs against institutions that have bypassed their rights.

Strategies of planned change, that derive their legitimacy from the direct participation of local citizens and service users, have had a stormy history since they were launched by the President's Committee on Juvenile Delinquency and Youth Crime in 1962. These developments must be seen in the context of the civil rights revolution and the emergence of militant demands for black power. In response to pressures, representative communitywide structures were broadened to include individuals and groups that were the targets of change. The principle of "maximum feasible participation" articulated in the Economic Opportunity Act was administratively interpreted in many ways including direct participation of the poor on policy-making boards of Community Action Agencies.[25] In some cities, such as San Francisco (and later Oakland under the Model Cities Program), participation was interpreted as control, and the poor dominated the board with the mayor retreating to a subordinate role.[26] As organizational resistance to social change was encountered, participation turned from planning to social protest and social action, taking the form of rent strikes, boycotts, picketing, and other strategies of confron-

---

24 Peter Bachrach, "Elite Consensus and Democracy," *Journal of Politics,* XXIV (1962), 451.

25 For a discussion of the critique of participation as policy-making, see John C. Donovan, *The Politics of Poverty* (New York: Pegasus, 1967), pp. 41–48

26 James Cunningham, "The Struggle of the American for Freedom and Power," a report prepared for the Ford Foundation, August 1967. See, pp. 57–69 for an account of community action in the city of San Francisco.

tation to promote change.[27] More recently, citizen participation has come to mean community control of social services, such as multiservice centers, health programs, and a decentralized public school system.[28] The Model Cities Program encouraged experimentation with advocacy planning, where local groups (Boston, for example) were able to win resources to hire their own planners to develop plans incorporating social and physical resources for the reduction of urban blight. Under the Nixon Administration, the Community Self-Determination Act of 1968, now before Congress, may usher in yet a new phase of user control for it is designed to create community-controlled business enterprises that would permit the people of the community "to utilize a share of the profits of (these) enterprises to provide needed social services."[29]

The acceptance of this argument leads to an anomalous position for it inadvertently supports a different interpretation of democracy for the poor than for other segments of society.[30] In the middle-income style of democratic involvement, citizens work through their representatives, whereas in low-income communities, democracy tends to be interpreted as a form of direct participation at the grassroots level. Community competence through self-help becomes defined as a therapeutic process for promoting social integration. Competent communities produce competent men, as each man is his own politician. Organizations are expected to develop spontaneously out of the mutual interests of residents working side by side on common problems. The rewards of participation are defined as civic pride, personal growth, and the reduction of community deviancy. The groups are not forged out of the more pragmatic interests in personal favors and economic advantages which more typically characterize the motives of those who join local political parties. The task might better be defined not as increasing the competence of low-income communities to manage their own affairs, but rather as creating more representative structures which will be more responsive to the special needs and interests of low-income groups. Paid politicians rather than paid community enablers may be necessary if representative rather than direct democracy is to be achieved. Direct democracy may thus be seen as a stage in the process of developing new political coalitions and new political leadership rather than as an ideal in the "good" community.

Richard Cloward and Frances Piven argue that a fundamental conflict between elite and low-income collective protests arises because they are based upon "quite divergent beliefs about the nature of social, economic, and political institutions and

27 For a thoughtful appraisal of the limits and strengths of protest, see Michael Lipsky, "Protest as a Political Resource" (Institute for Research on Poverty, University of Wisconsin, April 1967). (Mimeographed.)
28 Hans Spiegel, "How Much Neighborhood Control?" in *Citizen Participation in Urban Development* (Washington, D.C.: NTL Institute of Applied Behavioral Science, 1968), pp. 271–91.
29 *Congressional Record*, July 24, 1968.
30 See Martin Rein and S. M. Miller, "Citizen Participation and Poverty," *University of Connecticut Law Review*, 1 (December 1968), 221–43.

what it takes to change them." [31] The elitist approach assumes that institutions change by persuasion and education and that issues are largely technical and capable of analysis in terms analogous to a cost-benefit evaluation. Low-income collective protests, by contrast, view institutions as responsive to naked power and pressure; issues are defined in personalized terms; opponents are seen as culprits; and exploitation of the poor is rejected, whatever the benefits.

Efforts to organize low-income communities encounter difficulties in sustaining a high level of interest and participation, especially when programs have only marginal meaning for the residents and offer little opportunity for changes in jobs, housing, or other amenities. There is also the danger that issues are selected more for their capacity to rally interest than for their intrinsic merit. Protests can become ends in themselves instead of platforms for bargaining and negotiating. But without an issue for protest, organizations are likely to succumb to the meaningless ritual of organization for its own sake. Saul Alinsky's work is a prototype of one approach that attempts to sustain commitment by polarizing a community around an issue and then ruthlessly attacking the villain who is alleged to have created the problem.

While it has been exceedingly difficult to organize the poor on the basis of their poverty or social class in the occupational hierarchy, there is at least precedent for politicalization along ethnic and religious lines. Citizen participation reflects this aspect of American political life and extends it by inadvertently becoming a program for organizing the Negro community—the growing militancy of black urban action programs reflects the militants' discovery of the difficulties of change. The heightened sense of relative deprivation converted the process from reform (defined either as therapy and self-help to achieve a competent community or as provision of opportunities through organizational change to promote mobility) to revolution, which found expression in riots and the repudiation of integration as a realizable social ideal. How established power will respond to violence and assault on its citadels is unclear. There is evidence of both backlash and increased liberalization as the desire for social stability and social justice is joined and divided.

Lipsky has pointed out that "protest groups are uniquely capable of raising the saliency of issues, but are unequipped—by virtue of their lack of organizational resources—to participate in the formulation or adoption of solutions to problems they dramatize." [32] When protest groups are sponsored by social welfare organizations, they rapidly lose their authenticity as grassroots movements. They drift into labor-saving self-help projects and cleanup and fix-up programs. It is rather startling to note how many bureaucracies attempt to organize low-income residents to promote bureaucratic goals. Sanitation departments create block groups; settlements organize neighborhood

[31] Richard Cloward and Frances Piven, *Low-Income People and Political Process,* a paper presented at the Training Institute Program on Urban Community Development Projects (New York: Mobilization for Youth, May 1965).

[32] Michael Lipsky, "Protest as a Political Resource" (University of Wisconsin, Madison). (Mimeo.)

councils; the schools promote PTA's; and urban renewal in a similar fashion attempts to mobilize a community as a device for co-opting and reducing opposition to renewal plans. The professional comes to plan the agenda, and when the professional leaves, the organization collapses.

The process of involving the poor as a form of therapy and self-help on the one hand and legitimation of the activities of the planners on the other hand does not take adequate account of the potential role that citizen participation may have in politicalizing the poor. It can serve as well to create a new center of power by revitalizing the urban political machinery in low-income areas, replacing the atrophied structures that once helped generations of immigrants to adjust to American society. It is paradoxical that the targets of reform in one generation should become the ideals of the next generation: ethnic politics and the political machine were once seen as major impediments to good local government. However, many of the groups that do participate in these "establishment" sponsored programs are suspiciously regarded as having "sold out" their allegiance to the community from which they came. But this harsh assessment of betrayal fails to recognize that involvement, when seen from the point of view of its consumers, is a way of "buying in" to a system they aspire to be part of.

DILEMMAS IN THE SEARCH FOR LEGITIMACY

We have described, then, the three strategies that reformers and planners rely on to legitimate their actions. Each appeals to a different aspect of the democratic process: the need for consensus among elite institutional interests; the reverence for science and fact; and the validation of pluralism, diversity, and conflict on which democracy depends for its vitality. The dilemma seems to be the reform that works with the establishment, searching for a consensus, tends to lose its soul and its purpose. It abandons its real feeling and commitment for the poor as it sacrifices innovation and reform for survival and growth. Yet, any program that is based solely on a fight for the rights of the poor and that fails to work with established institutions not only is likely to create conflict, but also may fail to generate any constructive accommodation that can lead to real reform. Organizing the poor on a neighborhood basis cannot achieve very much fundamental change. Vision is limited to issues around which local initiative can be mobilized; most typically there is failure to give attention to broad social and economic policy. Research can interfere with both functions, for it can be used, in Gouldner's graphic term, as a "hamletic strategy" of delay and procrastination, responsive to political realities, while avoiding action that will provide authentic services for the poor. Research can compete with reform for resources, and it may pursue competing aims. The documentation of social injustice, which seeks action by confrontation, may embarrass the bureaucracies and make cooperation with the reformers more difficult. But without research, without some kind of objective analysis of the consequences of action, social policy moves from fashion to fashion without ever learning anything. It is, after all, useless to continue to create innovations and to spread new ideas if one never checks to see whether the new ideas and innovations are mere fads or whether they do indeed produce any kind of demonstrable change.

How then can these dilemmas be resolved? The answer, I believe, is that they cannot, for the contradictions are inherent in the nature of American social life.[33] It is futile to search for paradigms and prescriptions that will clear the whole problem out of the way and ultimately demonstrate that the strategies are indeed consistent and mutually reinforcing, not fundamentally in conflict. The search for a welfare monism that rejects pluralism and conflict only fosters utopian illusions. When all three strategies are pursued simultaneously in the same organization, internal conflict develops over time.

Eugene Litwak has suggested that we typically resolve such conflicts by having the conflicting functions carried out by separate organizations.

A society might stress both freedom and physical safety. These two values may conflict . . . yet the society seeks to maximize each. One way of assuring that each will be retained, despite the conflict, is to put them under separate organizational structures; i.e., have the police guard physical safety and the newspapers guard freedom of the press.[34]

Fragmentation of function does not, however, resolve the dilemma; it serves only to exacerbate the problem of interorganizational relationships as lack of coordination becomes a perpetual crisis. . . .

CONCLUSIONS

Physical and social planners have proceeded under the assumption that the consensus of values which binds society together offers the most compelling frame of reference for a "community regarding" planning process. However, when the divisions separating society become evident and the chasms dividing its groups become deep, planning at all levels comes to reflect these conditions. And although the need for disinterested planning becomes more urgent when the disharmonies in the society become more evident, it also becomes more difficult to perform as harmonizers and integrators. Rational planning is a myth when the value consensus on which it must depend is illusory and technology for eliminating arbitrary decisions is not available. But as the conditions of society become more complex and as each decision is a response to short range expediencies and accommodations of conflicting vested interests, the need to protect society's long-term interests becomes more insistent and the demands for rational solutions grow more urgent.

The crucial dilemma of planning cannot be altogether avoided: society's social problems require disinterested, rational, and politically independent solutions. However, we have no technology which lends itself to objective assesment, nor have we or can we ever devise a way to

---

[33] For a further discussion of each of these strategies and how they conflict, see Peter Marris and Martin Rein, *Dilemmas of Social Reform: Poverty and Community Action in the United States* (New York: Atherton Press, 1967).

[34] Eugene Litwak and Lydia F. Hylton, "Inter-organizational Analysis: A Hypothesis on Coordinating Agencies," *Administrative Science Quarterly*, IV (March 1962), 396.

detach planning from political pressure, without at the same time converting the detachment into irrelevance. Nor is advocacy planning a solution, for one planner as advocate implies yet another (not necessarily a planner) as judge. A judge is not simply a mediator among conflicting interests; what makes his decisions just is that they conform to some normative standard, some moral value judgment.[35] But the society has created neither mechanisms of adjudication nor a body of law and tradition to provide us with norms and standards to judge conflicting social policies. This situation arises because the effect of social policies tends to be distributional in that they leave some groups better off and others worse off. Social planning impels us to go beyond Pareto Optimality as a criterion for public decision-making. Even the choices of means are never neutral insofar as ends are concerned. Because the tools for intervention embody values, no simple calculus for distinguishing means and ends is at hand. As a result, social science alone cannot help us choose among conflicting goals, nor can it offer criteria when public policy requires interpersonal comparison of utilities, nor can it offer criteria other than efficiency and effectiveness in empirical studies that try to bring together means and ends.

Since resolution of these fundamental dilemmas is not at hand,

each source of authority that legitimates planning offers an alternative interpretation of its role. Thus one role can be seen as disinterested planning, which seeks to exploit whatever available consensus is at hand and to plan in terms of these areas of common agreement. Planning is then interpreted as a rational scientific process by which the relative efficiency of various means can be assessed when goals are known. Alternatively, as Reiner has suggested, the planner can be a rational goal technician, explicating the muffled goals among choices already made on other grounds.[36] Or, when agreement is lacking, planning can offer a forum through which the planner tries to forge harmony among conflicting interests. Or the planner may be seen as a bureaucrat acquiring his goals from elected officials' interpretation of his mission. When established political patterns are rigid, the planner may act as an advocate for rejected and excluded groups, organizing them to enter the political process. Or he may serve as a guerilla attempting to initiate change in bureaucracy by enhancing internal competence and responsiveness, having no explicit agenda of reform other than the wish to be relevant to current social problems.

35 Alvin W. Gouldner, "The Sociologist as Partisan," p. 113.

36 Thomas A. Reiner, "The Planner as Value Technician: Two Classes of Utopian Constructs and Their Impacts on Planning," in H. Wentworth Eldredge (ed.), *Taming Megalopolis* (Vol. I. New York: Doubleday and Company, 1967), 232–47.

Planning Models: The Analytic-Interactional Continuum

part II

The story is told of Martin and Marvin, two recent social welfare planning graduates. As a student, Martin was known to his classmates as "Marty the Modeler," in recognition of his remarkable ability to develop complex computer models for analyzing planning problems. His fellow student, Marvin, was dubbed "Marvin the Mover" in appreciation of his extraordinary ability to cultivate faculty friendships, secure positions on student committees, and to connect with all of the important people in the "power structure." After graduation, Martin and Marvin obtained positions as planning specialists for Health and Welfare Councils.

Marty the Modeler spent most of his first six months on the job in his office, the Council library, and the computer center, studying charts and figures and writing programs. At the end of that period he had designed a computerized program that would allow for comparison of the cost-benefit ratios of the Council's member agencies. To implement this plan, member agencies would have to complete certain forms on a monthly basis. Martin invited the executives of the twenty member agencies to a meeting to explain his plan and to elicit their support. Only three executives came—they sniped at the plan and left early.

Marvin the Mover devoted the first six months on the job to meetings with the staffs of member agencies, lunches with the executives, and sessions with the Council's board members. He then arranged for a series of weekly meetings to discuss possible changes in reporting procedures that would allow the Council to improve its cost-benefit assessments of the local health and welfare system. Meetings were well attended and lively. Marvin vigorously supported the position that a more accurate reporting system was essential for effective planning. The member-agency executives advocated the interests of their organizations and constituencies. One executive pointed out that implementing new procedures would be time consuming and costly, and that it would demand considerable work on the part of his staff. Another was concerned that the confidentiality of information might be compromised by the new data collection system. Most of the executives expressed their satisfaction with the current information system. Bit by bit, conflicts

71

were resolved and competing interests accommodated. At the end of six months the group reached consensus on a plan involving some minor modifications of the current reporting system—which really changed nothing.

Most of the literature on social welfare planning describes and analyzes the planning process from two perspectives: planning as a technomethodological process and planning as a sociopolitical process. These perspectives illuminate dual facets of the planner's role. Carried to the extreme, either of them may have debilitating effects on the planning process, as revealed in the account of Martin and Marvin's experiences. Generally, social welfare planners do not gravitate to these extremes; most are attentive to both the technomethodological and the sociopolitical aspects of the planning process.

The technomethodological aspects of the planning process involve "analytic" tasks, and the sociopolitical aspects involve "interactional" tasks. "Analytic" tasks include data collection, quantification of problems, ranking priorities, specification of objectives, program design, cost-benefit estimates, and the like. "Interactional" tasks involve structuring a planning system and facilitating communication, bargaining, and exchange among parties in planning decisions.[1] In light of these perspectives, the planning roles described in Part I may be seen as ordered along a continuum according to the degree to which they emphasize analytical tasks or interactional tasks; the technocrat operates at the analytic end of the continuum, the advocate at the interactional end, and the bureaucrat close to the center.

The distinction between analytic and interactional tasks applies not only to planner roles but also to general models of the planning process. The differential emphasis accorded technomethodological and sociopolitical aspects of the planning enterprise has been a major practice issue in social planning literature. To illustrate we will examine four models of planning: rational decision-making; mixed scanning; disjointed incrementalism; and transactive planning. Though these approaches to the planning process differ along a number of dimensions (e.g., degree of comprehensiveness, scope), this discussion will be focused upon their respective positions with regard to the analytic-interactional continuum as depicted in Table 1.

The *rational decision-making* approach conceives of planning as an orderly, logical progression from diagnosis to action based upon analysis of the relevant facts, theories, and values. The problem under consideration is diagnosed, solutions or ends (i.e. programmatic goals) are decided upon, programmatic means are designed to achieve the solution, and the effectiveness of these means is assessed. In this manner the correct (or "best") solution

1 *Readings in Community Organization Practice*, Ralph M. Kramer and Harry Specht, eds. (Englewood Cliffs, N.J.: Prentice-Hall, Inc., 1975), pp. 7–9; see also Robert Perlman and Arnold Gurin, *Community Organization and Social Planning* (New York: John Wiley and Sons, 1972), pp. 52–75.

TABLE 1. PLANNING ROLES AND MODELS ON THE
ANALYTIC-INTERACTION CONTINUUM

Planning Roles	Emphasis on Analytic Tasks	Planning Models
Technocrat		Rational Decision-making
		Mixed Scanning
Bureaucrat		
Advocate		Disjointed Incrementalism
		Transactive Planning
	Emphasis on Interactional Tasks	

can be found. In the literature on rational decision making, the number of stages and the terminology used to describe each stage in the planning process vary according to a particular author's predilection for specificity.[2] A representative example of the rational decision-making process is seen in the six stages, or anchor points, outlined by Alfred J. Kahn in Reading 5, "Definition of the Tasks: Facts, Projections, and Inventories." Of course, Kahn is cognizant of the sociopolitical aspects of planning. But his explication of this rational model emphasizes the analytic tasks and technical functions of assembling the facts and appraising relevant realities that must be performed to bring the process to fruition.

The *mixed scanning* approach to planning involves a combination of elements of the rationalistic model that emphasize the analytic tasks of research and fact-gathering and elements of the incremental approach that emphasize the interactional task of consensus building. This model, described in Reading 6 by Amitai Etzioni, "Mixed-Scanning: A 'Third' Approach to Decision-making," combines two levels of activity: "broad-angle scanning" through which data are collected and analyzed (though not in as much detail as in the rationalistic approach) and "narrow-scope scanning" through which a limited range of alternatives is examined in detail (similar to the incremental approach). The general direction of planning activities is based upon the information and knowledge obtained from broad-angle scanning, and within this context more specific and incremental planning choices are agreed upon.

Disjointed incrementalism involves choosing among a limited range of alternatives that differ in small degrees from existing policies. Reading 7, aptly entitled "The Science of 'Muddling Through,'" by Charles Lind-

2 For further discussion and comparisons of models developed on different levels of generalization, see Neil Gilbert and Harry Specht, *Dimensions of Social Welfare Policy* (Englewood Cliffs, N.J.: Prentice-Hall, Inc., 1974), pp. 14–21.

blom, deals with this model. Unlike the rationalistic approach, this model does not emphasize problem solving by in-depth analysis of cause-and-effect relationships and examination of all possible courses of action. Instead, the incremental approach seeks to achieve small remedial gains through successive limited comparisons between "what is" and "what is acceptable or feasible in the way of change." The technical aspects of designing the "best" programmatic solution are deemphasized. The test of a "good" plan is the extent to which it elicits agreement among relevant interest groups. In the model, interactional tasks such as exchange, compromise, and developing agreement are the predominant features of the planning process.

The *transactive* approach considers planning to be a social process not so much concerned with the activity of plan-making as with the ongoing guidance of change in which goals and means are continually being readjusted. Unlike the rational decision-making model, this approach fuses the various stages of problem analysis, plan, and implementation "into a two-part model in which designing the plan disappear[s] as a separate step, leaving analysis and action as the two principal components of a single process." [3] The fusion of analysis and action requires that an interpersonal relationship between planner and client be established to assure open dialogue and mutual learning. The crucial element of this model is the quality of the interaction between planner and client. This aspect of the model is elaborated in Reading 8, "The Transactive Style of Planning," an excerpt from John Friedmann's book *Retracking America,* in which the transactive model is fully developed.

The four models contain assumptions about the achievement of consensus and the degree of centralized or decentralized planning. Briefly, these assumptions are as follows: (1) With the *rational decision-making* approach, it is taken as a given that a general societal consensus on means and ends that serve the common good can be achieved; designation of the "best" plan is primarily a technical problem that will be solved by careful analysis of relevant data. This analysis can be accomplished more effectively and efficiently by a centralized planning mechanism that can deal with the "large picture" than by a group of decentralized units with a limited purview.

(2) *Mixed scanning* allows for greater or lesser degrees of consensus in any issue confronting the planner. When there is a moderate degree of consensus on an issue, general policy directions can be decided centrally, leaving latitude for decentralized planning around the specifics of program design. For example, in New York City a city-wide master plan sets a framework within which neighborhood "miniplans" are designed. This arrangement allows for flexible responses tailored to local needs and wishes, while

[3] John Friedmann, *Retracking America* (New York: Doubleday/Anchor Press, 1963), pp. 16–17.

continuing to keep the "big picture" in view. The merit of this combined approach is described in a *New York Times* editorial as follows:

. . . it would be a serious mistake to believe that "master planning" and "mini-planning" are mutually exclusive. They are mutually essential. A city must constantly evaluate its large picture in terms of trends, aims, and values, and relate special neighborhood requirements to it. That is the only way a city grows constructively and creatively.[4]

(3) *Disjointed incrementalism* rejects the likelihood that consensus can be built around broad planning issues. In this view, consensus is extremely difficult to achieve and is most likely to occur in proposals for incremental changes. This model calls for a decentralized planning mechanism through which different interest groups can be consulted, a mechanism that is versatile and flexible enough to construct consensus issue-by-issue and step-by-step. This arrangement also allows opposing groups to protect their interests by developing their own plans to compensate for the shortcomings of others; hence it allows for a process of mutual adjustment on the societal level.

(4) The *transactive* model proposes a planning process in which small, decentralized cells create meaningful face-to-face interaction among their members. Broad-scale consensus among these cells is not considered necessary for implementation. As Friedmann puts it:

. . . it is simply false to assert that the expression of a diversity of interests and value positions will inevitably result in chaos. A large and wealthy society like America's is quite capable of accommodating a multiplicity of life styles and simultaneous pursuit of many different interests. . . . Original ideas can arise at any point within the network of a cellular structure and can often be acted upon without infringing upon the central interests of others.[5]

Faced with these different approaches, the student inevitably will ask: Is there a preferred model of planning? Which approach is most useful? There are no definitive answers to these questions. Some professionals employ a mixture of approaches, and others favor one or another model because of their social values, their perceptions of reality, and their opinions concerning the cognitive capacities of planners. In addition, the particular planning environment in which the professional finds himself at a given time may be conducive to one or another of these approaches. The issue is too complex to yield a simple, firm, universal solution.

A more useful question is: Under what conditions are each of these models most appropriate? One must first consider the types of problems that confront the planner. Following this line of thought in Reading 9, "Problems, Solutions, and Strategies: A Contribution to the Theory and

[4] *New York Times,* June 27, 1974, p. 44.
[5] Friedmann, *op. cit.,* p. 204.

Practice of Planning," Timothy Cartwright has developed a typology of problems based on the number of variables in the problem definition and the precision with which these variables can be specified. Working with these characteristics, Cartwright identifies four types of problems ranging from lowest to highest in order of complexity: *simple, compound, complex,* and *metaproblems.* Cartwright's work is based on the following proposition:

The nature of the problem determines what is an appropriate strategy and, conversely, . . . the use of a particular strategy makes certain assumptions about the nature of the problem to which it is applied.[6]

Specifically, Cartwright argues that *simple* problems lend themselves to the rational decision-making approach while *metaproblems* are most adequately addressed through the disjointed-incrementalist or transactive approach. For the *compound* and *complex* problems, he suggests using strategies that correspond to variations of the mixed-scanning approach. According to this analysis, the balance between the analytic and interactional tasks of the planner is in a state of dynamic adjustment; and the emphases shift according to the characteristics of the problems and how they are defined. Some of these differential emphasis will be examined in Parts III and IV.

There is another outlook that is somewhat less optimistic about the planner's ability to use Cartwright's approaches. This perspective is presented by Horst Rittel and Melvin Webber in "Dilemmas in a General Theory of Planning," Reading 10. They agree that simple problems, as Cartwright defines them, are amenable to the rational decision-making approach and even that problems on the next order of difficulty might be dealt with through a combination of rational decision making and elements of the incremental approach. However, Rittel and Webber dismiss simple and compound problems as virtually irrelevant to social planning.

The kinds of problems that planners deal with—societal problems—are inherently different from the problems that scientists and perhaps some classes of engineers deal with. *Planning problems are inherently wicked.*[7] (Italics added.)

By "wicked problems" they are referring to the metaproblems in Cartwright's classification, for which the rational decision-making approach is clearly inadequate. Rittel and Webber's analysis even casts some doubt on the feasibility of achieving the limited degree of agreement required for incremental planning. They observe that society is becoming increasingly

6 Timothy J. Cartwright, "Problems, Solutions, and Strategies: A Contribution to the Theory and Practice of Planning," *Journal of the American Institute of Planners,* 39:3 (May 1973), 184.
7 Horst W. J. Rittel and Melvin M. Webber, "Dilemmas in a General Theory of Planning," *Policy Science,* 4:3 (September 1973).

heterogeneous with numerous groups pursuing diverse goals. Contrary to Friedmann's view concerning society's capacity to accommodate these various group interests, Rittel and Webber suggest that as differentiation continues, competing interests are likely to conflict so strongly that they will approximate zero-sum game situations that defy any possibility for compromise.

What is the appropriate combination of analytic and interactional skills for the social planner? How potent are these skills for resolving problems that must be approached through an increasingly heterogeneous social structure? While Cartwright's analysis of problem types and our description of planning approaches illuminate some of the paths that may be taken, Rittel and Webber identify the dark passages through which social planners must continue to grope.

5   *Rational Decision-Making*

DEFINITION OF THE TASK:
FACTS, PROJECTIONS, AND INVENTORIES

Alfred J. Kahn

Planning is a developmental process in which the several levels of intellectual undertaking are in constant interaction. Although a logical sequence may be listed, it is not necessarily a temporal one. Even as we organize for planning, we must provide for the interplay among levels. For our concern with assuring a planning outcome which gives appropriate weight to all relevant elements implies a readiness to refine and revise the outcomes of earlier stages as we move into later ones.

If a straight line depicts planning as a deductive process in which a sequence of specified formal steps is followed, our approach may best be seen as a series of interlocked spirals and circles. Changes in one place affect the entire system. . . .

In the real world, planning tends to begin because there is complaint, tension, disagreement, dissatisfaction, conflict, suffering, need for choice, a bill enacted by a legislative body with too little forethought, some combination of these—or a

Reprinted with permission of author and publisher from: Alfred J. Kahn, *Theory and Practice of Social Planning* (New York: Russell Sage Foundation, 1969), pp. 60–71.

dream. As these actions and feelings are pursued and their sources and rationales formulated, we emerge with a somewhat more formal statement of substantive issues and circumstances which may generate planning. A series of such statements has been presented in the first chapter [of *Theory and Practice of Social Planning*].

Since our present focus is not on the community organization, interest-group, or political aspects of the process, we merely assume for the moment that the planner, planners, or planning group are assigned the problem and have adequate sanction to begin. We assume, too, that the assigned or assumed charge takes the form of an expression of problem, need, or concen—or is presented in its broader frame as a case of priority determination, coping with serious social disorganization, need to build social services into physical redevelopment of an area, and so on.

The planner's most serious decision and major contribution is what may be called the *formulation or definition of the planning task*. The "task" is formulated through *a constant playing back between an assessment of the relevant aspects of social*

78

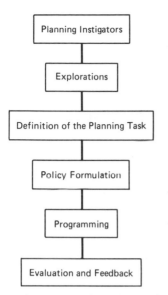

Simplified Outline of Anchor Points in Planning

reality and the preferences of the relevant community. Each of these two factors affects and modifies the perception of the other. The task definition appears as an integration of the two. Much else in social planning follows from the outcome of such integration.

Traditionally, planners talked of "goals" or "objectives" as given at the beginning of a planning process. Then, in fact, the assignment might be conceived of in deductive terms: one weighs resources and obstacles and one programs the approach to the goal. Similarly, the assumption that planning seeks to satisfy "needs," as though these were fixed and readily discoverable personal manifestations of social goals, tends to a static view of what is essentially a very complex and unstable reality.

In effect, "needs" are social definitions, representing a view of what an individual or group requires in order to play a role, meet a commitment, participate adequately in a social process, retain an adequate level of energy and productivity—at a given moment of history. "Needs" are biology interpreted through and very much supplemented by culture, to a point where the universal, stable biological core is a small component of the whole. The need is defined with a view of what the social institution or the broader society expects of the individual or the group, and what the resources and possibilities are to make a given level of expectation realistic. Entering into the definition is an assessment as to whether the social or economic price of meeting the need at a given level is justified in the perspective of the expected results. In short, a value judgment enters.

Thus to talk of the goal of "meeting" certain needs is to be involved in a complex human calculus—not starting with a fixed and readily formulated "given." The goal both derives from a concept of need and also helps shape that concept. For this reason we have tended to think of the definition of the planning task as the formulation of the appropriate *needs/task concept*—a concept to guide the planning in which needs and task are shaped together, each affecting and modifying the other. Only the clumsiness of the phrase in its written or oral form leads us to employ the less complete: *definition of the planning task.*

Almost all goal statements made at the beginning of planning enterprises are very complex statements in this sense. Once they have been made, much of the value debate and assessment of social priorities is over, at least temporarily. In fact, much

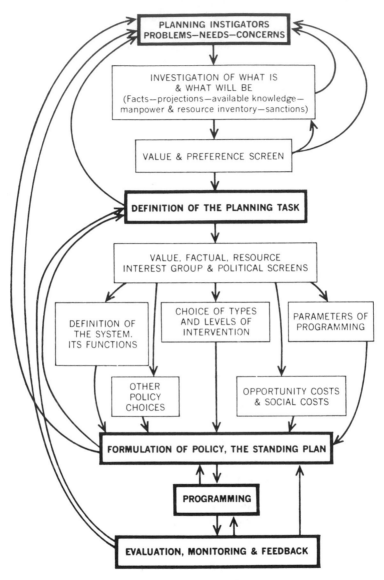

Interlocking Circles & Spirals: Planning in Action

of the evaluation of social reality has already taken place. The definition of the planning task is "the idea sword" in planning, to borrow Constantinos Doxiadis' phrase for the "processing" key through which the planner orders his learning and actions.[1]

An emphasis on the formulation of the planning task as a first phase

[1] C. A. Doxiadis, "Learning How to Learn," *Saturday Review*, January 1, 1966, 107.

may, therefore, be seen as an effort to make conscious and deliberate the entire process. . . .

SIGNIFICANCE OF THE DEFINITION OF THE PLANNING TASK

Recent American social welfare history provides a series of dramatic illustrations of the significance of this element in planning.

DELINQUENCY CONTROL TO YOUTH DEVELOPMENT

At one time, police, courts, and correctional institutions dealing with young people who committed crimes or were otherwise unmanageable viewed their jobs as one of controlling and punishing the deviants so as to protect the larger community. The offenders were seen as willful and deliberate sinners or exploiters of the larger community who deserved punishment and would be deterred by it. A "planner" in this field in the eighteen-eighties, if he existed, would have surveyed the efficiency of police in detection, the adequacy of court machinery to adjudicate, and the sufficiency of deterrent-oriented places of incarceration. True, some individuals at work in the system were operating on somewhat different concepts, but community decisions were directed by a general consensus.

It was during the second half of the last century that a series of forces, not here recapitulated, converged in the decision to define young offenders somewhat differently from adults who broke the law and to offer them opportunity for re-education and rehabilitation. The problem was lack of education or mis-education, and the deficit could be determined and filled in. The of-fender was considered capable of taking the help. The juvenile courts invented for him a status which was not to carry a stigma ("juvenile delinquent") and strengthened both community-based probation services and specialized institutional resources. Much emphasis was placed on character reform and vocational training. Again, there were some who went beyond this and many who never quite implemented the theory, but the guidelines were there and governed most policies and programs.

Gradually, from the late nineteen-twenties, but particularly after World War II, this general strategy was given new content by a combination of sociological and psychological findings, especially by psychoanalysis, and by shifts in the social ethic which were concurrent. The locus of the strategy shifted from character reform and retraining to treatment of the delinquent. From the premise of free will—or a large component thereof—the ideology of anti-delinquency programs shifted to emphasize "sickness" and lack of capacity to do otherwise. Because of the nature of their own institutional rationales, most police systems and many juvenile courts still conducted their "rituals" on the free will premise, but the dispositional authorities operating probationary, foster home, guidance clinic, and institutional services were charged with treating adjudicated delinquents on the assumption that environmental and intrapsychic life forces had created behavior patterns of which the antisocial action was a normal outcome. Moreover, with only a token effort to change the environmental part of the question, they could seek enough personality change to assure future adjustment. For this was the key: to help an unsocialized or disturbed personality to achieve enough control or rationality to adjust and to begin with the assumption that he needed treatment to achieve this.

Again, this is an oversimplification. Each of these views had its opponents and its variations, and the leading students of the subject were far more sophisticated than this summary allows.[2] For most workers in most agencies, and for the commissions, committees, and executives planning and projecting programs, these were the guiding areas.

The application to delinquency of a sociological approach known as "anomie theory" marked the transition to a new phase. As developed and modified by Richard A. Cloward and Lloyd E. Ohlin, in *Delinquency and Opportunity,* and then used in a planning context in a document called *A Proposal for the Prevention and Control of Delinquency by Expanding Opportunities,*[3] this theory held:

[2] A more comprehensive presentation of delinquency theory and a more detailed illustration of consequences for delinquency services of a re-definition of the planning task will be found in Alfred J. Kahn, "Social Work and the Control of Delinquency," *Social Work,* 10, No. 2 (April, 1965), 3–13, and his "Trends and Problems in Community Organization," in National Conference on Social Welfare, *Social Work Practice, 1964* (New York: Columbia University Press, 1964), 3–27, or his "From Delinquency Treatment to Community Development," in P. F. Lazarsfeld, W. H. Sewell, and H. L. Wilensky, Editors, *The Uses of Sociology* (New York: Basic Books, 1967).

[3] Richard A. Cloward and Lloyd E. Ohlin, *Delinquency and Opportunity* (Glencoe, Ill.: The Free Press, 1960) and *A Proposal for the Prevention and Control of Delinquency by Expanding Opportunities* (New York: Mobilization for Youth, 1961).

much delinquent behavior is engendered because opportunities for conformity are limited. Delinquency therefore represents not lack of motivation to conform but quite the opposite: the desire to meet social expectations itself becomes the source of delinquent behavior if the possibility of doing so is limited or non-existent.[4]

Therefore, according to Mobilization's plan, "in order to reduce the incidence of delinquent behavior or to rehabilitate persons who are already enmeshed in delinquent patterns, *we must provide the social and psychological resources that make conformity possible.*" Now, in place of the traditional delinquency-program emphasis on personal counseling and on psychiatrically guided treatment, programs such as job counseling, placement, job training, and cultural experience which would enhance capacity for participation in the larger society all became central. In fact, treatment programs became secondary to what were seen as these preventive efforts.

Furthermore, when confronted with the problem of disadvantaged and "closed out" youth, the new predilection was to ask what there is about the school, the job placement center, the social agency which closes them out, where once the only question asked was why they did not adjust or how they could be made competent to conform.

To phrase this somewhat differently, in the language of those who do not read sociological tracts, the adolescents congregating on the streetcorners of urban ghettos and constantly at war with the police

[4] Cloward and Ohlin, *A Proposal for the Prevention and Control of Delinquency by Expanding Opportunities. . . .*

were redefined from "drop-outs" to "push-outs," and the society had now directed its attention to the rejecting forces, where once it looked at the rejected only as a group to be treated.

Obviously, the shifts were generated not by the theories alone but by social forces which validated and gave them support. Thus, at the beginning of the Kennedy Administration, while traditional child welfare and mental health programs continued with their basic programs, a new organization, called the President's Committee on Delinquency and Youth Crime, was created as the vehicle for the new efforts—efforts based on redefinition of the task.

In sixteen cities community groups looked at the facts and trends anew and sought, in the general framework of the "opportunity theory" described above, to develop two-, three-, or five-year plans for assisting their youth. Given their social settings and the need to cope with a broader social welfare system, which emphasized treatment and deterrence of delinquency, they did not ignore the old entirely. They sought instead to improve treatment programs by "reaching out" efforts, which took the services to young people who could not enter agencies as they were set up, and which adapted treatment techniques to the social, economic, and ethnic groups served. Furthermore, they sought to implement proposals for service coordination and case integration as developed by critics of the current patterns of welfare organization. However, the core of the programs was job counseling, training, placement, educational services, and access to new kinds of socializing experiences. For the problem, to repeat, was defined as one of lack of access to relevant resources, knowledge, skills, habits, and attitudes.

Thus, the emphasis had moved from delinquency control to re-education, to treatment, to *youth development*. And once this transition had been made, most of the cities involved decided that the new programs should not be in the hands of judges, probation personnel, clinicians, youth gang workers, or family service agencies. All of these had parts to play, but new community coalitions concerned with youth development were to be created as sponsors and operators of the new efforts. In many cities or sections of cities the traditional community welfare councils were eclipsed entirely or assumed secondary roles as Mobilization for Youth, Action for Boston Community Development, Haryou, Action for Appalachian Youth, and others took the center of the stage.[5]

What had occurred was a new definition of the planning task and what emerged were new social strategies, service approaches, sponsoring organizations, staffing patterns, public definition of access, and much more. Furthermore, variations in the more detailed specifications of the planning task among the cities chosen for experiments by the President's Committee and granted funds for planning led to variations in emphasis significant enough to identify and characterize each.

Several stressed "target population" participation in community planning with obvious socio-therapeutic intent, in a community organization tradition, but Haryou,

[5] See detailed bibliography in Kahn, "From Delinquency Treatment to Community Development," *op. cit.*

which saw Negro "powerlessness" as the center of the problem of Harlem youth, gave training and organization for political participation a central position in the plan.

Most of the cities placed emphasis on improvement of educational and employment programs, the better to serve the formerly closed-out youth, but several undertook larger institutional change targets and found themselves fighting not only for improvements in the systems but for a role in controlling educational, housing, employment, or welfare policy. As they did this, they became aware of the artificiality of the pretence that a *youth* program could open opportunities or "change the opportunity structure" (Mobilization for Youth's attractive new slogan). Was this not a program for the total community?

New Haven defined its youth employment project in the context of its comprehensive manpower projections and plans and emerged with something quite distinct from those plans that coped with the needs of disadvantaged and delinquent youth as though the economy of their neighborhood were independent of the city-wide or regional economy. Several planners found it necessary either to attack or to ignore traditional case services (counseling, treatment, group guidance) in order to demonstrate that their efforts were basic and sought institutional change. Others viewed case services, basic educational and vocational programs, and more radical individual change as mutually interrelated aspects of a total approach. New Haven planners saw education and job training as the central "oppor-

tunity program" and decided to use counseling and treatment to support access to and use of such services.

By now the point has been illustrated: definition and re-definition of the planning task and variability in such re-definition carry visible consequences for the social plans which emerge. These, in turn, create vastly differing operational programs, professional balance, and staffing patterns.

This observation is further documented by what occurred in 1964 and 1965. Just as many of these community "opportunity" mobilizations were getting under way (and modifying their plans en route), a national shift occurred. For fundamental social reasons, the task definition changed. The central concern was no longer juvenile delinquency but poverty. Moreover, poverty was not merely to be alleviated, it was to be "conquered." Now, freed of the pretence that delinquent youth and specific delinquency prevention were adequate points of departure, local anti-poverty planners could consider more complete community development strategy or even go beyond it, depending on how they conceived of the roots of poverty. The various opportunity mobilizations were soon absorbed by Community Action Programs supported by the Office of Economic Opportunity. Youth employment and educational reform programs were emphasized, but in a far broader context. The President's Committee on Delinquency and Youth Crime now found itself with a far narrower charge, focused once again on individual and group deviance, and developed a more specific "corrections" program, which it, nonetheless, sought to implement with a view to the broader scene.[6]

"TASK," FACTS, VALUES

While the use of the terms "definition of the planning task" or "needs/task concept" may not be common, recognition of the intellectual process is not rare. Economic planners know the difference between a decision in Country A to see "the task ahead for economic policy as that of 'sustaining full employment without inflation,'" while Country B announces that "the main economic task of the current Five-Year Plan . . . [is] to insure a further considerable expansion of industry. . . ."

Rein and Miller, for example, illustrate the consequences of various possible task formulations for antipoverty policy.[7] If the problem is seen as inequality, one stresses redistribution; if it is the lack of a minimum of services, one emphasizes specific amenities. If the issue is defined as the absence of mobility, one "opens opportunities"; but if the concern is social stability, rehabilitative and re-educative measures may be stressed. Similarly, other definitions lead to their own strategies.

A Mobilization for Youth report notes how progressive task redefinition has major impact on an agency's programming, shifting it from individual case approaches to group methods, community organization, and social action.[8]

A United Nations report describes the consequences of task updating, over a period of time, for economic planning in Poland.[9] An economic analyst shows how understanding of the task formulation (growth, full employment without inflation, etc.) adds coherence to British economic planning.[10] Others remark that even the institutional arrangements for planning reflect concepts of the task.

On the other hand, one readily identifies considerable numbers of planning reports doomed to ineffectiveness, because participants could not or would not resolve conflicting concepts and thus emerged from the process without a beacon.

Clearly, the process of task definition and redefinition is critical in planning and offers the occasion for sterility as well as creativity. In the language of systems analysts, it is in the process of task definition that one may introduce new scenarios,

---

[6] The discussion of income maintenance programs in Chapter IV of the companion volume illustrates shifting task definitions and their impact. An equally clear illustration is offered by what is now called the field of child welfare after its journey from Poor Law to child-saving to child care. Currently one asks whether child welfare must not be sought through family-based social services and income policy. See Chapter VII in the companion volume, *Studies in Social Policy and Planning*.

[7] Martin Rein and S. M. Miller, "Poverty, Policy and Purpose: The Dilemmas of Choice," in Leonard H. Goodman, ed., *Economic Progress and Social Welfare* (New York: Columbia University Press, 1966), 20–64; Martin Rein, "Social Science and the Elimination of Poverty," *Journal of the American Institute of Planners*, XXXIII, No. 3 (May, 1967), 146–63.

[8] Mobilization for Youth, "Action on the Lower East Side" (New York: 1964, mimeographed), 68–69.

[9] United Nations Department of Economic and Social Affairs, *Planning for Balanced Social and Economic Development: Six Country Case Studies* (New York, 1964).

[10] Everett E. Hagen, *Planning Economic Development* (Homewood, Ill.: Richard D. Irwin, 1963), Chap. 10.

extrapolating beyond a currently perceived reality.

Formal task definition deals with the manifest: what is and what is sought. To those who inaugurate, carry out, and seek to implement planning, however, there is always alertness to the latent as well: what can the formulation mean; what does it mean; where may it lead beyond the goals which are stated and outlined? [11]. . .

We are now prepared to look at the *elements* involved in any systematic effort to define the task as part of a planning process. . . .

FACTS, PROJECTIONS, AND INVENTORIES

Given the availability of many research texts and manuals, the discussion here may be brief. However, what may be described as the exploration of relevant realities is generally the most time-consuming phase of a planning endeavor. The problem, need, concern, promise, or generalized social goal has launched the enterprise. Now one must do some or all of the following:

—define the problem in detail
—"diagnose" the causes
—seek relevant theories
—get realistic estimates of scope and scale
—consider the interrelationship of component parts
—project relevant variables into the future

[11] See Bertram M. Gross, prefatory comment, "The 'Drifting Cloud' of Guided Development," in John Friedman, *Venezuela: From Doctrine to Dialogue* (Syracuse: Syracuse University Press, 1965, paperback).

—inventory present resources and estimate future resources
—compute presently available and potentially available manpower
—examine relevant legal rights, sanctions, precedents
—translate all this as appropriate into geographic units, time units, or subdivide it by other critical variables
—assemble interpretations placed by others on these facts and appraise such interpretations
—estimate consequences of various possible interventions.

The above list is long, but it is not complete, since there are many variations in scale, substance, and point of departure in social planning, and this condition obviously affects just what is known and given and what needs to be determined or tested if the process is to move forward.

Planning without adequate investigation of relevant realities, relevant social facts, is utopian thinking or traveling blind. Planning that assembles volumes of data without imposing criteria of relevance and priority in their appraisal is useless ritual. Actually, one does not know what facts to assemble and how to weight such facts without simultaneous attention to preference and value questions. It is for this reason that, while we begin with the discussion of relevant factual investigation, the preference matter is here presented as a co-equal and certainly temporally overlapping phase in the determination of the planning task. Both fact-finding and preference analysis recur (and sometimes are concentrated) at the policy development or programming phases of a planning enterprise that follow task definition. . . .

6   *Mixed Scanning*

MIXED-SCANNING: A "THIRD" APPROACH TO DECISION-MAKING

Amitai Etzioni

In the concept of social decision-making, vague commitments of a normative and political nature are translated into specific commitments to one or more specific courses of action. Since decision-making includes an element of choice, it is the most deliberate and voluntaristic aspect of social conduct. As such, it raises the question: To what extent can social actors decide what their course will be, and to what extent are they compelled to follow a course set by forces beyond their control? Three conceptions of decision-making are considered here with assumptions that give varying weights to the conscious choice of the decision-makers.

Rationalistic models tend to posit a high degree of control over the decision-making situation on the part of the decision-maker. The incrementalist approach presents an alternative model, referred to as the art of "muddling through," which assumes much less command over the environment. Finally, the article outlines a third approach to social decision-making which, in combining elements of both earlier approaches, is neither as utopian in its assumptions as the first model nor as conservative as the second. For reasons which will become evident, this third approach is referred to as mixed-scanning.

THE RATIONALISTIC APPROACH

Rationalistic models are widely held conceptions about how decisions are and ought to be made. An actor becomes aware of a problem, posits a goal, carefully weighs alternative means, and chooses among them according to his estimates of their respective merit, with reference to the state of affairs he prefers. Incrementalists' criticism of this approach focuses on the disparity between the requirements of the model and the capacities of decision-makers.[1] Social decision-making centers,

Reprinted with permission of author and publisher from: Amitai Etzioni, "Mixed-Scanning: A 'Third' Approach to Decision-making," *Public Administration Review*, 1 (December 1967), 385–92.

[1] See David Braybrooke and Charles E. Lindblom, *A Strategy of Decision* (New York: Free Press, 1963), pp. 48–50 and pp. 111–43; Charles E. Lindblom, *The Intelligence of Democracy* (New York: Free Press, 1965), pp. 137–39. See also Jerome S. Bruner, Jacqueline J. Goodnow,

it is pointed out, frequently do not have a specific, agreed upon set of values that could provide the criteria for evaluating alternatives. Values, rather, are fluid and are affected by, as well as affect, the decisions made. Moreover, in actual practice, the rationalistic assumption that values and facts, means and ends, can be clearly distinguished seems inapplicable:

. . . Public controversy . . . has surrounded the proposal to construct a branch of the Cook County Hospital on the South Side in or near the Negro area. Several questions of policy are involved in the matter, but the ones which have caused one of the few *public* debates of an issue in the Negro community concern whether, or to what extent, building such a branch would result in an all-Negro or "Jim Crow" hospital and whether such a hospital is desirable as a means of providing added medical facilities for Negro patients. Involved are both an issue of *fact* (whether the hospital would be segregated, intentionally or unintentionally, as a result of the character of the neighborhood in which it would be located) and an issue of *value* (whether even an all-Negro hospital would be preferable to no hospital at all in the area). In reality, however, the factions have aligned themselves in such a way and the debate has proceeded in such a manner that the fact issue and the value issue have been collapsed into the single question of whether to build or not to build. Those in favor of the proposal will argue that the facts do not bear out the charge of "Jim Crowism" —"the proposed site . . . is not considered to be placed in a segregated area for the exclusive use of one racial or minority group"; or "no responsible officials would try to develop a new hospital to further segregation"; or "establishing a branch hospital for the . . . more adequate care of the indigent patient load, from the facts thus presented, does not represent Jim Crowism." At the same time, these proponents argue that whatever the facts, the factual issue is secondary to the overriding consideration that "there is a here-and-now need for more hospital beds. . . . Integration may be the long-run goal, but in the short-run we need more facilities." [2]

In addition, information about consequences is, at best, fractional. Decision-makers have neither the assets nor the time to collect the information required for rational choice. While knowledge technology, especially computers, does aid in the collection and processing of information, it cannot provide for the computation required by the rationalist model. (This holds even for chess playing, let alone "real-life" decisions.) Finally, rather than being confronted with a limited universe of relevant consequences, decision-makers face an open system of variables, a world in which all consequences cannot be surveyed.[3] A decision-maker, attempting to adhere to the tenets of a rationalistic model, will become frustrated, exhaust his resources without coming to a decision, and remain without an effective decision-making model to guide him.

2 James Q. Wilson, *Negro Politics* (New York: Free Press, 1960), p. 189.

3 See review of *A Strategy of Decision* by Kenneth J. Arrow in *Political Science Quarterly*, Vol. 79 (1964), p. 585. See also Herbert A. Simon, *Models of Man* (New York: Wiley, 1957), p. 198, and Aaron Wildavsky, *The Politics of the Budgetary Process* (Boston: Little, Brown and Co., 1964), pp. 147–52.

and George A. Austin, *A Study of Thinking* (New York: John Wiley, 1956), chapters 4–5.

Rationalistic models are thus rejected as being at once unrealistic and undesirable.

THE INCREMENTALIST APPROACH

A less demanding model of decision-making has been outlined in the strategy of "disjointed incrementalism" advanced by Charles E. Lindblom and others.[4] Disjointed incrementalism seeks to adapt decision-making strategies to the limited cognitive capacities of decision-makers and to reduce the scope and cost of information collection and computation. Lindblom summarized the six primary requirements of the model in this way: [5]

1. Rather than attempting a comprehensive survey and evaluation of all alternatives, the decision-maker focuses only on those policies which differ incrementally from existing policies.
2. Only a relatively small number of policy alternatives are considered.
3. For each policy alternative, only a restricted number of "important" consequences are evaluated.
4. The problem confronting the decision-maker is continually redefined: Incrementalism allows for countless ends-means and means-ends adjustments which, in effect, make the problem more manageable.

4 Charles E. Lindblom, "The Science of 'Muddling Through,'" *Public Administration Review*, Vol. 19 (1959), pp. 79-99 [reprinted here, pp. 98–112]; Robert A. Dahl and Charles E. Lindblom, *Politics, Economics and Welfare* (New York: Harper and Brothers, 1953); *Strategy of Decision, op. cit.;* and *The Intelligence of Democracy, op. cit.*
5 Lindblom, *The Intelligence of Democracy, op. cit.,* pp. 144–48.

5. Thus, there is no one decision or "right" solution but a "never-ending series of attacks" on the issues at hand through serial analyses and evaluation.
6. As such, incremental decision-making is described as remedial, geared more to the alleviation of present, concrete social imperfections than to the promotion of future social goals.

MORPHOLOGICAL ASSUMPTIONS OF THE INCREMENTAL APPROACH

Beyond a model and a strategy of decision-making, disjointed incrementalism also posits a structure model; it is presented as the typical decision-making process of pluralistic societies, as contrasted with the master planning of totalitarian societies. Influenced by the free competition model of economics, incrementalists reject the notion that policies can be guided in terms of central institutions of a society expressing the collective "good." Policies, rather, are the outcome of a give-and-take among numerous societal "partisans." The measure of a good decision is the decision-makers' agreement about it. Poor decisions are those which exclude actors capable of affecting the projected course of action; decisions of this type tend to be blocked or modified later.

Partisan "mutual-adjustment" is held to provide for a measure of coordination of decisions among a multiplicity of decision-makers and, in effect, to compensate on the societal level for the inadequacies of the individual incremental decision-maker and for the society's inability to make decisions effectively from one center. Incremental decision-making is claimed to be both a realistic account of how the American polity and other modern democracies decide and the most effective approach to societal decision-making, i.e., both a descriptive and a normative model.

A CRITIQUE OF THE INCREMENTAL APPROACH AS A NORMATIVE MODEL

Decisions by consent among partisans without a societywide regulatory center and guiding institutions should not be viewed as the preferred approach to decision-making. In the first place, decisions so reached would, of necessity, reflect the interests of the most powerful, since partisans invariably differ in their respective power positions; demands of the underprivileged and politically unorganized would be underrepresented.

Secondly, incrementalism would tend to neglect *basic* societal innovations, as it focuses on the short run and seeks no more than limited variations from past policies. While an accumulation of small steps could lead to a significant change, there is nothing in this approach to guide the accumulation; the steps may be circular—leading back to where they started, or dispersed—leading in many directions at once but leading nowhere. Boulding comments that, according to this approach, "we do stagger through history like a drunk putting one disjointed incremental foot after another." [6]

In addition, incrementalists seem to underestimate *their* impact on the

[6] Kenneth E. Boulding in a review of *A Strategy of Decision* in the *American Sociological Review*, Vol. 29 (1964), 931.

decision-makers. As Dror put it, "Although Lindblom's thesis includes a number of reservations, these are insufficient to alter its main impact as an ideological reinforcement of the pro-inertia and anti-innovation forces." [7]

A CONCEPTUAL AND EMPIRICAL CRITIQUE OF INCREMENTALISM

Incrementalist strategy clearly recognizes one subset of situations to which it does not apply—namely, "large" or fundamental decisions,[8] such as a declaration of war. While incremental decisions greatly outnumber fundamental ones, the latter's significance for societal decision-making is not commensurate with their number; it is thus a mistake to relegate nonincremental decisions to the category of exceptions. Moreover, it is often the fundamental decisions which set the context for the numerous incremental ones. Although fundamental decisions are frequently "prepared" by incremental ones in order that the final decision will initiate a less abrupt change, these decisions may still be considered relatively fundamental. The incremental steps which follow cannot be understood without them, and the preceding steps are useless unless they lead to fundamental decisions.

Thus, while the incrementalists hold that decision-making involves a choice between the two kinds of decision-making models, it should be noted that (a) *most incremental de-*

[7] Yehezkel Dror, "Muddling Through— 'Science' or Inertia?" *Public Administration Review*, Vol. 24 (1964), 155.

[8] Braybrooke and Lindblom, *A Strategy of Decision, op. cit.*, pp. 66–69.

cisions specify or anticipate funda-mental decisions, and (b) *the cumu-lative value of the incremental decisions is greatly affected by the related fundamental decisions.*

Thus, it is not enough to show, as Fenno did, that Congress makes pri-marily marginal changes in the fed-eral budget (a comparison of one year's budget for a federal agency with that of the preceding year showed on many occasions only a 10 percent difference [9]), or that for long periods the defense budget does not change much in terms of its per-centage of the federal budget, or that the federal budget changes little each year in terms of its percentage of the Gross National Product.[10] These in-cremental changes are often the un-folding of trends initiated at critical turning points at which fundamental decisions were made. The American defense budget jumped at the begin-ning of the Korean War in 1950 from 5 percent of the GNP to 10.3 percent in 1951. The fact that it stayed at about this level, ranging between 9 and 11.3 percent of the GNP after the war ended (1954–1960), did re-flect incremental decisions, but these were made within the context of the decision to engage in the Korean War.[11] Fenno's own figures show al-most an equal number of changes above the 20 percent level as below

it; seven changes represented an in-crease of 100 percent or more and 24 changes increased 50 percent or more.[12]

It is clear that, while Congress or other societal decision-making bodies do make some cumulative incremen-tal decisions without facing the fun-damental one implied, many other decisions which appear to be a series of incremental ones are, in effect, the implementation or elaboration of a fundamental decision. For exam-ple, after Congress set up a national space agency in 1958 and consented to back President Kennedy's space goals, it made "incremental" addi-tional commitments for several years. Initially, however, a fundamental de-cision had been made. Congress in 1958, drawing on past experiences and on an understanding of the dynamics of incremental processes, could not have been unaware that once a fundamental commitment is made it is difficult to reverse it. While the initial space budget was relatively small, the very act of set-ting up a space agency amounted to subscribing to additional budget in-crements in future years.[13]

Incrementalists argue that incre-mental decisions tend to be remedial; small steps are taken in the "right" direction, or, when it is evident the direction is "wrong," the course is altered. But if the decision-maker evaluates his incremental decisions

[9] Richard Fenno, Jr., *The Power of the Purse* (Boston: Little, Brown and Co., 1966), pp. 266ff. See also Otto A. Davis, M. A. H. Dempster, and Aaron Wildavsky, "A Theory of the Budgetary Process," *American Political Science Review*, Vol. 60 (1966), esp. pp. 530–31.

[10] Samuel P. Huntington, quoted by Nelson E. Polsby, *Congress and the Presidency* (Englewood Cliffs, N.J.: Prentice-Hall, 1964), p. 86.

[11] *Ibid.*

[12] Fenno, *The Power of the Purse, loc. cit.*

[13] For an example involving the Supreme Court's decision on desegregation, see Martin Shapiro, "Stability and Change in Judicial Decision-Making: Incremen-talism or *Stare Decisis*," *Law in Transi-tion Quarterly,* Vol. 2 (1965), 134–57. See also a commentary by Bruce L. R. Smith, *American Political Science Review*, Vol. 61 (1967), esp. p. 151.

and small steps, which he must do if he is to decide whether or not the direction is right, his judgment will be greatly affected by the evaluative criteria he applies. Here, again, we have to go outside the incrementalist model to ascertain the ways in which these criteria are set.

Thus, while actors make both kinds of decisions, the number and role of fundamental decisions are significantly greater than incrementalists state, and when the fundamental ones are missing, incremental decision-making amounts to drifting—action without direction. A more active approach to societal decision-making requires two sets of mechanisms: (a) high-order, fundamental policy-making processes which set basic directions and (b) incremental processes which prepare for fundamental decisions and work them out after they have been reached. This is provided by mixed-scanning.

THE MIXED-SCANNING APPROACH

Mixed scanning provides both a realistic description of the strategy used by actors in a large variety of fields and the strategy for effective actors to follow. Let us first illustrate this approach in a simple situation and then explore its societal dimensions. Assume we are about to set up a worldwide weather observation system using weather satellites. The rationalistic approach would seek an exhaustive survey of weather conditions by using cameras capable of detailed observations and by scheduling reviews of the entire sky as often as possible. This would yield an ava-

lanche of details, costly to analyze and likely to overwhelm our action capacities (e.g., "seeding" cloud formations that could develop into hurricanes or bring rain to arid areas). Incrementalism would focus on those areas in which similar patterns developed in the recent past and, perhaps, on a few nearby regions; it would thus ignore all formations which might deserve attention if they arose in unexpected areas.

A mixed-scanning strategy would include elements of both approaches by employing two cameras: a broad-angle camera that would cover all parts of the sky but not in great detail, and a second one which would zero in on those areas revealed by the first camera to require a more in-depth examination. While mixed-scanning might miss areas in which only a detailed camera could reveal trouble, it is less likely than incrementalism to miss obvious trouble spots in unfamiliar areas.

From an abstract viewpoint mixed-scanning provides a particular procedure for the collection of information (e.g., the surveying or "scanning" of weather conditions), a strategy about the allocation of resources (e.g., "seeding"), and—we shall see—guidelines for the relations between the two. The strategy combines a detailed ("rationalistic") examination of some sectors—which, unlike the exhaustive examination of the entire area, is feasible—with a "truncated" review of other sectors. The relative investment in the two kinds of scanning—full detail and truncated—as well as in the very act of scanning, depends on how costly it would be to miss, for example, one hurricane;

the cost of additional scanning; and the amount of time it would take.

Scanning may be divided into more than two levels; there can be several levels with varying degrees of detail and coverage, though it seems most effective to include an all-encompassing level (so that no major option will be left uncovered) and a highly detailed level (so that the option selected can be explored as fully as is feasible).

The decision on how the investment of assets and time is to be allocated among the levels of scanning is, in fact, part of the strategy. The actual amount of assets and time spent depends on the total amount available and on experimentation with various interlevel combinations. Also, the amount spent is best changed over time. Effective decision-making requires that sporadically, or at set intervals, investment in encompassing (high-coverage) scanning be increased to check for far removed but "obvious" dangers and to search for better lines of approach. Annual budget reviews and the State of the Union messages provide, in principle, such occasions.

An increase in investment of this type is also effective when the actor realizes that the environment radically changes or when he sees that the early chain of increments brings no improvement in the situation or brings even a "worsening." If, at this point, the actor decides to drop the course of action, the effectiveness of his decision-making is reduced, since, through some high-coverage scanning, he may discover that a continuation of the "loss" is about to lead to a solution. (An obvious example is the selling of a declining stock

if a further review reveals that the corporation is expected to improve its earning next year, after several years of decline.) Reality cannot be assumed to be structured in straight lines where each step towards a goal leads directly to another and where the accumulation of small steps in effect solves the problem. Often what from an incremental viewpoint is a step away from the goal ("worsening") may from a broader perspective be a step in the right direction, as when the temperature of a patient is allowed to rise because this will hasten his recovery. Thus mixed-scanning not only combines various levels of scanning but also provides a set of criteria for situations in which one level or another is to be emphasized.

In the exploration of mixed-scanning, it is essential to differentiate fundamental decisions from incremental ones. Fundamental decisions are made by exploring the main alternatives the actor sees in view of his conception of his goals, but –unlike what rationalism would indicate–details and specifications are omitted so that an overview is feasible. Incremental decisions are made but within the contexts set by fundamental decisions (and fundamental reviews). Thus, each of the two elements in mixed-scanning helps to reduce the effects of the particular shortcomings of the other; incrementalism reduces the unrealistic aspects of rationalism by limiting the details required in fundamental decisions, and contextuating rationalism helps to overcome the conservative slant of incrementalism by exploring longer-run alternatives. Together, empirical tests and comparative study of decision-makers would show that these elements make for a third approach which is at once more realistic and more effective than its components.

CAN DECISIONS BE EVALUATED?

The preceding discussion assumes that both the observer and the actor have a capacity to evaluate decision-making strategies and to determine which is the more effective. Incrementalists, however, argue that since values cannot be scaled and summarized, "good" decisions cannot be defined and, hence, evaluation is not possible. In contrast, it is reasonable to expect that the decision-makers, as well as the observers, can summarize their values and rank them, at least in an ordinal scale.

For example, many societal projects have one primary goal such as increasing birth control, economically desalting sea water, or reducing price inflation by one-half over a two-year period. Other goals which are also served are secondary, e.g., increasing the country's R & D sector by investing in desalting. The actor, hence, may deal with the degree to which the *primary* goal was realized and make this the central evaluative measure for a "good" policy, while noting its effects on secondary goals. When he compares projects in these terms, he, in effect, weighs the primary goal as several times as important as all the secondary goals combined. This procedure amounts to saying, "As I care very much about one goal and little about the others, if the project does not serve the first goal, it is no good and I do not have to worry about measuring and total-

ing up whatever other gains it may be providing for my secondary values."

When there are two or even three primary goals (e.g., teaching, therapy, and research in a university hospital), the actor can still compare projects in terms of the extent to which they realize each primary goal. He can establish that project X is good for research but not for teaching while project Y is very good for teaching but not as good for research, etc., without having to raise the additional difficulties of combining the effectiveness measures into one numerical index. In effect, he proceeds as if they had identical weights.

Finally, an informal scaling of values is not as difficult as the incrementalists imagine. Most actors are able to rank their goals to some extent (e.g., faculty is more concerned about the quality of research than the quality of teaching).

One of the most imaginative attempts to evaluate the effectiveness of programs with hard-to-assess objectives is a method devised by David Osborn, Deputy Assisant Secretary of State for Educational and Cultural affairs. . . . Osborn recommends a scheme of cross-multiplying the costs of the activities with a number representing the rank of its objectives on a scale. For instance, the exchange of Fulbright professors may contribute to "cultural prestige and mutual respect," "educational development," and gaining "entrée," which might be given scale numbers such as 8, 6, and 5, respectively. These numbers are then multiplied with the costs of the program, and the resulting figure is in turn multiplied with an ingenious figure called a "country number." The latter is an attempt to get a rough measure of the importance to the U.S.

of the countries with which we have cultural relations. It is arrived at by putting togther in complicated ways certain key data, weighed to reflect cultural and educational matters, such as the country's population, Gross National Product, number of college students, rate of illiteracy, and so forth. The resulting numbers are then revised in the light of working experience, as when, because of its high per capita income, a certain tiny middle-eastern country turns out to be more important to the U.S. than a large eastern European one. At this point, country numbers are revised on the basis of judgment and experience, as are other numbers at other points. But those who make such revisions have a basic framework to start with, a set of numbers arranged on the basis of many factors, rather than single arbitrary guesses.[14]

Thus, in evaluation as in decision-making itself, while full detailed rationalism may well be impossible, truncated reviews are feasible, and this approach may be expected to be more effective in terms of the actors' goal than "muddling through."

MORPHOLOGICAL FACTORS

The structures within which interactions among actors take place become more significant the more we recognize that the bases of decisions neither are nor can be a fully ordered set of values and an exhaustive examination of reality. In part, the strategy followed is determined neither by values nor by information

14 Virginia Held, "PPBS Comes to Washington," *The Public Interest*, No. 4 (Summer 1966), 102–115, quotation from pp. 112–13.

but by the positions of and power relations among the decision-makers. For example, the extent to which one element of mixed-scanning is stressed as against the other is affected by the relationship between higher and lower organizational ranks. In some situations, the higher in rank, concerned only with the overall picture, are impatient with details, while lower ranks—especially experts—are more likely to focus on details. In other situations, the higher ranks, to avoid facing the overall picture, seek to bury themselves, their administration, and the public in details.

Next, the environment should be taken into account. For instance, a highly incremental approach would perhaps be adequate if the situation were more stable and the decisions made were effective from the start. This approach is expected to be less appropriate when conditions are rapidly changing and when the initial course was wrong. Thus, there seems to be no one effective decision-making strategy in the abstract, apart from the societal environment into which it is introduced. Mixed-scanning is flexible; changes in the relative investment in scanning in general as well as among the various levels of scanning permit it to adapt to the specific situation. For example, more encompassing scanning is called for when the environment is more malleable.

Another major consideration here is the capacities of the actor. This is illustrated with regard to interagency relations by the following statement: ". . . the State Department was hopelessly behind. Its cryptographic equipment was obsolescent, which slowed communications, and it had no central situation room at all." [15] The author goes on to show how as a consequence the State Department was less able to act than was the Defense Department.

An actor with a low capacity to mobilize power to implement his decision may do better to rely less on encompassing scanning; even if remote outcomes are anticipated, he will be able to do little about them. More generally, the greater a unit's control capacities the more encompassing scanning it can undertake, and the more such scanning, the more effective its decision-making. This points to an interesting paradox: The developing nations, with much lower control capacities than the modern ones, tend to favor much more planning, although they may have to make do with a relatively high degree of incrementalism. Yet modern pluralistic societies—which are much more able to scan and, at least in some dimensions, are much more able to control—tend to plan less.

Two different factors are involved which highlight the difference in this regard among modern societies. While all have a higher capacity to scan and some control advantages as compared to nonmodern societies, they differ sharply in their capacity to build consensus. Democracies must accept a relatively high degree of incrementalism (though not as high as developing nations) because of their greater need to gain support for new decisions from many and conflicting subsocieties, a need which

reduces their capacity to follow a long-run plan. It is easier to reach consensus under noncrisis situations, on increments similar to existing policies, than to gain support for a new policy. However, the role of crises is significant; in relatively less passive democracies, crises serve to build consensus for major changes of direction which are overdue (e.g., desegregation).

Totalitarian societies, more centralist and relying on powers which are less dependent on consensus, can plan more but they tend to overshoot the mark. Unlike democracies which first seek to build up a consensus and then proceed, often doing less than necessary later than necessary, totalitarian societies, lacking the capacity for consensus-building or even for assessing the various resistances, usually try for too much too early. They are then forced to adjust their plans after initiation, with the revised policies often scaled down and involving more "consensus" than the original one. While totalitarian gross misplanning constitutes a large waste of resources, some initial overplanning and later down-scaling is as much a decision-making strategy as is disjointed incrementalism, and is the one for which totalitarian societies may be best suited.

A society more able to effectively handle its problems (one referred to elsewhere as an *active society*) [16] would require:

1. A higher capacity to build consensus than even democracies command.
2. More effective though not necessarily

15 Roger Hilsman, *To Move a Nation: The Politics of Foreign Policy in the Administration of John F. Kennedy* (Garden City, N.Y.: Doubleday & Co., 1967), p. 27.

16 Amitai Etzioni, *The Active Society: A Theory of Societal and Political Processes* (New York: Free Press, 1968).

more numerous means of control than totalitarian societies employ (which new knowledge technology and better analysis through the social sciences may make feasible).

3. A mixed-scanning strategy which is not as rationalistic as that which the totalitarian societies attempt to pursue and not as incremental as the strategy democracies advocate.

7   *Disjointed Incrementalism*

THE SCIENCE OF "MUDDLING THROUGH"

CHARLES E. LINDBLOM

Suppose an administrator is given responsibility for formulating policy with respect to inflation. He might start by trying to list all related values in order of importance, e.g., full employment, reasonable business profit, protection of small savings, prevention of a stock market crash. Then all possible policy outcomes could be rated as more or less efficient in attaining a maximum of these values. This would of course require a prodigious inquiry into values held by members of society and an equally prodigious set of calculations on how much of each value is equal to how much of each other value. He could then proceed to outline all possible policy alternatives. In a third step, he would undertake systematic comparison of his multitude of alternatives to determine which attains the greatest amount of values.

In comparing policies, he would take advantage of any theory available that generalized about classes of policies. In considering inflation, for example, he would compare all

Reprinted with permission of author and publisher from: Charles E. Lindblom, "The Science of 'Muddling Through,'" *Public Administration Review*, 19 (Spring 1959), 79–88.

policies in the light of the theory of prices. Since no alternatives are beyond his investigation, he would consider strict central control and the abolition of all prices and markets on the one hand and elimination of all public controls with reliance completely on the free market on the other both in the light of whatever theoretical generalizations he could find on such hypothetical economies.

Finally, he would try to make the choice that would in fact maximize his values.

An alternative line of attack would be to set as his principal objective, either explicitly or without conscious thought, the relatively simple goal of keeping prices level. This objective might be compromised or complicated by only a few other goals, such as full employment. He would in fact disregard most other social values as beyond his present interest, and he would for the moment not even attempt to rank the few values that he regarded as immediately relevant. Were he pressed, he would quickly admit that he was ignoring many related values and many possible important consequences of his policies.

As a second step, he would outline those relatively few policy alternatives that occurred to him. He would then compare them. In comparing his limited number of alternatives, most of them familiar from past controversies, he would not ordinarily find a body of theory precise enough to carry him through a comparison of their respective consequences. Instead he would rely heavily on the record of past experience with small policy steps to predict the consequences of similar steps extended into the future.

Moreover, he would find that the policy alternatives combined objectives or values in different ways. For example, one policy might offer price level stability at the cost of some risk of unemployment; another might offer less price stability but also less risk of unemployment. Hence, the next step in his approach—the final selection—would combine into one the choice among values and the choice among instruments for reaching values. It would not, as in the first method of policymaking, approximate a more mechanical process of choosing the means that best satisfied goals that were previously clarified and ranked. Because practitioners of the second approach expect to achieve their goals only partially, they would expect to repeat endlessly the sequence just described, as conditions and aspirations changed and as accuracy of prediction improved.

BY ROOT OR BY BRANCH

For complex problems, the first of these two approaches is of course impossible. Although such an approach can be described, it cannot be practiced except for relatively simple problems and even then only in a somewhat modified form. It assumes intellectual capacities and sources of information that men simply do not possess, and it is even more absurd as an approach to policy when the time and money that can be allocated to a policy problem is limited, as is always the case. Of particular importance to public administrators is the fact that public agencies are in effect usually instructed not to practice the first method. That is to say, their prescribed functions and constraints—the politically or legally possible—restrict their attention to relatively few values and relatively few alternative policies among the countless alternatives that might be imagined. It is the second method that is practiced.

Curiously, however, the literatures of decision-making, policy formulation, planning, and public administration formalize the first approach rather than the second, leaving public administrators who handle complex decisions in the position of practicing what few preach. For emphasis I run some risk of overstatement. True enough, the literature is well aware of limits on man's capacities and of the inevitability that policies will be approached in some such style as the second. But attempts to formalize rational policy formulation—to lay out explicitly the necessary steps in the process—usually describe the first approach and not the second.[1]

1 James G. March and Herbert A. Simon similarly characterize the literature. They also take some important steps, as have Simon's recent articles, to describe a less heroic model of policy-making. See *Organizations* (John Wiley and Sons, 1958), p. 137.

The common tendency to describe policy formulation even for complex problems as though it followed the first approach has been strengthened by the attention given to, and successes enjoyed by, operations research, statistical decision theory, and systems analysis. The hallmarks of these procedures, typical of the first approach, are clarity of objective, explicitness of evaluation, a high degree of comprehensiveness of overview, and, wherever possible, quantification of values for mathematical analysis. But these advanced procedures remain largely the appropriate techniques of relatively small-scale problem-solving where the total number of variables to be considered is small and value problems restricted. Charles Hitch, head of the Economics Division of RAND Corporation, one of the leading centers for application of these techniques, has written:

I would make the empirical generalization from my experience at RAND and elsewhere that operations research is the art of sub-optimizing, i.e., of solving some lower-level problems, and that difficulties increase and our special competence diminishes by an order of magnitude with every level of decision making we attempt to ascend. The sort of simple explicit model which operations researchers are so proficient in using can certainly reflect most of the significant factors influencing traffic control on the George Washington Bridge, but the proportion of the relevant reality which we can represent by any such model or models in studying, say, a major foreign-policy decision, appears to be almost trivial.[2]

Accordingly, I propose in this paper to clarify and formalize the

second method, much neglected in the literature. This might be described as the method of *successive limited comparisons.* I will contrast it with the first approach, which might be called the rational-comprehensive method.[3] More impressionistically and briefly—and therefore generally used in this article—they could be characterized as the branch method and root method, the former continually building out from the current situation, step-by-step and by small degrees; the latter starting from fundamentals anew each time, building on the past only as experience is embodied in a theory, and always prepared to start completely from the ground up.

Let us put the characteristics of the two methods side by side in simplest terms.

Assuming that the root method is familiar and understandable, we proceed directly to clarification of its alternative by contrast. In explaining the second, we shall be describing how most administrators do in fact approach complex questions, for the root method, the "best" way as a blueprint or model, is in fact not workable for complex policy ques-

particular points made in the article to which his paper is a reply; his claim that operations research is for low-level problems is widely accepted.

For examples of the kind of problems to which operations research is applied, see C. W. Churchman, R. L. Ackoff, and E. L. Arnoff, *Introduction to Operations Research* (John Wiley and Sons, 1957); and J. F. McCloskey and J. M. Coppinger (eds.), *Operations Research for Management,* Vol. II (Johns Hopkins Press, 1956).

[3] I am assuming that administrators often make policy and advise in the making of policy and am treating decision-making and policy-making as synonymous for purposes of this paper.

[2] "Operations Research and National Planning—A Dissent," 5 *Operations Research* 718 (October, 1957). Hitch's dissent is from

Rational-Comprehensive Root	Successive Limited Comparisons (Branch)
1a. Clarification of values or objectives distinct from and usually prerequisite to empirical analysis of alternative policies.	1b. Selection of value goals and empirical analysis of the needed action are not distinct from one another but are closely intertwined.
2a. Policy-formulation is therefore approached through means-end analysis: First the ends are isolated, then the the means to achieve them are sought.	2b. Since means and ends are not distinct, means-end analysis is often inappropriate or limited.
3a. The test of a "good" policy is that it can be shown to be the most appropriate means to desired ends.	3b. The test of a "good" policy is typically that various analysts find themselves directly agreeing on a policy (without their agreeing that it is the most appropriate means to an agreed objective).

4a. Analysis is comprehensive; every important relevant factor is taken into account.	4b. Analysis is drastically limited:
	  i) Important possible outcomes are neglected.
	  ii) Important alternative potential policies are neglected.
	  iii) Important affected values are neglected.

5a. Theory is often heavily relied upon.	5b. A succession of comparisons greatly reduces or eliminates reliance on theory.

tions, and administrators are forced to use the method of successive limited comparisons.

INTERTWINING EVALUATION AND EMPIRICAL ANALYSIS (1b)

The quickest way to understand how values are handled in the method of successive limited comparisons is to see how the root method often breaks down in *its* handling of values or objectives. The idea that values should be clarified, and in advance of the examination of alternative policies, is appealing. But what happens when we attempt it for complex social problems? The first difficulty is that on many critical values or objectives, citizens disagree, congressmen disagree, and public administrators disagree. Even where a fairly specific objective is prescribed for the administrator, there remains considerable room for disagreement on subobjectives. Consider, for example, the conflict with respect to locating public housing, described in Meyerson and Banfield's study of the Chicago Housing Authority [4]—disagreement which occurred despite the clear objective of providing a certain number of public housing units in the city. Similarly conflicting are objectives in highway location, traffic control, minimum wage administration, development of tourist facilities in national parks, or insect control. Administrators cannot escape these conflicts by ascertaining the major-

[4] Martin Meyerson and Edward C. Banfield, *Politics, Planning, and the Public Interest* (Free Press, 1955).

ity's preference, for preferences have not been registered on most issues; indeed, there often *are* no preferences in the absence of public discussion sufficient to bring an issue to the attention of the electorate. Furthermore, there is a question of whether intensity of feeling should be considered as well as the number of persons preferring each alternative. By the impossibility of doing otherwise, administrators often are reduced to deciding policy without clarifying objectives first.

Even when an administrator resolves to follow his own values as a criterion for decisions, he often will not know how to rank them when they conflict with one another, as they usually do. Suppose, for example, that an administrator must relocate tenants living in tenements scheduled for destruction. One objective is to empty the buildings fairly promptly, another is to find suitable accommodation for persons displaced, another is to avoid friction with residents in other areas in which a large influx would be unwelcome, another is to deal with all concerned through persuasion if possible, and so on.

How does one state even to himself the relative importance of these partially conflicting values? A simple ranking of them is not enough; one needs ideally to know how much of one value is worth sacrificing for some of another value. The answer is that typically the administrator chooses—and must choose—directly among policies in which these values are combined in different ways. He cannot first clarify his values and then choose among policies.

A more subtle third point underlies both the first two. Social objectives do not always have the same relative values. One objective may be highly prized in one circumstance, another in another circumstance. If, for example, an administrator values highly both the dispatch with which his agency can carry through its projects *and* good public relations, it matters little which of the two possibly conflicting values he favors in some abstract or general sense. Policy questions arise in forms which put to administrators such a question as: Given the degree to which we are or are not already achieving the values of dispatch and the values of good public relations, is it worth sacrificing a little speed for a happier clientele, or is it better to risk offending the clientele so that we can get on with our work? The answer to such a question varies with circumstances.

The value problem is, as the example shows, always a problem of adjustments at a margin. But there is no practicable way to state marginal objectives or values except in terms of particular policies. That one value is preferred to another in one decision situation does not mean that it will be preferred in another decision situation in which it can be had only at great sacrifice of another value. Attempts to rank or order values in general and abstract terms so that they do not shift from decision to decision end up by ignoring the relevant marginal preferences. The significance of this third point thus goes very far. Even if all administrators had at hand an agreed set of values, objectives, and constraints, and an agreed ranking of these values, objectives, and constraints, their marginal values in actual choice situations would be impossible to formulate.

Unable consequently to formulate

the relevant values first and then choose among policies to achieve them, administrators must choose directly among alternative policies that offer different marginal combinations of values. Somewhat paradoxically, the only practicable way to disclose one's relevant marginal values even to oneself is to describe the policy one chooses to achieve them. Except roughly and vaguely, I know of no way to describe—or even to understand—what my relative evaluations are for, say, freedom and security, speed and accuracy in governmental decisions, or low taxes and better schools than to describe my preferences among specific policy choices that might be made between the alternatives in each of the pairs.

In summary, two aspects of the process by which values are actually handled can be distinguished. The first is clear: evaluation and empirical analysis are intertwined; that is, one chooses among values and among policies at one and the same time. Put a little more elaborately, one simultaneously chooses a policy to attain certain objectives and chooses the objectives themselves. The second aspect is related but distinct: the administrator focuses his attention on marginal or incremental values. Whether he is aware of it or not, he does not find general formulations of objectives very helpful and in fact makes specific marginal or incremental comparisons. Two policies, X and Y, confront him. Both promise the same degree of attainment of objectives *a, b, c, d,* and *e.* But X promises him somewhat more of *f* than does Y, while Y promises him somewhat more of *g* than does X. In choosing between them, he is in fact offered the alternative of a marginal or incremental amount of *f* at the expense of a marginal or incremental amount of *g.* The only values that are relevant to his choice are these increments by which the two policies differ; and, when he finally chooses between the two marginal values, he does so by making a choice between policies.[5]

As to whether the attempt to clarify objectives in advance of policy selection is more or less rational than the close intertwining of marginal evaluation and empirical analysis, the principal difference established is that for complex problems the first is impossible and irrelevant, and the second is both possible and relevant. The second is possible because the administrator need not try to analyze any values except the values by which alternative policies differ and need not be concerned with them except as they differ marginally. His need for information on values or objectives is drastically reduced as compared with the root method; and his capacity for grasping, comprehending, and relating values to one another is not strained beyond the breaking point.

RELATIONS BETWEEN MEANS AND ENDS (2b)

Decision-making is ordinarily formalized as a means-ends relationship: means are conceived to be evaluated and chosen in the light of ends finally selected independently of and prior to the choice of means. This is the means-ends relationship of the root method. But it follows from all that has just been said that

---

[5] The line of argument is, of course, an extension of the theory of market choice, especially the theory of consumer choice, to public policy choices.

such a means-ends relationship is possible only to the extent that values are agreed upon, are reconcilable, and are stable at the margin. Typically, therefore, such a means-ends relationship is absent from the branch method, where means and ends are simultaneously chosen.

Yet any departure from the means-ends relationship of the root method will strike some readers as inconceivable. For it will appear to them that only in such a relationship is it possible to determine whether one policy choice is better or worse than another. How can an administrator know whether he has made a wise or foolish decision if he is without prior values or objectives by which to judge his decisions? The answer to this question calls up the third distinctive difference between root and branch methods: how to decide the best policy.

THE TEST OF "GOOD" POLICY (3b)

In the root method, a decision is "correct," "good," or "rational" if it can be shown to attain some specified objective, where the objective can be specified without simply describing the decision itself. Where objectives are defined only through the marginal or incremental approach to values described above, it is still sometimes possible to test whether a policy does in fact attain the desired objectives; but a precise statement of the objectives takes the form of a description of the policy chosen or some alternative to it. To show that a policy is mistaken one cannot offer an abstract argument that important objectives are not achieved; one must instead argue

that another policy is more to be preferred.

So far, the departure from customary ways of looking at problem-solving is not troublesome, for many administrators will be quick to agree that the most effective discussion of the correctness of policy does take the form of comparison with other policies that might have been chosen. But what of the situation in which administrators cannot agree on values or objectives, either abstractly or in marginal terms? What then is the test of "good" policy? For the root method, there is no test. Agreement on objectives failing, there is no standard of "correctness." For the method of successive limited comparisons, the test is agreement on policy itself, which remains possible even when agreement on values is not.

It has been suggested that continuing agreement in Congress on the desirability of extending old age insurance stems from liberal desires to strengthen the welfare programs of the federal government and from conservative desires to reduce union demands for private pension plans. If so, this is an excellent demonstration of the ease with which individuals of different ideologies often can agree on concrete policy. Labor mediators report a similar phenomenon: the contestants cannot agree on criteria for settling their disputes but can agree on specific proposals. Similarly, when one administrator's objective turns out to be another's means, they often can agree on policy.

Agreement on policy thus becomes the only practicable test of the policy's correctness. And for one administrator to seek to win the other over to agreement on ends as well would accomplish nothing and create quite unnecessary controversy.

If agreement directly on policy as a test for "best" policy seems a poor substitute for testing the policy against its objectives, it ought to be remembered that objectives themselves have no ultimate validity other than they are agreed upon. Hence agreement is the test of "best" policy in both methods. But where the root method requires agreement on what elements in the decision constitute objectives and on which of these objectives should be sought, the branch method falls back on agreement wherever it can be found.

In an important sense, therefore, it is not irrational for an administrator to defend a policy as good without being able to specify what it is good for.

NON-COMPREHENSIVE ANALYSIS (4b)

Ideally, rational-comprehensive analysis leaves out nothing important. But it is impossible to take everything important into consideration unless "important" is so narrowly defined that analysis is in fact quite limited. Limits on human intellectual capacities and on available information set definite limits to man's capacity to be comprehensive. In actual fact, therefore, no one can practice the rational-comprehensive method for really complex problems, and every administrator faced with a sufficiently complex problem must find ways drastically to simplify.

An administrator assisting in the formulation of agricultural economic policy cannot in the first place be competent on all possible policies. He cannot even comprehend one policy entirely. In planning a soil bank program, he cannot successfully anticipate the impact of higher or lower farm income on, say, urbanization—the possible consequent loosening of family ties, possible consequent eventual need for revisions in social security and further implications for tax problems arising out of new federal responsibilities for social security and municipal responsibilities for urban services. Nor, to follow another line of repercussions, can he work through the soil bank program's effects on prices for agricultural products in foreign markets and consequent implications for foreign relations, including those arising out of economic rivalry between the United States and the U.S.S.R.

In the method of successive limited comparisons, simplification is systematically achieved in two principal ways. First, it is achieved through limitation of policy comparisons to those policies that differ in relatively small degree from policies presently in effect. Such a limitation immediately reduces the number of alternatives to be investigated and also drastically simplifies the character of the investigation of each. For it is not necessary to undertake fundamental inquiry into an alternative and its consequences; it is necessary only to study those respects in which the proposed alternative and its consequences differ from the status quo. The empirical comparison of marginal differences among alternative policies that differ only marginally is, of course, a counterpart to the incremental or marginal comparison of values discussed above.[6]

RELEVANCE AS WELL AS REALISM

It is a matter of common observation that in Western democracies public administrators and policy analysts in general do largely limit their analyses to incremental or marginal differences in policies that are chosen to differ only incrementally. They do not do so, however, solely because they desperately need some way to simplify their problems; they also do so in order to be relevant. Democracies change their policies almost entirely through incremental adjustments. Policy does not move in leaps and bounds.

The incremental character of political change in the United States has often been remarked. The two major political parties agree on fundamentals; they offer alternative policies to the voters only on relatively small points of difference. Both parties favor full employment, but they define it somewhat differently; both favor the development of water power resources, but in slightly different ways; and both favor unemployment compensation, but not the same level of benefits. Similarly, shifts of policy within a party take place largely through a series of relatively small changes, as can be seen in their only gradual

6 A more precise definition of incremental policies and a discussion of whether a change that appears "small" to one observer might be seen differently by another is to be found in my "Policy Analysis," 48 *American Economic Review* 298 (June 1958).

acceptance of the idea of governmental responsibility for support of the unemployed, a change in party positions beginning in the early 30s and culminating in a sense in the Employment Act of 1946.

Party behavior is in turn rooted in public attitudes, and political theorists cannot conceive of democracy's surviving in the United States in the absence of fundamental agreement on potentially disruptive issues, with consequent limitation of policy debates to relatively small differences in policy.

Since the policies ignored by the administrator are politically impossible and so irrelevant, the simplification of analysis achieved by concentrating on policies that differ only incrementally is not a capricious kind of simplification. In addition, it can be argued that, given the limits on knowledge within which policy-makers are confined, simplifying by limiting the focus to small variations from present policy makes the most of available knowledge. Because policies being considered are like present and past policies, the administrator can obtain information and claim some insight. Nonincremental policy proposals are therefore typically not only politically irrelevant but also unpredictable in their consequences.

The second method of simplification of analysis is the practice of ignoring important possible consequences of possible policies, as well as the values attached to the neglected consequences. If this appears to disclose a shocking shortcoming of successive limited comparisons, it can be replied that, even if the exclusions are random, policies may nevertheless be more intelligently formulated than through futile attempts to achieve a comprehensiveness beyond human capacity. Actually, however, the exclusions, seeming arbitrary or random from one point of view, need be neither.

ACHIEVING A DEGREE OF COMPREHENSIVENESS

Suppose that each value neglected by one policy-making agency were a major concern of at least one other agency. In that case, a helpful division of labor would be achieved, and no agency need find its task beyond its capacities. The shortcomings of such a system would be that one agency might destroy a value either before another agency could be activated to safeguard it or in spite of another agency's efforts. But the possibility that important values may be lost is present in any form of organization, even where agencies attempt to comprehend in planning more than is humanly possible.

The virtue of such a hypothetical division of labor is that every important interest or value has its watchdog. And these watchdogs can protect the interests in their jurisdiction in two quite different ways: first, by redressing damages done by other agencies; and, second, by anticipating and heading off injury before it occurs.

In a society like that of the United States in which individuals are free to combine to pursue almost any possible common interest they might have and in which government agencies are sensitive to the pressures of these groups, the system described is approximated. Almost every interest

has its watchdog. Without claiming that every interest has a sufficiently powerful watchdog, it can be argued that our system often can assure a more comprehensive regard for the values of the whole society than any attempt at intellectual comprehensiveness.

In the United States, for example, no part of government attempts a comprehensive overview of policy on income distribution. A policy nevertheless evolves, and one responding to a wide variety of interests. A process of mutual adjustment among farm groups, labor unions, municipalities and school boards, tax authorities, and government agencies with responsibilities in the fields of housing, health, highways, national parks, fire, and police accomplishes a distribution of income in which particular income problems neglected at one point in the decision processes become central at another point.

Mutual adjustment is more pervasive than the explicit forms it takes in negotiation between groups; it persists through the mutual impacts of groups upon each other even where they are not in communication. For all the imperfections and latent dangers in this ubiquitous process of mutual adjustment, it will often accomplish an adaptation of policies to a wider range of interests than could be done by one group centrally.

Note, too, how the incremental pattern of policy-making fits with the multiple pressure pattern. For when decisions are only incremental—closely related to known policies, it is easier for one group to anticipate the kind of moves another might make and easier too for it to make correction for injury already accomplished.[7]

Even partisanship and narrowness, to use pejorative terms, will sometimes be assets to rational decision-making, for they can doubly insure that what one agency neglects, another will not; they specialize personnel to distinct points of view. The claim is valid that effective rational coordination of the federal administration, if possible to achieve at all, would require an agreed set of values [8]—if "rational" is defined as the practice of the root method of decision-making. But a high degree of administrative coordination occurs as each agency adjusts its policies to the concerns of the other agencies in the process of fragmented decision-making I have just described.

For all the apparent shortcomings of the incremental approach to policy alternatives with its arbitrary exclusion coupled with fragmentation, when compared to the root method, the branch method often looks far superior. In the root method, the inevitable exclusion of factors is accidental, unsystematic, and not defensible by any argument so far developed, while in the branch method the exclusions are deliberate, systematic, and defensible. Ideally, of course, the root method does not exclude; in practice it must.

Nor does the branch method necessarily neglect long-run considerations and objectives. It is clear that important values must be omitted in considering policy, and sometimes the only way long-run objectives can be given adequate attention is through the neglect of short-run considerations. But the values omitted can be either long-run or short-run.

SUCCESSION OF COMPARISONS (5b)

The final distinctive element in the branch method is that the comparisons, together with the policy choice, proceed in a chronological series. Policy is not made once and for all; it is made and re-made endlessly. Policy-making is a process of successive approximation to some desired objectives in which what is desired itself continues to change under reconsideration.

Making policy is at best a very rough process. Neither social scientists, nor politicians, nor public administrators yet know enough about the social world to avoid repeated error in predicting the consequences of policy moves. A wise policy-maker consequently expects that his policies will achieve only part of what he hopes and at the same time will produce unanticipated consequences he would have preferred to avoid. If he proceeds through a *succession* of incremental changes, he avoids serious lasting mistakes in several ways.

In the first place, past sequences of policy steps have given him knowledge about the probable consequences of further similar steps. Second, he need not attempt big jumps toward his goals that would require predictions beyond his or anyone else's knowledge, because he

---

[7] The link between the practice of the method of successive limited comparisons and mutual adjustment of interests in a highly fragmented decision-making process adds a new facet to pluralist theories of government and administration.

[8] Herbert Simon, Donald W. Smithburg, and Victor A. Thompson, *Public Administration* (Alfred A. Knopf, 1950), p. 434.

never expects his policy to be a final resolution of a problem. His decision is only one step, one that if successful can quickly be followed by another. Third, he is in effect able to test his previous predictions as he moves on to each further step. Lastly, he often can remedy a past error fairly quickly—more quickly than if policy proceeded through more distinct steps widely spaced in time.

Compare this comparative analysis of incremental changes with the aspiration to employ theory in the root method. Man cannot think without classifying, without subsuming one experience under a more general category of experiences. The attempt to push categorization as far as possible and to find general propositions which can be applied to specific situations is what I refer to with the word "theory." Where root analysis often leans heavily on theory in this sense, the branch method does not.

The assumption of root analysts is that theory is the most systematic and economical way to bring relevant knowledge to bear on a specific problem. Granting the assumption, an unhappy fact is that we do not have adequate theory to apply to problems in any policy area, although theory is more adequate in some areas—monetary policy, for example—than in others. Comparative analysis, as in the branch method, is sometimes a systematic alternative to theory.

Suppose an administrator must choose among a small group of policies that differ only incrementally from each other and from present policy. He might aspire to "understand" each of the alternatives—for example, to know all the conse-

quences of each aspect of each policy. If so, he would indeed require theory. In fact, however, he would usually decide that, *for policy-making purposes,* he need know, as explained above, only the consequences of each of those aspects of the policies in which they differed from one another. For this much more modest aspiration, he requires no theory (although it might be helpful, if available), for he can proceed to isolate probable differences by examining the differences in consequences associated with past differences in policies, a feasible program because he can take his observations from a long sequence of incremental changes.

For example, without a more comprehensive social theory about juvenile delinquency than scholars have yet produced, one cannot possibly understand the ways in which a variety of public policies—say on education, housing, recreation, employment, race relations, and policing—might encourage or discourage delinquency. And one needs such an understanding if he undertakes the comprehensive overview of the problem prescribed in the models of the root method. If, however, one merely wants to mobilize knowledge sufficient to assist in a choice among a small group of similar policies—alternative policies on juvenile court procedures, for example—he can do so by comparative analysis of the results of similar past policy moves.

THEORISTS AND PRACTITIONERS

This difference explains—in some cases at least—why the administrator often feels that the outside expert or academic problem-solver is sometimes not helpful and why they in turn often urge more theory on him. And it explains why an administrator often feels more confident when "flying by the seat of his pants" than when following the advice of theorists. Theorists often ask the administrator to go the long way round to the solution of his problems, in effect ask him to follow the best canons of the scientific method, when the administrator knows that the best available theory will work less well than more modest incremental comparisons. Theorists do not realize that the administrator is often in fact practicing a systematic method. It would be foolish to push this explanation too far, for sometimes practical decision-makers are pursuing neither a theoretical approach nor successive comparisons, nor any other systematic method.

It may be worth emphasizing that theory is sometimes of extremely limited helpfulness in policy-making for at least two rather different reasons. It is greedy for facts; it can be constructed only through a great collection of observations. And it is typically insufficiently precise for application to a policy process that moves through small changes. In contrast, the comparative method both economizes on the need for facts and directs the analyst's attention to just those facts that are relevant to the fine choices faced by the decision-maker.

With respect to precision of theory, economic theory serves as an example. It predicts that an economy without money or prices would in certain specified ways misallocate resources, but this finding pertains to an alternative far removed from the kind of policies on which ad-

ministrators need help. On the other hand, it is not precise enough to predict the consequences of policies restricting business mergers, and this is the kind of issue on which the administrators need help. Only in relatively restricted areas does economic theory achieve sufficient precision to go far in resolving policy questions; its helpfulness in policy-making is always so limited that it requires supplementation through comparative analysis.

SUCCESSIVE COMPARISON AS A SYSTEM

Successive limited comparisons is, then, indeed a method or system; it is not a failure of method for which administrators ought to apologize. None the less, its imperfections, which have not been explored in this paper, are many. For example, the method is without a built-in safeguard for all relevant values, and it also may lead the decision-maker to overlook excellent policies for no other reason than that they are not suggested by the chain of successive policy steps leading up to the present. Hence, it ought to be said that under this method, as well as under some of the most sophisticated variants of the root method—operations research, for example—policies will continue to be as foolish as they are wise.

Why then bother to describe the method in all the above detail? Because it is in fact a common method of policy formulation, and is, for complex problems, the principal reliance of administrators as well as of other policy analysts.[9] And because it will be superior to any other decision-making method available for complex problems in many circumstances, certainly superior to a futile attempt at superhuman comprehensiveness. The reaction of the public administrator to the exposition of method doubtless will be less a discovery of a new method than a better acquaintance with an old. But by becoming more conscious of their practice of this method, administrators might practice it with more skill and know when to extend or constrict its use. (That they sometimes practice it effectively and sometimes not may explain the extremes of opinion on "muddling through," which is both praised as a highly sophisticated form of problem-solv-

---

[9] Elsewhere I have explored this same method of policy formulation as practiced by academic analysts of policy ("Policy Analysis," 48 *American Economic Review* 298 [June, 1958]). Although it has been here presented as a method for public administrators, it is no less necessary to analysts more removed from immediate policy questions, despite their tendencies to describe their own analytical efforts as though they were the rational-comprehensive method with an especially heavy use of theory. Similarly, this same method is inevitably resorted to in personal problem-solving, where means and ends are sometimes impossible to separate, where aspirations or objectives undergo constant development, and where drastic simplification of the complexity of the real world is urgent if problems are to be solved in the time that can be given to them. To an economist accustomed to dealing with the marginal or incremental concept in market processes, the central idea in the method is that both evaluation and empirical analysis are incremental. Accordingly, I have referred to the method elsewhere as "the incremental method."

ing and denounced as no method at all. For I suspect that in so far as there is a system in what is known as "muddling through," this method is it.)

One of the noteworthy incidental consequences of clarification of the method is the light it throws on the suspicion an administrator sometimes entertains that a consultant or adviser is not speaking relevantly and responsibly when in fact by all ordinary objective evidence he is. The trouble lies in the fact that most of us approach policy problems within a framework given by our view of a chain of successive policy choices made up to the present. One's thinking about appropriate policies with respect, say, to urban traffic control is greatly influenced by one's knowledge of the incremental steps taken up to the present. An administrator enjoys an intimate knowledge of his past sequences that "outsiders" do not share, and his thinking and that of the "outsider" will consequently be different in ways that may puzzle both. Both may appear to be talking intelligently, yet each may find the other unsatisfactory. The relevance of the policy chain of succession is even more clear when an American tries to discuss, say, antitrust policy with a Swiss, for the chains of policy in the two countries are strikingly different and the two individuals consequently have organized their knowledge in quite different ways.

If this phenomenon is a barrier to communication, an understanding of it promises an enrichment of intellectual interaction in policy formulation. Once the source of difference is understood, it will sometimes be stimulating for an administrator to seek out a policy analyst whose recent experience is with a policy chain different from his own.

This raises again a question only briefly discussed above on the merits of like-mindedness among government administrators. While much of organization theory argues the virtues of common values and agreed organizational objectives, for complex problems in which the root method is inapplicable, agencies will want among their own personnel two types of diversification: administrators whose thinking is organized by reference to policy chains other than those familiar to most members of the organization and, even more commonly, administrators whose professional or personal values or interests create diversity of view (perhaps coming from different specialties, social classes, geographical areas) so that, even within a single agency, decision-making can be fragmented and parts of the agency can serve as watchdogs for others parts.

8   The Transactive Approach

THE TRANSACTIVE STYLE OF PLANNING

John Friedmann

. . . Transactive planning is a response to the widening gulf in communication between technical planners and their clients. To simplify the discussion, let us assume that planners as well as clients are individual persons rather than institutions, and that clients generate streams of action on which they wish to be advised.

This assumption is not altogether unrealistic. Institutions do not relate to each other as wholes, but through a complex series of exchanges among individuals. Although these individuals behave primarily according to their formal role prescriptions, each role masks a singular personality. Roles are defined by a set of abstract behavior patterns, but the person assuming a particular role may be straightforward or devious, disposed to be tranquil or angry, approachable or remote, eager for power or reluctant to assume responsibility. The planner steeped in the practice of the transactive style will try to reach out to the person who stands behind the formal role. . . .

Planners talk primarily to other

Reprinted with permission of author and publisher from: John Friedmann, *Retracking America: A Theory of Transactive Planning* (New York: Anchor Books, 1973), pp. 171–90.

planners, and their counsel falls on unresponsive ears. As we shall see, however, the establishment of a more satisfactory form of communication is not simply a matter of translating the abstract and highly symbolic language of the planner into the simpler and more experience-related vocabulary of the client. The real solution involves a restructuring of the basic relationship between planner and client. . . .

The language of clients—so difficult to incorporate into the formalized vocabulary of the planner—is tied to specific operational contexts. Its meanings shift with changes in the context, and its manner of expression is frequently as important as the actual words employed. This is probably the reason why planners prefer written to verbal communications, and why the latter tend to be in the form of highly stylized presentations. Tone of voice, emphasis, subtle changes in grammatical structure and word sequence, so important in the face-to-face communications of action-oriented persons, are consistently de-emphasized by planners. Whereas planners' formal communications could be translated by a computer into a foreign language without substantial loss of meaning, a tape-recorded conversation among clients could not.

Planners relate primarily to other members of their profession and to the university departments responsible for the transmission and advancement of professional knowledge. Clients, on the other hand, relate chiefly to organizations of their own kind. The reference group of each acts as a cultural matrix that helps to confirm and strengthen differences of approach and behavior. . . .

What can be done to overcome these barriers to effective communication between planners and clients? The traditional means, an exchange of formal documents, has not proved spectacularly successful in the past. Strangely enough, most planners are probably still unaware of this.

A few years ago, I served as an advisor to the government of Chile on questions of urban and regional development. Several foreign experts working with me were connected with a number of central institutions, such as the National Planning Office and the Ministry of Housing. My own office, however, was independent and not formally associated with any agency of the government.

After a few months of initial reconnaissance, I thought that I had obtained a sufficient grasp of the situation to make a series of far-reaching recommendations. I set forth these recommendations very carefully in a lengthy memorandum, which, translated into Spanish, was carried by messenger to a number of leading government figures. A covering letter explained the general purpose of my effort. After letting two weeks go by, I arranged for an interview with each person who had received a copy. During the inter-

views, formal courtesies were exchanged, and some noncommittal references were made to the memorandum on which I had labored for several months. Afterwards I returned to my office to wait for a formal reply, but none ever came.

What had gone wrong? A good part of the answer can be found in my failure to establish, long before I ever set to work on the memorandum, a transactive relationship with the people whose encouragement I wanted. There was, indeed, no compelling reason why the government of Chile should have adopted any part of my recommendations. Who was I, after all, except an expert with a vague professional reputation abroad? Was it not presumptuous, not to say arrogant, for me, a foreigner who had spent only a few months in Chile, to suggest a whole series of sweeping reforms to responsible people who had been working for a good part of their political lives on problems of which I myself had only recently become aware?

All these questions converge upon a single answer. If the communication gap between planner and client is to be closed, a continuing series of personal and primarily verbal transactions between them is needed, through which processed knowledge is fused with personal knowledge and both are fused with action. . . .

Transactive planning is carried on the ground swell of dialogue. When I prepared the memorandum for the Chilean Government, the basis for dialogue had not yet been established. Later, all this changed. In recruiting the advisory staff, emphasis was given to the personal qualities of each advisor—his ability to be a person (not a role-playing professional alone), to establish direct relations with others that would not be perceived as threatening, to be sensitive to the needs of others, and to learn quickly from complex, novel situations. Technical qualifications were also considered important, but they carried less weight.

At the start, the newly recruited advisor spent from six months to a year learning about the multi-faceted situation in which he had been placed and establishing relations of dialogue with a few key persons in the offices to which he was assigned. Although his formal role was not eliminated, it was so loosely structured that the advisor was able to emerge as a person. And once a relationship of this kind had been established, transactive planning could begin in earnest. . . .

THE TAO OF TRANSACTIVE PLANNING

Planners are often inspired by a wish to change existing reality. This almost compulsive desire stands in direct relationship to their inability to influence the requisite behavior to produce a change. The head of a large technical assistance operation once exclaimed in my presence, pounding his first on the table: "We have to show controlled impatience." It was not clear to me then, nor is it clear to me now, why impatience was called for. He had neither the power nor the responsibility to act. His job was simply to advise the government, not to replace it.

This incident has remained with me over the years. It reflects, I think, a complete lack of understanding of the essential tasks of planning.

Clearly, the man was eager to step into the driver's seat. Lack of sufficient progress, according to his lights, was due entirely to the laziness, corruption, recalcitrance, decadence, cupidity, political irresponsibility, and irrationality of the guidance institutions of the country to which he had been called. He knew what needed to be done, and he had told his clients how to do it. Why did they not follow his advice?

His model of the planning process was exceedingly simplistic. The planner plans; the client buys the plans and uses all the means at his disposal to see them carried out. If planning follows a transactive style, however, a different, more complex model has to be considered (Figure 1). The Taoist philosophy of *wu-wei*—doing nothing—would seem to be more appropriate to this model than controlled impatience.

The Tao says: *All things go through their own transformations.* All systems obey their own laws of internal change. These laws cannot be arbitrarily reversed without causing substantial harm to the system. Both the maintenance and the change of a system are the result of processes that relate the system's elements to one another. A good deal of system behavior is regulated automatically, but sometimes there is insufficient change, or the change is not the kind we would like, or changes are too rapid, causing the system to fall into disorder. If the planner wants to rectify any of these conditions, he must concentrate upon the processes of maintenance and transformation in order to see how to accelerate, decelerate, or contain them; occasionally a new process should be introduced or a process

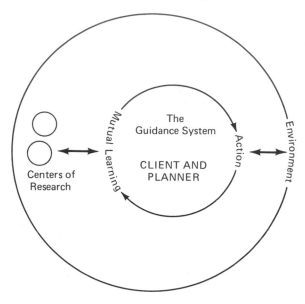

Planners Contribute	Clients Contribute
• concepts	• initimate knowledge
• theory	of context
• analysis	• realistic alternatives
• processed knowledge	• norms
• new perspectives	• priorities
• systematic search	• feasibility judgments
procedures	• operational details

FIGURE 1. A Model of Transactive Planning

that has lost its vital functions should be discarded. To change a process means to act upon the sources that generate the lawful behavior of the system. But both planner and client must respect the laws of transformation and be mindful of their limited abilities to control the flow of events.

The same principle applies to mutual learning. Learning cannot be imposed; it obeys the laws by which a structure of thinking, feeling, and valuing is changed. The planner may learn rapidly. But the more he assimilates his client's knowledge, the greater the complexity of which he is aware. To change the reasons why people act the way they do and produce the results they do, one must respect the processes by which they learn. Anxieties have little influence upon the outcome. Students do not learn because their teachers want them to. They learn only when they are ready to accept the new perceptions and to make new images their own.

The Tao says: *Truly, a great cutter does not cut.* Knowing the laws of transformation, the planner need not slash wildly into the tangle of social relationships, tearing out whole living tissues here and grafting others there, piling control upon control to make the process bend to his will. He will use the "natural" forces at work in society to produce the desired results. This means selective intervention and methods of indirect or field control. A knowledge of the consequences of strategic intervention is essential to the art of planning.

Similarly, the planner involved in mutual learning will not start by destroying the world view of his client. He will withhold his judgments, respecting his client's freedom and autonomy. To begin a restructuring of the client's field of cognition, the planner must discover within that field itself the points that provide an opening. What are the client's interests? What are the inconsistencies in his way of thinking and feeling? What are his secret doubts? What aspects of his knowledge are not supported by the values he affirms? It is through a process of selective focusing at such critical points that the planner can achieve the transformation and expansion of his client's learning.

The Tao says: *Tao invariably does nothing, yet there is nothing that is not done.* Under conditions of mutual learning, the planner appears to be doing nothing: he learns, and, learning, he imparts new knowledge. As perceptions and images are changed, so is the behavior that flows from them. Time is necessary for changes in behavior to occur. In the natural course of things, little appears to happen, yet everything happens in due time. Persons change, institutions change, the environ-

ment for action changes. The ideas of the learner take root, are themselves transformed, and pass into action, affecting the behavior of society.

The Tao says: *The most yielding of things outruns the most unyielding.* Mutual learning cannot be compelled; the planner cannot accelerate the processes of understanding and behavior change. Time is needed; listening is needed. If the planner listens carefully and long enough, his own thoughts may eventually be given back to him as the ideas of others. Only then can the planner truly be said to have succeeded in his task.

The future cannot be conquered by the present; compulsion destroys the generative forces in society. The planner must learn to yield when necessary, but also to persuade. Dialogue is essential to learning. Through dialogue, mutual learning occurs; and through mutual learning changes are brought about in the collective behavior of society.

The Tao says: *To give life, but not to own, to achieve but not to cherish, to lead but not to be master —that is the mystic virtue.* This is the most important, and also the most difficult of the five teachings of the Tao. It says: let everyone be free to choose himself, do not desire what is not your own, do not hold back on what you know. As a teacher, fade into the background and let the student speak; as a student, take new learning and use it to advantage. But when there are neither teachers nor students, as in mutual learning, the property of learning is held in common trust: no one is master, each has something to give and something to receive. From period to period, you pass to higher levels of understanding. Do not cherish them. Keep your mind open to what is yet to come.

If the processed knowledge of planners is serviceable only insofar as it is used as an instrument for learning; if learning cannot be imparted to others except through dialogue; and if dialogue creates a process in which each partner has as much to give as to receive, then the Tao provides good counsel.

TRANSACTIVE PLANNING IN THE CONTEXT OF SOCIETY

American society needs a heightened capacity for learning about itself and, to make what it learns effective in guiding its own development, a way to transform learning into appropriate actions. This implies that we must find a way to join scientific and technical intelligence with personal knowledge at the critical points for social intervention. I have argued that transactive planning is the most appropriate method for achieving this linkage.

The transactive style is not, admittedly, applicable to every situation where expert knowledge is joined to action. It is inappropriate, for instance, *where expertise carries suffiicent authority to act without the benefit of mutual learning.* The mechanic, the airplane pilot, or the surgeon is each prepared to do his job without elaborate discussion with his clients. There is no need for dialogue. Few questions will be asked and fewer answered. Nor are situations of mutual learning between expert and client common in highly stratified societies, where technical expertise enjoys high social esteem and clients unhesitatingly accept its judgments simply because they are offered under a prestigious professional label. In all other situations, however, the transactive style is essential to the ultimate success of planning. And this holds true with particular force in American society today. . . .

9   *Differential Application of Models*

PROBLEMS, SOLUTIONS AND STRATEGIES:

A CONTRIBUTION TO THE THEORY

AND PRACTICE OF PLANNING

T. J. CARTWRIGHT

The purpose of this paper is to examine the validity and some of the implications of the following proposition: that the nature of a problem determines the strategy appropriate for dealing with it and, conversely, that the use of a particular strategy makes certain assumptions about the nature of the problem to which it is applied. Such a proposition, it is argued, can help to clarify some aspects of planning theory as well as to provide a useful

Reprinted with permission of author and publisher from: Timothy J. Cartwright, "Problems, Solutions and Strategies: A Contribution to the Theory and Practice of Planning," *Journal of the American Institute of Planners*, 39: 3 (May 1973), 179–87. The author would like to express his gratitude to his colleagues, Professors Michel Chevalier and James Fenwick, who contributed to the development of these ideas in a joint course on planning theory at the Université de Montréal. Earlier versions of this paper were presented to the Regional Management Development Seminar of the Canadian Welfare Council in Lévis, Québec, in March 1969, and to the Transportation Planning Committee of the Roads and Transportation Association of Canada (R.T.A.C.) at a seminar in Toronto in April 1971.

guideline for the practicing planner.

The paper has five sections. The first argues that problems are not objective things, inherent in the so-called real world, but "images" of that world defined by people in a variety of more or less precise ways. The second section describes a general model of a problem and shows how the solution to a problem lies necessarily within the definition of the problem. The third section presents a four-part typology of problems for use (in the fourth section) in the definition of a framework for assessing the appropriateness of planning strategies. A final section discusses some of the implications of these arguments for the theory and practice of planning.

PLANNING AND PERCEPTION

Planning, like any other human activity, is based on individual perceptions of the world we live in. These perceptions may, of course, be shared by a greater or smaller number of people; but the fact that the basis of planning is ultimately subjective leaves the planner a certain amount of discretion in the set

119

of perceptions that he chooses as a basis for planning.

There are many possible definitions of planning, but it is assumed here that, as a minimum, planning means deliberate intervention in some process. Planning may mean something more precise than this for some people but, for most people, it probably means *at least* what is entailed in the above definition.

It should be noted that intervention in a process which is not deliberate (i.e., accidental intervention) is not normally considered to be planning. The bridge-player, for example, who (accidentally!) deals himself a handful of spades is unlikely to claim on that basis that he is a good player (or a good planner). In other words, intervention must be designed to achieve a specified purpose or goal. The good planner, like the good billiards player, "calls his shots."

Moreover, the purpose or goal of the intervention normally has to be defined in terms of the process at which the intervention is directed. The chess-player plans to move his rook in an effort to win the game he is playing, and not normally for some ulterior reason unconnected with the game. In short, intervention must be directed toward some deliberate modification of the process in question for it to be called planning.

All this may seem rather obvious, but these points form the basis for another important implication of the above definition of planning. This is that planning presupposes at least two different states of the process in which the planning (i.e., the deliberate intervention) is to occur and that one of these states is regarded as being, in some sense, more desirable than the other. The less desirable state of affairs may conveniently be called a *problem* situation and the more desirable state of affairs may similarly be termed a *solution* situation. Other situations may also be defined, of course; but, at the very least, any kind of planning automatically entails the definition of both a problem and a solution situation.

Problems and solutions are, however, based on the perceptions of individuals. They are not objective conditions of the real world. They are subjective constructions—what Kenneth Boulding would call "images" of the real world—although such perceptions may be and often are shared in roughly the same form by many people (1956:16).[1] Nevertheless, problems may appear in different forms to different people. What is a critical problem for one person may appear unimportant, or even not a problem at all, to another person. To paraphrase Boulding, a problem is what somebody or something perceives as a problem; and, without somebody or something to perceive it, a problem is an absurdity.

Social problems, therefore, are what somebody or some organization perceives as problems. In turn, the nature of these problems is determined by the manner in which each is perceived. Thus, social problems may be perceived as having a single root cause or as being the product of many interrelated factors. On the one hand, poverty (for example) may be seen as the result of inadequate

[1] See also David Lowenthal (1967). [Full citations can be found in the References section to this article, p. 132—Eds.]

incomes (hence proposals for a guaranteed minimum income), delinquency as the result of broken homes, slums as caused by inadequate housing, unemployment as a lack of jobs, and so on.[2] On the other hand, social problems can be defined almost infinitely broadly. For example, the authors of a study of public housing projects in Chicago suggest that, conceivably, the way in which a single carpenter drives a single nail into a single house could be relevant to the problem of providing public housing (if, for example, certain union practices are sacrosanct) (Meyerson and Banfield, 1965: preface). Obviously, neither kind of approach to defining a social problem is "right" and the other "wrong." Each is the result of a different perception of the problem.

Although no one perception of a social problem is inherently more correct than any other, the planner must still choose among them in deciding how broadly or how narrowly, how vaguely or how precisely, to define his problem. In making this decision, the planner will have many sources of advice. His clients, whether public servants, businessmen, or private citizens, may have one or several perceptions of the problem at issue. There may also be a different set of "popular" perceptions of the same problem. Moreover, any of these perceptions may change over time. Perceptions of poverty and pollution in North America, for example, have changed dramatically over the past decade

2 For a concrete example, see the Moynihan Report on "The Negro Family: The Case for National Action," in Lee Rainwater and W. L. Yancey (1967).

or so. In Latin America, one observer has suggested that popular perceptions of social problems tend to pass through four distinct stages:

1. The problem does not exist subjectively. The problem exists but no one is preoccupied with it; no one pays much attention to those few who study it or try to arouse some interest in it.

2. Utopian proposals. Suddenly the problem projects itself into people's consciousness. People begin to talk about it; solutions are suggested, always radical, definitive, absolute and recognized as utopian even by those who advance them.

3. The utopia is converted into law. The solutions, somewhat mellowed, are accepted even by those opposed to them before. The problem seems so urgent that even utopian solutions seem possible, and in the Spanish tradition the solution takes the shape of a law or of a constitutional text.

4. The reform of the reform. The law is not obeyed or else it is applied with excessive rigidity. Sometimes the law brings out new, unsuspected aspects of the problem. Here enters not the counter-reform but rather a reform of the reform, an adaptation of the principles to fit the reality in order better to change the latter. (Alba, 1961: 47–48)

Problems, in short, are not immutable in their nature, and the planner often retains a degree of discretion in deciding just what kind of problem he is trying to solve.

It is the contention of this paper that, while no one perception of a problem is more correct than another, some perceptions can be more *useful* than others for planning purposes. There are two principal reasons for this:

a. The way in which a problem is perceived determines the range of possible solutions to that problem.
b. The way in which a problem is perceived determines the kind of strategy that is appropriate for its solution.

For these reasons, the effective planner capitalizes on whatever discretion he may have in defining the problem he is to help solve.

PROBLEMS AND SOLUTIONS

That the perception of a problem implies a particular range of possible solutions to it appears intuitively obvious. If the problem of poverty (for example) is defined in terms of family income, then solutions to that problem must equally be capable of definition in terms of family income. Or, to give another example, the civil engineer faced with the problem of designing a high-speed urban roadway would never suppose that a solution to his problem might require taking into account, say, the training of future highway engineers —unless, of course, this factor had been perceived as part of the problem in the first place (as it might in a developing country, for instance). It seems, in short, that the definition of a problem specifies the nature of the possible solutions to it.

The nature of the relationship between problems and solutions is capable of more precise demonstration.[3] In the previous section, a problem

[3] There is an interesting parallel between the argument which follows and the attempts to design computerized general problem-solving programs for heuristic problems. See Allen Newell, J. C. Shaw, and Herbert A. Simon (1959) and Simon and Newell (1962).

and its solution were defined as different states of a single process, with the latter being in some sense a more desirable state than the former. Consider the simplest kind of social problem: for example, a house is said to be too small for a particular family. Suppose that the problem is perceived (defined) in terms of only two variables: the size of the house and the size of the family. Accordingly, the problem (denoted as P) can be expressed as a function (using the mathematical notation) of the size of the family (say, f) and the size of the house (say, h): viz.,

$$P = P(f, h).$$

This relationship is illustrated in more graphic terms in Figure 1, in which any point (such as P_1) indicates a specific housing situation in which a family of size f_1 lives in a house of size h_1. P_1 is a problem because, according to some criterion or set of criteria, the house is too small. For the present purposes, it is not necessary to specify the source of the criterion; it is illustrated in Figure 1 by the curve MN. Since P_1 lies above and to the left of MN, it is a problem situation.

There are two obvious solutions to this problem: give the house to a smaller family or find a larger house for the original family. (These two solutions could be illustrated by points S_1 and S_2 respectively in Figure 1). Other solutions may also be possible, solutions reflecting changes in both variables at once. But the important thing is not how many solutions are possible but that, whatever solution may be adopted, it is going to be a function of family size and house size. The problem as it

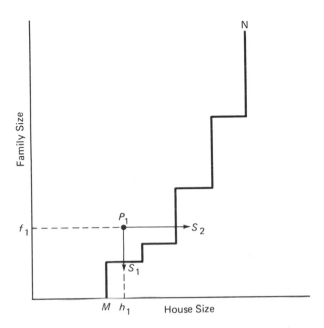

FIGURE 1.   Housing as a function of family size and house size.

has been defined is not going to be solved by changing the income of the family or the quality of the house —unless these changes can in turn affect the defining variables of the problem. In short, the solution to a problem is, by definition, a preferred configuration of the same variables as are entailed in the problem itself.

To put this in more general terms, if any problem (P) is defined as

$$P = P (x_1, x_2, x_3, \ldots, x_n),$$

where x_n represents the nth variable in terms of which the problem is defined, then any solution (S) to that problem must similarly be capable of expression as

$$S = S(x_1, x_2, x_3, \ldots, x_n).$$

Thus, the way in which a problem is defined determines the nature of its solution. Or, as Herbert Simon (1962) has described it,

Problem-solving requires continual translation between the state and process descriptions of the same complex reality. Plato, in the *Meno,* argued that all learning is remembering. He could not otherwise explain how we can discover or recognize the answer to a problem unless we already know the answer. . . . We pose a problem by giving the state description of the solution. The task is to discover a sequence of processes that will produce the goal state [i.e., the solution] from an initial state [i.e., the problem].

This task will be examined in due course, but it is useful first to look at a typology of problems.

A TYPOLOGY OF PROBLEMS

Consider again the general definition of a problem proposed in the previous section. This formulation of a problem can be characterized in two fundamental ways: according to the number of variables entailed in the definition of the problem (i.e., the value of n), and according to the precision of each of those variables. First, the number of variables in the problem may be specified in its definition (i.e., n has a known value of five, ten, twenty, a hundred, a thousand, or some such finite number), or the number of variables is not specified and the problem is defined as being open-ended (i.e., n has no fixed value). Second, the variables themselves may be either known or unknown—or, as will be said here, calculable or incalculable.[4] Accordingly, the general definition of a problem suggests two basic ways of classifying problems.

Putting these two distinctions together suggests four fundamentally different types of problems (see Figure 2). These four types may conveniently be termed:

I. simple problems,
II. compound problems,
III. complex problems, and
IV. metaproblems.

The names, however, are not so im-

[4] This second dichotomy is really the same as the first one but at a "lower" level, since each variable can itself be defined as a function of n subvariables of its own. On this basis, the calculability of each variable depends on *its* n having a specified value—just as was argued in the case of the first dichotomy. For this reason, the somewhat broader dimension of calculability is preferred to that of quantifiability, which implies that the variable must be capable of being measured according to some scale. A variable may be calculable, however, in the sense that all its elements are known, and yet not necessarily be quantifiable as well.

portant as the distinctions they reflect.

Simple problems are problems which are completely understood: they are defined in terms of a specified number of calculable variables. It should be added that to denote a problem as simple (in the sense implied here) need have no bearing on how easy or how difficult it is to implement a solution to that problem. Unless implementation is explicitly defined as forming part of the problem—which it frequently is *not* in the case of problems defined in simple terms—the solution to a simple problem may turn out to be either relatively easy or relatively difficult to implement. The definition of a problem as a simple problem may or may not be appropriate in a given case; for example, a planner may decide that a simple definition of his problem is somewhat academic in circumstances where implementation is expected to be relatively difficult. But that is not the point here; the point is that a simple problem is one which, wisely or unwisely, is defined in terms that are finite and calculable.

Compound problems are problems some, but not all, of whose parts are known: they are defined in terms of an unspecified number of calculable variables. This means that a compound problem may consist in part of one or more simple problems, if it includes among its variables one or more subsets which can be defined as problems in their own right.

Complex problems are problems which look like simple problems but are not: they are defined in terms of a specified number of variables, but

Nature of variables

		Calculable	Incalculable
Number of variables	Specified	I Simple problem	| III | Complex | problem
	Unspecified (i.e., open-ended)	II Compound problem	| IV | Metaproblem

FIGURE 2. A Typology of Problems.
Note: The significance of the dotted line is explained in the text.

the variables are incalculable rather than calculable.

Metaproblems, on the other hand, are the least precise of all: they are defined in terms of an unspecified number of incalculable variables.[5] In other words, a metaproblem acknowledges that a problem is perceived to exist and that some particular variables are involved in its definition; but precisely what these particular variables are and with what other variables they might be involved is not specified. Thus, a metaproblem is distinguished by its lack of precision.

In fact, the four types of problem represent varying degrees of precision, from the quite precise simple problem to the least precise metaproblem. But it should not be concluded from this that simple problems are better or more "scientific"

5 One of the leading proponents over the past several years of the term "metaproblem" has been Michel Chevalier; see his *Social Science and Water Management: A Planning Strategy* (1969). Chevalier also originated the calculable-incalculable distinction in this context.

than metaproblems. Precision of meaning in planning, as in other branches of science, can be functional or dysfunctional in different circumstances. As Abraham Kaplan has explained in his book on methodology in the behavioral sciences,

The demand for exactness of meaning and for precise definition of terms can easily have a pernicious effect, as I believe it often has had in behavioral science. It results in what has been aptly named the *premature closure* of our ideas. That the progress of science is marked by successive closures can be stipulated; but it is just the function of inquiry to instruct us how and where closure can best be achieved. . . . That a cognitive situation is not as well structured as we would like does not imply that no inquiry made in that situation is really scientific. On the contrary, it is the dogmatisms outside science that proliferate closed systems of meaning; the scientist is in no hurry for closure. Tolerance of ambiguity is as important for creativity in science as it is anywhere else. (1964: 70 71)

Similarly, the planner may be best served by a precise definition of a problem in one case and an imprecise definition in another case.

In practice, of course, things may not work out as neatly as the previous paragraphs imply. For a problem may be defined as having some variables which are calculable and some which are incalculable. (Thus, in Figure 2, the line between calculable and incalculable variables is shown as a dotted line.) However, this fact does not invalidate the distinction in theory.[6] In practice, it is necessary merely to add a stipulation to the effect that the existence in the definition of a problem of at least one incalculable variable is sufficient to have the problem as a whole classified as a complex problem or as a metaproblem, as the case may be.

It may be useful to take a specific example again at this point: consider the problem of poverty. According to what has been suggested before, it should be possible to define poverty in four fundamentally different ways. One example of each different type of definition is as follows:

I. As a simple problem: poverty means having an annual income of less than three thousand dollars.
II. As a compound problem: poverty means having an annual income of less than three thousand dollars, having an education below the level of grade eight, living in substandard housing (according to

[6] Max Weber himself once pointed out, "If one perceives that concepts are primarily analytical instruments for the intellectual mastery of empirical data . . . , the fact that concepts . . . are ideal types will not cause him to desist from constructing them." E. A. Shils and H. A. Finch (1947) 106.

some specific criteria), and/or other characteristics.
III. As a complex problem: poverty means the inability to obtain for oneself the minimum basic necessities of life (i.e., adequate food and shelter).
IV. As a metaproblem: poverty means relative social deprivation.

Of course, these are not the only definitions of poverty that can be proposed, tested, and found useful. The point is that each of the above definitions is possible and each illustrates one of the four different types of problems identified earlier in this section.

Consider more briefly another example: say, the construction of a highway through a city. As a matter of engineering, building the highway can be regarded as a simple problem (although not necessarily, of course, an easy problem to solve). If to this definition is added an unspecified number of other calculable variables (such as the taking of land, financing of the project, landscaping and maintenance of the highway, and so on), the problem becomes compound in nature. On the other hand, if the problem of constructing the highway is regarded as one of location and design, in which incalculable factors such as community participation are considered relevant, then the problem becomes complex. Finally, if all these factors (engineering, maintenance, location, design, and so on) as well as other factors related to an overall transportation policy for the city and region concerned are included in the definition of the problem, then the problem of constructing a highway can be defined as a metaproblem. Again, other definitions are possible; but the ones used here show how the "same" problem can be defined in four fundamentally different ways.

THE APPROPRIATENESS OF STRATEGY TO PROBLEM

Given this typology of problems, it becomes possible to deal with the basic proposition set out at the beginning of the paper: that the nature of a problem determines what is an appropriate strategy and, conversely, that the use of a particular strategy makes certain assumptions about the nature of the problem to which it is applied.

It will be recalled that planning was defined as deliberate intervention in some process; this, in turn, was held to imply the existence of a problem and a solution. For the purposes of this paper, a strategy is defined simply as a process of analysis and action leading to the determination of the deliberate intervention that constitutes the planning and ultimately transforms the problem into the solution. To quote Herbert Simon (1962) again, "Given a desired state of affairs and an existing state of affairs, the task . . . is to find the difference between these two states and then to find the correlating process that will erase the difference." It should be noted here that the nature of a problem may, of course, change over time; indeed, to induce such a change deliberately may form part of a planning strategy in a given case.

If planning strategies consist of analysis and action, then the central question posed in this paper can be rephrased in operational terms as follows: *Do the four fundamental types of problems identified earlier imply any special conditions for carrying out analysis and action and, if so, what are these conditions?*

One set of answers to these questions is given in Table 1. Essentially, the table shows that simple problems permit comprehensive analysis —and, therefore, maximization or optimization—but that the other three types of problems do not. Compound, complex, and metaproblems permit no more than varying degrees of less-than-comprehensive analysis and, therefore, various degrees of improvement or amelioration short of optimization.

The reason for this is that a simple problem amounts to a closed system of information, and so it can be maximized or optimized. There are many techniques available to planners for this purpose, including some which can be programed for use with computers. None of the other three kinds of problems, however, is closed like a simple problem; so they cannot be optimized or maximized in the same way.

Because, therefore, a compound problem permits a complete understanding of only some of its variables, optimization is possible among only those variables which are completely understood. This process has been called by a variety of names, including suboptimization, "second best," and *"satisficing."* [7]

In the case of complex problems, however, only a partial understanding of all the variables is possible;

[7] See, for example, H. A. Simon, *Models of Man, Social and Rational* (1957), Chaps. 14–16; and Kelvin Lancaster and R. G. Lipsey (1956–1957).

TABLE 1. LIMITS OF ANALYSIS AND ACTION BY TYPE OF PROBLEM

Type of Problem	Limits of Analysis	Limits of Action
I. *Simple* (a specified number of calculable variables)	Complete understanding of all of the variables (comprehensive analysis)	Maximization or optimization
II. *Compound* (an unspecified number of calculable variables)	Complete understanding of some of the variables (in-depth analysis of subproblems)	Suboptimization (second best, "satisficing," etc.)
III. *Complex* (a specified number of incalculable variables)	Partial understanding of all of the variables (quick surveys)	Overall improvements (Pareto optima)
IV. *Metaproblem* (an unspecified number of incalculable variables)	Partial understanding of some of the variables (points of departure, benchmarks, etc.)	Partial improvements (Pareto "suboptima")

but the fact that all of the variables are known does mean that action can be directed at improvements in the whole situation and not just part of it. On the other hand, such overall improvements as may be possible will clearly not amount to optimization, since there is no possible way of knowing what is the optimum value of an incalculable variable. The most that can be said about the solution to a complex problem, therefore, is that it is better than the problem situation. Economists sometimes describe this kind of improvement as a "Pareto optimum," which is defined as a situation in which no one is any worse off and at least someone is better off than in some alternative situation.[8] Similarly, the solution to a complex problem may be a situation in which none of the defining variables is made worse and at least one of them is made better.

[8] See, for example, I. M. D. Little, *A Critique of Welfare Economics* (1957), and Richard Zeckhauser and Elmer Schaefer (1968).

Not even this is possible in the case of metaproblems. For metaproblems yield only a partial understanding of only some of their component variables. Thus, where quick surveys (to identify all of the variables) were appropriate analytical techniques for complex problems, metaproblems warrant no more than the identification of points of departure or benchmarks.[9] Furthermore, without a definite knowledge of even the number (to say nothing of the nature) of the variables involved, it does not make sense to seek even an improvement (let alone an optimum) in the situation as a whole. The most that can be expected from the solution to a metaproblem is an improvement in some part of the situation—a condition which economists might be induced to call a "Pareto suboptimum"! It is impossi-

[9] An interesting parallel to the difference between making quick surveys and finding benchmarks or points of departure may be found in the distinction between "simultaneous scanning" and "successive scanning," as described by J. S. Bruner *et al.* (1956).

ble to foresee all the "side-effects" of trying to solve a metaproblem; hence, solving metaproblems is also likely to put a premium on experimentation and adaptability.[10]

It is perhaps open to question whether, under the circumstances described above, it makes very much sense to talk about the "solution" to a metaproblem or even to a compound or complex problem. Such problems obviously cannot be "solved" in the same way that a simple problem can. The solution to a simple problem, in a sense, does away with or eliminates the problem; but this is clearly not the case with compound, complex, and metaproblems. Thus, it is sometimes argued that there is no solution to problems like poverty or pollution: the poor will always be with us, it is said; or, as long as there is man, there will be pollution. But this obviously does not mean that nothing can or should be done to improve the lot of the poor or to reduce the level of pollution. In fact, the difficulty is largely a semantic one. The practice in this paper has been to use the term "solution" to apply to any situation perceived as being more desirable than the problem to which it corresponds. The assumption in this paper is that any problem can be solved.

To summarize, therefore: *simple* problems are solved by comprehensive analysis and planned optimization; *compound* problems are solved by analyzing those parts of the problem which are amenable to analysis

(i.e., the known calculable variables) and planning to optimize those parts; *complex* problems are solved by analyzing all the variables of the problem to the extent necessary to permit the planning of improvements in the situation as a whole; and *metaproblems* are solved by analyzing some of the variables to the extent that some improvements can be planned in some parts of the problem.

It should be noted that analysis governs action in the case of simple and compound problems, but that action governs analysis in the case of complex and metaproblems.

Finally, the terminology of David Braybrooke and Charles Lindblom suggests a still more concise summary (1963). Braybrooke and Lindblom describe a strategy called "disjointed incrementalism," which they present as an alternative to the traditional kind of "comprehensive rationalism." If "comprehensive rationalism" is taken to describe the kind of strategy appropriate for simple problems and if "disjointed incrementalism" is taken as a paradigm for the kind of strategy appropriate for metaproblems, then it is convenient to suggest that strategies appropriate for compound problems be described as "disjointed rationalism" and those appropriate for complex problems as "comprehensive incrementalism." This is summarized in Table 2, which should be compared with Table 1.

CONCLUSION

If true, the implications of all this are of not inconsiderable importance for both the planning theorist and

---

[10] One of the major proponents of experimentation and adaptability in an organizational context has been Warren Bennis; see, for example, his "Beyond Bureaucracy" (1965).

TABLE 2. PROBLEMS AND STRATEGIES

Type of Problem	Nature of Strategy Appropriate to Problem
Simple	Comprehensive and rational
Compound	Disjointed and rational
Complex	Comprehensive and incremental
Metaproblem	Disjointed and incremental

the practicing planner. For what they suggest is that the definition of a problem is a vital part of the planning process. The planner may not always enjoy as much discretion in this respect as he might like; he may find that others (such as his clients or society at large) have already arrived at a fairly definite idea of the nature of a problem. He is, however, obliged to recognize that the way in which a problem is defined governs the kind of strategy which is appropriate for dealing with it.

Ignorance of this relationship may lead a planner into a position where there is a serious lack of "fit" between his problem and the strategy he is using on it. Thus, a planner may unwittingly find himself in the impossible position of trying to solve a problem he does not actually have.

For example, a planner may define (or have defined for him) a simple problem but be using a strategy appropriate for a metaproblem. As a result, his analysis is likely to be superficial and his proposals for action correspondingly facile. On the other hand, a planner may define (or have defined for him) a metaproblem but be using a strategy appropriate for a simple problem. As a result, his analysis is likely to be of limited value and his proposals for action correspondingly inadequate.

Ultimately, things may resolve themselves. Either the strategy will force a change in the problem, or the problem will force a change in the strategy. For example, persistent efforts to apply comprehensive rational strategies to a metaproblem will eventually reduce it to a simple problem—whether the planner intends it or not. Thus, insistence on a guaranteed annual income as the solution to the problem of poverty leads to perceiving poverty as a simple problem of inadequate income. The fact that some people may still have no job, insufficient education and training, inadequate housing, and so on become separate (if no less important) problems.

Similarly, clinging to a metaproblem kind of definition will eventually force adoption of a strategy of disjointed incrementalism—whether the planner intends it or not. Thus, there is some evidence that the problem of pollution is having this sort of effect. Insistence on defining pollution in relation to economic progress and population growth, for example, makes traditional strategies of regulation and standards inadequate by themselves. New kinds of strategies are required.[11]

[11] The effect of pollution problems in encouraging the development of new forms of planning strategies is described in Michel Chevalier and T. J. Cartwright (1972), "An Institutional Perspective of

Either way, however, if the planner does not understand the kind of adjustments which are taking place between problems and strategies, he stands much less chance of being able to influence them in any effective way.

In fact, planning has for some time been faced with a cruel dilemma in this respect. On the one hand, there has been a growing willingness to perceive social, and especially urban, problems (such as poverty, pollution, housing, transportation, and others) as broader, more complicated, and more interrelated in their nature than was hitherto appreciated—in short, as being more complicated than just simple problems. On the other hand, planning techniques and strategies over the last few decades have improved far more rapidly and extensively in the opposite direction. In other words, planners have found themselves in the position of wanting to broaden many of their simple definitions of problems, yet relatively better and better able to solve the original simple types of problems.

Faced with this dilemma, practicing planners have had to avoid both the myopia of sticking to the old simple definitions of problems and using the new, more sophisticated techniques designed for them and the illusion of adopting the broader problem-definitions and then using the new techniques anyway.

But the dilemma persists. Is it pre-

Environmental Perception: The Delaware Estuary Comprehensive Study," in W. R. D. Sewell and Ian Burton, eds., *Perceptions and Attitudes in Resource Management* (Ottawa: Information Canada, 1972), Chap. 12.

ferable to have the wrong strategy for the right problem, or the right strategy for the wrong problem? Is it, to paraphrase Raymond Bauer (1966) talking about social indicators, better to have a crude and less-than-comprehensive strategy for the problem you are really interested in, or a precise and comprehensive strategy for a problem which is only an approximation of what you are interested in?

If the desirable problem-definition (say, a metaproblem) does not "fit" the desirable strategy (say, a comprehensive rational one), where should the planner give way? Should he accept a constraining of his problem (to suit the strategy) or should he be content with a less certain strategy (to suit the problem)?

There is, of course, no easy answer to this dilemma; yet practicing planners must make, and planning theorists must explain, everyday operational decisions about problems and strategies. Herein, perhaps, lies that part of planning which is more of an art than a science: knowing how best to define a problem given the trade-off with strategy.

But whether problem-definition is largely a matter for art or for science, its relationship to the choice of strategy should in any case be clearly understood in theory and consciously applied in practice. Not to do so is to risk, on the one hand, forcing problems to conform to the assumptions of a chosen strategy, and, on the other hand, wasting time and money looking for impossibly precise solutions instead of being content with "the art of the possible" —all of which is, in the final analysis, what planning is really all about.

REFERENCES

ALBA, VICTOR (1961). "The Latin American Style and the New Social Forces." In Albert O. Hirschman, ed., *Latin American Issues: Essays and Comments.* New York: Twentieth Century Fund.

BAUER, RAYMOND, ed. (1966). *Social Indicators.* Cambridge, Mass.: The MIT Press.

BENNIS, WARREN (1965). "Beyond Bureaucracy," *Trans-Action,* July–August.

BOULDING, KENNETH (1956). *The Image.* Ann Arbor, Mich.: University of Michigan Press.

BRAYBROOKE, DAVID, and CHARLES E. LINDBLOM (1963). *A Strategy of Decision.* New York: The Free Press.

BRUNER, J. S., *et al.* (1956). *A Study of Thinking.* New York: Wiley. Chaps. 4–5.

CHEVALIER, MICHEL (1969). *Social Science and Water Management: A Planning Strategy.* Ottawa: Queen's Printer. For the Policy and Planning Branch of the Department of Energy, Mines and Resources.

LITTLE, I. M. D. (1957). *A Critique of Welfare Economics,* 2nd ed. Cambridge, Eng.: Oxford University Press.

KAPLAN, ABRAHAM (1964). *The Conduct of Inquiry.* San Francisco: Chandler.

LANCASTER, KELVIN, and R. G. LIPSEY (1956–1957). "The General Theory of Second-Best." *Review of Economic Studies* XXIV (1): 63.

LOWENTHAL, DAVID, ed. (1967). *Environment and Perception.* Department of Geography, Occasional Paper No. 109. Chicago: University of Chicago Press.

MEYERSON, MARTIN, and EDWARD C. BANFIELD (1955). *Politics, Planning, and Public Interest.* New York: Free Press of Glencoe.

NEWELL, ALLEN, J. C. SHAW, and HERBERT A. SIMON (1959). "A General Problem Solving Program for Heuristic Problems." *Computers and Automation* 8 (July): 10–17.

RAINWATER, LEE, and W. L. YANCEY (1967). *The Moynihan Report and the Politics of Controversy.* Cambridge, Mass.: The MIT Press.

SHILS, E. A., and H. A. FINCH, eds. (1947). *The Methodology of the Social Sciences.* Glencoe, Ill.: The Fress Press.

SIMON, H. A. (1957). *Models of Man, Social and Rational.* New York: Wiley.

——— (1962). "The Architecture of Complexity." *Proceedings of the American Philosophical Society* 106 (Dec.). Reprinted in H. A. Simon, *The Science of the Artificial.* Cambridge, Mass.: M.I.T. Press.

——— and ALLEN NEWELL. "Simulation of Human Thinking." In Martin Greenberger, ed. *Management and the Computer of the Future.* Cambridge, Mass.: The MIT Press.

ZECKHAUSER, RICHARD, and ELMER SCHAEFER. "Public Policy and Economic Theory." In R. A. Bauer and K. J. Gergen, eds., *The Study of Policy Formation.* New York: The Free Press, 1968.

10   Where Models Fail

DILEMMAS IN A GENERAL THEORY
OF PLANNING

Horst W. J. Rittel/Melvin M. Webber

George Bernard Shaw diagnosed the case several years ago; in more recent times popular protest may have already become a social movement. Shaw averred that "every profession is a conspiracy against the laity." The contemporary publics are responding as though they have made the same discsovery.

Few of the modern professionals seem to be immune from the popular attack—whether they be social workers, educators, housers, public health officials, policemen, city planners, highway engineers or physicians. Our restive clients have been telling us that they don't like the educational programs that schoolmen have been offering, the redevelopment projects urban renewal agencies have been proposing, the law enforcement styles of the police, the administrative behavior of the welfare agencies, the locations of the highways, and so on. In the courts, the streets, and the political campaigns, we've been hearing everlouder public protests against the

Reprinted with permission of authors and publisher from: Horst W. J. Rittel and Melvin M. Webber, "Dilemmas in a General Theory of Planning," *Policy Sciences*, 4: 2 (June 1973), 155–69.

professions' diagnoses of the clients' problems, against professionally designed governmental programs, against professionally certified standards for the public services.

It docs seem odd that this attack should be coming just when professionals in the social services are beginning to acquire professional competencies. It might seem that our publics are being perverse, having condoned professionalism when it was really only dressed-up amateurism and condemning professionalism when we finally seem to be getting good at our jobs. Perverse though the laity may be, surely the professionals themselves have been behind this attack as well.

Some of the generators of the confrontation have been intellectual in origin. The anti-professional movement stems in part from a reconceptualization of the professional's task. Others are more in the character of historical imperatives, i.e. conditions have been thrown up by the course of societal events that call for different modes of intervention.

The professional's job was once seen as solving an assortment of problems that appeared to be definable, understandable and consensual. He was hired to eliminate those conditions that predominant opinion judged undesirable. His record has been quite spectacular, of course; the contemporary city and contemporary urban society stand as clean evidences of professional prowess. The streets have been paved, and roads now connect all places; houses shelter virtually everyone; the dread diseases are virtually gone; clean water is piped into nearly every building; sanitary sewers carry wastes from them; schools and hospitals serve virtually every district; and so on. The accomplishments of the past century in these respects have been truly phenomenal, however short of some persons' aspirations they might have been.

But now that these relatively easy problems have been dealt with, we have been turning our attention to others that are much more stubborn. The tests for efficiency, that were once so useful as measures of accomplishment, are being challenged by a renewed preoccupation with consequences for equity. The seeming consensus, that might once have allowed distributional problems to be dealt with, is being eroded by the growing awareness of the nation's pluralism and of the differentiation of values that accompanies differentiation of publics. The professionalized cognitive and occupational styles that were refined in the first half of this century, based in Newtonian mechanistic physics, are not readily adapted to contemporary conceptions of interacting open systems and to contemporary concerns with equity. A growing sensitivity to the waves of repercussions that ripple through such systemic networks and to the value consequences

of those repercussions has generated the recent reexamination of received values and the recent search for national goals. There seems to be a growing realization that a weak strut in the professional's support system lies at the juncture where goal-formulation, problem-definition and equity issues meet. . . .

By now we are all beginning to realize that one of the most intractable problems is that of defining problems (of knowing what distinguishes an observed condition from a desired condition) and of locating problems (finding where in the complex causal networks the trouble really lies). In turn, and equally intractable, is the problem of identifying the actions that might effectively narrow the gap between what-is and what-ought-to-be. As we seek to improve the effectiveness of actions in pursuit of valued outcomes, as system boundaries get stretched, and as we become more sophisticated about the complex workings of open societal systems, it becomes ever more difficult to make the planning idea operational.

Many now have an image of *how* an *idealized* planning system would function. It is being seen as an ongoing, cybernetic process of governance, incorporating systematic procedures for continuously searching out goals; identifying problems; forecasting uncontrollable contextual changes; inventing alternative strategies, tactics, and time-sequenced actions; stimulating alternative and plausible action sets and their consequences; evaluating alternatively forecasted outcomes; statistically monitoring those conditions of the publics and of systems that are judged to be germane; feeding back information to the simulation and decision channels so that errors can be corrected—all in a simultaneously functioning government process. That set of steps is familiar to all of us, for it comprises what is by now the modern-classical model of planning. And yet we all know that such a planning system is unattainable, even as we seek more closely to approximate it. It is even questionable whether such a planning system is desirable.

PLANNING PROBLEMS ARE WICKED PROBLEMS

A great many barriers keep us from perfecting such a planning governing system: theory is inadequate for decent forecasting; our intelligence is insufficient to our tasks; plurality of objectives held by pluralities of politics makes it impossible to pursue unitary aims; and so on. The difficulties attached to rationality are tenacious, and we have so far been unable to get untangled from their web. This is partly because the classical paradigm of science and engineering—the paradigm that has underlain modern professionalism—is not applicable to the problems of open societal systems. One reason the publics have been attacking the social professions, we believe, is that the cognitive and occupational styles of the professions —mimicking the cognitive style of science and the occupational style of engineering—have just not worked on a wide array of social problems. The lay customers are complaining because planners and other professionals have not succeeded in solving the problems they claimed they could solve. We shall want to suggest that the social professions were misled somewhere along the line into assuming they could be applied scientists—that they could solve problems in the ways scientists can solve their sorts of problems. The error has been a serious one.

The kinds of problems that planners deal with—societal problems— are inherently different from the problems that scientists and perhaps some classes of engineers deal with. Planning problems are inherently wicked.

As distinguished from problems in the natural sciences, which are definable and separable, and may have solutions that are findable, the problems of governmental planning —and especially those of social or policy planning—are ill-defined; and they rely upon elusive political judgment for resolution. (Not "solution." Social problems are never solved. At best they are only re-solved—over and over again.) Permit us to draw a cartoon that will help clarify the distinction we intend.

The problems that scientists and engineers have usually focused upon are mostly "tame" or "benign" ones. As an example, consider a problem of mathematics, such as solving an equation; or the task of an organic chemist in analyzing the structure of some unknown compound; or that of the chessplayer attempting to accomplish checkmate in five moves. For each the mission is clear. It is clear, in turn, whether or not the problems have been solved.

Wicked problems, in contrast, have neither of these clarifying traits; and they include nearly all public policy issues—whether the question concerns the location of a

by also formulated a solution. To find the problem is thus the same thing as finding the solution; the problem can't be defined until the solution has been found.

The formulation of a wicked problem *is* the problem! The process of formulating the problem and of conceiving a solution (or re-solution) are identical, since every specification of the problem is a specification of the direction in which a treatment is considered. Thus, if we recognize deficient mental health services as part of the problem, then —trivially enough—"improvement of mental health services" is a specification of solution. If, as the next step, we declare the lack of community centers one deficiency of the mental health services system, then "procurement of community centers" is the next specification of solution. If it is inadequate treatment within community centers, then improved therapy training of staff may be the locus of solution, and so on.

This property sheds some light on the usefulness of the famed "systems-approach" for treating wicked problems. The classical systems-approach of the military and the space programs is based on the assumption that a planning project can be organized into distinct phases. Every textbook of systems engineering starts with an enumeration of these phases: "understand the problems or the mission," "gather information," "analyze information," "synthesize information and wait for the creative leap," "work out solution," or the like. For wicked problems, however, this type of scheme does not work. One cannot understand the problem without knowing about its

context; one cannot meaningfully search for information without the orientation of a solution concept; one cannot first understand, then solve. The systems-approach "of the first generation" is inadequate for dealing with wicked-problems. Approaches of the "second generation" should be based on a model of planning as an argumentative process in the course of which an image of the problem and of the solution emerges gradually among the participants, as a product of incessant judgment, subjected to critical argument. The methods of Operations Research play a prominent role in the systems-approach of the first generation; they become operational, however, only *after* the most important decisions have already been made, i.e., after the problem has already been tamed.

Take an optimization model. Here the inputs needed include the definition of the solution space, the system of constraints, and the performance measure as a function of the planning and contextual variables. But setting up and constraining the solution space and constructing the measure of performance is the wicked part of the problem. Very likely it is more essential than the remaining steps of searching for a solution which is optimal relative to the measure of performance and the constraint system.

2. WICKED PROBLEMS HAVE NO STOPPING RULE

In solving a chess problem or a mathematical equation, the problem-solver knows when he has done his job. There are criteria that tell when *the* or *a* solution has been found.

Not so with planning problems. Because (according to Proposition 1) the process of solving the problem is identical with the process of understanding its nature, because there are no criteria for sufficient understanding and because there are no ends to the causal chains that link interacting open systems, the would-be planner can always try to do better. Some additional investment of effort might increase the chances of finding a better solution.

The planner terminates work on a wicked problem, not for reasons inherent in the "logic" of the problem. He stops for considerations that are external to the problem: he runs out of time, or money, or patience. He finally says, "That's good enough," or "This is the best I can do within the limitations of the project," or "I like this solution," etc.

3. SOLUTIONS TO WICKED PROBLEMS ARE NOT TRUE-OR-FALSE, BUT GOOD-OR-BAD

There are conventionalized criteria for objectively deciding whether the offered solution to an equation or whether the proposed structural formula of a chemical compound is correct or false. They can be independently checked by other qualified persons who are familiar with the established criteria; and the answer will be normally unambiguous.

For wicked planning problems, there are no true or false answers. Normally, many parties are equally equipped, interested, and/or en-

titled to judge the solutions, although none has the power to set formal decision rules to determine correctness. Their judgments are likely to differ widely to accord with their group or personal interests, their special value-sets, and their ideological predilections. Their assessments of proposed solutions are expressed as "good" or "bad" or, more likely, as "better or worse" or "satisfying" or "good enough."

4. THERE IS NO IMMEDIATE AND NO ULTIMATE TEST OF A SOLUTION TO A WICKED PROBLEM

For tame-problems one can determine on the spot how good a solution-attempt has been. More accurately, the test of a solution is entirely under the control of the few people who are involved and interested in the problem.

With wicked problems, on the other hand, any solution, after being implemented, will generate waves of consequences over an extended— virtually an unbounded—period of time. Moreover, the next day's consequences of the solution may yield utterly undesirable repercussions which outweigh the intended advantages or the advantages accomplished hitherto. In such cases, one would have been better off if the plan had never been carried out.

The full consequences cannot be appraised until the waves of repercussions have completely run out, and we have no way of tracing *all* the waves through *all* the affected lives ahead of time or within a limited time span.

5. EVERY SOLUTION TO A WICKED PROBLEM IS A "ONE-SHOT OPERATION"; BECAUSE THERE IS NO OPPORTUNITY TO LEARN BY TRIAL-AND-ERROR, EVERY ATTEMPT COUNTS SIGNIFICANTLY

In the sciences and in fields like mathematics, chess, puzzle-solving or mechanical engineering design, the problem-solver can try various runs without penalty. Whatever his outcome on these individual experiment runs, it doesn't matter much to the subject-system or to the course of societal affairs. A lost chess game is seldom consequential for other chess games or for non-chess-players.

With wicked planning problems, however, *every* implemented solution is consequential. It leaves "traces" that cannot be undone. One cannot build a freeway to see how it works, and then easily correct it after unsatisfactory performance. Large public-works are effectively irreversible, and the consequences they generate have long half-lives. Many people's lives will have been irreversibly influenced, and large amounts of money will have been spent—another irreversible act. The same happens with most other large-scale public works and with virtually all public-service programs. The effects of an experimental curriculum will follow the pupils into their adult lives.

Whenever actions are effectively irreversible and whenever the half-lives of the consequences are long, *every trial counts*. And every attempt to reverse a decision or to correct for the undesired conse-

quences poses another set of wicked problems, which are in turn subject to the same dilemmas.

6. WICKED PROBLEMS DO NOT HAVE AN ENUMERABLE (OR AN EXHAUSTIVELY DESCRIBABLE) SET OF POTENTIAL SOLUTIONS, NOR IS THERE A WELL-DESCRIBED SET OF PERMISSIBLE OPERATIONS THAT MAY BE INCORPORATED INTO THE PLAN

There are no criteria which enable one to prove that all solutions to a wicked problem have been identified and considered.

It may happen that *no* solution is found, owing to logical inconsistencies in the "picture" of the problem. (For example, the problem-solver may arrive at a problem description requiring that both A and not-A should happen at the same time.) Or it might result from his failing to develop an idea for solution (which does not mean that someone else might be more successful). But normally, in the pursuit of a wicked planning problem, a host of potential solutions arises; and another host is never thought up. It is then a matter of *judgment* whether one should try to enlarge the available set or not. And it is, of course, a matter of judgment which of these solutions should be pursued and implemented.

Chess has a finite set of rules, accounting for all situations that can occur. In mathematics, the tool chest of operations is also explicit; so, too, although less rigorously, in chemistry.

But not so in the world of social policy. Which strategies-or-moves are permissible in dealing with crime in the streets, for example, have been enumerated nowhere. "Anything goes," or at least, any new idea for a planning measure may become a serious candidate for a re-solution: What should we do to reduce street crime? Should we disarm the police, as they do in England, since even criminals are less likely to shoot unarmed men? Or repeal the laws that define crime, such as those that make marijuana use a criminal act or those that make car theft a criminal act? That would reduce crime by changing definitions. Try moral rearmament and substitute ethical self-control for police and court control? Shoot all criminals and thus reduce the numbers who commit crime? Give away free loot to would-be-thieves, and so reduce the incentive to crime? And so on.

In such fields of ill-defined problems and hence ill-definable solutions, the set of feasible plans of action relies on realistic judgment, the capability to appraise "exotic" ideas and on the amount of trust and credibility between planner and clientele that will lead to the conclusion, "OK let's try that."

7. EVERY WICKED PROBLEM IS ESSENTIALLY UNIQUE

Of course, for any two problems at least one distinguishing property can be found (just as any number of properties can be found which they share in common), and each of them is therefore unique in a trivial sense. But by *"essentially* unique" we mean that, despite long lists of similarities between a current prob-

lem and a previous one, there always might be an additional distinguishing property that is of overriding importance. Part of the art of dealing with wicked problems is the art of not knowing too early which type of solution to apply.

There are no *classes* of wicked problems in the sense that principles of solution can be developed to fit *all* members of a class. In mathematics there are rules for classifying families of problems—say, of solving a class of equations—whenever a certain, quite-well-specified set of characteristics matches the problem. There are explicit characteristics of tame problems that define similarities among them, in such fashion that the same set of techniques is likely to be effective on all of them.

Despite seeming similarities among wicked problems, one can never be *certain* that the particulars of a problem do not override its commonalities with other problems already dealt with.

The conditions in a city constructing a subway may look similar to the conditions in San Francisco, say; but planners would be ill-advised to transfer the San Francisco solutions directly. Differences in commuter habits or residential patterns may far outweigh similarities in subway layout, downtown layout and the rest. In the more complex world of social policy planning, every situation is likely to be one-of-a-kind. If we are right about that, the direct transference of the physical-science and engineering thoughtways into social policy might be dysfunctional, i.e. positively harmful. "Solutions" might be applied to seemingly familiar problems which are quite incompatible with them.

8. EVERY WICKED PROBLEM CAN BE CONSIDERED TO BE A SYMPTOM OF ANOTHER PROBLEM

Problems can be described as discrepancies between the state of affairs as it is and the state as it ought to be. The process of resolving the problem starts with the search for causal explanation of the discrepancy. Removal of that cause poses another problem of which the original problem is a "symptom." In turn, it can be considered the symptom of still another, "higher level" problem. Thus "crime in the streets" can be considered as a symptom of general moral decay, or permissiveness, or deficient opportunity, or wealth, or poverty, or whatever causal explanation you happen to like best. The level at which a problem is settled depends upon the self-confidence of the analyst and cannot be decided on logical grounds. There is nothing like a natural level of a wicked problem. Of course, the higher the level of a problem's formulation, the broader and more general it becomes: and the more difficult it becomes to do something about it. On the other hand, one should not try to cure symptoms; and therefore one should try to settle the problem on as high a level as possible.

Here lies a difficulty with incrementalism, as well. This doctrine advertises a policy of small steps, in the hope of contributing systematically to overall improvement. If, however, the problem is attacked on too low a level (an increment), then success of resolution may result in making things worse, because it may become more difficult to deal with the higher problems. Marginal improvement does not guarantee overall improvement. For example, computerization of an administrative process may result in reduced cost, ease of operation, etc. But at the same time it becomes more difficult to incur structural changes in the organization, because technical perfection reinforces organizational patterns and normally increases the cost of change. The newly acquired power of the controllers of information may then deter later modifications of their roles.

Under these circumstances it is not surprising that the members of an organization tend to see the problems on a level below their own level. If you ask a police chief what the problems of the police are, he is likely to demand better hardware.

9. THE EXISTENCE OF A DISCREPANCY REPRESENTING A WICKED PROBLEM CAN BE EXPLAINED IN NUMEROUS WAYS. THE CHOICE OF EXPLANATION DETERMINES THE NATURE OF THE PROBLEM'S RESOLUTION

"Crime in the streets" can be explained by not enough police, by too many criminals, by inadequate laws, too many police, cultural deprivation, deficient opportunity, too many guns, phrenologic aberrations, etc. Each of these offers a direction for attacking crime in the streets. Which one is right? There is no rule or procedure to determine the "correct" explanation or combination of them. The reason is that in dealing with wicked problems there are several more ways of refuting a hypothesis than there are permissible in the sciences.

The mode of dealing with conflicting evidence that is customary in science is as follows: "Under conditions C and assuming the validity of hypothesis H, effect E must occur. Now, given C, E does not occur. Consequently H is to be refuted." In the context of wicked problems, however, further modes are admissible: one can deny that the effect E has not occurred, or one can explain the nonoccurrence of E by intervening processes without having to abandon H. Here's an example: Assume that somebody chooses to explain crime in the streets by "not enough police." This is made the basis of a plan, and the size of the police force is increased. Assume further that in the subsequent years there is an increased number of arrests, but an increase of offenses at a rate slightly lower than the increase of GNP. Has the effect E occurred? Has crime in the streets been reduced by increasing the police force? If the answer is no, several nonscientific explanations may be tried in order to rescue the hypothesis H ("Increasing the police force reduces crime in the streets"): "If we had not increased the number of officers, the increase in crime would have been even greater;" "This case is an exception from rule H because there was an irregular influx of criminal elements;" "Time is too short to feel the effects yet;" etc. But also the answer "Yes, E has occurred" can be defended: "The number of arrests was increased," etc.

In dealing with wicked problems, the modes of reasoning used in the argument are much richer than those permissible in the scientific discourse. Because of the essential uniqueness of the problem (see Proposition 7) and lacking opportunity for rigorous experimentation (see Proposition 5), it is not possible to put H to a crucial test.

That is to say, the choice of explanation is arbitrary in the logical sense. In actuality, attitudinal criteria guide the choice. People choose those explanations which are most plausible to them. Somewhat but not much exaggerated, you might say that everybody picks that explanation of a discrepancy which fits his intentions best and which conforms to the action-prospects that are available to him. The analyst's "world view" is the strongest determining factor in explaining a discrepancy and, therefore, in resolving a wicked problem.

10. THE PLANNER HAS NO RIGHT TO BE WRONG

As Karl Popper argues in *The Logic of Scientific Discovery*,[1] it is a principle of science that solutions to problems are only hypotheses offered for refutation. This habit is based on the insight that there are no proofs to hypotheses, only potential refutations. The more a hypothesis withstands numerous attempts at refutation, the better its "corroboration" is considered to be. Consequently, the scientific community does not blame its members for postulating hypotheses that are later refuted—so long as the author abides by the rules of the game, of course.

In the world of planning and wicked problems no such immunity is tolerated. Here the aim is not to find the truth, but to improve some characteristics of the world where

[1] Science Editions, New York, 1961.

people live. Planners are liable for the consequences of the actions they generate; the effects can matter a great deal to those people that are touched by those actions.

We are thus led to conclude that the problems that planners must deal with are wicked and incorrigible ones, for they defy efforts to delineate their boundaries and to identify their causes, and thus to expose their problematic nature. The planner who works with open systems is caught up in the ambiguity of their causal webs. Moreover, his would-be solutions are confounded by a still further set of dilemmas posed by the growing pluralism of the contemporary publics, whose valuations of his proposals are judged against an array of different and contradicting scales. Let us turn to these dilemmas next.

THE SOCIAL CONTEXT

There was a time during the 'Fifties when the quasi-sociological literature was predicting a Mass Society—foreseen as a rather homogeneously shared culture in which most persons would share values and beliefs, would hold to common aims, would follow similar life-styles, and thus would behave in similar ways. (You will recall the popular literature on suburbia of ten years ago.) It is now apparent that those forecasts were wrong.

Instead, the high-scale societies of the Western world are becoming increasingly heterogeneous. They are becoming increasingly differentiated, comprising thousands of minority groups, *each* joined around common interests, common value systems, and shared stylistic preferences that differ from those of other groups. As the sheer volume of information and knowledge increases, as technological developments further expand the range of options, and as awareness of the liberty to deviate and differentiate spreads, more variations are *possible*. Rising affluence or, even more, growing desire for at least subcultural identity induces groups to exploit those options and to invent new ones. We almost dare say that irregular cultural permutations are becoming the rule. We have come to realize that the melting pot never worked for large numbers of immigrants to America,[2] and that the unitary conception of *"The* American Way of Life" is now giving way to a recognition that there are numerous ways of life that are also American.

It was *pre*-industrial society that was culturally homogeneous. The industrial age greatly expanded cultural diversity. Post-industrial society is likely to be far more differentiated than any in all of past history.

It is still too early to know whether the current politicization of subpublics is going to be a long-run phenomenon or not. One could write scenarios that would be equally plausible either way. But one thing is clear: large population size will mean that small minorities can comprise large numbers of people; and, as we have been seeing, even small minorities can swing large political influence.

In a setting in which a plurality of publics is politically pursuing a

[2] See an early sign of this growing realization in Nathan Glazer and Daniel Patrick Moynihan, *Beyond the Melting Pot* (Cambridge: Harvard and MIT Press, 1963).

diversity of goals, how is the larger society to deal with its wicked problems in a planful way? How are goals to be set, when the valuative bases are so diverse? Surely a unitary conception of *a* unitary "public welfare" is an anachronistic one.

We do not even have a theory that tells us how to find out what might be considered a societally best state. We have no theory that tells us what distribution of the social product is best—whether those outputs are expressed in the coinage of money income, information income, cultural opportunities, or whatever. We have come to realize that the concept of *the* social product is not very meaningful; possibly there is no aggregate measure for the welfare of a highly diversified society, if this measure is claimed to be objective and nonpartisan. Social science has simply been unable to uncover a social-welfare function that would suggest which decisions would contribute to a societally best state. Instead, we have had to rely upon the axioms of individualism that underlie economic and political theory, deducing, in effect, that the *larger-public* welfare derives from summation of individualistic choices. And yet, we know that *this* is not necessarily so, as our current experience with air pollution has dramatized.

We also know that many societal processes have the character of zero-sum games. As the population becomes increasingly pluralistic, intergroup differences are likely to be reflected as inter-group rivalries of the zero-sum sorts. If they do, the prospects for inventing positive non-zero-sum development strategies would become increasingly difficult.

Perhaps we can illustrate. A few years ago there was a nearly universal consensus in America that full-employment, high productivity, and widespread distribution of consumer durables fitted into a development strategy in which all would be winners. That consensus is now being eroded. Now, when substitutes for wages are being disbursed to the poor, the college student, and the retired, as well as to the more traditional recipient of nonwage incomes, our conceptions of "employment" and of a full-employment economy are having to be revised. Now, when it is recognized that raw materials that enter the economy end up as residuals polluting the air mantle and the rivers, many are becoming wary of rising manufacturing production. And, when some of the new middle-class religions are exorcising worldly goods in favor of less tangible communal "goods," the consumption-oriented society is being challenged—oddly enough, to be sure, by those who were reared in its affluence.

What was once a clear-cut win-win strategy, that had the status of a near-truism, has now become a source of contentious differences among subpublics.

Or, if these illustrations seem to be posed at too high a level of generality, consider the sorts of intergroup conflicts imbedded in urban renewal, roadway construction, or curriculum design in the public schools. Our observation is not only that values are changing. That is true enough, and the probabilities of parametric changes are large enough to humble even the most perceptive observer of contemporary norms. Our point, rather, is that diverse values are held by different groups of individuals—that what satisfies one may be abhorrent to another, that what comprises problem-solution for one is problem-generation for another. Under such circumstances, and in the absence of an overriding social theory or an overriding social ethic, there is no gainsaying which group is right and which should have its ends served.

One traditional approach to the reconciliation of social values and individual choice is to entrust *de facto* decision-making to the wise and knowledgeable professional experts and politicians. But whether one finds that ethically tolerable or not, we hope we have made it clear that even such a tactic only begs the question, for there are no value-free, true-false answers to any of the wicked problems governments must deal with. To substitute expert professional judgment for those of contending political groups may make the rationales and the repercussions more explicit, but it would not necessarily make the outcomes better. The one-best answer is possible with tame problems, but not with wicked ones.

Another traditional approach to the reconciliation of social values and indivdual choice is to bias in favor of the latter. Accordingly, one would promote widened differentiation of goods, services, environments, and opportunities, such that individuals might more closely satisfy their individual preferences. Where large-system problems are generated, he would seek to ameliorate the effects that he judges most deleterious. Where latent opportunities become visible, he would seek to exploit them. Where positive non-zero-sum developmental strategies can be designed, he would of course work hard to install them.

Whichever the tactic, though, it should be clear that the expert is also the player in a political game, seeking to promote his private vision of goodness over others'. Planning is a component of politics. There is no escaping that truism.

We are also suggesting that none of these tactics will answer the difficult questions attached to the sorts of wicked problems planners must deal with. We have neither a theory that can locate societal goodness, nor one that might dispel wickedness, nor one that might resolve the problems of equity that rising pluralism is provoking. We are inclined to think that these theoretic dilemmas may be the most wicked conditions that confront us.

Interactional Tasks: Perspectives on Planning as a Sociopolitical Process

part III

This section is addressed especially to potential planners like "Martin the Modeler" with the hope that meetings in which attendance is disappointing and participation is disaffected should not be forever their lot.

When planning is viewed as a sociopolitical process, the characteristics of the community and relationships with clients and other relevant actors are among the chief concerns of the planner.

The community provides the climate and structure within which the planning process evolves. However, the developing body of knowledge in this area is not entirely coherent for planning purposes. There is no grand theory that planners can draw upon to comprehend the relative impact of different contextual variables. Indeed, even the conceptual distinctions among these variables are still only roughly developed. Nevertheless this growing body of knowledge is of heuristic value to the planner. Within the last decade, many studies have examined the impact of different characteristics of the community context on planning efforts.[1] Reading 11, "Community Structure and Innovation: The Case of Urban Renewal," by

[1] See, for example, Terry N. Clark, ed., *Community Structures and Decision-Making: Comparative Analysis* (San Francisco: Chandler Publishing Co., 1968); Terry Clark, "Urban Typologies and Political Outputs: Causal Models Using Discrete Variables and Orthogonal Factors, or Precise Distortion Versus Model Muddling," *Social Science Information,* 9:6 (December 1970), 7–33; Michael Aiken and Robert Alford, "Comparative Urban Research and Community Decision-Making," *The New Atlantis,* 1:2 (Winter 1970), 85–110; Neil Gilbert and Harry Specht, "Sociopolitical Correlates of Community Action: An Analysis of Conflict, Political Integration, and Citizen Influence," *Sociological Review Monographs,* No. 21 (November 1975), 93–111; and Neil Gilbert, Harry Specht, and Charlane Brown, "Demographic Correlates of Citizen Participation: Race, Community Size, and Citizen Influence," *Social Service Review* (December 1974), 517–30.

Michael Aiken and Robert Alford, provides an overview of theory and research in this area. Aiken and Alford's study sensitizes the planner to the ways that contextual variables such as political culture, community size, concentration of power, form of government, and planning experience may contribute to the community's general planning capacity.

The community context that Aiken and Alford describe, provides the overall setting within which planners engage in a variety of relationships to move the planning process forward. These relationships include:

a. planner relationships with clients (i.e., employers—usually public or private organizations);

b. relationships of planner and client with other organizations in the planning environment whose interests are affected by the planning (i.e., the interorganizational context); and

c. relationships of the planner with citizens and consumers of the planning product (usually those people served by the public or private organization employing the planner).

When the planner's client is an organization, interorganizational relationships can be ambiguous because individual members of the client organization may be affiliated in different ways and with varying commitments to other agencies in the planning environment. Thus, although it may be useful for analytic purposes to describe clients, organizations in the planning environment, and citizen-consumer groups as though they were distinct entities, the distinctions may not be entirely clear in reality. The network in which planners operate and many of the variables that influence planner-client interaction are identified in Reading 12, Richard Bolan's analysis, "The Social Relations of the Planner." In working with clients, planners must be sensitive to certain factors in their relationships in order to avert unnecessary tensions. As Bolan observes, for example, the planner must clearly discern the client's capacities (i.e., legal powers as well as organizational competencies) for policy implementation. In addition, the planner's effectiveness depends not only upon his technical competence, but also upon his social skills in organizing a planning system and developing communications. Beyond this, at a more fundamental level, personal qualities such as tolerance, objectivity, patience, and the creative use of self come into play.

Some of the ways in which these skills and qualities are applied to interactional tasks are suggested in Reading 13, Neil Gilbert's case study of neighborhood planning and coordination in the Community Action Program. In this case the planner is accountable to three client groups and charged with the responsibility for design and coordination of a local service-delivery system that includes a variety of social welfare organizations. Gilbert notes that the planner's influence upon clients and agencies is based primarily on the use of normative power. This case study illustrates the complicated nature of the social relations of the planner. For instance, planners may be employed directly by citizen-consumer groups with funds provided to these groups by public or private agencies. In this case the citizen-consumer group is both client and employer. However, the role of planner can become complicated because the funding agency may believe that it has some claims on the planner's loyalty and commitment. Indeed, the planner frequently finds his services and loyalties divided among different parties in the planning environment.

When planning is viewed mainly as a sociopolitical process, the planner often becomes an advocate for his client's interests. Paul Davidoff, in "Advocacy and Pluralism in Planning," Reading 14, describes some of the advocate planner's responsibilities. The most important of these responsibilities, Davidoff suggests, involves carrying out the planning process for the organization and persuasively arguing its cause.

Davidoff recognizes that one of the obstacles to pluralistic planning is that the most vulnerable groups in society, those most often affected by social planning, cannot afford the entry fee. Rarely is the advocate planner's dedication to his client expected to extend to work without pay. Many disadvantaged interest groups lack the means to sponsor planning. Government is a possible source of financial support for these groups, but political constraints are frequently attached to such funds. If Gilbert's case study of the antipoverty program is any indication, government-funded planners who advocate for local citizen groups are bound to find themselves under a great deal of political strain, with more "clients" demanding their loyalty and trying to hold them accountable than they bargained for.

The network of relationships among planner and client may range from neighborhood agencies to departments of the federal government, depending upon the planning issue. The nature of interorganizational relationships is the topic of Reading 15, "The Interaction of Community Decision Organizations: Some Basic Concepts and Needed Research," by Roland Warren. Focusing upon relationships among planning organizations within the local community (i.e., "Community Decision Organizations"), Warren offers some observations gleaned from community studies and raises a number of questions that are germane to the planner's management of interactional tasks. For example, the relationships of a planning organization may be conceptualized broadly in terms of an "in-put constituency" (i.e., groups that perform supporting functions to whom the organization is accountable) and an "out-put constituency" (i.e., the target groups or consumers on whose behalf program plans are developed). Warren observes that planning organizations are more sensitive to the interests of in-put constituencies. If the planner desires to change organizational objectives, one major task will be to create linkages and overlap among in-put and out-put constituencies. Warren also notes that the "interactional field" in which planning takes place is fertile ground for research on such questions as: How do planning organizations respond to factors such as density of events and turbulence in the field? And more generally: What variations in this field in different cities account for different behaviors of planning organizations?

Apropos of this line of questioning, in Reading 16, "Decision-makers and Influentials," Robert Connery and his associates provide an insightful comparative analysis of the influence exercised by various units at different levels of the interorganizational field for mental health services in six metropolitan areas. To understand the forces affecting mental health programming in these communities, they examine the planning environment from two perspectives: the roles played by state, local, and private groups interested in mental health, and the local community power structure. They found that the participation of different interest groups varied considerably: state legislators played primarily a ratifying role in mental health planning; organized professional groups did not play a significant role in program development; state mental health administrative agencies contributed importantly to policy development; local private agencies influenced policy in cities where their activities were well coordinated; and voluntary state mental health associations varied in their ability to exercise influence. The local community power structure contained a diversity of decision-making patterns generally characterized by pluralistic tendencies. Overall, in the communities they studied, the planning environment was considerably fragmented.

As already noted, the interaction between the planner and the citizens and consumers of the planning product is one of the significant relationships in the planning environment. (Citizen-consumer units are part of the "out-put constituency" described by Warren.) This particular relationship is qualitatively different from relationships between the planner and other organizational units in the field. For example, the interaction between planner and citizen-consumer units usually centers upon efforts to involve the latter in the planning process. The precise form of involvement will vary depending upon the interests and motives of the client organization and the planner's commitment to the views of his client organization. That is, where the client organization is interested in appeasing or controlling the citizen-consumer unit, involvement may take the form of therapy or education. Where the objective is to transform the citizen-consumer into part of the in-put constituency, involvement may take the form of partnership. In some cases, usually when the client organization *is* the citizen-consumer unit, the citizen-consumer may actually obtain major control over policy-making. Various typologies of forms of citizen participation can be found in the literature. Sherry Arnstein, for example, has designed a typology that identifies eight modes of citizen involvement based on the degree of power the citizen-consumer unit exercises in the planning process. "Citizen participation," she explains, "is a categorical term for citizen power. It is the redistribution of power that enables the have-not citizens, presently excluded from the political and economic processes, to be deliberately included in the future." [2]

A substantial redistribution of power does not come about without resistance. Faced with the task of involving citizen-consumer units in decision making, planners employ various tactics to overcome resistance. The mode of intervention most appropriate for the interactional tasks in planner-citizen relationships depends upon the degree to which citizen-consumer participation is intended to alter the prevailing distribution of power and resources. In Reading 17 George Brager and Harry Specht analyze three basic alternative modes of intervention: collaboration, campaign, and contest. They explain the conditions that give rise to these modes of intervention and also offer some practical advice about the timing of action and about image management; these matters are pointedly illustrated in the two parts of Reading 18, which analyzes citizen participation in community planning for Philadelphia's Model Cities Program. The first analysis is "Maximum Feasible Manipulation," Told to Sherry Arnstein by the North City Area Wide Council, Inc. The analysis is made from the perspective of the citizen organization, the North City Area Wide Council, Inc. (AWC). It is the story of a spirited struggle as revealed in AWC's month-by-month, blow-by-blow description of events. The AWC analysis presents one view of a complicated series of issues and events. The second analysis, Michelle Osborn's "Postscript," presents the picture from the perspective of other units in the interactional field. In comparing the two reports, it is interesting to observe how important the tactics of image management are in the struggle between contending interests. The Arnstein analysis presents the AWC as a cohesive, highly representative, democratic, grassroots organization. The image presented in Osborn's analysis is less likely to inspire confidence in either the representativeness or the accountability of AWC.

It is apparent from this brief review of the sociopolitical aspects of the planning process that the planner must be able to function in a complex network of social relationships. To maintain productive contacts with clients, consumers, and other units in the planning environment requires a high degree of interactional skill and political savvy. Without these abilities the planner is limited in his capacity to generate and guide the dynamics of

2 Sherry Arnstein, "A Ladder of Citizen Participation," *Journal of the American Institute of Planners*, 35:4 (July 1969), 216; other typologies of citizen participation are presented by Ralph M. Kramer, *Community Development in Israel and the Netherlands* (Berkeley: Institute of International Studies, University of California, Berkeley, 1970), p. 127; and Peter H. Rossi and Robert Dentler, *The Politics of Urban Renewal* (New York: The Free Press of Glencoe, Inc., 1961), pp. 283–88.

social planning in a pluralistic environment. But with *only* these abilities the planner is relegated to the political domain. Relying on social skills alone, the planner's contribution to the planning process will be difficult to distinguish from that of other political actors on the scene—which is to say that the social planner must have more than socialability to get the job done: technical skills are also required. In the next section we will examine the technical aspects of social planning.

11   *Contextual Factors*

COMMUNITY STRUCTURE AND INNOVATION:
THE CASE OF URBAN RENEWAL

Michael Aiken/Robert R. Alford

The search for determinants of public policy innovation in American cities has received little attention from social scientists. The controversy over "community power structure" focused almost entirely upon case studies of "who governs" in particular cities and barely at all upon the policy consequences of different configurations of power in the local community (Jacob and Lipsky, 1968; Alford, 1969; Aiken, 1970). However, a number of comparative studies have appeared recently focusing upon such policy outputs as urban renewal, fluoridation, and desegregation. The data used in these studies, often rather crudely, indicate the concepts they allegedly represent. Such slippage between available data and theoretical constructs has resulted in the proliferation of diffuse explanations of public policy innovations and identical or even contradictory empirical indicators.

In this paper we shall review a number of theories of community

Reprinted with permission of author and publisher from: Michael Aiken and Robert R. Alford, "Community Structure and Innovation: The Case of Urban Renewal," *American Sociological Review*, 35: 4 (August 1970), 650–65.

policy innovation, examine some empirical findings about innovation in urban renewal, and conclude by suggesting an alternative theory which conceives of the community as an interorganizational system.[1] Parallel papers to this one analyze innovation in public housing and in poverty programs (Aiken and Alford, 1970 a, b).

THE NATURE OF COMMUNITY INNOVATION

Little attention has been given to innovation in communities, although they are continually introducing new ideas, activities, processes, and services. In the comparative perspective

[1] This research was supported in part by funds granted to the Institute for Research on Poverty at the University of Wisconsin by the Office of Economic Opportunity pursuant to the provisions of the Economic Opportunity Act of 1964. The conclusions are the sole responsibility of the authors. We are indebted to Terry N. Clark, Robert L. Crain, and Paul E. Mott for their detailed and helpful comments. We are grateful to the Institute for its research and administrative support, and to Elizabeth Balcer, Janet Jensen, and Ann Wallace for their competent and vital research assistance.

utilized here, we are interested not only in knowing those structures and processes in communities that are associated with the *adoption* of an innovation, but also with the *speed* of the innovation and the *level of output* or performance of the innovative activity. In particular, we are interested in identifying the underlying structural properties and community processes that explain why some communities moved quickly to enter the urban renewal program while others were either slow to innovate or have never participated at all in this federal program. At least five theories of innovation which are relevant to this question can be found in the recent social science literature. Nowhere have these various explanations of community innovation been brought together. In part this lack of theoretical integration is due to the diverse concepts used; what we consider to be innovation has also been called community decision-making, community decision outcomes, and policy outputs.

SOME THEORIES OF COMMUNITY INNOVATION

The five general hypotheses of community innovation are as follows:

1. *Political Culture:* Cities with majorities holding "public-regarding" values are more innovative with respect to policies benefiting the community as a whole than cities dominated by groups with "private-regarding" values (Wolfinger and Field, 1966; cf. Wilson, 1966).

2. *Centralization of Formal Political Structure:* Cities with central-

ized administrative arrangements and a strong mayor, that is, cities with city manager or partisan mayor-council governmental structures, are more innovative (Crain *et al.,* 1969; Greenstone and Peterson, 1968).

3. *Concentration or Diffusion of Community Power:* There are two aspects to this argument: concentration of systemic power (Hawley, 1963) and diffusion of power through mass citizen participation (Crain and Rosenthal, 1967). In both cases the hypothesis is the same: the greater the concentration of power, the greater the degree of innovation.

4. *Community Differentiation and Continuity:* Older and larger cities are more bureaucratic and consequently less receptive to policy innovations than younger and smaller cities (Dye, 1968).

5. *Community Integration:* Cities in which community integration breaks down or is extremely low have a lower probability of innovation or other collective actions. Consequently innovation should be highest in integrated communities (Coleman, 1957; Pinard, 1963).

We have presented these five explanations separately because it is possible to conceive of them as five independent factors. However, one or more of these factors may be either spurious or intervening variables for the operation of another more fundamental factor, such as the sheer need for a program. Also, as we shall see, the indicators of the theoretical variables have been quite diverse, overlapping, and are sometimes used for quite different concepts. This diversity in the use of the same empirical indicators is partly a result of the great "distance" of the easily available quantitative indicators from the theoretical variables of greatest concern to most scholars.

Most of the data we use are no better, but we have the advantage of bringing together most of the various indicators used in the previous literature, as well as adding several measures which have the merit of being considerably closer to the theoretical variables to which they refer, although they have defects of their own.

DATA AND METHODS

Urban renewal programs have been the most frequently studied aspect of public policy making in American cities in recent years. In the scholarly literature, the aspects studied have been diverse, including whether or not a program had reached a planning or execution stage in a given city, urban renewal expenditures, and the number of years a city took to enter the program. The problems which have led to its study include community power structure, the political ethos of the city, and the capacity of shrewd political leaders to generate support. (There seems to be little doubt that the main effect of the program has been to reduce the stock of low-cost housing, since the original legislation explicitly forbade local governments to use income from the sale of land to build new low-rent housing, and relatively few cities have built public housing with other funds, whether federal or non-federal.)

The findings of this study are based on the universe of 582 American cities in 1960 with the following characteristics: (1) incorporated ur-ban places of size 25,000 population or more, (2) location in states that had state enabling legislation prior to 1958 permitting cities to enter the urban renewal program, and (3) cities in existence in 1950. Of the 676 incorporated urban places of size 25,000 population or more in 1960, 74 are omitted because they were located in 11 states which did not get enabling legislation until 1958 or later (Idaho, Montana, New Mexico, Utah, and Wyoming), or which had highly restrictive enabling legislation, reversals of decision, or no enabling legislation at all as of June 30, 1966, or had a combination of these (Florida, Louisiana, Maryland, Mississippi, Oklahoma, and South Carolina). Another 20 cities that did not exist in 1950 are also omitted. . . .

The various measures of community structure were taken from the *Municipal Year Books* of 1963 and 1964, the 1950 Census of Housing, and the 1960 Census of Population. Information about the innovation measure, i.e., participation in the urban renewal program, was taken from the *Urban Renewal Directory: June 30, 1966,* Department of Housing and Urban Development, U.S. Government, Washington, D. C., 1966.

We shall ignore in this paper changes in federal urban renewal legislation from 1949 on, although such changes may alter the incentives of different cities to obtain such resources. The original 1949 act required that 55 percent or more, of the project area be residential either before or after renewal in order to qualify for federal assistance. This requirement was gradually eased by subsequent legislation. Undoubtedly the incentives of local industrialists, real estate investors, and local groups of residents to initiate, support, or oppose urban renewal were altered by these changes, and therefore the probabilities of a given program being carried through, but we do not have the data to investigate this possibility (Ventre, 1966).

We measure the presence or absence of innovation by whether or not a community has ever participated in the urban renewal program. Of the 582 cities in the analysis here, 372 (or 64 percent) had innovated an urban renewal program, although 32 of these later dropped out of the program. Among the remaining 340 cities, 187 had completed at least one urban renewal program as of June 30, 1966; 130 others had reached the execution stage of the program; and another 23 were still in planning. There were 210 communities that had never innovated an urban renewal program.

The speed of community innovation is measured by the number of years after 1949 before the city entered the urban renewal program. This is similar to a measure developed by Straits (1965) in his critique of Hawley's (1963) work, although Straits used 1951 to calculate the speed with which a community entered the urban renewal program. The distribution of this variable was slightly skewed toward the lower end of the distribution, but skewness was not of sufficient magnitude to warrant a transformation of this variable.

Since some cities were located in states that did not enact enabling legislation until after 1949, another measure of speed in innovation was constructed: the number of years it took the city to enter the program after state enabling legislation was enacted.

The level of output measure is the number of urban renewal dollars reserved per capita as of June 30, 1966. This measure is similar to those used by Wolfinger and Field (1966) and Clark (1968b), although not strictly comparable. The measure used here was computed by determining the total number of dollars reserved for all urban renewal projects as of June 30, 1966, and then standardizing this figure by the population size, thus yielding a dollar amount reserved per capita for all urban renewal projects. This distribution was highly skewed toward the upper end of the scale so that a natural logarithm transformation of this variable (which was approximately normally distributed) was used in the computation of correlation coefficients.

The relationships among these measures of innovation are quite high, as shown in Table 1, although not so high as to make them equivalent measures. Nor are they logically the same. . . .

STRUCTURAL DIFFERENTIATION AND COMMUNITY INNOVATION

Let us start negatively by reviewing the rejected explanations.[2] Glo-

2 [Readers interested in the details of the Aiken and Alford analysis should consult the complete article. Also see the following articles by Aiken and Alford: "Community Structure and Innovation: The Case of Public Housing," *American Political Science Review*, 65: 3 (September 1970) and "Comparative Urban Research and Community Decision-making," *The New Atlantis*. 1: 2 (Winter 1970)—Eds.]

TABLE 1. RELATIONSHIPS AMONG INDICATORS OF COMMUNITY INNOVATION

	Presence of Innovation	Speed of Innovation		Level of Output
	Presence of Urban Renewal Program	*Number of Years After 1949 Before Entering the Urban Renewal Program*	*Number of Years It Took After State Enabling Legislation Was Present*	*Number of Dollars Reserved Per Capita (Natural Log)*
Presence of participation in the urban renewal program		−.69***	−.62***	.86***
Number of years after 1949 before the community entered the urban renewal program			.88***	−.80***
Number of years it took after state enabling legislation was present				−.71***
Number of urban renewal dollars reserved per capita (natural logarithm)				

*** p<.001.

NOTE: The number of cases is 582 except for the proportion of registrants voting, which was 370. The presence of urban renewal programs of one or another form of political structure was treated as a "dummy" (binary) variable for purposes of correlations and regressions in subsequent analysis. The natural logarithm of four highly skewed variables was used for correlation analysis, in order to produce an approximately normal distribution.

bal properties of the political ethos of majorities and integration seemed to fare most poorly. While the zero-order predictions of Hawley and Crain and Rosenthal were as predicted, we have shown that even these relationships can be removed by partialing procedures. That is, hypotheses referring to properties of the city as a whole rather than properties of groups or organizations making up that city seemed (1) to use concepts most distant from the available data and (2) to be supported most weakly by the data. If anything, the data point in the opposite direction. Cities that appear to be heterogeneous, differentiated, and fragmented—as indicated by ethnicity, a large working class, nonwhite composition, size, and the

qualitative data on centralization (elite participation) in the works of Clark (1968b) and Aiken (1970)—are most likely to have innovated in urban renewal. The same studies show that the more groups and actors participating in current decisions, the higher is the level of innovation and outputs.

Additional and more directly relevant data support the proposition that the more differentiated the organizational structure of a city, the more innovative it will be. A more direct measure of organizational complexity than simply city size would be a count of the number of organizations of various types which play some role in community life. We have data on three such types of organizations—manufacturing firms, banks, and trade unions—although only for a subsample of cities in each case. Unfortunately, we lack data on other more crucial types of organizations such as political parties, voluntary associations or the local government.

Not only the sheer number of organizations may be important, but also the number having sufficient resources to affect critically the course of community innovation. For this reason we have chosen the number of manufacturing establishments with 100 or more employees and the number of independent banks with assets of at least fifty million dollars as our measures of organizational complexity and differentiation. Unfortunately, the unionization data cannot be treated in exactly the same way. But because larger firms are more likely to be unionized and because the data include all establishments in which a majority of the plant workers are unionized, we believe that this measure is an appropriate indicator of the organizational complexity of a community.

These data relating structural differentiation and community innovation are presented in Table 2. Because the level and character of unionization can be presumed to be different in the North and the South, the data for that variable are presented by region. The results are consistent with our expectations. The more manufacturing establishments, the more independent banks, and the more unionized plants that a city has, the more innovative it is.

These measures of structural differentiation can be regarded as ways of spelling out more precisely what it means to be a large city as far as capacity to innovate is concerned.

Large cities have a greater diversity of social organizations, and they also have greater innovation.

AN ALTERNATIVE EXPLANATION

Because we find none of the previously discussed theories completely satisfactory, we here propose one approach that seems to be more consistent with the previous findings. Our alternative explanation of the findings can be only a suggestion since we do not have the empirical data to test directly our ideas. Therefore, we shall only suggest here some of the concepts that appear to us at this time to be most relevant in explaining innovation in such decision-areas as urban renewal, public housing, and the war on poverty.

Our tentative alternative explanation is that such innovations are a product of the nature and state of interorganizational networks in communities (cf. Turk, 1970). Such networks are properties of community systems that have developed historically through the interaction of organizational units and their leaders. If the population of a community is relatively stable, these interorganizational networks are not likely to be disrupted by the continuous influx of new citizens and organizations, and thus greater potential exists for increasing their capacity for coordination over time.

The degree of historical continuity in a community structure—especially as it affects interorganizational networks—may also influence innovation. Presumably older cities have had a longer time for existing organizations to work out patterns of interactions, alliances, factions, or

TABLE 2. DIFFERENTIATION OF ECONOMIC STRUCTURE AND INNOVATION IN URBAN RENEWAL IN AMERICAN CITIES [a]

	Manufacturing Number of Establishments of Size 100 or More	Banking Number of Independent Banks with Assets of Fifty Million Dollars or More	Unionization Per Cent of Plant Workers Unionized among All Industries North	South
Innovation				
Presence of urban renewal	.27***	.33***	.22*	.33**
Speed of Innovation				
Number of years after 1949 it took the city to enter the urban renewal program	−.42***	−.46***	−.15	−.48***
Number of years it took after state enabling legislation was present	−.33***	−.37***	−.03	−.03
Outputs				
Log N urban renewal dollars reserved per capita	.32***	.36***	.24**	.40**
	N = (217)	(217)	(77)	(35)

[a] Source: Manufacturing and banking data are available for the 217 nonsuburban cities in the size range 25,000 to 250,000 population which had 20 percent or more of their labor force in manufacturing in 1960. The unionization of manufacturing establishments is available for 84 metropolitan areas, which provide an estimate of unionization in 112 cities within them. See Michael Aiken, "Economic Concentration and Community Innovation," unpublished manuscript, 1969, for details on the construction of the measures. The banking data were taken from *Polk's Bank Directory* (Nashville: R. L. Polk and Co., March, 1966). The data on unions are drawn from Bulletin No. 1465–86, Bureau of Labor Statistics, U.S. Department of Labor, Washington, D.C., October, 1966, titled *Wages and Related Benefits: Part I, 84 Metropolitan Areas, 1965–66*. The measure is the approximate percent of all plant workers employed in establishments in which a union contract covered a majority of workers during the period July, 1964 to June, 1966. We have assigned the degree of unionization in the SMSA to the urban place as the best estimate we have of the unionization of the city itself.

* $p < .05$.
** $p < .01$.
*** $p < .001$.

coalitions. In such communities the state of knowledge in the community system about the orientations, needs, and probable reactions to varying proposals for community action is likely to be quite high, thus increasing the probability of developing a sufficiently high level of coordination in order to implement successfully a community innovation.

The degree of structural differentiation and complexity of a community may also influence innovation for two reasons. First, larger cities are likely to have more organizations devoted to specific kinds of decision-areas—i.e., more likely to have a redevelopment agency, a housing agency, a community action agency, a city development agency for Model Cities, welfare councils and other community decision organizations. Such organizations are likely to have larger, more specialized, and more professional staffs to provide the technical, administrative, and political knowledge required to innovate successfully, not only within their organizations, but also in the activation of interorganizational relationships and establishment of critical coalitions (cf. Mohr, 1969). Secondly, it is precisely in the larger, more structurally differentiated communities that coalitions that can implement an innovation will be easiest to establish. If we assume that only a limited number of organizational units need to be mobilized to bring about a successful innovation, then it follows that in large, highly differentiated communities a lower proportion of the available organizations will participate in such decisions, and that there will be wider latitude in selecting organizations for these critical coalitions. In other words, the "issue arena" involved in the innovation will require the participation of only a few of the organizations that exist in the community system. In one sense, this proposition is simply a spelling out of what is meant by "structural differentiation" or "functional specialization." The more highly differentiated or specialized a community system, the higher the proportion of decisions that are likely to be made by subsystems and the less likely the

entire system will be activated on most issues.

The extent to which the interorganizational field is "turbulent" may also influence innovation (cf. Terreberry, 1968). Where many people are moving out of the city, the existing historically developed network of organizational relationships may be relatively undisturbed, except insofar as outmigration indicates an economic or perhaps political crisis which existing institutions cannot handle. Conversely, where many people are moving in, bringing with them different ideas about the appropriate functions of local government, and perhaps creating demands for new services, newly established organizations may be severely limited since they are less likely to be in an organizational network which can aid in achieving an adequate level of coordination for a proposed community innovation.

We thus suggest that three properties—structural differentiation, the accumulation of experience and information, and the stability and extensiveness of interorganizational networks—may contribute to the capacity of a community to innovate. Let us turn to more concrete concepts and hypotheses that might be consistent with this particular approach.

Community systems can be conceived of as interorganizational fields in which the basic interacting units are *centers of power*. A center of power can be defined as an organization which possesses a high degree of autonomy, resources, and cohesion. The linking mechanisms among centers of power in a community system we call *interfaces* (see Mott, 1970).

Interfaces are not only the current set of interorganizational relationships in the community, but more importantly include the historical accumulation of knowledge and experience among various centers of power. An *issue arena* is the organization set (Evan, 1966) of centers of power which must be activated on a given issue in order to effectuate a decision.

We hypothesize that the greater the number of centers of power in a community and the more pervasive and encompassing the interfaces, the higher the probability of innovation in a given issue arena. In other words, the more choice among acting units in the system—centers of power—and the greater the state of information about organizational actors, the higher the probability that a minimum coalition can be formed. For many issues this will mean the creation of an organization whose specific task is the implementation of the decision to innovate. Warren (1967a, b) refers to these as "community decision organizations," and he cites community action agencies, housing authorities, welfare councils, health departments as examples. The community decision organization is a special type of center of power whose mission is to supervise the planning, coordination, and delivery of the innovated activity. The professional staffs of such organizations are likely to generate further innovations.

The structural conditions in the community that lead to the introduction of an innovation in a given activity—organizational differentiation and historical continuity—may not be the factors that are most conducive to high levels of performance by community decision organizations. Once the innovation has been introduced, the community decision organization may seek to develop relatively tightly controlled relationships with cooperating organizations in their issue arena and thus gain legitimacy for an exclusive mandate from other community decision organizations. If so, communities with high levels of performance in various community action activities may well be those in which relatively autonomous issue arenas have emerged. It may be that the structures of relationships within such subsystems are indeed "centralized" in the sense of a given organization having strong control over units within that issue arena. If this is true, it would suggest that Hawley's thesis may be appropriate if a community subsystem is taken as the unit of analysis.

It is possible, however, that this model is only applicable to decisions for which the major actors are organizations. To the extent that private citizens are mobilized on a given decision—such as in the case of fluoridation—this model may not be appropriate, or at least it may be incomplete.

What we have suggested is a two-stage process in which the overall state of a community system may be most important for understanding the community's propensity for innovation across a wide spectrum of issues, but that the appropriate analytic unit for understanding specific innovations, as well as performance in such innovations, is a subsystem of a community in which the central actor is the community decision organization. Our data do not permit us to test the validity of assertions such as these; that would require a completely different type of comparative study. But this particular approach appears to us to be as consistent with the data presented in this paper as any of the theories we have examined, if not more so.

REFERENCES

AIKEN, MICHAEL, 1970. "The Distribution of Community Power: Structural Bases and Social Consequences." In Michael Aiken and Paul E. Mott, eds., *The Structure of Community Power: An Anthology*. New York: Random House.

———— and ROBERT R. ALFORD, 1970a. "Community Structure and Innovation: The Case of Public Housing." *American Political Science Review*, 64, September.

————, 1970b. "Community Structure and the War on Poverty: Theoretical and Methodological Considerations." In Mattei Dogan, ed., *Studies in Political Ecology*. Paris.

ALFORD, ROBERT R., with the collaboration of Harry M. Scoble, 1969. *Bureaucracy and Participation: Political Cultures in Four Wisconsin Cities*. Chicago: Rand McNally.

BARNETT, H. G., 1953. *Innovation: The Basis of Cultural Change*. New York: McGraw-Hill.

BELLUSH, JEWEL, and MURRAY HAUSKNECHT, 1967. *Urban Renewal: People, Politics, and Planning*. New York: Doubleday Anchor Books.

CLARK, TERRY N., 1968a. "Community Structure and Decision-making." Pp. 91–126 in Terry N. Clark, ed., *Community Structure and Decision-Making: Comparative Analyses*. San Francisco: Chandler.

————, 1968b. "Community Structure, Decision-making, Budget Expenditures, and Urban Renewal in 51 American Communities." *American Sociological Review*, 33 (August), 576–93.

COLEMAN, JAMES S., 1957. *Community Conflict*. New York: Free Press.

CRAIN, ROBERT L., and DONALD B. ROSEN-

THAL, 1967. "Community Status as a Dimension of Local Decision-making." *American Sociological Review*, 32 (December), 970–84.

————, ELIHU KATZ, and DONALD B. ROSENTHAL, 1969. *The Politics of Community Conflict: The Fluoridation Decision*. Indianapolis: Bobbs-Merrill.

DAHL, ROBERT A., 1961. *Who Governs? Power and Democracy in an American City*. New Haven: Yale University Press.

DUGGAR, GEORGE, 1961. "The Relationship of Local Government Structures to Urban Renewal." *Law and Contemporary Problems*, 26 (Winter), 49–69.

DYE, THOMAS R., 1968. "Urban School Segregation: A Comparative Analysis." *Urban Affairs Quarterly*, 4 (December), 141–65.

ELAZAR, DANIEL J., 1967. " 'Fragmentation' and Local Organizational Response to Federal-City Programs." *Urban Affairs Quarterly*, 4 (June), 30–46.

EVAN, WILLIAM, 1966. "The Organization-Set: Toward a Theory of Interorganizational Relations." Pp. 173–91 in James D. Thompson, ed., *Approaches to Organizational Design*. Pittsburgh: University of Pittsburgh Press.

FROMAN, LEWIS A., JR., 1968. "An Analysis of Public Policies in Cities." *Journal of Politics*, 29 (February), 94–108.

GREENSTONE, J. DAVID, and PAUL E. PETERSON, 1968. "Reformers, Machines, and the War on Poverty." Pp. 267–92 in James Q. Wilson, ed., *City Politics and Public Policy*. New York: Wiley.

HAWLEY, AMOS H., 1963. "Community Power Structure and Urban Renewal Success." *American Journal of Sociology*, 68 (January) 422–31.

HUNTER, FLOYD, 1953. *Community Power Structure*. Chapel Hill: University of North Carolina Press. Anchor edition, 1963.

JACOB, HERBERT, and MICHAEL LIPSKY, 1968. "Outputs, Structure, and Power: An Assessment of the Changes in the Study of State and Local Politics." *Journal of Politics*, 30 (May), 510–38.

LINEBERRY, ROBERT L. and EDMUND P. FOWLER, 1967. "Reformism and Public Policies in American Cities." *American Political Science Review*, 61 (September), 701–16.

LOWI, THEODORE J., 1964a. *At the Pleasure of the Mayor*. New York: Free Press.

———, 1964b. "American Business, Public Policy, Case Studies, and Political Theory." *World Politics*, 16 (July), 677–715.

MANSFIELD, EDWIN, 1963. "The Speed of Response of Firms to New Techniques." *Quarterly Journal of Economics*, 22 (May), 290–311.

MOHR, LAWRENCE B., 1969. "Determinants of Innovation in Organization." *American Political Science Review*, 63 (March), 111–26.

MOTT, PAUL E., 1970. "Configurations of Power." In Michael Aiken and Paul E. Mott, eds., *The Structure of Community Power: An Anthology*. New York: Random House.

PINARD, MAURICE, 1963. "Structural Attachments and Political Support in Urban Politics: A Case of a Fluoridation Referendum." *American Journal of Sociology*, 68 (March), 513–26.

ROGERS, EVERETT M., 1962. *Diffusion of Innovations*. New York: Free Press.

SALISBURY, ROBERT H., 1968. "The Analysis of Public Policy: A Search for Theories and Roles." Pp. 151–75 in Austin Ranney, ed., *Political Science and Public Policy*. Chicago: Markham.

SHARKANSKY, IRA, 1969. *Spending in the American States*. Chicago: Rand McNally.

SOGG, WILTON S. and WARREN WERTHEIMER, 1967. "Legal and Governmental Issues in Urban Renewal." Pp. 126–88 in James Q. Wilson, ed., *Urban Renewal: The Record and the Controversy*. Cambridge: The M.I.T. Press.

STINCHCOMBE, ARTHUR, 1968. *Constructing Social Theories*. New York: Harcourt, Brace and World.

STRAITS, BRUCE C., 1965. "Community Adoption and Implementation of Urban Renewal." *American Journal of Sociology*, 71 (July), 77–82.

TERREBERRY, SHIRLEY, 1968. "The Evolution of Organizational Environments." *Administrative Science Quarterly*, 12 (March), 590–613.

THOMPSON, VICTOR A., 1965. "Bureaucracy and Innovation." *Administrative Science Quarterly*, 10 (June), 1–20.

TURK, HERMAN, 1970. "Interorganizational Networks in Urban Society: Initial Perspective and Comparative Research." *American Sociological Review*, 35 (February), 1–19.

VENTRE, FRANCIS T., 1966. "Local Initiatives in Urban Industrial Development." *Urban Affairs Quarterly*, 2 (December), 53–67.

WALTER, BENJAMIN, 1962. "Political Decision-making in Arcadia." Pp. 141–87 in F. Stuart Chapin, Jr., and Shirley F. Weiss, eds., *Urban Growth Dynamics*. New York: Wiley.

WARREN, ROLAND L., 1967a. "Interaction of Community Decision Organizations: Some Basic Concepts and Needed Research." *Social Service Review*, 41 (September), 261–70.

———, 1967b. "The Interorganizational Field as a Focus for Investigation." *Administrative Science Quarterly*, 12 (December), 396–419.

WILSON, JAMES Q., 1966. "Innovation in Organization: Notes Toward a Theory." Pp. 193–218 in James D. Thompson, ed., *Approaches to Organizational Design*. Pittsburgh: University of Pittsburgh Press.

———, and EDWARD C. BANFIELD, 1966. Communication to the editor. *American Political Science Review*, 60 (December), 998–99.

WOLFINGER, RAYMOND E., and JOHN OSGOOD FIELD, 1966. "Political Ethos and the Structure of City Government." *American Political Science Review*, 60 (June), 306–26.

freeway, the adjustment of a tax rate, the modification of school curricula, or the confrontation of crime.

There are at least ten distinguishing properties of planning-type problems, i.e., wicked ones, that planners had better be alert to and which we shall comment upon in turn. As you will see, we are calling them "wicked" not because these properties are themselves ethically deplorable. We use the term "wicked" in a meaning akin to that of "malignant" (in contrast to "benign") or "vicious" (like a circle) or "tricky" (like a leprechaun) or "aggressive" (like a lion, in contrast to the docility of a lamb). We do not mean to personify these properties of social systems by implying malicious intent. But then, you may agree that it becomes morally objectionable for the planner to treat a wicked problem as though it were a tame one, or to tame a wicked problem prematurely, or to refuse to recognize the inherent wickedness of social problems.

1. THERE IS NO DEFINITIVE FORMULATION OF A WICKED PROBLEM

For any given tame problem, an exhaustive formulation can be stated containing all the information the problem-solver needs for understanding and solving the problem—provided he knows his "art," of course.

This is not possible with wicked-problems. The information needed to *understand* the problem depends upon one's idea for *solving* it. That is to say: in order to *describe* a wicked-problem in sufficient detail, one has to develop an exhaustive inventory of all conceivable *solutions* ahead of time. The reason is that every question asking for additional information depends upon the understanding of the problem—and its resolution—at that time. Problem understanding and problem resolution are concomitant to each other. Therefore, in order to anticipate all questions (in order to anticipate all information required for resolution ahead of time), knowledge of all conceivable solutions is required.

Consider, for example, what would be necessary in identifying the nature of the poverty problem. Does poverty mean low income? Yes, in part. But what are the determinants of low income? Is it deficiency of the national and regional economies, or is it deficiencies of cognitive and occupational skills within the labor force? If the latter, the problem statement and the problem "solution" must encompass the educational processes. But, then, where within the educational system does the real problem lie? What then might it mean to "improve the educational system"? Or does the poverty problem reside in deficient physical and mental health? If so, we must add those etiologies to our information package, and search inside the health services for a plausible cause. Does it include cultural deprivation? spatial dislocation? problems of ego identity? deficient political and social skills?—and so on. If we can formulate the problem by tracing it to some sorts of sources —such that we can say, "Aha! That's the locus of the difficulty," i.e. those are the root causes of the differences between the "is" and the "ought to be" conditions—then we have there-

12   The Network of Social Relations

THE SOCIAL RELATIONS OF THE PLANNER

RICHARD S. BOLAN

City planning in the broadest sense is a social process.[1] For plans to be accepted and acted upon, planners of all persuasions must become involved in social relations with other people, groups, and organizations. While the community decision process has been examined often from the viewpoints of the sociologist and the political scientist,[2] few analyses have been attempted of the interpersonal interactions intrinsic to the process of getting plans adopted and carried out. Yet, as John Friedmann (1969) has suggested:

In action-planning . . . the planner moves to the foreground as a person and autonomous agent. His success will in large measure depend on his skill in managing interpersonal relations.

Reprinted with permission of author and publisher from: Richard S. Bolan, "The Social Relations of the Planner," *Journal of the American Institute of Planners,* 37: 6 (November 1971), 386–96.

[1] For a small sample of literature contributing to this conclusion, see: Burke (1968); *Journal of the American Institute of Planners* (1969a, 1969b, 1969c); Kahn (1969); and Speigel (1968).

[2] See: Bolan (1969); Clark (1968); Clavel (1968); Connolly (1967); Curtis and Petras (1970); Mann (1964); and Rabinovitz (1969).

This article sketches a framework of factors involved in the planner's interpersonal relations, drawing on work in group dynamics, role theory, and organizational studies.[3] It is intended to be a general sketch and to suggest the range of variables influencing social relations in any planning setting. From such a framework, one can begin to imagine some of the implications that interpersonal relations holds for planning theory and method.

THE PLANNER'S SOCIAL NETWORK

At the outset, the planner can be viewed as part of a social interaction network which Talcott Parsons (1968) has suggested is comprised of four "analytically distinguishable aspects":

(1) a set of "units" which interact with each other; (2) a set of rules or other "code" factors, the terms of which structure both the orientations of the units

[3] For an excellent review of the literature on groups, see: Olmstead (1959) and Luft (1970). Basic sources include: Bales (1950); Cartwright and Zander (1953); Homans (1961); Berger and Luckman (1967); Sarbin (1954); Argyris (1962); March and Simon (1958); and Sullivan (1953).

and the interaction itself; (3) an ordered or patterned system or process of the interaction itself; and (4) an environment in which the system operates and with which systematic interchange takes place.[4]

The units, rules, system, and environment of the planner's social network are related in Figure 1. In the diagram, the planner is viewed as playing his role only when linked to a specific client group, although he must be concerned with interaction processes at two quite distinct levels: (1) the interchange within his client group; and (2) the interchange with the broader community (or, in Parsonian terms, the environment).[5]

Some planners may find it difficult to imagine the client as separate and distinct from the total community. Most work for government agencies and not for "private" clients. They would argue that they work for organizations charged with the responsibility of planning for the total public interest. Planners are not doctors; they do not deal with individuals.

It is argued here, however, that one can view any planner as serving a specific client group, even when such a group is labeled "government" or "planning commission." When a city planning commission makes a decision, it does not necessarily follow that the community at large will concur. This is also true if the city planner's client is the mayor or the governor. In short, government planning agencies are one interest group among many. They are specialized formal organizations whose manifest role is to perform a specific function for the entire community. The members of such organizations, however, tend to make decisions which justify and maintain their own position and power. Government decisions represent the interests of the group in power first, and a total public second.[6]

In the overall pattern of social relations, then, the planner has a first line of communication with his client. Together, they attempt to move the larger community decision system to achieve goals which are purportedly in the interests of the total community but also are always in the interests of the client. The relationships involved are subject to definitions of rules, or norms, and functional roles.

The client group holds certain expectations of professional performance from the planner, and the planner seeks to motivate the client group to appropriately respond to the demands of the environment. Discerning or interpreting such demands may be done by the client, the planner, or, more usually, both. Both attempt to interact with the broader community when widescale action is required to carry out plans.

PLANNER—CLIENT INTERACTION

Essentially the planner and the client group are viewed as a social

---

[4] It should be noted that I do not wholly subscribe to all the equilibrating tendencies implied in Parsons' statement nor are they necessary to the analysis.

[5] See, Lippitt, Watson, and Westley (1958), Chapters 1, 2, and 3. Also, Olmstead (1959), p. 139.

[6] This is not an unusual view of government. Talcott Parsons (1960: Chapter 1) suggests that government is one organizational entity among many. As might be expected, this view is shared by Jacques Maritain (1951: Chapters 1, 2, and 3).

structure bound together by *roles*—much as a family unit is defined by various roles and their relation to each other. It is also assumed that one cannot talk about the role of the planner except in reference to the role of the client group. As Thompson and Van Houton (1970) have suggested:

Role is always a social unit, part of a system or network of roles, and hence is always defined with regard to other roles. . . . The reciprocity involved in pairs of roles constitutes an essential "glue" which holds social relationships together. *Only so long as each role is the source of rewards for the other role can we expect the relationship to continue.* (Emphasis added.)

Also assumed in the planner-client interaction is a basic sense of *exchange.* The planner performs his role under the terms of an employment contract with his client.[7] The contract's terms express rewards and obligations, inducements and contributions.[8] As in any employment contract, the client sets forth the rules, norms, and specifications of the planner's participation (as shown in Figure 1), while the planner specifies the requirements and needs necessary to perform the role and, finally, acts out the role (Parsons, 1960). Although the terms of a planner's contract usually allow wide latitude in behavior, perceived violation of such terms will obviously damage (and possibly sever) the planner-client relationship.

[7] This, of course, is implicit in the definition of the term "client."
[8] See: Barnard (1938), Chapter 8; March and Simon (1958), pp. 47–81; Parsons (1960), Chapter 1; Levi-Strauss (1957), pp. 84–94.

THE CLIENT GROUP

The client group—that social entity which engages the planner's services—may be an individual, a loosely allied group, a formal organization, or a coalition of organizations or parts of organizations. It may represent narrow specific interests or broad general interests. It may be a sub-group which is part of a larger entity. Figure 2 illustrates some factors influencing the planner-client interaction.

Control and Guidance Capacities. An important aspect of the client group that planners usually ignore is its basic capacity to influence community decisions or alter community behavior. This capacity is a primary concern of professionals dealing with private clients, but is seldom considered when speaking of a city government or a public authority. Parsons has suggested four functional properties as essential for the maintenance and survival of a social system and of individual organizations within a system. Shown in Figure 2, these properties include: (1) performance capacities; (2) supportive capacities; (3) integrative capacities; and (4) managerial capacities.[9] These are vital, since too often planners propose plans which extend well beyond their client's abilities. These functional capacities are concerned not merely with legal powers but also with internal operating skills, strengths, and weaknesses. Many central city plans for urban renewal, for example, rest on an

[9] For Parsons these functions are, respectively: the adaptive, goal attainment, integrative and pattern maintenance functions.

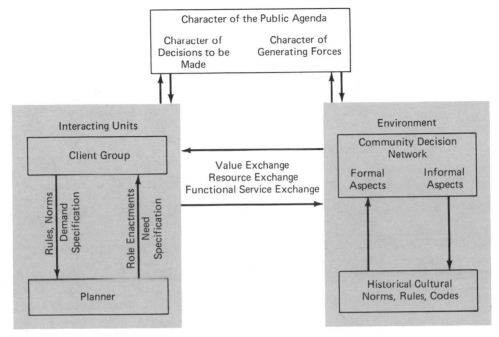

FIGURE 1. Basic Social Network in the Planning Process

assumption that the central city school board will improve its educational services, making them attractive for all segments of the metropolitan community. This has not been the case, and, consequently, a key assumption of these plans—the ability of the central city renewal authority to coordinate and control the central city school board—is invalidated.

Very often, in fact, the planner offers plans which express how he *wishes* the client would behave or might be capable of behaving, without really considering the client's realistic capacities or his state of readiness to accept new patterns of behavior. Failure to account for these realities can result in frustration and anxiety for all concerned. *External Competing Demands.*

Another important property of the client group stems from competing loyalties of individual members to other external roles. Planners often find themselves serving client groups whose members are volunteer, part-time actors. Frequently, members of planning groups also hold competing occupational or community roles, with ties to groups whose interests may conflict with the planning group interest. Conflict between the interests and norms of the different groups to which an individual belongs creates emotional stress. (Alleviation of this stress will tend to be in the direction of the strongest group ties.[10]) And, such stress can impede the cohesiveness and effectiveness of the group as a whole.

10 See Berelson and Steiner (1964), p. 329.

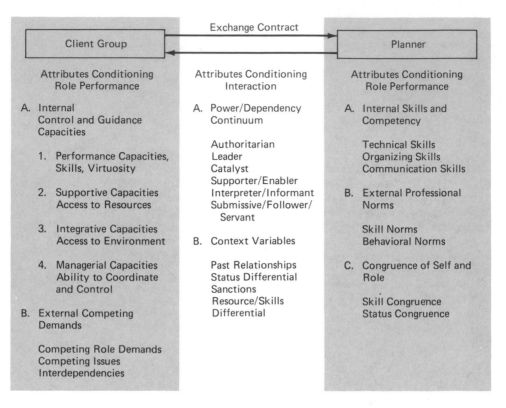

FIGURE 2.   Factors Influencing Planner and Client Interaction

The degree of commitment individual members hold toward the client group affects the internalization (and strength) of group norms and the capabilities of the group for task achievement.[11]

A client group often faces many issues simultaneously, limiting the resources (time, effort, and funds) available for any one issue. Client groups who can focus on planning around a single problem are usually able to perform more effectively than if their attention is diffused. In general, the more issues occupying the attention of a client group at any given moment, the less effective the effort on any single issue is likely to be.

Interdependencies with other decision units can be of two kinds; each is basically opposite in its effect. Supportive interdependencies would tend to aid the planning process and would include such examples as a planning agency's links to a federal agency which supplies financial and technical aid. A blocking relationship, on the other hand, might be the relationship of a planning agency with a city council which holds veto power over its budget

[11] See Olmstead (1959), pp. 111–14 and 121.

and perhaps over other activities as well.[12]

THE PLANNER

Figure 2 also suggests some basic factors influencing the performance of the planner's role.

Internal Skills and Competency. To assert that the greater the skills, the more effective the role performance is a trivial statement. What is not quite so obvious, however, is that technical skills alone do not make an effective planner. Social abilities (in the form of organizing and communications skills) are also required. Role performance depends on qualities of personality as well as job skills (as an illustration, one would not expect to see a jovial, back-slapping personality as a funeral director, regardless of his embalming skills).[13]

External Norms. Professional norms and doctrine exert important external influences on the planner. Not only will his behavior and role performance be judged by his client group and community, but also by his professional peers. The conflict between professional-centered norms and client-centered norms can create great tension in professional roles, especially those which are ambiguous or vague. While most planners respond directly to client norms and demands, many planners harbor strong feelings of guilt for failing to carry out the tasks and activities which professional doctrine has prescribed. One example, of course, is where professional doctrine has in-sisted the prime task of the planner is to prepare a comprehensive, long-range master plan, while specific clients have pressed other demands.

Congruence of Self and Role. Role theory holds that the effectiveness of role performance depends on the degree of congruence between self and role. When a planner is playing his role as planner, he should feel he is doing what "comes naturally" (or in current jargon, "doing his own thing"). If the planner does not enjoy or feel comfortable engaging in the planning process—that is, in interaction with the client group and the larger community, then the effectiveness of his role performance will probably be diminished. Congruence of self and role implies social status dimensions as well as functional dimensions (Smelser, 1961). Serious conflict between self and role results in what has been termed by Festinger (1957) as "cognitive dissonance" which may yield behavior that adversely affects role performance, such as withdrawal from or rejection of one or more of the reference groups underlying the conflict. A planner whose social and political background is strongly liberal would experience this type of conflict if employed by an extremely conservative client.

PLANNER-CLIENT RELATIONS

Conditioning the relationship between the planner and his client is an overarching climate of instability. One source of this is the limited commitment of individual members of the client group. Another equally important source is the ambiguous nature of the planner's role. Within a given client group, different mem-

---

[12] See Lippitt, Watson, and Wesley (1958), pp. 219–21 and 251–52.
[13] See Sarbin and Jones (1955), pp. 236–41.

bers can have quite different perceptions (and thus expectations) of the planner's role, and these can change over time.

One of the manifest goals of the planner-client interaction is to induce the client group to bring about change in the larger social network for its presumed progress and betterment. Also, since the planner operates in a real world rather than an ideal one, he is attempting to induce action which satisfies the status needs of his client. In short, the planner has a fundamental task of motivating his client group to change in its (the group's) own behalf. If city planners have not previously seen their role in this light, those in the social work and community organization professions have had this as a major concern. Planning, for these professionals, is a process in which the client is helped to identify his problems, develop an ability to analyze them, find the resources to deal with them, and take action with respect to them (Ross, 1955). In this view, engagement and commitment of the client are of greater importance, as a measure of professional skill and service, than the methodological skills with which the problem has been analyzed and a solution developed.

The Power/Dependency Continuum. The ability to affect the behavior of others is the essence of most conceptions of power. Thus, for a planner to affect his client group, the nature of the power relationship between them is fundamental. Richard Emerson (1962) views power as a *reciprocal* relation where the power of one person derives from the dependency of an-

other.[14] Figure 2 suggests a power continuum ranging from a totally authoritarian relationship to a totally submissive one. In an authoritarian relationship, the planner holds maximum power and the client group is maximally dependent. Such a relationship would be marked by broad, far-reaching expectations regarding the extent and nature of the planner's skills—the greater the dependency of the client, the broader the planner's policy influence.

Seldom, of course, is the planner really in an authoritarian position in relation to his client. Almost as rare is a totally submissive relationship, where the planner is totally dependent on the client, who would be in the authoritarian position.[15]

Usually the planner finds himself in a mixed power-dependency relationship with his client. The various terms suggested in Figure 2 illustrate this diversity: leader, catalyst, enabler, informant. The choice of which relation will prevail is not up to the planner alone but, rather, is the product of interaction with the client. In a real sense, each new planning episode shared by the planner and his client involves *learning* and consequent mutual adjustment of role perception. Each such adjustment alters the power-dependency status of the actors. Thus, the power relationship is constantly in a state of flux.

Context Variables. A number of situational variables operate on the power relationship, defining both its

14 For other work on the concept of power as it relates to this discussion, see, Bell, Edwards, and Wagner (1969).

15 For one example, see Banfield (1961), pp. 154–58.

context and its boundaries. Of primary importance is the past history of the relationship or the degree to which needs and demands of each party in the relationship have been fulfilled in previous episodes. This history can exert both positive and negative influences on the current status of the relationship as the parties keep score of credits (plus and minus) from prior episodes.

Another key factor is the perceived status differential between the client group and the planner. If the client group enjoys high status in the community, it is difficulty to imagine the planner in an authoritarian relationship. Presumably, such a high status is held because of past success, social class of members, legal authority, control of significant political or economic resources, or a combination of any of these. There is little need or motivation for a high status client group to defer to the planner. One would expect, in these circumstances, that the planner's role would tend toward the submissive end of the continuum. Only when the planner serves his perceived social inferiors is the authoritarian relation likely to occur.[16] A client group low in status has a higher degree of dependency on the planner's skills and must pay greater attention to survival needs and enhancement opportunities.

A third variable consists of the sanctions available to the planner to discourage or raise the cost of "negative" behavior by his client. Doctors, and lawyers to a lesser degree, tend to have role and power relationships with clients which come very close to the authoritarian end of the continuum. Among numerous reasons for this is the client's perception of fairly substantial costs in not behaving as the professional has suggested (in the medical situation the client's life may be at stake). For the planner, it is always difficult to convey the dire results of negative social action (or inaction) since the planner must admit to only a limited understanding of a complex environment and to a large degree of uncertainty in his predictions. The planner is always in the position of having to offer more than one prescription, and each usually entails as many uncertainties and risks as no action at all.

Some research efforts have suggested that in conditions of great uncertainty and complexity, the most effective problem-solving efforts are found in groups where status and power differentials are minimal; that is, where participants are viewed as peers or equals.[17] This effectiveness is thought to be due to a number of factors: the openness of communication; the respect afforded the ideas each individual offers to the group; the cohesiveness arising from the social gratification group membership provides; and the understanding of and commitment of members to decisions in which they have participated. One normative inference that might be drawn is that more effective planner-client interaction might be achieved through efforts to equalize status and power both within the client group and

---

[16] This is not to suggest that an authoritarian role will necessarily occur; other factors will be operative. The planner, himself, may shun the role because of personal value characteristics.

[17] See: Lippitt and White (1952); Kelley and Thibaut (1954); and Bavelas (1953).

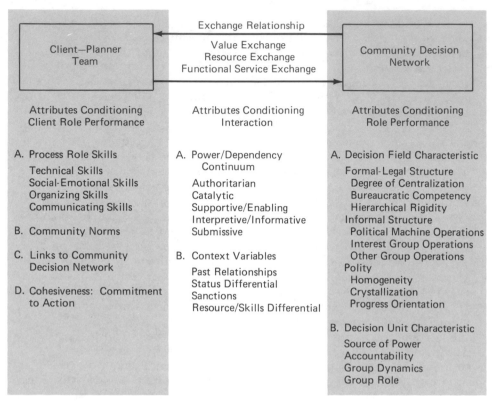

FIGURE 3.   Factors Influencing Client and Community Interaction

between the planner and client group members. Attempting to alter power-dependency relationships to achieve parity requires special group dynamics skills, as well as skill in controlling the exchange of resources (including information). The problem situation or agenda item itself might be the source of such alteration (by alteration of the influence of sanctions); alternatively, the social context of the group might be the basis for changing power relations (by making group membership more rewarding or attractive).[18]

CLIENT—COMMUNITY INTERACTION

The community decision field has been analyzed by many authors.[19] Figure 3 lists some basic structural factors affecting community political behavior, including the distinguishing characteristics of the total community decision field as well as the social attributes of particular decision units within the field. These internal characteristics will not be discussed further here, since it is the relationships of the client-plan-

[18] See: Emerson (1962); also Thompson and Van Houten (1970), pp. 149–53.

[19] For a summary framework, see Bolan (1969).

ner team with the community decision network that we are concerned with.

In specific instances, the client group may also comprise the decision unit (planners working directly for a mayor with highly centralized powers for example). Often, however, the client group and the planner together are involved in attempting to stir action in some other decision-making body (a redevelopment agency, for example, must secure city council adoption of an urban renewal plan). Occasionally, a planner may work for more than one client group in the same community, thereby providing direct links between the two groups. (Such a planner is quickly in trouble if his clients should come into conflict.)

RELATIONSHIP TO COMMUNITY DECISION NETWORK

The planner approaches the community decision network as an *agent* of his client. Their joint basic objective is to activate the broader community to change on the client's behalf. In doing this, the planner and client are acting together. Under certain circumstances, the planner might play a leading role; in others the client may be required to play the major role. This relationship is analogous to that between the lawyer and his client when they face the larger judicial system together. The client can often best express his values and objectives, while the professional provides the technical considerations to support them.

The notion that the community is asked to change on the client's behalf is a subtle one. Most planners would

assume, for example, that a neighborhood plan benefits a neighborhood rather than a planning commission which may be promulgating the plan. But the motivation of the planning commission in pursuing a program for a specific neighborhood is crucial. It is superficial to say that the area is blighted or has critical problems to be solved. The planning commission, in giving consideration to such difficulties, is ultimately seeking the approbation of some or all of its varied constituencies as a way of maintaining or enhancing its own legitimation and status.

Attributes Conditioning Interaction. Once more, the power-dependency continuum is vital, and again the planner seldom finds situations involving the extreme ends of the scale. Even in societies with highly centralized (even dictatorial) decision systems, a totally authoritarian relationship, in which the planner and the client have all the power, is rare. Seldom can deference be absolute without massive force. A totally submissive relationship, in which the planner and his client have no power, is equally unlikely, since such a planner-client could not long survive in a pluralistic, competitive environment—it would simply lose too often.

The planner and his client, abroad in the larger community, usually find themselves between the two extremes —attempting to initiate and control exchange tasks including enlistment of supporters, development of consensus groups among supportive elements, exchange of sanctions and inducements, and other forms of social negotiation. They attempt to assemble the coalition that will move the action system.

An important distinction should be noted here. Previously in discussing relations between the planner and his client, it was suggested that efforts to *equalize* power and status relationships would enhance the problem-solving or task-achievement capability of the group. In dealing with the larger community, however, the effort is to assemble power (through coalition building) and then to expend it (through exchanges required to secure positive action). This distinction recognizes that the much higher degree of pluralism and competition to be found in the community contributes to the survival of the client group as an important latent goal. The client group hopes that the final result of this process will be a net positive *gain* of power which can result in a more secure and more effective position for the next issue to be faced.

Figure 3 also lists the variables which influence the power-dependency continuum of the client group vis-a-vis the larger community. As before, these include the past history of the client group, the sanctions available to it, its social status, and its legal and financial resources.

It is important to note that it is the role and status of the *client* that are governing here—not those of the planner. The planner may affect client status and role, but in the eyes of the community, he is an agent of the client group which means that, to outsiders, he is an integral part of it. He thus inherits his client's previous history and current posture in the community.

Client Role Performance. The situational attributes affecting the client's role in the community decision field are shown in Figure 3.

The skills involved in the planner-client interaction are extrapolated to the larger scene, but these skills must be employed in ways consistent with the community's perception and expectations (one does not expect a school board to be issuing plans for highways, even though it might be within its staff's technical competence to do so). Thus, the community norms applicable to the client group can act to constrain behavior. External links (such as those to federal agencies) have already been cited as affecting internal relations within the client group. They are also important levers in relations with the larger community. Finally, and of most importance, the impact of the client group on the community will be only as strong as the client group's cohesiveness and strength of purpose. Should the community actors detect cleavages or dissension within the client group, their own engagement (either in support or opposition) is likely to be substantially altered.

THE COMMUNITY DECISION NETWORK

The complexity of the community decision network can be formidable, especially when one is trying to conceive of mechanisms that will induce interaction leading to positive implementation of plans. How to build an effective coalition requires a high degree of sophistication regarding roles, sentiments, capacities, and resources of organizations and individuals within a given community. Moreover, it is always risky to assume that the network is in any way stable or moving toward some "steady-state" equilibrium. It is in continual dynamic motion, but this

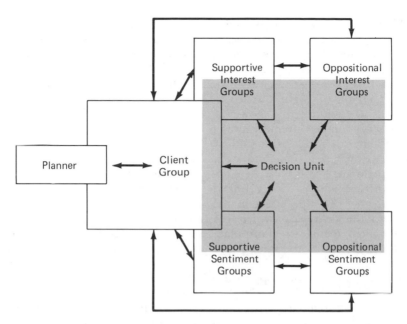

FIGURE 4.   Illustrative Conception of Decision Field Structure

is not to suggest that it defies organization or control.

One way to conceptualize the decision field is illustrated in Figure 4.[20] At the center of all interactions are the specific actors who will cast the decisive votes in deciding to adopt and implement a plan. These actors comprise the decision unit previously referred to. In some instances, the planner's client group may also be the decision unit; this greatly simplifies the situation. In very complex settings, there may be more than one decisive, or requisite, group of actors. In any event, these people are the key individuals who will have to be moved to act.

Figure 4 suggests that there may be overlaps between the decision unit and other groups of actors. For example, a member of a city council may also be in real estate or active

[20] This conception is adapted from Warren (1965), pp. 317–20.

in a labor union. Ideally, such actors might also be induced to join the client group itself ("co-optation" in Selznick's [1948] terms, for example, placing a key member of a city council on an advisory body to the planning commission). There exists within both formal and informal structures, a group of actors who can be identified as sharing sentiment or interests in any given planning effort. Such actors would make up a group of "supportive" elements. This supportive group can be further differentiated as (1) cooperating *interest* groups who stand to benefit directly and materially from change; and (2) cooperating *sentiment* groups who see indirect benefit in symbolic or ideological terms or in some potential adjustment in status.

Such cooperative relationships require *mutual* gratifications. Cooperating actors, in short, are part of an exchange process represented by the arrows in Figure 4. Behavior and actions which support the planner-client team always have a price. For actors who will realize direct benefits, this exchange is most obvious and predictable. For those who merely share sentiments, however, the exchange can be extremely subtle, and actions can range from mildly passive to overtly active (and even violent) support. The level of emotional involvement is highly linked to the degree of value stress in the plan and the degree to which the planner-client team can manipulate or control the emotional symbols involved.

Finally, there are opposition groups. These actors have to be accounted for in some form of interaction relationship, unless they are so lacking in resources or political skills as to constitute no threat to the planning enterprise. Since such situations are rare, opponents must also be dealt with in terms of some form of reciprocal exchange. Opponents can be differentiated between those who stand to be directly penalized in some way by a plan and those who disagree with a plan on principle. As suggested before, the behavior of the former is usually much more predictable than the latter. Negotiation, bargaining, and compromise become intrinsic and time-consuming elements of the planning process.

THE CHARACTER OF THE PUBLIC AGENDA

The nature of the issue facing the client and the community affects behavior in all relationships and in all stages of social network development. For simple issues affecting few people, costing little money, and seeming to entail few risks, the social relations of the actors may become quite simple, and, indeed, many may not arise at all. Routine administrative decisions fall into this category. But as complexities, risks, effects, and value stresses rise, social relations multiply and spread throughout the community.

Also involved are the *kinds* of stresses and the *sources* of stress, both of which will affect relationships between the systems. A civil rights issue arising from a specific neighborhood affects the community, the client, and the planner in different ways than an issue developed by a planning staff as the result of a technical survey. The pressures of an aggrieved neighborhood or minority group may produce greater *felt* stress than, say, a plan for a series of downtown parking lots. Presumably, in such cases, motivation to act is quite different for all participants. The planner develops different relationships with his client when the issue is forced on the client by outside pressures than when the issue is one of the client's own making. In the former case, the client may be faced with the task of reconciling a number of competing interests; in the latter, he is very likely to be concerned with the maintenance and enhancement of his own interest (or furthering his version of the "public interest").

PLANNING TASK STRATEGIES

Using this conceptual framework of interaction, the planner can approach his role with greater awareness of situational variables facing him. Consequently, his criteria for selection of planning method becomes somewhat less influenced by his traditional utopian instincts or pedantic tendencies, and more concerned with the relationship of planning method to the processes of social interaction in decision-making. None of the many possible strategies of planning style (Bolan, 1967), can be ruled out, but it is evident that, in considering our more comprehensive and more sophisticated methodologies, we make a number of simplistic assumptions about the planner's required social interaction.

To a varying degree, different planning methods implicitly assume differing levels of pluralism and competition within society. They also entail implicit assumptions about the client's role and status within the local political ecology. The classical comprehensive planning method, for example, tends to make the most extreme assumptions, seemingly endowing the planner's client with extensive social capacities. Those utilizing this method normally presume the client's rather complete ability to coordinate and control a substantial portion of the community's resources. The client is presumed to exercise broad, sweeping powers to regulate wide segments of private life. In harshest terms, the classical comprehensive method would seem most appropriate to a highly centralized, authoritarian government.

The classical comprehensive method also makes extreme assumptions about the planner himself. The very notion of a long-range, comprehensive plan requires the client to make broad-scale commitments, the de-

tailed consequences of which he cannot possibly know. He is thus presumed to relinquish to the planner a great deal of his (and his successors') decision-making power. Also entailed in the classical model is a society with a stable ideology, relatively homogenous interests and goals, and a substantial degree of societal and interest group deference to governmental authority. The community is presumed to defer to the planner.

Each of these assumptions is relaxed by degrees as planning methods are adjusted toward opportunism or incrementalism. The presumption of client control over society and resources is abandoned as pluralism and interest group or factional competition are presumed to increase. In pure opportunism, virtual laissez-faire conditions are assumed with the planner's client competing on roughly even terms with all other interests.

Variations in program content (scope, time-horizon, means-ends emphasis, and information selectivity) can be comparably analyzed in relation to situational variables. Wide-scope, long-term horizons and emphasis on goals, rather than means, imply assumptions about the planner, the client, and the community corresponding to those suggested for the comprehensive method. These assumptions can be adjusted or relaxed to provide better accord with actual conditions.

Perhaps more important, however, is the issue of the appropriate mix of planning and *other skills*. Clearly, the less status, power, and resources held by the client, the more the client is in need of *organizing and political skills rather than planning skills* (in the traditional city planner's use of the term). This has been a major factor in the experience of advocacy planners (Peattie, 1968). At the other end of the scale, where the planner is employed by a highly centralized, authoritarian government exercising major control over resources (public and private), strictly technical planning skills might prevail. Society under these circumstances is already tightly organized and has delegated a substantial share of authority to the planner's client. In this situation, technically competent planning (again in the traditional sense) might be the best political strategy (presuming adequate backup by a competent, loyal military force).

The issue, however, is more focused in the pluralistic communities prevalent in the United States. To what extent does the planner employ political and organizing skills over and above his purely technical skills? What, in his training and education, provides him with the rudiments of such skills? In what circumstances do role expectations and client capabilities force him into developing and exercising such skills? The framework developed in this article implies that such skills are an integral part of the planning process in the broadest sense of the term.[21]

Hopefully, this framework of the social relations of the planner will provide a useful operational guide for the practicing planner. It should be viewed with some caution, however. Abstract, simplified views of complex social arrangements can be highly mischievous if followed blind-ly. The framework should be looked upon primarily as a preliminary hypothesis for future research. It is immediately useful, however, in that once again it emphasizes the poverty of traditional approaches of city planning which cling to a naive, simple view of social change and societal decision-making.

To prepare a plan is to promote a cause. This is never a purely technical task; nor is it ever done simply in the privacy of a planning office. It is a social process and necessarily entails social relations.

REFERENCES

ALTSHULER, A. (1965). *The City Planning Process*. Ithaca: Cornell University Press.

ARGYRIS, C. (1962). *Interpersonal Competence and Organizational Effectiveness*. Homewood, Ill.: Richard D. Irwin, Inc.

BALES, R. F. (1950). *Interaction Process Analysis*. Cambridge, Mass.: Addison-Wesley Press.

BANFIELD, E. C. (1961). *Political Influence*. New York: The Free Press.

BARNARD, C. (1938). *The Functions of the Executive*. Cambridge, Mass.: Harvard University Press.

BAVELAS, A. (1953). "Communication Patterns in Task Oriented Groups." Pp. 493–506 in Cartwright and Zander, eds., *Group Dynamics*.

BELL, R., D. V. EDWARDS, and R. H. WAGNER (1969). *Political Power: A Reader in Theory and Research*. New York: The Free Press.

BERELSON, B. and G. A. STEINER (1964). *Human Behavior: An Inventory of Scientific Findings*. New York: Harcourt, Brace and World Inc.

BERGER, P. and T. LUCKMAN (1967). *The Social Construction of Reality*. Garden City, N.Y.: Doubleday & Co., Inc., Anchor Books Edition.

BOLAN, R. S. (1967). "Emerging Views of Planning." *Journal of the American Institute of Planners*, 33 (July), 233–45.

---

[21] For this same point, see Friedmann (1969), p. 317.

BOLAN, R. S. (1969). "Community Decision Behavior: The Culture of Planning." *Journal of the American Institute of Planners,* 35 (September), 301–10.

BURKE, E. M. (1968). "Citizen Participation Strategies." *Journal of the American Institute of Planners,* 34 (September), 287–94.

CARTWRIGHT, D. and A. ZANDER (1953). *Group Dynamics: Research and Theory.* Evanston, Ill.: Row, Peterson and Company.

CLARK, T. N., ed. (1968). *Community Structure and Decision Making.* San Francisco: Chandler Publishing Company.

CLAVEL, P. (1968). "Planners and Citizen Boards: Some Applications of Social Theory to the Problem of Plan Implementation." *Journal of the American Institute of Planners,* 34 (May), 130–39.

CONNOLLY, W. E. (1967). *Political Science and Ideology.* New York: Atherton Press.

CURTIS, J. E., and J. W. PETRAS (1970). "Community Power, Power Studies and the Sociology of Knowledge." *Human Organization,* 29 (Fall), 204–18.

EMERSON, R. (1962). "Power-Dependence Relations." *American Sociological Review,* 27 (February), 31–40.

FESTINGER, L. (1957). *A Theory of Cognitive Dissonance.* Evanston, Ill.: Row, Peterson.

FRIEDMANN, J. (1969). "Notes on Societal Action." *Journal of the American Institute of Planners,* 35 (September), 311–18.

HOMANS, G. C. (1961). *Social Behavior: Its Elementary Forms.* New York: Harcourt, Brace and World.

Special Issue: *Journal of the American Institute of Planners* (1969a). "The Cities, The Black and The Poor." 35 (March).

Special Issue: *Journal of the American Institute of Planners* (1969b). "Planning and Citizen Participation." 35 (July).

Special Issue: *Journal of the American Institute of Planners* (1969c). "The Practical Uses of Planning Theory: A Symposium." 35 (September).

KAHN, A. J. (1969). *Theory and Practice of Social Planning.* New York: Russell Sage Foundation.

KELLEY, H. and J. THIBAUT (1954). "Experimental Studies of Group Problem Solving and Process." In G. Lindzey, ed., *Handbook of Social Psychology.* Cambridge, Mass.: Addison-Wesley Press. Vol. 2.

LEVI-STRAUSS, C. (1957). "The Principle of Reciprocity." Pp. 84–94 in L. Closer and

B. Rosenberg, eds. *Sociological Theory.* New York: The Macmillan Company.

LIPPITT, R. and R. K. WHITE (1952). "An Experimental Study of Leadership and Group Life." In G. Swanson, T. Newcomb, and E. Hartley, eds., *Readings in Social Psychology.* New York: Henry Holt & Co.

LIPPITT, R., J. WATSON, and B. WESTLEY (1958). *The Dynamics of Planned Change.* New York: Harcourt, Brace and World.

LUFT, J. (1970). *Group Processes: An Introduction to Group Dynamics,* Second edition. Palo Alto, Calif.: National Press Books.

MANN, L. D. (1964). "Studies in Community Decision-Making." *Journal of the American Institute of Planners,* 30 (February), 58–65.

MARCH, J. G. and H. A. SIMON (1958). *Organizations.* New York: John Wiley and Sons.

MARITAIN, J. (1951). *Man and the State.* Chicago: University of Chicago Press.

OLMSTEAD, M. S. (1959). *The Small Group.* New York: Random House, Inc.

PARSONS, T. (1960). *Structure and Process in Modern Society.* Glencoe: The Free Press.

PARSONS, T. et al., eds. (1964). *Theories of Society.* Glencoe: The Free Press. Vol. 1.

PARSONS, T. (1968). "Social Interaction." *International Encyclopedia of the Social Sciences.* New York: The Macmillan Company and the Free Press. Vol. 7.

PEATTIE, L. R. (1968). "Reflections on Advocacy Planning." *Journal of the American Institute of Planners,* 34 (March), 80–88.

RABINOVITZ, F. F. (1969). *City Politics and Planning.* New York: Atherton Press.

ROSS, M. (1955). *Community Organization: Theory and Principles.* New York: Harper and Brothers.

SARBIN, T. R. (1954). "Role Theory." In G. Lindzey, ed., *Handbook of Social Psychology.* Cambridge, Mass.: Addison-Wesley Press. Vol. 1.

SARBIN, T. R. and D. S. JONES (1955). "An Experimental Analysis of Role Behavior." *Journal of Abnormal and Social Psychology,* 51, 236–41.

SELZNICK, P. (1948). "Foundations of the Theory of Organization." *American Sociological Review,* 13 (February), 33–35.

SMELSER, W. T. (1961). "Dominance as a Factor in Achievement and Perception in Cooperative Problem Solving Interactions." *Journal of Abnormal and Social Psychology*, 62, 535–42.

SPEIGEL, H. B. C. (1968). *Citizen Participation in Urban Development: Vol. 1, Concepts and Issues*. Washington: Center for Community Affairs, National Training Laboratory Institute for Applied Behavioral Science.

SULLIVAN, H. S. (1953). *The Interpersonal Theory of Psychiatry*. New York: W. W. Norton & Co.

THOMPSON, J. D. and D. R. VAN HOUTEN (1970). *The Behavioral Sciences: An Interpretation*. Reading, Mass.: Addison-Wesley Press.

WARREN, R. L. (1965). *The Community in America*. Chicago: Rand McNally & Co.

13 Community Action: A Case Study in Advocacy and Social Relations

THE NEIGHBORHOOD COORDINATORS

Neil Gilbert

Eight neighborhood coordinators, with their respective staffs of two to six assistant coordinators, work out of Pittsburgh's eight target areas. These individuals come from varied backgrounds: four were experienced social workers, two were public housing administrators, one was a Peace Corps volunteer, and one was an editor of a community newspaper. All have college degrees, and none live in the neighborhoods in which they work. Thus, they are "outsiders" in almost every sense.

These coordinators have two key qualities in common: a stamina that allows them to work about sixty hours a week, and a temperament that permits them to function under conditions of "chaotic ambiguity." This ambiguity is reflected even in the title "coordinator." The verb "to coordinate" is variously defined as meaning to equalize, to harmonize, to adjust, or to organize; and the co-

Reprinted with permission of author and publisher from: Neil Gilbert, *Clients or Constituents* (San Francisco: Jossey Bass, Inc., 1970), pp. 69–89.

ordinator is expected to fulfill all four functions—organizing the citizens, adjusting the service system, harmonizing the relationships between citizens' groups and between citizens and agencies, and equalizing the opportunity for citizens to participate in community decision making. These tasks are, obviously, not always congruent; often, choices must be made between them, as between harmony and equality; and, in making this type of choice, there are no established guidelines to follow and no clear set of priorities. The chaotic dimension of this position is largely manifest in the day-to-day crises that emerge in working with the poor. For example, many cases of individual problems come to the attention of the coordinator; although some may be handled by referral (to one of the service components in the neighborhood center), others require immediate and personal assistance. The coordinator must frequently take the initiative and the time to obtain anything from a bus to a bed, to find shelter for an evicted tenant, or to have the heat turned on in a client's home. . . .

181

SELECTION PROCESS

The selection of neighborhood co-ordinators was a sensitive process. The citizens, the contracting agencies, and the Mayor's Committee on Human Resources, Inc., [MCHR] each had their particular interests to be satisfied, the main one being the employment of an individual loyal to their particular organization. The citizens were interested in a person they could work with and trust, one who was strongly committed to popular participation. The coordinating agencies, for their part, sought a person acceptable to the citizens but whose first loyalty would be to the agency, a person not so committed to popular participation that he would, for example, support the citizens in an attack on the agency. The MCHR, as the official city-wide agency responsible for both the co-ordination and the direct-service aspects of the antipoverty program, is in a somewhat tenuous position if and when conflict arises between these components; both would turn to the MCHR for support, using whatever forms of political pressures that are available—which would make life at the MCHR somewhat uncomfortable and could even jeopardize the entire program. Thus, the MCHR had an implicit preference for a coordinator predisposed toward a cooperative, as opposed to a conflict-oriented, approach to his job, a preference that essentially coincided with that of the contracting agencies. . . .

STRUCTURAL RESTRAINTS

The selection process illustrates how the coordinator is responsible to three groups, with overlapping but not coincident interests. This is a structural arrangement that operates to divide loyalties, confuse roles, and inhibit functioning. In evaluating the coordination structure, the citizens of at least one neighborhood explicitly noted that it creates an "inoperative relationship," one in which the coordinator "is torn among the wishes of the citizens' council, the financial control of the funding [contracting] agency, and the policies of the Mayor's Committee on Human Resources." [1]

If not totally inoperative, the structure is certainly unwieldy, anchored more in the principle of control than of action. Each of the three groups employing the coordinator wants to know, in terms of its own needs, what was accomplished yesterday, what is being worked on today, and what is planned for tomorrow. These demands are realized in the form of reports, phone calls, meetings, and a sea of paperwork; the coordinator spends an inordinate amount of time just trying to stay afloat. Multiple accounting of this sort sacrifices time, energy, and productivity to control, and, as a by-product, inhibits flexibility and action. This common bureaucratic phenomenon is here intensified by the presence of three sets of organizational interests and by the volatile political nature of the job.[2] To escape or minimize the pressures to

1 South Oakland Citizen's Council, "An Evaluation of Neighborhood Coordination," March 1967, p. 2 (mimeographed).
2 For example, see Robert K. Merton, *Social Theory and Social Structure* (Glencoe, Ill.: Free Press, 1964), pp. 197–202; and Peter M. Blau, *Bureaucracy in Modern Society* (New York: Random House, 1963), pp. 105–110.

satisfy a diversity of interests, the coordinator must often act on the principle of least friction, or he must maneuver furtively. Sometimes, through selective response to one or another of these pressures, the coordinator is able to guide his own course of action; but this involves the willingness and—more important —the ability to play politics.

Political considerations enter in as seemingly simple a task as designating the outdoor sign for the office. Should it be identified with the citizens' council, the contracting agency, or the MCHR? If all three, in what order should they appear? Who should get the biggest letters? Issues like this, which have little effect upon the core of the program, nip away with vexation at its husk.

More significant and complex problems exist, particularly the ones generated by the role of the coordinating agencies within the overall antipoverty structure. These agencies not only employ the coordinating staff, but they also contract with the MCHR to provide direct services in program areas like housing, employment, and family life. In the North Side, for example, the employment, family service, and coordination units all are contracted to Neighborhood Centers Association, a local settlement house. The North Side coordinator, as he aids citizens in their evaluatory review of proposed or actual programs in these areas, is thereby faced with a distinct and serious conflict of interests. The citizens are entitled to his services and honesty, his integrity and professionalism call for objectivity, while his job security, economic welfare, and bureaucratic status are controlled by a settlement house that is certainly not anxious

to have criticism directed at any of its operations.

In some areas, such as the North Side, East Liberty-Garfield, and the Hill, the contracting agency also employs neighborhood development units that are funded outside the antipoverty structure (through the Community Chest or other sources). The philosophy and responsibilities of neighborhood development and coordination staffs are very similar, any difference being more of degree than of kind. Generally, the neighborhood development worker provides service to smaller or sectional groups within the larger target area, and the coordinator focuses upon community-wide organizations. However, there are many exceptions to this arrangement, with both staffs often working simultaneously on both levels. Although the stated goal is to maintain a cooperative and reinforcing relationship between these units, neither is functionally dependent upon the other for fulfillment of its specific tasks.[3] Instead, both often compete for the time, energy, and confidence of citizen leaders, and both seek special recognition for the roles they play in whatever local victories are achieved. Such a structure places the contracting agency in a particularly strategic position to control both staffs, and, through them, the citizenry; for example, by physically separating these units in different facilities, regulating the flow of information between them, and judi-

3 The implications of "functional autonomy" for intraorganizational conflict are discussed by Alvin W. Gouldner in "Organizational Analysis," *Sociology Today*, ed. Robert K. Merton, Leonard Broom, and Leonard S. Cottrell, Jr. (New York: Harper, 1965), pp. 419–23.

ciously utilizing incentives and sanctions, the agency, if so inclined, could discourage the development and consolidation of power in one community-wide citizens' group.

Although the formal structure does not facilitate clearly defined bureaucratic relationships, interdependence, and cooperation, it is possible that a harmonious relationship between coordination and neighborhood development staffs could be established informally. To a large extent, the success of such a structure would depend upon personal variables such as age, experience, and attitudes; the staffs could transcend the formal structure and collaborate in a fruitful effort if these variables were complementary. For instance, this result could be expected if either the coordinator or the neighborhood development worker were clearly the "top man" by virtue of status characteristics, skill, and personality, and the other were clearly the junior partner. Informal hierarchy would fill the void of formal hierarchy. However, in reality, the nature of these positions is such that they demand similar individuals.

Thus, the coordination structure in almost half of Pittsburgh's target neighborhoods provides fertile ground for internal conflict. The fact that internal conflict has been confined to seemingly minor skirmishes rather than being expressed in all-out warfare testifies not to any logic of structure, but to the ingenuity of the professionals involved and their ability to operate under strain.

RUNNING THE ENTERPRISE

In addition to organizing citizens and helping them to plan and evaluate neighborhood services, the co-

ordinator is responsible for assuring that these component services are effectively working together in a comprehensive effort to eradicate poverty. Ideally, this means that the units must be willing to pool their skills, knowledge, manpower, and resources in a cooperative venture. To illustrate, take the hypothetical case of a welfare client entering the neighborhood service center to report to the receptionist that the ceiling in her apartment has collapsed, damaging some of the furniture. What should follow is something like this: the case is referred to a family service worker, who gets all the details from the client; the neighborhood lawyer is asked by the family service worker to find out if the landlord is responsible for making repairs and paying the cost of damages; in the course of his investigation, the lawyer learns that the landlord owns a number of slum dwellings in the neighborhood; he reports this to the coordinator, who, in turn, calls a meeting with the citizens' housing committee to discuss the problem; the committee decides to approach the landlord, requesting that he upgrade his properties, but he refuses; the health aides are sent out to inspect the properties, the lawyer is asked to review the ramifications of a rent strike, and the citizens form a picket line around the landlord's home in suburbia. While the landlord is taking an impromptu vacation in Florida, the family service worker has not forgotten the client; the public-assistance consultant is asked to obtain a relocation grant, the employment worker is called upon to place the client in a work-training program, the client's children are enrolled in the local day-care center, and other local resources, such as homemakers and planned parenthood, are also utilized in an exhaustive effort to move the client out of poverty.

This example suggests how the component services might be integrated in a comprehensive attack on poverty—an ideal rarely achieved. In the actual situation, it would be discovered that the lawyer could provide service to the individual client and thereby advise on the landlord's responsibility for damages. However, he could not counsel the citizens' committee on the legality of a rent strike, since providing service to a group is against agency policy; the rationale is that, by pooling resources, the group could afford to buy this service in a private market. The health aides would need organizational permission to leave the area that they were currently inspecting in order to focus an intense effort upon the landlord's properties, dispersed throughout the neighborhood; their moving would conflict with the Allegheny County Health Department's service strategy, which involves saturating the neighborhood with inspections section-by-section. The Planned Parenthood unit could provide immediate birth control assistance only if the client was graced by holy matrimony; otherwise, this agency's policy dictates that certain procedures, such as obtaining parental consent for girls under 21 or somehow establishing that they are "clearly emancipated," first be fulfilled. Although the public assistance consultant could check on the availability of a relocation grant, like the others he has no power to transcend the rules and regulations of his agency, and grants of this nature are generally not provided by the Alle-

gheny County Department of Public Assistance.

Each service unit is thus part of an autonomous organization with its own goals, policies, and needs—which are at times different than those of the coordinator, the client, and the citizens. These service units work together in the sense of being situated, usually, under one roof in one neighborhood service center. Although this proximity facilitates communications, it does not dictate cooperation. The neighborhood service center is structured to operate not along the lines of traditional bureaucratic organization, but as an "enterprise"— an impermanent and loose association of relatively autonomous organizations seeking to achieve common goals.[4] Four important features of the enterprise are: (a) *Complexity*—The neighborhood-center enterprise represents a mixture of public, private, civic, and religious organizations. Some are neighborhood-based, others have city, county, or nation-wide affiliations. The sheer number of participants is enough to complicate adminstration.   (b)   *Authority*—The participants are not bound to a formal hierarchy of positions based upon the element of rational-legal authority. Thus, informal relationships are more significant and be-

---

4 For an analysis of the "enterprise" concept as it applies to urban renewal, see George S. Duggar, "The Relation of Local Government Structure to Urban Renewal," and Jewel Bellush and Murray Hausknecht, "Entrepreneurs and Urban Renewal: The New Men of Power," in *Urban Renewal: People Politics and Planning*, ed. Jewel Bellush and Murray Hausknecht (New York: Anchor Books, 1967), pp. 179–88, 209–223. This concept is also discussed by Scott Greer in *Urban Renewal and American Cities* (New York: Bobbs-Merrill, 1967), p. 36.

havior less predictable than in a traditional bureaucracy. For example, in one neighborhood, the director of a family service unit even refused to allow the coordination staff (who were professional social workers like herself) access to case files because of personal incompatibility. (c) *Reciprocity*—The lack of formal hierarchy means that some element other than rational-legal authority is needed to coordinate membership activities. In the enterprise, this element is reciprocity; members respond to one another more on the basis of mutual benefit than of individual advantage. This type of relationship may the established if members have similar norms and conceptions of reality and if a degree of solidarity exists within the organization.[5] (d) *Fluidity*—Organizational participation in the enterprise may expand and constrict because of spontaneous or prearranged action. Such shifting of participation may reflect an agreed-upon plan (as with the Summer Headstart program) or an arbitrary unilateral decision (as when the Bureau of Employment Security, without notice, reduced its staff commitment to the neighborhood employment units).

COMPLIANCE STRUCTURE

As one participant among many in the neighborhood-center enterprise, the coordinator does not possess coercive power and has only very indirect, if any, access to remunerative power. Thus, compliance with his administrative directives is not very much influenced by the threat of punishment or by the incentive of financial gain. Instead, it is the "ideal motives of solidarity" (Weber) or the "inculcation of motives" (Barnard) upon which the authority structure rests.[6] Essentially, this involves the use of normative power—the allocation and manipulation of symbolic rewards and deprivations—to produce acceptance or rejection, encouragement or embarrassment.[7]

Socialization is an important mechanism for ensuring the effectiveness of normative power. Through this process, organizational norms are internalized and commitments to goals are developed.[8] At the beginning of the Pittsburgh program, training and orientation sessions were held for the professional and nonprofessional staff of most agencies participating in the enterprise. These sessions ostensibly focused upon the etiology of poverty and the community-action strategy for attacking this social disease. Most significant here

---

[5] Coordination through reciprocity as an alternative to a bureaucratic hierarchy is discussed by Robert A. Dahl and Charles E. Lindblom in *Politics, Economics, and Welfare* (New York: Harper, 1953), pp. 237–38.

[6] Max Weber, *The Theory of Social and Economic Organization*, ed. Talcott Parsons (New York: Free Press, 1947), p. 325; Chester Barnard, *The Functions of the Executive* (Cambridge: Harvard University Press, 1938), pp. 149–53. Also see Terence Hopkins, "Bureaucratic Authority: The Convergence of Weber and Barnard," *Sociological Theory*, eds. Lewis Coser and Bernard Rosenberg (New York: Macmillan, 1957), pp. 159–71.

[7] Amitai Etzioni suggests that there are two kinds of normative power: pure normative power and social power. The latter is more common in horizontal relations and is based upon the allocation of acceptance and positive response as opposed to esteem and prestige. See Etzioni, *A Comparative Analysis of Complex Organizations* (New York: Free Press, 1964), pp. 4–6.

[8] Etzioni, pp. 40–44.

was not learning the facts of poverty, but developing an "esprit de corps" and a broad identification with the antipoverty movement; the necessity of transcending agency goals and building staff commitments to the goals of the enterprise was continually stressed. This indoctrination also helped to confirm the legitimacy of the coordinator's authority by weaving it into the fabric of the program's philosophy and goals.

Although these sessions undoubtedly had some impact, it would be an exaggeration to suggest that, in terms of establishing the coordinator's authority, they did more than set the stage. The coordinator's ability to elicit cooperation was actually determined through the interaction of personalities when the community-action drama unfolded in the neighborhoods. In the traditional bureaucracy, the lines are already written and the play is performed more or less in the spirit of formalistic impersonality—" 'Sine ira et studio' without hatred or passion, and hence without affection or enthusiasm. The dominant norms are concepts of straightforward duty without regard to personal consideration." [9] In contrast, the enterprise is less of a play and more of a "happening"; the actors move on and off stage at will, and the expression of individual personality is central to the performance. . . .

The coordinators in the North Side and South-West are both professional social workers, aggressive but affable, and without any apparent personality disorders. Their attempts to integrate the legal aid component into the neighborhood-center enterprise were, to begin with, hindered by

their lack of formal authority and complicated by the status differential that exists between social work and law. The attorneys were both formally qualified professionals working under the rules and regulations of the same legal service agency. Thus, in each situation, there were two professionals working within the same types of structures under similar constraints. Only the personalities of those involved account for the relatively easy integration in one setting and the almost completely independent legal operation in the other. . . . The coordinator is able to exert his authority upon those at the cooperative end of this continuum through the use of normative power. At the other end of the continuum are those who respond very erratically, if at all, to this form of authority; these are usually staff from the more powerful and more established of the participating agencies, such as the Bureau of Employment Security, the Board of Public Education, and the Allegheny County Health Department. The rigid bureaucratic mode of operation characteristic of these agencies extends right out to their antipoverty staff in the neighborhood centers. More than in the case of other members of the enterprise, the actions of these personnel are circumscribed by the firm rules and regulations of their agencies. Worth noting is the outstanding and somewhat unanticipated exception to the sluggish cooperation of the larger component agencies—the Catholic Diocese, whose staff was remarkably flexible and dynamic. This exception may be explained in part by the quest for relevancy, among religious organizations, through involvement in secular movements.

9 Weber, p. 340.

In situations in which normative power is not sufficient to elicit compliance, the coordinator may, through a complicated and very indirect process, attempt to exercise remunerative power over personnel and agencies. This process is accomplished by means of the formal periodic citizen evaluation of programs, agencies, and personnel. In these evaluations, the citizens rely heavily upon the coordinator for information, advice, and technical assistance. Thus, more than any other staff person in the neighborhood, the coordinator is able to influence the recommendations that emerge from these investigations, recommendations that may advise expanding, limiting, or eliminating a component service. Frequently, after investigating a program and conferring with the coordinator, citizens delegate to him the task of writing up the evaluation. Sometimes when they are extraordinarily busy, tired, or apathetic, they leave to him the total responsibility for the entire investigation and evaluation. In either case, the evaluation must have the final approval and support of the citizens before it is sent to the MCHR.

The attempt to exercise this type of power encounters many difficulties. First, practically speaking, for this power to be viable, those who are expected to respond must perceive a cause-effect relationship between their behavior and any consequences. Since evaluation and refunding is a months-long process, the reaction, if any, is a delayed one. In terms of reinforcing authority, this procedure is far less potent than the swift allocation of sanctions and rewards—the bonus or the "pink slip"—employed by most organiza-

tions operating on the principle of remuneration. Also practically speaking, the actual impact and consequences of these evaluations are, at best, minor; that this secret is not very well kept certainly does not add to the coordinator's authority, and may even detract from it.

Another problem relates to the simultaneous utilization of a dual compliance structure—normative and remunerative—in the neighborhood-center enterprise. The exercise of remunerative power is necessarily based upon an alliance between the coordinator and a specific party to the enterprise, the citizens; here the coordinator is functioning as a citizen advocate. The coordinator's right to exercise normative power, on the other hand, rests on an alliance of professionals dedicated to the abstract enterprise—with the coordinator functioning as a middleman. Once the coordinator behaves publicly as an advocate and uses this role to exercise remunerative power, he ceases to be viewed as an essentially neutral middleman; thus, his capacity to utilize normative power is subsequently reduced.

ROLES AND LOYALTIES

Given the restraints, ambiguities, and conflicts in the coordinator's role, how does this professional perform? Is he an advocate or is he a middleman? Does he manage a delicate balance between these two positions? Some insights into the actual performance of the coordinator may be gleaned from the perceptions of those with whom he works. In terms of the coordinator's role, the data in Table 1 reveal that the staff of ser-

TABLE 1. CITIZEN AND STAFF PERCEPTIONS OF
COORDINATOR'S ROLE AND LOYALTY [a]

	Percentage of Citizens	Percentage of Staff
Coordinator's Role:		
Primarily helps welfare agencies develop services for the neighborhood	4.7	3.8
Primarily helps citizens plan services for the neighborhood	28.1	15.4
Equally helps both citizens and welfare agencies to develop services	57.4	73.1
Helps neither of the above to develop services	5.5	7.7
No answer	4.3	—
Total	100	100
	(N = 256)	(N = 26)
First Loyalty of Coordinator:		
To MCHR or contracting agencies	27.3	38.5
To citizens	66.4	42.3
To none of the above	2.0	3.8
No answer	4.3	15.4
Total	100	100
	(N = 256)	(N = 26)

[a] The data on citizen board members and staff presented here and in subsequent tables come from a survey conducted in the spring of 1967. For further details see the Appendix [of *Clients and Constituents*].

vice agencies participating in the neighborhood-center enterprise describe him as a predominantly neutral agent, one who is equally helpful to citizens and agencies. Staff perceptions are much less consistent on the question of loyalty; here they are almost evenly divided between those who describe the coordinator's first loyalty as being to citizens and those who see it as being to agencies. The general picture of the coordinator that emerges from a staff perspective resembles more closely that of a middleman than of an advocate. The citizens, on the other hand, are more likely to see the coordinator as their advocate; although more than half the citizens view the coordinator as helping both groups, proportionately almost twice as many citizens

as staff see his primary role as helping citizens, and two-thirds of the citizens see themselves as the object of his first loyalty. This suggests that the coordinators have mastered the essential political and social tools for operating under conflicting pressures in the public spotlight—mainly, the ability to present different faces to different people and interest groups.

Most of Pittsburgh's coordinators view themselves as advocates, and are personally committed to increasing the power and influence of neighborhood citizens; but their performance, with few exceptions, rarely measures up to full advocate status. An advocate must be single-minded, almost fanatical, in the dedication of his time, energy, and sympathy. The selection   process,   the   delegate agency-coordination structure, and the neighborhood-center enterprise—each, in its own way, militates against the enactment of this role; there are too many tasks to be accomplished and too many interests to be pacified. For example, in the summer of 1967, the North Side coordinator organized a neighborhood-wide program to upgrade slum housing—mainly through rent strikes. He was reprimanded by the MCHR and Neighborhood Centers Association (the coordinating agency), not because this activity was especially threatening to these organizations, but because it left him little time for other responsibilities relevant to the neighborhood-center enterprise. In this case advocacy did not involve a direct confrontation with agencies operating in the antipoverty structure. Nevertheless, the enactment of this role still posed real problems.

Thus, in answer to the question raised earlier, most coordinators respond to both agency and citizen interests, and in doing so walk the tightrope between advocate and middleman. To maintain this balance, they became masters at negotiation, accommodation, and manipulation of citizens and agency staff. This role is not one conducive to democratization and reform of social welfare.

14   The Advocate Relationship

ADVOCACY AND PLURALISM IN PLANNING

PAUL DAVIDOFF

The present can become an epoch in which the dreams of the past for an enlightened and just democracy are turned into a reality. The massing of voices protesting racial discrimination have roused this nation to the need to rectify racial and other social injustices. The adoption by Congress of a host of welfare measures and the Supreme Court's specification of the meaning of equal protection by law both reveal the response to protest and open the way for the vast changes still required.

The just demand for political and social equality on the part of the Negro and the impoverished requires the public to establish the bases for a society affording equal opportunity to all citizens. The compelling need

Reprinted with permission of author and publisher from: Paul Davidoff, "Advocacy and Pluralism in Planning," *Journal of the American Institute of Planners*, 31: 4 (November 1965), pp. 331–37. Author's Note: The author wishes to thank Melvin H. Webber for his insightful criticism and Linda Davidoff for her many helpful suggestions and for her analysis of advocate planning. Special acknowledgment is made of the penetrating and brilliant social insights offered by the eminent legal scholar and practitioner, Michael Brodie, of the Philadelphia Bar.

for intelligent planning, for specification of new social goals and the means for achieving them, is manifest. The society of the future will be an urban one, and city planners will help to give it shape and content.

The prospect for future planning is that of a practice which openly invites political and social values to be examined and debated. Acceptance of this position means rejection of prescriptions for planning which would have the planner act solely as a technician. It has been argued that technical studies to enlarge the information available to decision makers must take precedence over statements of goals and ideals:

We have suggested that, at least in part, the city planner is better advised to start from research into the functional aspects of cities than from his own estimation of the values which he is attempting to maximize. This suggestion springs from a conviction that at this juncture the implications of many planning decisions are poorly understood, and that no certain means are at hand by which values can be measured, ranked, and translated into the design of a metropolitan system.[1]

[1] Britton Harris, "Plan or Projection," *Journal of the American Institute of Planners*, XXVI (November 1960), 265–72.

While acknowledging the need for humility and openness in the adoption of social goals, this statement amounts to an attempt to eliminate, or sharply reduce, the unique contribution planning can make: understanding the functional aspects of the city and recommending appropriate future action to improve the urban condition.

Another argument that attempts to reduce the importance of attitudes and values in planning and other policy sciences is that the major public questions are themselves matters of choice between technical methods of solution. Dahl and Lindblom put forth this position at the beginning of their important textbook, *Politics, Economics, and Welfare*.[2]

In economic organization and reform, the "great issues" are no longer the great issues, if they ever were. It has become increasingly difficult for thoughtful men to find meaningful alternatives posed in the traditional choices between socialism and capitalism, planning and the free market, regulation and laissez faire, for they find their actual choices neither so simple nor so grand. Not so simple, because economic organization poses knotty problems that can only be solved by painstaking attention to technical details—how else, for example, can inflation be controlled? Nor so grand, because, at least in the Western world, most people neither can nor wish to experiment with the whole pattern of socio-economic organization to attain goals more easily won. If for example, taxation will serve the purpose, why "abolish the wages system" to ameliorate income inequality?

These words were written in the early 1950s and express the spirit of that decade more than that of the 1960s. They suggest that the major battles have been fought. But the "great issues" in economic organization, those revolving around the central issue of the nature of distributive justice, have yet to be settled. The world is still in turmoil over the way in which the resources of nations are to be distributed. The justice of the present social allocation of wealth, knowledge, skill, and other social goods is clearly in debate. Solutions to questions about the share of wealth and other social commodities that should go to different classes cannot be technically derived; they must arise from social attitudes.

Appropriate planning action cannot be prescribed from a position of value neutrality, for prescriptions are based on desired objectives. One conclusion drawn from this assertion is that "values are inescapable elements of any rational decision-making process"[3] and that values held by the planner should be made clear. The implications of that conclusion for planning have been described elsewhere and will not be considered in this article.[4] Here I will say that the planner should do more than explicate the values underlying his prescriptions for courses of action; he should affirm them; he should be an advocate for what he deems proper.

Determinations of what serves the public interest, in a society containing many diverse interest groups, are almost always of a highly contentious nature. In performing its role of

---

[2] Robert Dahl and Charles Lindblom, *Politics, Economics and Welfare* (New York: Harper and Brothers, 1953), p. 3

[3] Paul Davidoff and Thomas Reiner, "A Choice Theory of Planning," *Journal of the American Institute of Planners,* XXVIII (May 1962), 103–115.

[4] *Ibid.*

prescribing courses of action leading to future desired states, the planning profession must engage itself thoroughly and openly in the contention surrounding political determination. Moreover, planners should be able to engage in the political process as advocates of the interests both of government and of such other groups, organizations, or individuals who are concerned with proposing policies for the future development of the community.

The recommendation that city planners represent and plead the plans of many interest groups is founded upon the need to establish an effective urban democracy, one in which citizens may be able to play an active role in the process of deciding public policy. Appropriate policy in a democracy is determined through a process of political debate. The right course of action is always a matter of choice, never of fact. In a bureaucratic age great care must be taken that choices remain in the area of public view and participation.

Urban politics, in an era of increasing government activity in planning and welfare, must balance the demands for ever-increasing central bureaucratic control against the demands for increased concern for the unique requirements of local, specialized interests. The welfare of all and the welfare of minorities are both deserving of support; planning must be so structured and so practiced as to account for this unavoidable bifurcation of the public interest.

The idealized political process in a democracy serves the search for truth in much the same manner as due process in law. Fair notice and hearings, production of supporting evidence, cross examination, reasoned decision are all means employed to arrive at relative truth: a just decision. Due process and two- (or more) party political contention both rely heavily upon strong advocacy by a professional. The advocate represents an individual, group, or organization. He affirms their position in language understandable to his client and to the decision makers he seeks to convince.

If the planning process is to encourage democratic urban government then it must operate so as to include rather than exclude citizens from participating in the process. "Inclusion" means not only permitting the citizen to be heard. It also means that he be able to become well informed about the underlying reason for planning proposals, and be able to respond to them in the technical language of professional planners.

A practice that has discouraged full participation by citizens in plan making in the past has been based on what might be called the *"unitary plan."* This is the idea that only one agency in a community should prepare a comprehensive plan; that agency is the city planning commission or department. Why is it that no other organization within a community prepares a plan? Why is only one agency concerned with establishing both general and specific goals for community development, and with proposing the strategies and costs required to effect the goals? Why are there not plural plans?

If the social, economic, and political ramifications of a plan are politically contentious, then why is it that those in opposition to the agency plan do not prepare one of their own? It is interesting to observe that "rational" theories of planning have called for consideration of alternative courses of action by planning agencies. As a matter of rationality it has been argued that all of the alternative choices open as means to the ends sought be examined.[5] But those, including myself, who have recommended agency consideration of alternatives have placed upon the agency planner the burden of inventing "a few representative alternatives." [6] The agency planner has been given the duty of constructing a model of the political spectrum, and charged with sorting out what he conceives to be worthy alternatives. This duty has placed too great a burden on the agency planner, and has failed to provide for the formulation of alternatives by the interest groups who will eventually be affected by the completed plans.

Whereas in a large part of our national and local political practice contention is viewed as healthy, in city planning where a large proportion of the professionals are public employees, contentious criticism has not always been viewed as legitimate. Further, where only government prepares plans, and no minority plans are developed, pressure is often ap-

[5] See, for example, Martin Meyerson and Edward Banfield, *Politics, Planning and the Public Interest* (Glencoe: The Free Press, 1955), p. 314 ff. The authors state "By a *rational* decision, we mean one made in the following manner: (1) the decision-maker considers all of the alternatives (courses of action) open to him; . . . (2) he identifies and evaluates all of the consequences which would follow from the adoption of each alternative; . . . (3) he selects that alternative the probable consequences of which would be preferable in terms of his most valued ends."

[6] Davidoff and Reiner, *op. cit.*

plied to bring all professionals to work for the ends espoused by a public agency. For example, last year a Federal official complained to a meeting of planning professors that the academic planners were not giving enough support to Federal programs. He assumed that every planner should be on the side of the Federal renewal program. Of course government administrators will seek to gain the support of professionals outside of government, but such support should not be expected as a matter of loyalty. In a democratic system opposition to a public agency should be just as normal and appropriate as support. The agency, despite the fact that it is concerned with planning, may be serving undesired ends.

In presenting a plea for plural planning I do not mean to minimize the importance of the obligation of the public planning agency. It must decide upon appropriate future courses of action for the community. But being isolated as the only plan maker in the community, public agencies as well as the public itself may have suffered from incomplete and shallow analysis of potential directions. Lively political dispute aided by plural plans could do much to improve the level of rationality in the process of preparing the public plan.

The advocacy of alternative plans by interest groups outside of government would stimulate city planning in a number of ways. First, it would serve as a means of better informing the public of the alternative choices open, *alternatives strongly supported by their proponents.* In current practice those few agencies which have portrayed alternatives have not been equally enthusiastic about each.[7] A standard reaction to rationalists' prescription for consideration of alternative courses of action has been "it can't be done; how can you expect planners to present alternatives which they don't approve?" The appropriate answer to that question has been that planners like lawyers may have a professional obligation to defend positions they oppose. However, in a system of plural planning, the public agency would be relieved of at least some of the burden of presenting alternatives. In plural planning the alternatives would be presented by interest groups differing with the public agency's plan. Such alternatives would represent the deep-seated convictions of their proponents and not just the mental exercises of rational planners seeking to portray the range of choice.

A second way in which advocacy and plural planning would improve planning practice would be in forcing the public agency to compete with other planning groups to win political support. In the absence of opposition or alternative plans presented by interest groups the public agencies have had little incentive to improve the quality of their work or the rate of production of plans. The political consumer has been offered a yes–no ballot in regard to the comprehensive plan; either the public agency's plan was to be adopted or no plan would be adopted.

A third improvement in planning practice which might follow from plural planning would be to force those who have been critical of "es-

[7] National Capital Planning Commission, *The Nation's Capital: A Policies Plan for the Year 2000* (Washington, D.C.: The Commission, 1961).

tablishment" plans to produce superior plans, rather than only to carry out the very essential obligation of criticizing plans deemed improper.

THE PLANNER AS ADVOCATE

Where plural planning is practiced, advocacy becomes the means of professional support for competing claims about how the community should develop. Pluralism in support of political contention describes the process; advocacy describes the role performed by the professional in the process. Where unitary planning prevails, advocacy is not of paramount importance, for there is little or no competition for the plan prepared by the public agency. The concept of advocacy as taken from legal practice implies the opposition of at least two contending viewpoints in an adversary proceeding.

The legal advocate must plead for his own and his client's sense of legal propriety or justice. The planner as advocate would plead for his own and his client's view of the good society. The advocate planner would be more than a provider of information, an analyst of current trends, a simulator of future conditions, and a detailer of means. In addition to carrying out these necessary parts of planning, he would be a *proponent* of specific substantive solutions.

The advocate planner would be responsible to his client and would seek to express his client's views. This does not mean that the planner could not seek to persuade his client. In some situations persuasion might not be necessary, for the planner would have sought out an employer with whom he shared common views about desired social conditions and the means toward them. In fact one of the benefits of advocate planning is the possibility it creates for a planner to find employment with agencies holding values close to his own. Today the agency planner may be dismayed by the positions affirmed by his agency, but there may be no alternative employer.

The advocate planner would be above all a planner. He would be responsible to his client for preparing plans and for all of the other elements comprising the planning process. Whether working for the public agency or for some private organization, the planner would have to prepare plans that take account of the arguments made in other plans. Thus the advocate's plan might have some of the characteristics of a legal brief. It would be a document presenting the facts and reasons for supporting one set of proposals, and facts and reasons indicating the inferiority of counter-proposals. The adversary nature of plural planning might, then, have the beneficial effect of upsetting the tradition of writing plan proposals in terminology which makes them appear self-evident.

A troublesome issue in contemporary planning is that of finding techniques for evaluating alternative plans. Technical devices such as cost-benefit analysis by themselves are of little assistance without the use of means for appraising the values underlying plans. Advocate planning, by making more apparent the values underlying plans, and by making definitions of social costs and benefits more explicit, should greatly assist the process of plan evaluation.

Further, it would become clear (as it is not at present) that there are no neutral grounds for evaluating a plan; there are as many evaluative systems as there are value systems.

The adversary nature of plural planning might also have a good effect on the uses of information and research in planning. One of the tasks of the advocate planner in discussing the plans prepared in opposition to his would be to point out the nature of the bias underlying information presented in other plans. In this way, as critic of opposition plans, he would be performing a task similar to the legal technique of cross-examination. While painful to the planner whose bias is exposed (and no planner can be entirely free of bias) the net effect of confrontation between advocates of alternative plans would be more careful and precise research.

Not all the work of an advocate planner would be of an adversary nature. Much of it would be educational. The advocate would have the job of informing other groups, including public agencies, of the conditions, problems, and outlook of the group he represented. Another major educational job would be that of informing his clients of their rights under planning and renewal laws, about the general operations of city government, and of particular programs likely to affect them.

The advocate planner would devote much attention to assisting the client organization to clarify its ideas and to give expression to them. In order to make his client more powerful politically the advocate might also become engaged in expanding the size and scope of his client organization. But the advocate's most important function would be to carry out the planning process for the organization and to argue persuasively in favor of its planning proposals. . . .

Pluralism and advocacy are means for stimulating consideration of future conditions by all groups in society. But there is one social group which at present is particularly in need of the assistance of planners. This group includes organizations representing low-income families. At a time when concern for the condition of the poor finds institutionalization in community action programs, it would be appropriate for planners concerned with such groups to find means to plan with them. The plans prepared for these groups would seek to combat poverty and would propose programs affording new and better opportunities to the members of the organization and to families similarly situated.[8]

The difficulty in providing adequate planning assistance to organizations representing low-income families may in part be overcome by funds allocated to local anti-poverty councils. But these councils are not the only representatives of the poor; other organizations exist and seek help. How can this type of assistance be financed? This question will be examined below, when attention is turned to the means for institutionalizing plural planning.

[8] The first conscious effort to employ the advocacy method was carried out by a graduate student of city planning as an independent research project. The author acted as both a participant and an observer of a local housing organization. See Linda Davidoff, "The Bluffs: Advocate Planning," *Comment,* Dept. of City Planning, University of Pennsylvania (Spring 1965), p. 59.

THE STRUCTURE OF PLANNING

PLANNING BY SPECIAL INTEREST GROUPS

The local planning process typically includes one or more "citizens" organizations concerned with the nature of planning in the community. The Workable Program requirement for "citizen participation"[9] has enforced this tradition and brought it to most large communities. The difficulty with current citizen participation programs is that citizens are more often *reacting* to agency programs than *proposing* their concepts of appropriate goals and future action.

The fact that citizens' organizations have not played a positive role in formulating plans is to some extent a result of both the enlarged role in society played by government bureaucracies and the historic weakness of municipal party politics. There is something very shameful to our society in the necessity to have organized "citizen participation." Such participation should be the norm in an enlightened democracy. The formalization of citizen participation as a required practice in localities is similar in many respects to totalitarian shows of loyalty to the state by citizen parades.

Will a private group interested in preparing a recommendation for community development be required to carry out its own survey and analysis of the community? The answer would depend upon the quality of the work prepared by the public agency, work which should be public

[9] See Section 101(c) of the United States Housing Act of 1949, as amended.

information. In some instances the public agency may not have surveyed or analyzed aspects the private group thinks important; or the public agency's work may reveal strong biases unacceptable to the private group. In any event, the production of a useful plan proposal will require much information concerning the present and predicted conditions in the community. There will be some costs associated with gathering that information, even if it is taken from the public agency. The major cost involved in the preparation of a plan by a private agency would probably be the employment of one or more professional planners.

What organizations might be expected to engage in the plural planning process? The first type that comes to mind are the political parties; but this is clearly an aspirational thought. There is very little evidence that local political organizations have the interest, ability, or concern to establish well-developed programs for their communities. Not all the fault, though, should be placed upon the professional politicians, for the registered members of political parties have not demanded very much, if anything, from them as agents.

Despite the unreality of the wish, the desirability for active participation in the process of planning by the political parties is strong. In an ideal situation local parties would establish political platforms which would contain master plans for community growth and both the majority and minority parties in the legislative branch of government would use such plans as one basis for appraising individual legislative proposals. Further, the local administration would use its planning agency to carry out the plans it proposed to the electorate. This dream will not turn to reality for a long time. In the interim other interest groups must be sought to fill the gap caused by the present inability of political organizations.

The second set of organizations which might be interested in preparing plans for community development are those that represent special interest groups having established views in regard to proper public policy. Such organizations as chambers of commerce, real estate boards, labor organizations, pro- and anti-civil rights groups, and anti-poverty councils come to mind. Groups of this nature have often played parts in the development of community plans, but only in a very few instances have they proposed their own plans.

It must be recognized that there is strong reason operating against commitment to a plan by these organizations. In fact it is the same reason that in part limits the interests of politicians and which limits the potential for planning in our society. The expressed commitment to a particular plan may make it difficult for groups to find means for accommodating their various interests. In other terms, it may be simpler for professionals, politicians, or lobbyists to make deals if they have not laid their cards on the table.

There is a third set of organizations that might be looked to as proponents of plans and to whom the foregoing comments might not apply. These are the ad hoc protest associations which may form in opposition to some proposed policy. An example of such a group is a neighborhood association formed to combat a renewal plan, a zoning change, or the proposed location of a public facility. Such organizations may seek to develop alternative plans, plans which would, if effected, better serve their interests.

From the point of view of effective and rational planning it might be desirable to commence plural planning at the level of city-wide organizations, but a more realistic view is that it will start at the neighborhood level. Certain advantages of this outcome should be noted. Mention was made earlier of tension in government between centralizing and decentralizing forces. The contention aroused by conflict between the central planning agency and the neighborhood organization may indeed be healthy, leading to clearer definition of welfare policies and their relation to the rights of individuals or minority groups.

Who will pay for plural planning? Some organizations have the resources to sponsor the development of a plan. Many groups lack the means. The plight of the relatively indigent association seeking to propose a plan might be analogous to that of the indigent client in search of legal aid. If the idea of plural planning makes sense, then support may be found from foundations or from government. In the beginning it is more likely that some foundation might be willing to experiment with plural planning as a means of making city planning more effective and more democratic. Or the Federal Government might see plural planning, if carried out by local anti-poverty councils, as a strong means of generating local interest in community affairs.

Federal sponsorship of plural planning might be seen as a more effective tool for stimulating involvement of the citizen in the future of his community than are the present types of citizen participation programs. Federal support could only be expected if plural planning were seen, not as a means of combating renewal plans, but as an incentive to local renewal agencies to prepare better plans.

THE PUBLIC PLANNING AGENCY

A major drawback to effective democratic planning practice is the continuation of that non-responsible vestigial institution, the planning commission. If it is agreed that the establishment of both general policies and implementation policies are questions affecting the public interest and that public interest questions should be decided in accord with established democratic practices for decision making, then it is indeed difficult to find convincing reasons for continuing to permit independent commissions to make planning decisions. At an earlier stage in planning the strong arguments of John T. Howard [10] and others in support of commissions may have been persuasive. But it is now more than a decade since Howard made his defense against Robert Walker's position favoring planning as a staff function under the mayor.

[10] John T. Howard, "In Defense of Planning Commissions," *Journal of the American Institute of Planners,* XVII (Spring 1951).

With the increasing effect planning decisions have upon the lives of citizens the Walker proposal assumes great urgency.[11]

Aside from important questions regarding the propriety of independent agencies which are far removed from public control determining public policy, the failure to place planning decision choices in the hands of elected officials has weakened the ability of professional planners to have their proposals effected.

[11] Robert Walker, *The Planning Function in Urban Government,* second edition (Chicago: University of Chicago Press, 1950). Walker drew the following conclusions from his examination of planning and planning commissions. "Another conclusion to be drawn from the existing composition of city planning boards is that they are not representative of the population as a whole." p. 153. "In summary the writer is of the opinion that the claim that planning commissions are more objective than elected officials must be rejected." p. 155. "From his observations the writer feels justified in saying that very seldom does a majority of any commission have any well-rounded understanding of the purposes and ramifications of planning." p. 157. "In summary, then, it was found that the average commission member does not comprehend planning nor is he particularly interested even in the range of customary physical planning." p. 158. "Looking at the planning commission at the present time, however, one is forced to conclude that, despite some examples of successful operations, the unpaid board is not proving satisfactory as a planning agency," p. 165. ". . . [it] is believed that the most fruitful line of development for the future would be replacement of these commissions by a department or bureau attached to the office of mayor or city manager. This department might be headed by a board or by a single director, but the members or the director would in any case hold office at the pleasure of the executive on the same basis as other department heads." p. 177.

Separating planning from local politics has made it difficult for independent commissions to garner influential political support. The commissions are not responsible directly to the electorate and in turn the electorate is, at best, often indifferent to the planning commission.

During the last decade in many cities power to alter community development has slipped out of the hands of city planning commissions, assuming they ever held it, and has been transferred to development coordinators. This has weakened the professional planner. Perhaps planners unknowingly contributed to this by their refusal to take concerted action in opposition to the perpetuation of commissions.

Planning commissions are products of the conservative reform movement of the early part of this century. The movement was essentially anti-populist and pro-aristocracy. Politics was viewed as dirty business. The commissions are relics of a not-too-distant past when it was believed that if men of good will discussed a problem thoroughly, certainly the right solution would be forthcoming. We know today, and perhaps it was always known, that there are no right solutions. Proper policy is that which the decision-making unit declares to be proper.

Planning commissions are responsible to no constituency. The members of the commissions, except for their chairman, are seldom known to the public. In general the individual members fail to expose their personal views about policy and prefer to immerse them in group decision. If the members wrote concurring and dissenting opinions, then at least the commissions might stimulate thought about planning issues. It is difficult to comprehend why this aristocratic and undemocratic form of decision making should be continued. The public planning function should be carried out in the executive or legislative office and perhaps in both. There has been some question about which of these branches of government would provide the best home, but there is much reason to believe that both branches would be made more cognizant of planning issues if they were each informed by their own planning staffs. To carry this division further, it would probably be advisable to establish minority and majority planning staffs in the legislative branch. . . .

The independent planning commission and unitary plan practice certainly should not co-exist. Separately they dull the possibility for enlightened political debate; in combination they have made it yet more difficult. But when still another hoary concept of city planning is added to them, such debate becomes practically impossible. This third of a trinity of worn-out notions is that city planning should focus only upon the physical aspects of city development.

AN INCLUSIVE DEFINITION
OF THE SCOPE OF PLANNING

The view that equates physical planning with city planning is myopic. It may have had some historic justification, but it is clearly out of place at a time when it is necessary to integrate knowledge and techniques in order to wrestle effectively with the myriad of problems afflicting urban populations.

The city planning profession's historic concern with the physical environment has warped its ability to see physical structures and land as servants to those who use them.[12] Physical relations and conditions

12 An excellent and complete study of the bias resulting from reliance upon physical or land use criteria appears in David Farbman, *A Description, Analysis and Critique of the Master Plan,* an unpublished mimeographed study prepared for the Univ. of Pennsylvania's Institute for Urban Studies, 1959–1960. After studying more than 100 master plans Farbman wrote:

"As a result of the predominantly physical orientation of the planning profession many planners have fallen victims to a malaise which I suggest calling the 'Physical Bias.' This bias is not the physical orientation of the planner itself but is the result of it. . . . The physical bias is an attitude on the part of the planner which leads him to conceive of the principles and techniques of *his profession* as the key factors in determining the particular recommendations to be embodied in his plans. . . .

"The physically biased planner plans on the assumption (conviction) that the physical problems of a city can be solved within the framework of physical desiderata; in other words, that physical probems can be adequately stated, solved and remedied according to physical criteria and expertise. The physical bias produces both an inability and an unwillingness on the part of the planner to 'get behind' the physical recommendations of the plan, to isolate, examine or discuss more basic criteria. . . .

". . . There is room, then, in plan thinking, for physical principles, i.e., theories of structural inter-relationships of the physical city; but this is only a part of the story, for the structural impacts of the plan are only a part of the total impact. This total impact must be conceived as a web of physical, economic and social causes and effects." pp. 22–26.

have no meaning or quality apart from the way they serve their users. But this is forgotten every time a physical condition is described as good or bad without relation to a specified group of users. High density, low density, green belts, mixed uses, cluster developments, centralized or decentralized business centers are per se neither good nor bad. They describe physical relations or conditions, but take on value only when seen in terms of their social, economic, psychological, physiological, or aesthetic effects upon different users.

The profession's experience with renewal over the past decade has shown the high costs of exclusive concern with physical conditions. It has been found that the allocation of funds for removal of physical blight may not necessarily improve the over-all physical condition of a community and may engender such harsh social repercussions as to severely damage both social and economic institutions. Another example of the deficiencies of the physical bias is the assumption of city planners that they could deal with the capital budget as if the physical attributes of a facility could be understood apart from the philosophy and practice of the service conducted within the physical structure. This assumption is open to question. The size, shape, and location of a facility greatly interact with the purpose of the activity the facility houses. Clear examples of this can be seen in public education and in the provision of low cost housing. The racial and other socio-economic consequences of "physical decisions" such as location of schools and housing projects have

been immense, but city planners, while acknowledging the existence of such consequences, have not sought or trained themselves to understand socio-economic problems, their causes or solutions.

The city planning profession's limited scope has tended to bias strongly many of its recommendations toward perpetuation of existing social and economic practices. Here I am not opposing the outcomes, but the way in which they developed. Relative ignorance of social and economic methods of analysis have caused planners to propose solutions in the absence of sufficient knowledge of the costs and benefits of proposals upon different sections of the population.

Large expenditures have been made on planning studies of regional transportation needs, for example, but these studies have been conducted in a manner suggesting that different social and economic classes of the population did not have different needs and different abilities to meet them. In the field of housing, to take another example, planners have been hesitant to question the consequences of locating public housing in slum areas. In the field of industrial development, planners have seldom examined the types of jobs the community needed; it has been assumed that one job was about as useful as another. But this may not be the case where a significant sector of the population finds it difficult to get employment.

"Who gets what, when, where, why, and how" are the basic political questions which need to be raised about every allocation of public resources. The questions cannot be answered if land use criteria are the sole or major standards for judgment.

The need to see an element of city development, land use, in broad perspective applies equally well to every other element, such as health, welfare, and recreation. The governing of a city requires an adequate plan for its future. Such a plan loses guiding force and rational basis to the degree that it deals with less than the whole that is of concern to the public.

The implications of the foregoing comments for the practice of city planning are these. First, state planning enabling legislation should be amended to permit planning departments to study and to prepare plans related to any area of public concern. Second, planning education must be redirected so as to provide channels of specialization in different parts of public planning and a core focused upon the planning process. Third, the professional planning association should enlarge its scope so as to not exclude city planners not specializing in physical planning. . . .

CONCLUSION

The urban community is a system comprised of interrelated elements, but little is known about how the elements do, will, or should interrelate. The type of knowledge required by the new comprehensive city planner demands that the planning profession be comprised of groups of men well versed in contemporary philosophy, social work, law, the social sciences, and civic design. Not every planner must be knowledgeable in all these areas, but each planner must have a deep understanding of one or more of these areas and he must be able to give persuasive expression to his understanding.

As a profession charged with making urban life more beautiful, exciting, and creative, and more just, we have had little to say. Our task is to train a future generation of planners to go well beyond us in its ability to prescribe the future urban life.

15   The Interorganizational Field

THE INTERACTION OF COMMUNITY DECISION
ORGANIZATIONS: SOME BASIC CONCEPTS
AND NEEDED RESEARCH

Roland L. Warren

It is a commonplace that unified economic, physical, and social planning at the community level is a will-o'-the-wisp whose possibility for realization, if it was ever present, is rapidly diminishing. Rather, the situation in all but the smallest cities can be characterized as follows: There is a large and increasing number of organizations at the city or metropolitan level, each of which is more or less legitimated for program-planning or -operation in some particular sector of the community's interest. Almost without exception, these community decision organizations[1] receive a

large portion of their funding from agencies of the federal government, from which they also receive varying amounts of program stimulation. While they have different fields of emphasis and activity, the pursuit of these fields often involves them in various types of relationship with one another. Sometimes these relationships are co-operative, as when a housing authority and an urban-renewal authority and a united community service agency may collaborate in planning for a particular type of service to low-income people. At other times (or even simultaneously) they may compete for a major say in decisions which affect them all, for funds, or for "clout" in the mayor's office.

Indeed, as one goes from city to city, one sees with remarkable con-

Reprinted with permission of author and publisher from: Roland L. Warren, "The Interaction of Community Decision Organization: Some Basic Concepts and Needed Research," *Social Service Review*, 41: 3 (September 1967), 261–70.

[1] We had originally approached this study thinking of "planning" organizations, but it soon became apparent that the usual ambiguity around the term "planning" applied here as well, but, even more importantly, that "planning," regardless of definition, was one of the variables, rather than a differentia, of these organizations. What seemed important was not the extent to which they fitted some definition

of planning but whether or not they were legitimated to "speak for" or represent the community in some aspect of its interests, whether this be schools, land-use, industrial base, health care, vertical mobility for the poor, low-cost housing, or whatever. The term "community decision organization" was coined by James J. Callahan, Jr., a doctoral candidate at Brandeis University.

sistency the same general types of community decision organizations, however they may vary in details of organization or program. There are the city-planning commissions, the urban renewal authorities, the local poverty organizations, the chambers of commerce, united community services, united funds, housing authorities, welfare departments, health departments, industrial development corporations, and so on. Although many of these organizations confine their activities to the city limits, others encompass roughly the metropolitan area. The aggregate of their activity governs, to a large extent, the amount of conscious, co-ordinated direction given to the affairs of the community.

Yet such organizations do not constitute the sole influence on decision-making at the community level. On the one hand, they themselves are subject to various types of social, political, and economic pressures, and, although many of them are set up autonomously, presumably to apply rational, deliberate effort toward accomplishing their stated goals, they are not immune from the pressures of the marketplace. On the other hand, many decisions which they are presumably legitimated to make are actually made under other auspices at quiet meetings between the mayor and a few business leaders or other members of one or another top "power structure." Or they are hammered out inside and around the city council in a bargaining process with Washington, or in various combinations of such settings.

The behavior of these community decision organizations is seldom neatly confined to the community arena, whether this is considered roughly as the central city or as the metropolitan area. On various types of projects, it has been observed that the interaction of these organizations is only a part of a larger process of interaction concerning any particular project. Other agencies and organizations at a less inclusive level of the community, such as neighborhood organizations or direct-service agencies, or organizations at a more inclusive level, such as agencies of the state or federal government, are also involved. In the complex, multileveled interaction surrounding the development of most community projects, there does not appear to be a distinct field of interaction at the community level which is clearly distinguishable from the total process of multilevel, mixed-level interaction. Nevertheless, there is little doubt that such community decision organizations, in their interaction, play a large role in the multicentered decision-making (and decision-avoiding) processes that characterize most American cities. There is some indication that large cities have a greater number of such relatively autonomous legitimated community decision organizations than do the smaller ones.

There is every indication that this situation, in which interrelated concerns of the city or metropolitan area are largely—though not exclusively—determined through the interaction of such major community decision organizations, will characterize the predictable future. This opinion is held by many agency executives who differ as to the desirability of having such a large number of relatively autonomous organizations each planning as a separate entity, or the desirability of setting up a superagency or some other mechanism for concerted planning efforts and programs. . . .

PREVIOUS RESEARCH ON COMMUNITY DECISION ORGANIZATIONS

In view of the importance of community decision organizations in "comprehensive and co-ordinated planning" and the presence of more or less the same types and combinations of them in different cities, the paucity of systematic research on their behavior is surprising. Once one considers the presence of roughly the same types of organizations in various cities, a dozen interesting and researchable questions arise regarding the differences in the structure and behavior of any one type of organization in various cities—urban-renewal authorities, chambers of commerce, or welfare departments—and their relation to a number of environmental variables. Likewise, the development of a systematic body of knowledge concerning the behavior of these organizations with respect to each other, as they go about planning or operating programs in fields which often overlap, seems desirable.

The existing social science knowledge base for understanding the behavior of community decision organizations consists principally of intensive case studies of particular organizations, conducted mainly by sociologists, and studies and conceptualizations from the burgeoning field of organizational and administrative theory, in which research is widely interdisciplinary. . . .

While few studies from the organizational literature deal with community decision organizations as such, a number of organizational studies and conceptualizations have direct relevance to possible future research in this field. Etzioni, Simpson and Gulley, and Marschak [2] give varied typologies for classifying different types of organizations. Rushing, Hage, Blau, and Litwak [3] all attempt to specify and in preliminary fashion to operationalize a number of variables of presumed importance in accounting for various aspects of organizational behavior. From the wide literature on conceptualizations of organizational decision-making, those by Gore, Thompson and Tuden, and Simon [4] can be taken as

[2] Amitai Etzioni, *A Comparative Analysis of Complex Organizations: On Power, Involvement, and Their Correlates* (New York: Free Press of Glencoe, 1961); Richard L. Simpson and William H. Gulley, "Goals, Environmental Pressures, and Organizational Characteristics," *American Sociological Review*, 27 (June, 1962), 344–51; Jacob Marschak, "Towards an Economic Theory of Organization and Information," in *Decision Processes,* ed. Robert McDowell Thrall, C. H. Combs, and R. L. Davis (New York: John Wiley & Sons, 1954).

[3] William A. Rushing, "Organizational Rules and Surveillance: Propositions in Comparative Organizational Analysis," *Administrative Science Quarterly*, 10 (March, 1966), 423–43; Jerald Hage, "An Axiomatic Theory of Organizations," *Administrative Science Quarterly*, 10 (December, 1965), 289–320; Peter M. Blau, "The Comparative Study of Organizations," *Industrial and Labor Relations Review*, 18 (April, 1965), 323–38; Eugene Litwak, "Models of Bureaucracies Which Permit Conflict," *American Journal of Sociology,* 67 (September, 1961), 177–84.

[4] William J. Gore, "Decision-making Research: Some Prospects and Limitations," in *Concepts and Issues in Administrative Behavior,* ed. Sydney Mailick and Edward H. Van Ness (Englewood Cliffs, N.J.:

useful analytical schemes that lend themselves to empirical research in behavior of community decision organizations. Kammerer has made an interesting study of city managers, in which she was able to operationalize Gore's three types of decision-making.[5]

A question of increasing importance is that of the circumstances under which organizations display innovative behavior, as opposed to routine or adaptive behavior, to follow a distinction developed by Gore.[6] A literature on organizational innovation is growing, from which the contributions of Simon, Wilson, and Thompson [7] are particularly pertinent for research on community decision organizations.

Likewise, there are a number of pertinent studies and articles on the relation of organizations to their general environment, although most of them do not address themselves to this specific type of organization.[8] There is also a growing body of possibly relevant literature on the specific relations of various organizations to each other.[9]

VARIABLES FOR POSSIBLE STUDY . . .

INPUT AND OUTPUT CONSTITUENCIES

In analysis of the structure of large community decision organizations in relation to their environments, the distinction between input and output constituencies was found useful.[10] "Input constituency" is con-

Prentice-Hall, 1962); James D. Thompson and Arthur Tuden, "Strategies, Structures, and Processes of Organizational Decision," in James D. Thompson et al., Comparative Studies in Administration (Pittsburgh: University of Pittsburgh Press, 1959); Herbert A. Simon, Administrative Behavior: A Study of Decision-making Processes in Administrative Organization (2d ed.; New York: Free Press, 1965).

[5] Gladys M. Kammerer, "Role Diversity of City Managers," Administrative Science Quarterly, 8 (March, 1964), 421–42.

[6] Loc. cit.

[7] Herbert A. Simon, "The Decision-maker as Innovator," in Mailick and Van Ness, op cit.; James Q. Wilson, "Innovation in Organization: Notes Toward a Theory," in Approaches to Organizational Design, ed. James D. Thompson (Pittsburgh: University of Pittsburgh Press, 1966); Victor A. Thompson, "Bureaucracy and Innovation," Administrative Science Quarterly, 10 (June, 1965), 1–20.

[8] For example, Simpson and Gulley, op. cit.; James D. Thompson and William J. McEwen, "Organizational Goals and Environment: Goal-setting as an Interaction Process," American Sociological Review, 23 (February, 1958), 23–31; William R. Dill, "The Impact of Environment on Organizational Development," in Mailick and Van Ness, op. cit.; Eugene Litwak and Lydia F. Hylton, "Interorganizational Analysis: A Hypothesis on Co-ordinating Agencies," Administrative Science Quarterly, 6 (March, 1962), 395–420; James D. Thompson, "Organizations and Output Transactions," American Journal of Sociology, 68 (November, 1962), 309–24.

[9] For example, Sol Levine and Paul E. White, "Exchange as a Conceptual Framework for the Study of Interorganizational Relationships," Administrative Science Quarterly, 5 (March, 1961), 583–601; Sol Levine, Paul E. White, and Benjamin D. Paul, "Community Interorganizational Problems in Providing Medical Care and Social Services," American Journal of Public Health, 53 (August, 1963), 1183–95; and William M. Evan, "The Organization-Set: Toward a Theory of Interorganizational Relations," in Approaches to Organizational Design, ed. James D. Thompson (Pittsburgh: University of Pittsburgh Press, 1966).

[10] These concepts are modifications of Evan's "Input Set" and "Output Set" (cf. Evan, op. cit.).

ceived of as those other organizations or actors acknowleged by the organization as supporting, financing, promoting, providing program material, or making decisions regarding the functioning of an organization. In other terms, it is the group of parties to which the organization acknowledges a responsibility in determining its policy and program. "Output constituency" is conceived of as those other organizations or actors acknowleged by an organization as being the appropriate target of the organization's activity.[11]

One preliminary result of the use of this conceptualization has been to suggest the importance of the relationship between the input constituency and the output constituency. As an example, the recipients of social services are not usually members of the input constituencies of the social service agencies, but community-action programs involving the participation of the poor, tenants' councils, and organizations of relief recipients are examples of the effort to gain recognition as part of the input constituency of poverty organizations, housing authorities, and welfare departments, respectively.

A second preliminary outcome from this conceptualization is the suggested hypothesis that organization policy and program are more sensitive to the interests of the input

constituency than to those of the output constituency.

A third preliminary implication is that the nature of the interaction between two or more organizations will be determined—in part—by their respective presence or absence in each other's input or output constituencies.

ORGANIZATIONAL STRUCTURES AND LEADERSHIP TYPES

Any analysis of organizational behavior, to be complete, must account for the impact of personality as well as situational variables. Preliminary study in the three cities indicated that the possibly vast difference in the behavior of an organization and the behavior of other organizations toward it can be attributed to differences in style of behavior on the part of the top leader, usually, though not always, the principal staff executive. This is particularly evident in intercity comparisons. Preliminary study indicates that a classification of leadership styles into "charismatic," "bureucratic," and "collegial" appears to capture many of the differences which the interview data have revealed.

The concept of charismatic leadership is substantially, though not completely, an inventory of the characteristics described by Max Weber.[12] The emphasis here is on personal innovativeness and *ad hoc* structuring of specific projects, rather than on following "normal channels," either in interorganizational proce-

---

11 Obviously, there are other organizations and actors that are affected by, or affect, an organization, which are not part of its output or input constituency. These relationships are treated in two ways: first, as side effects, insofar as the behaivor is not deliberately related to them, or, second, as various interorganizational interaction processes, for which a typology is presently being developed.

12 *The Theory of Social and Economic Organization,* trans. A. M. Henderson and Talcott Parsons (New York: Oxford University Press, 1947).

dures or in intraorganizational procedures.

The concept of bureaucratic leadership likewise follows Weber's general description, but with some minor modifications. Emphasis is placed on following normal channels, both within the organization and outside of it; on decision-making according to rules, policies, and precedents; and on the hierarchical organization of decision-making following the organization's structure.

The concept of collegial leadership receives its description and rationale largely from the "human relations" and "group dynamics" literature, but also from the literature of community organization in social work. The two principal elements, as we conceive them, are flexibility in the decision-making process and greater initiative coming from subordinates at any point in the administrative hierarchy.

Two questions from these considerations suggest more extensive research. One has to do with whether the specific structure and setting of certain organizations encourages one type of leadership rather than another. A number of such considerations, for example, might suggest that public welfare departments would be more congenial to bureaucratic leadership; antipoverty boards and urban renewal authorities might be more amenable to charismatic leadership; and community welfare councils, hospital councils, and church federations might be more amenable to collegial leadership. Even if this preliminary hypothesis is proved valid, it is nevertheless quite obvious that there are also variations based on the particular "style" of the incumbent leaders, and

that these, as well as the structural variables, may have important effects on organizational behavior. Hence, one must differentiate the structural aspects of these leadership styles from the personality aspects.

INNOVATIVENESS IN COMMUNITY DECISION ORGANIZATIONS

A related question is that of innovativeness in organizations. The past five years have been characterized by widespread expression of the need for creative, innovative solutions to urban problems and by disillusionment with routine methods, particularly in the social-planning field. For example, the antipoverty program initially was committed to innovation, and it apparently based much of its operating policy on the conclusion that existing organizations in its field, particularly the community welfare councils, were unable to innovate sufficiently to bring about "system change," as distinguished from "system maintenance" through customary, largely palliative, modes of service. The Office of Economic Opportunity, structurally, operationally, and in terms of the personal style of its director, showed many of the characteristics of charismatic leadership. In its encouragement of innovativeness in the local community; its impatience with "normal operating procedures" and channels and with the mere expansion of existing services by alleged unimaginative local organizations; its encouragement of setting up new, flexible organizations and of keeping them flexible; its emphasis on "getting things done" and on "the man with the idea," . . . seemingly has demanded a charismatic type of structure with charismatic types of leaders relatively unencumbered by the constraints of bureaucratic routine or by the slow process of consensus-seeking among peers which characterizes the collegial style.

Many meaningful and researchable questions are raised by such a conceptualization. One such question has to do with whether the local community-action programs, from the administrative point of view (as distinguished from the controverted and highly volatile aspect of the participation of the poor in policy-making), followed the course of most new innovative structures—namely, development toward routinization and bureaucratization or what Weber described as "the routinization of charisma." [13] Unfortunately, space does not permit a fuller elaboration of the interesting research questions related to the above analysis, but it is hoped that enough has been said to indicate the relevance and significance of a systematic study of leadership styles in community decision organizations.

A TYPOLOGY OF EXPLICIT FUNCTIONS

A variable which preliminary investigation indicates may be useful in studying the behavior of community decision organizations is that of the explicit functions which the organization is expected to perform and legitimated to perform. Presumably, the constraints on an organization's behavior will be somewhat different if it is designed primarily for joint planning among a number of member agencies or if it has to maintain an operating program of its own. For example, the constraints on a hospital council will be rather different if it is conceived as an organization to promote joint services (common laundry, common purchases) for its member institutions or if it is legitimated by them and others for broad health-planning functions in the community.

OTHER ASPECTS OF ORGANIZATIONAL BEHAVIOR

In this preliminary study, it was found that decisions were being made in four different contexts and that the nature of the context appeared to influence the type of interaction that took place in the decision-making. These contexts varied from that of units within a formal, hierarchically structured organization at the one extreme to the loose sort of individualistic pursuit of goals by various independent persons or organizations without any formal structure for decision-making. These four contexts, extending from unitary through federative and coalitional to "social choice" contexts, are described in detail in a different report.[14]

In conclusion, it might be well to indicate, in the briefest fashion, other important aspects of the problem, to be developed more fully in other papers.

There are two levels for studying the interaction of organizations. The first concentrates on the individual organization. This field has been

---

13 *Op. cit.*

14 Roland L. Warren, "The Interorganizational Field as a Focus of Investigation," *Administrative Science Quarterly*, forthcoming.

treated so far in two different inter-related ways. From the point of view, as it were, of the individual organization, one may consider that organization's own behavior in relation to the configuration of its environment, or one may examine the nature of exchange transactions between organizations. These approaches take as their focus the individual organization in its interaction with other organizations.

The second level deals, not with individual organizational behavior in the interaction process, but with the field in which the interaction takes place. Community decision organizations themselves are a response to a situation described by Mannheim, who stated that "the increasing *density of events (Dichtigkeit des Geschehens)* makes the possibility of a natural balance through competition or through mutual adaptation more and more hopeless." [15] More recently, Emery and Trist have analyzed what they call the causal texture of organizational environments and pointed out that under contemporary conditions, in which the environment is characterized as a turbulent field, "individual organizations, however large, cannot expect to adapt successfully simply through their own direct actions." [16] Such considerations give rise to the desirability of studying the interactional field within which community decision organizations interact, as a

level of analysis quite distinct from that of the action of any individual organization.

As in other analogous fields, there are the alternatives of studying "relationships" as a more or less steady state of the system and, on the other hand, studying interactional behavior as it flows through time in response to changing situations. They are not mutually exclusive. The second, however, seems particularly attractive in that it lends itself to a type of "flow" study, with both practical and theoretical implications—for example, the study of the interaction of community decision organizations in the process of the development of specific federally sponsored programs.

A number of questions immediately arise. What differences in the "interactional field" in various cities account for the differential utilization and implementation of available federal grant-in-aid programs? What variables appear to be related to the specific locus which a program is given in different cities—which body is chosen as the local public authority for urban-renewal programs, or as the community-action agency for antipoverty programs? What differences do these loci make in program development and operation? Under what circumstances and for what purposes are project decisions made largely within the normal operating procedures of the organizations themselves, and under what circumstances are they made in other settings—at the banker's club, at city hall, etc.? What circumstances are associated with program innovativeness? Do "co-ordination" among organizations and innovativeness and quality of pro-

15 Karl Mannheim, *Man and Society in an Age of Reconstruction: Studies in Modern Social Structure* (New York: Harcourt, Brace & World, 1951), p. 157.

16 F. E. Emery and E. L. Trist, "The Causal Texture of Organizational Environments," *Human Relations*, 18 (February, 1965), 28.

gram vary in inverse relationship to each other, as some bits of theory from analogous settings might suggest?

Finally, what of the "public welfare"? Are there researchable forms into which questions can be put regarding the type of interorganizational structure which would maximize utility for the community as a whole? Must these questions—loaded as they are with hidden assumptions and value postulates—remain in the field of armchair debate, or are there ways of setting reasonable criteria for a "healthy" situation regarding the interrelation of organizations in a given community? Are there methods of calculation—welfare economics, cost-benefit analysis, game theory, simulation—which can make significant contributions to the question? Given a plurality of community decision organizations—each legitimated to speak on behalf of some segment of the community's welfare, but whose interests overlap and whose goals cannot all be simultaneously maximized—what are the relevant criteria which will help improve the "mix"? This question, like the others immediately preceding it, will have to wait for treatment elsewhere. Meantime, it is hoped that a case has been made for further research on the interaction of community decision organizations.

16 The Interorganizational Field: A Case Study in Community Mental Health

DECISION-MAKERS AND INFLUENTIALS

ROBERT H. CONNERY/CHARLES H. BACKSTROM
DAVID R. DEENER/JULIAN R. FRIEDMAN
MORTON KROLL/ROBERT H. MARDEN
CLIFTON MCCLESKEY/PETER MEEKISON
JOHN A. MORGAN, JR.

Both the existing patterns of mental health services and the prospects for the federal Act depend upon the structure of influence and decision making in mental health in the various state and local communities. Who wields effective power over mental health services? What is the role of public officials? How influential are the various voluntary organizations in shaping mental health policy? What do the field studies contribute in answering these questions about decision making at the state and local level?

Two analytical approaches fre-

Reprinted with permission of authors and publisher from: Robert H. Connery, Charles H. Backstrom, David R. Deener, Julian R. Friedman, Morton Kroll, Robert H. Marden, Clifton McCleskey, Peter Meekison, and John A. Morgan, Jr., *The Politics of Mental Health: Organizing Community Mental Health in Metropolitan Areas* (New York: Columbia University Press, 1968).

quently employed by political and social scientists have been used in the field studies: interest groups have been examined and the community power structure outlined. Used with discretion both methods can add greatly to available knowledge about the decision-making process in mental health programs.

Influence is as deceptive as it is important. If influence is conceived as the capacity to control operations and shape program and policy decisions, then there are numerous gradations associated with the various groups and individuals involved in the policy field, and the influence of any one of them will vary with time and circumstance. . . .

PUBLIC OFFICIALS IN THE DECISION PROCESS

The group theory of politics, formulated by Bentley and elaborated by Truman, has often been accused—rightly or wrongly—of failing to take into account the role and influence of public officials.[1] According to some critics, the group theorists have portrayed the nongovernmental interest groups as the sole agents of influence, and the course of public policy as a vector of those forces, with official policy makers cast as essentially passive or helpless bystanders. What light do the field studies shed on the actual roles of public officials?

Since state legislatures are formally designated as official policy-makers for those within their jurisdictions, it might be well to begin by considering the role of their members in general and with particular reference to mental health programing. Viewed in general terms, and with a few exceptions, the fifty state legislatures have a low estate that contrasts sharply with their position atop the formal policy structure. To some extent this is a matter of personnel. Particularly in the lower houses there is a staggering rate of turnover among members, due partially to the tendency to view the state legislature as the first step toward higher office. This general political inexperience,

coupled with rawness in the legislative process, low pay, lack of office space, and the like, exacts a heavy toll in the lawmakers' performance.

There are also institutional forces at work to downgrade the state legislators. Often they are handicapped by state constitutional limitations. Biennial sessions, though declining in use, are still the prevailing pattern, so that many matters demanding careful attention can never get it. In some states the political context leaves legislators highly vulnerable to pressure group influence. The assemblies themselves seem determined to compound their difficulties by clinging to archaic or obsolete practices.

It does not necessarily follow, however, that state legislatures are therefore of no significance in the state policy process. In some states the legislative branch remains the dominant one; in others, it has been overshadowed by the executive. Probably the greater part of the legislatures fall in the intermediate position, neither dominating state policy nor relegated to an insignificant role. . . .

The greatest impact of these bodies may very well be found in the tendency of leadership elements to limit their proposals in anticipation of legislative disapproval. Particularly in the states where mental health programs are low in priority, there is some scattered indication of the emergence of a "self-fulfilling prophecy" in this respect, for an estimate of legislative coolness to mental health policy proposals may very well result in lack of proper effort to cultivate the lawmakers. While the field data do not bear directly on this question, there is reason to be-

---

[1] Arthur F. Bentley, *The Process of Government* (Bloomington, Ind.: The Principia Press, 1949); David B. Truman, *The Government Process* (New York: Alfred A. Knopf, 1951). For critical assessments of the group theory of politics, see Peter Odegard, "A Group Basis of Politics: A New Name for an Old Myth," *Western Political Quarterly*, Vol. 11 (Sept. 1958), 689; Stanley Rothman, "Systematic Political Theory: Observations on the Group Approach," *American Political Science Review*, Vol. 54 (March 1960), 15; and R. E. Dowling, "Pressure Group Theory: Its Methodological Range," *American Political Science Review*, Vol. 54 (Dec. 1960), 944.

lieve that the basic difficulty in getting increased legislative support for mental health is not so much hostility as indifference and ignorance. It is less a problem of changing legislative opinion than a matter of getting opinions formed at all. The function of "educating" the state's legislators on the needs and problems of mental health has not always been properly performed.

While state legislatures have been declining in status and power, the governors of the various states have been slowly improving their overall position. The governor's position as political leader has been strengthened, with the inevitable result that he has become more and more responsible for legislative and policy leadership. . . .

Although overshadowed both in constitutional theory and in political activity by the governor and the legislature, officials in state agencies are able to influence greatly the course of public policy. By pressing for legislative enactments, by winning budgetary support, and by implementing patterns, they give policy their distinctive imprint. Whether this potential is realized depends partly on the political context in which it functions, and partly on the drive and capabilities of the agency's leaders.

In considering the role and influence of state mental health administrative agencies it is helpful to note that their opportunities really begin with utilization of their expertise to identify policy needs and alternatives in the care of mentally ill persons. While there were naturally variations in the degree of accomplishment, in all six states studied, with the exception of Texas, there

was a real concern with this function. . . .

But such is the influence of the political environment that success in the next stage of influence, "educating" other participants, varied tremendously. In what is undoubtedly a cause and effect relationship, the Department of Public Welfare in Minnesota both contributes to and benefits from a climate of public and political opinion that is well disposed toward mental health programs. The Department of Mental Hygiene in New York, the Department of Mental Health in Massachusetts, and the Department of Hospitals in Louisiana also appear to be properly attentive to their "educational" responsibilities. In Washington the conditions operate to limit sharply the efforts of the Department of Institutions. In Texas, again with the exception of those dealing with the mentally retarded, the state agencies were not proceeding with any apparent vigor to press the case for better services with either the public or with state political leaders.

The final stage of the influence process for these agencies is the mobilization of public and governmental support for their proposals, and here one finds the widest range of accomplishment. In Minnesota, Louisiana, and New York, it would appear, the agencies have with other elements been especially successful in winning support. In Massachusetts strong agency efforts have produced considerable gains within the limitations imposed by broader state fiscal considerations. In Washington the mobilization of support by agencies has been hampered by rivalry and conflict between the Department of Institutions and the Health Department, as well as by general budgetary problems. One finds in Texas perhaps the least effective performance by agencies in attempting to mobilize for purposes of influencing state policy, although it is worth noting that they played an important role in organizing the mental health planning committee that did eventually weld together a structure of influence.

Thus, although conditions did not always enable these officials to have a great deal of impact, individual leaders of state agencies, such as Jack Ewalt in Massachusetts, did have considerable effect in all states except Texas. Deserving to be called professionals by virtue of their approach to administration as well as by their medical training, these administrators have undoubtedly contributed importantly to an atmosphere of administrative sophistication in the total state picture. Their approach was often described as expansive, but it is difficult to label innovative and pioneering thrusts as empire building or aggrandizement when existing levels of service are so low and the needs so shockingly evident.

On the local level, the influence of public officials is most evident in Minneapolis–St. Paul, New Orleans, and Syracuse. In each case an unusually effective county official played a very important role in furthering the development of local mental health programs, and other local officials have taken supportive positions. In Massachusetts the constitutional arrangements leave little room for local public mental health services, and hence it is not surprising that there has been virtually no influence exer-

cised by local officials. In Seattle local officials have generally shown little interest in or concern with mental health problems, but they are clearly a key element in the decisional process, since their unwillingness to provide funds for mental health services are felt, and felt heavily, in that community. The same generalization holds for Houston, although there are conspicuous exceptions. Thus the county judge has labored consistently if not always effectively for expanded services, and administrators in the Galena Park school district have gone far beyond most other districts in their mental health program. Still, it is generally true that local officialdom has given ungrudging support to mental health services only when they put no strain on the budget.

One can say, then, that local officials are acquiescent in a field that is dominated by state officialdom on the one hand and by private organizations on the other. Operating in an atomized, fragmented, often chaotic atmosphere, local officials are not apt themselves to produce a unified approach to the handling of problems in a field so broadly defined. The studies of the six communities reveal occasional instances of vigorous effort by political leaders seeking to realize mental health goals, but on the whole one cannot detect widespread involvement. However, if there is a further growth of local public mental health programs, then local officials, particularly county officials, may emerge as brokers between state, federal, local, and private interests in mental health.

Another vital part of the total context of mental health policy making is the existence of several major professional groups with an important stake in existing and proposed programs. These include such directly involved groups as psychiatrists, psychologists, psychiatric nurses, psychiatric social workers, therapists, and the like, and also such secondarily involved groups as the entire medical profession. Professionals in any complex industrial society such as our own are highly functional, and one of the questions to be considered is whether they play equally important roles in the policy process.

Certainly the most important organized medical group is the American Medical Association. It is a federation of 54 state, commonwealth, and territorial associations, which in turn are composed of more than 1,900 component medical societies. Authority moves up from the component societies through the state and territorial associations to the national body, through the process of electing delegates. With a membership of some 202,000, the AMA includes approximately 70 percent of the nation's physicians.

The extent of AMA activities is reflected in the total cost of operating the association. In 1965 expenses totaled almost $28 million. Among its many educational activities are the sponsoring of more than a thousand scientific meetings a year, postgraduate programs for physicians, several programs of educational and research grants and fellowships, the maintenance of an extensive medical library, a comprehensive information service providing guidance for physicians on drugs, and cooperation with other organizations in fostering health education. The AMA also serves the public as well as the medical profession through its activities on behalf of medical standards.

The activities that have the most direct bearing, both actual and potential, on the success of a particular public program are the AMA's legislative and publications programs. The association or the state medical societies analyze pending legislation of medical interest at both the national and state levels. It is an active pressure organization, supporting, opposing, even initiating various types of governmental activity.

Psychiatrists are, of course, physicians, and as such most are members of the AMA. And among the thirteen association councils set up to deal with professional or technical areas is the Council on Mental Health. The fundamental role of the council is to recommend policies and develop programs in mental health. In this role, the Council on Mental Health has played an important part in furthering mental health programs. Yet it must be remembered that while the AMA supported that part of the 1963 legislation authorizing construction grants, the House of Delegates overrode the Council on Mental Health to oppose successfully the initial staffing grants and that, when the 1965 amendments reinstated the staffing money, they were passed over the AMA's opposition.

The American Psychiatric Association is the oldest national medical society in the United States. Founded in Philadelphia in 1844 by thirteen distinguished physicians who administered mental hospitals, the association gradually broadened in scope from its origin as an organization of superintendents. Operating under its present name since 1921, the APA's membership has roughly doubled each decade since the 1930s. The membership now totals about 15,000, which is 80 per cent of the association's estimate of the total number of psychiatrists and psychiatric residents in the United States.

There is a district branch of the association in nearly every state, and some states have more than one. Requirements for membership in a branch are the same as for membership in the association, and since 1963 new members must belong to a district branch provided there is one in the area where they reside.

While lacking the resources and political muscle of the AMA, the APA has long been an active proponent of extensive governmental activity on behalf of mental health. It has been a consistent supporter of ever-higher appropriations for the National Institute of Mental Health and has vigorously urged the adoption of a new approach to the mentally ill through the community mental health center model. The association's role in bringing about the Joint Commission's study and its active support of the 1963 legislation were discussed in a preceding chapter [of *The Politics of Mental Health*]. The association exerted every effort on behalf of the staffing provisions in 1963 and redoubled its efforts after the initial failure. Only a little over a month after President Johnson's 1965 health message, for instance, the APA convened a conference for leaders in state mental health planning from all over the country; it was clearly designed to stimulate grassroots support for the staffing amendments, which it hoped

would be translated effectively to key congressmen. . . .

. . . While the situation reported varies from one area to another, there are certain elements of similarity that need to be noted. As a general rule professional groups tend to function most effectively in the political system as "veto" groups, and the field of mental health provides no exception to that rule. The hostility of any of the major professional groups would in most instances suffice to force accommodative modifications, and certain of them, most notably the psychiatrists and the medical societies, can probably block all efforts at policy innovation if sufficiently aroused.

On the whole the professional groups were more or less won over to the idea of a new departure in mental health services. None chose or was forced to exercise its veto power. That is not to say that there was uncritical acceptance, or that they did not seek modifications in the mental health centers plan. The AMA opposed staffing grants. There was some professional opposition in Massachusetts to separating the centers from general hospitals, and the medical profession in Texas was apparently ready to block the administrative reorganization of services unless the statute specified that the commissioner of mental health services had to be a psychiatrist. But despite these qualifications it is generally true that the various professional groups have acquiesced in the decision to develop community mental health centers.

Third, this acquiescent role should not be confused with an innovative one. While professionals in either public or private practice were invariably involved in the decisions to seek state and local implementation of the federal statutes, their organizations played minor parts. It appears that the organized professional groups were not in the policy vanguard.

It is worth considering why the professional groups failed to play a more significant role. There are at least three factors that seem to be important in that failure. One is the division of professional opinion regarding public mental health programs, and particularly those with the potential impact of community mental health centers. One confronts in almost every case the doubts and reservations of physicians about public psychiatry, sometimes expressed openly as in Massachusetts, sometimes implicitly as in Texas. The psychiatrists themselves are divided on a host of professional issues, ranging from the question of the wisdom of varying from the traditional one-to-one relationship of doctor and patient to the merits and demerits of the psychoanalytic approach. The proposals for community mental health centers added new issues, such as the advantages of a community-centered approach versus the state hospital tradition, or the proper location of community centers (general hospitals or physically separate facilities). Psychologists and social workers, and some psychiatrists, tend to prefer more emphasis on the preventive aspects of mental health services rather than relying on treatment after the onset of mental illness. With these and other professional differences so much in evidence, it is hardly surprising that the organized groups fail to stand out as policy innovators and leaders.

A second factor militating against a group role is the well-known conservatism of the professional groups involved. While this term can be applied in a political sense particularly to the medical profession in general and to some but certainly not all psychiatrists, it is used here in a broader sense to refer to the cautiousness, resistance to change, and lack of innovative spirit that are so often found among the professionals involved, social workers no less than physicians.

A third explanatory factor is that the organized groups, with the conspicuous exception of the American Medical Association, are not geared for involvement in the policy process. In some instances the organizations exist locally only on paper, and even when there is a functioning structure and a dues-paying membership the orientation is apt to be narrowly professional and/or social in nature. Rarely, if ever, is there a paid staff or office facilities. The means for propagandizing members and the general public, for research and analysis of substantive policy issues, for mobilization of group resources—all these prerequisites for successful entry into the policy sphere are largely absent. The preoccupation of the professionals with their private practices or with their own agencies and programs undoubtedly contributes heavily to this pattern, but whatever its causes the consequence is a marginal involvement in policy affairs.

It cannot be stressed too heavily that the foregoing has dealt only with the role of organized professional groups. These generalizations, however, are applicable as well to the vast majority of professional personnel, for the field studies are unanimous in reporting that most of them were not involved in policy affairs even in individual, unorganized ways. However, in each case it was found that a few professionals were deeply concerned with public policy matters, often playing leading roles. Thus one should not conclude that there is no professional influence on decisions, but rather that it is the product of individual motivation and effort, rather than being group-inspired and directed.

There is still another category of groups involved in mental health programing, which for want of a better term will be labeled "voluntary." It includes basically two types of organizations: the local, private, nonprofit agencies providing mental health services; and the lay associations organized at the state and local levels essentially as pressure groups, typically without providing any direct services. The former includes a variety of agencies dispensing a wide range of services; often they are at least partially supported by United Fund or Community Chest programs. These will for purposes of this discussion be designated as "private" agencies. The second category has several components, but the most prominent ones are the various state and local mental health and mental retardation associations.

For many years the private agencies have been the backbone of community mental health operations. They have often been the instruments if not the innovators of such successes as have been achieved, but on occasion they have represented stumbling blocks to successful program development. Typically each has its own niche carved out in the local spectrum of programs. As a general rule each is an indepedent agency, locally based and supported in most part. Normally a governing board operating under a charter serves as the official policy maker for the agency, but with day-to-day affairs in the hands of a professional staff. Depending on the size of the agency and the nature of its operations, the executive director who heads the staff may be either a psychiatrist or a social worker. Membership in the organization is open to all, but in practice it is apt to be limited to a relatively few interested persons.

The field studies suggest three perennial concerns of the private agencies. The first is originating, developing, and overseeing specific programs. Administrative structures must be organized, clientele accepted, administrative and professional personnel recruited, governing boards constituted. In some cases the agency must fit its efforts and ambitions into some sort of planning by a community council or its equivalent; in other cases each agency is on its own in developing and managing programs. It becomes literally a program instigator, implementer, and protector.

A second type of concern is financing. A certain element of uncertainty and insecurity is introduced by the lack of fixed and foreseeable sources of funds. Although it is true that few agencies ever suffer complete economic collapse, many do find it necessary from time to time to reorient their program to adapt to the financial realities of the situation.

Usually a great variety of sources is tapped: membership dues and contributions, fees from clients, United Fund support, and grants from foundations and governments.

Finally, private agencies are concerned with a number of what might be broadly termed communication needs and problems. Each must somehow fit into the total pattern of voluntary and public agency programs in a functional way. While this is always troublesome, it is particularly so when there is no effective coordinating or planning body to facilitate such integration. . . .

Although their professionals were often involved in state mental health planning activities, there is no evidence that the agencies as such played important roles. At the local level the private agencies would seem to have considerable potential for influencing the shape and structure of local mental health because of their linkages through their boards of directors with social and economic dominants or their lieutenants. Unfortunately, in this respect the agencies tend to be undone by their parochialism. Where unchecked, each agency functions more or less independently, expanding or reorienting its own activities largely as it can and as it pleases. In thus retaining freedom to chart its own course, each agency at the same time tacitly surrenders any claim to influence over similar decisions by other agencies. Justifying and protecting against encroachment their individual spheres of action become the major preoccupations of the private agencies.

Effective coordination to overcome these centrifugal tendencies is thus an important prerequisite to agency influence. The inability of private agencies to do much to mold mental health policy in Seattle and Houston despite their predominance in the provision of services is undoubtedly due in substantial measure to weakness of the coordinating body in each case (the Community Council in Houston, the United Fund organization in Seattle). By contrast, the finding of a more important role for the private agencies in Minneapolis and in Syracuse is paralleled by a report of a stronger structure of coordination in those cities.

While the unchecked parochialism of private agencies hinders their effectiveness in the development of broader programs, there is another factor at work that should not be neglected. The private agencies loom particularly large in Seattle and Houston mostly because of the paucity of publicly provided services, but that very paucity is testimony to a lack of community interest and involvement that relentlessly saps the private sector as well.

In concluding this discussion of the private agencies it might be well to recall the questions raised in the Syracuse study concerning their long-range future, for in greater or lesser degrees the same questions apply to other cities as well. Reduced to their starkest form, these questions ultimately concern the capacity of private agencies to retain their distinctive character and roles. They are apt to decline in relative importance as more comprehensive public mental health programs are increasingly extended to the various communities. Survival will demand increased bureaucratization and professionalization, bringing them closer and closer to resembling their public counterparts. Their uniqueness may then consist essentially of the element of private financing. This fate is hardly inevitable, but to escape it will require more concern with the nature and functions of private agencies than has been in evidence so far.

The second type of voluntary organization to be considered here concentrates not on the provision of services but on the many activities involved in mobilizing support for mental health programs. It is best exemplified by the mental health associations and associations for the mentally retarded operating at all three levels of government.

By far the most important supportive group is the National Association for Mental Health (NAMH) and its state and local affiliates. Indeed, in a directory of national, state, and local agencies "to which individuals can turn for psychiatric help and mental health services" included in the *Encyclopedia of Mental Health,* the only "State Sources" listed other than public authorities were state divisions of NAMH.

Supported entirely by voluntary contributions from individuals, business firms, and foundations, the NAMH includes well over 800 state and local affiliates and has member organizations in 48 states and the District of Columbia. These local associations vary considerably from one area to another in size and strength, but through its affiliates the association has over a half million members. In addition, more than a half million nonmember volunteers serve in the work of the NAMH during the year. The state and local programs are carried on with assistance, guidance, and materials from the national headquarters.

Among the numerous local activities of the mental health associations are the sponsoring and supporting of research; consultation, fund raising, and public information programs for the improvement of mental hospital conditions; recruitment, training, and placement of volunteer workers in mental hospitals; assistance of various types to the families of the mentally ill; and social, vocational, and medical rehabilitation programs. But from the standpoint of generating public support or opposition to any particular public program, by far the most important functions of the National Association for Mental Health are its widespread informational and educational activities. . . .

In some of the field studies the state mental health associations were found lacking in effectiveness. Although their representatives often participated in policy conferences, planning committees, and legislative arenas, these associations were seldom perceived as key elements in the policy process. This assessment may reflect in part a tendency to see the state associations as essentially auxiliaries or fronts for the dominant state agency involved in mental health (e.g., the Department of Mental Health in Massachusetts or the former Department of State Hospitals and Special Schools in Texas). It may also be that the state associations lack the capacity to attract the dedicated and devoted laborers necessary to give a voluntary group the means for exerting influence. Finally, it may well be that the state groups simply lack knowledge of the ways in which influence is gained and exerted, both in public and private arenas. . . .

COMMUNITY POWER STRUCTURE

No less significant for an understanding of mental health programing is that aspect involving informal and/or unorganized groupings of influentials in a community, summed up in the phrase "community power and decision making." The way in which influence is exerted in a community in general has obvious relevance for a consideration of mental health policy making, and each of the field studies deals with the issue of how the community under scrutiny generally goes about making decisions before examining the process with specific reference to mental health. Explicitly or implicitly, each field investigator in his analysis of community power in general tended to do so within the framework of two polar models: the elitist model and the pluralist model. The elitist model, associated with such figures as Floyd Hunter and Robert Presthus, is pretty well summed up in the following statement by Presthus: "Elitism connotes domination of the decisional process by a single group or a few men, limited rank-and-file access, little or no opposition and a failure on the part of most of the adult community to use their political resources to influence important decisions." [2]

In sharp contrast is the pluralist model, associated with such scholars as Robert Dahl and Nelson Polsby.[3] Its essential features are the absence of any ruling elite, with power and influence effectively dispersed among various strata, and with significant opportunities for many people to participate in decisions. . . .

What overall significance is there in the data . . . summarized for the six field studies? One of the most obvious points is the diversity of the patterns of general community influence. On the whole the areas discussed are characterized by somewhat pluralistic tendencies in the decision-making process, with little indication of a monolithic power structure in any of the communities. However, there are almost infinite varieties and degrees of pluralism, and each community is to some extent unique.

A second noteworthy point is that there appears in each case to be a reasonably close resemblance between the general pattern of influence and the pattern for mental health policy making. One does not find examples of highly centralized decision making in mental health; the pluralism of the general community carries over into that specific field.

A third and closely related point is the absolute necessity of understanding the community's influence system and of knowing how to function effectively within it. Given the de-

2 Robert Presthus, *Men at the Top* (New York: Oxford University Press, 1964), p. 25.

3 Robert Dahl, *Who Governs: Democracy and Power in an American City* (New Haven: Yale University Press, 1961); Nelson Polsby, *Community Power and Political Theory* (New Haven: Yale University Press, 1963).

gree of pluralism present, this is not an easy undertaking. There are few manuals available for the beginner, and in any case it is necessary to temper general rules to particular situations. In each of the field studies there are examples of failures or inadequacies in mental health programing that can be traced to poor comprehension of the policy-making process. Those in the mental health field are not necessarily any more lacking in this respect than others, for this appears to be a fairly common problem. But it may be that the training and folkways of the mental health professionals make the acquisition of such knowledge more difficult for them. It would be interesting to compare their political and community involvement with that of other professions.

It follows from these observations that the task of mobilizing community support for mental health programs calls for certain highly developed skills. The point is made most emphatically in the Syracuse study, where a sketch of the desirable characteristics of mediators pointed to a full-time job for them. The same report also brought out the possibility that there may be long-term trends toward change in the nature of the skills involved in community influence. It also follows from the pluralistic context of mental health programing that policy proposals must be designed with clear understanding of the various influences that must be brought into supportive roles.

But perhaps the most important conclusion to be drawn from the summaries touching the influence structure and the decision-making process is that the time span from program conception to adoption is apt to be far longer than is commonly anticipated. The five years of careful work that was behind the adoption of a mental health center for Dakota county, as noted in the Minneapolis–St. Paul study, may be far more typical than one would like to believe. The amount of time required undoubtedly varies greatly from one city or state to another and from one type of program to another, but it is to be expected that mobilization of community support will be a slow, sometimes glacial, process. It is true that shortcuts sometimes can be found, but such good fortune is not common and may carry with it unfortunate consequences of the tendency to use the budgetary process, with its one- or two-year cycle, as an instrument of policy development.

But even in the states where there is more leadership in evidence, there are often conspicuous gaps and failures. Without in any way denigrating the leaders who have performed ably, it appears that there have been countless opportunities for even more effective leadership. It seems likely that the failure of adequate leadership to emerge under even relatively more favorable conditions, as well as under the less favorable ones, is related to several factors. Among them is the existence of considerable fragmentation at all levels, for governmental and program fragmentation impedes leadership by discouraging attempts and by exacting a heavy toll in time, effort, and failures. Another factor appears to be the lack of sufficient knowledge of the system of community influence and decision making. One cannot play the game well if the rules and players are not sufficiently familiar, and there is evidence that among mental health personnel there is a decided unfamiliarity with the rules and players of the power and influence games.

17 Tactics in the Field

A PERSPECTIVE ON TACTICS

Geoge Brager/Harry Specht

. . . In this chapter we discuss the different interventions which constitute the spectrum of tactical choices, choices which range from collaboration to disruption. We first explore how the perceptions of the actors, their resources for influence, and their relationships to each other are associated with particular types of tactics. In a final section, we deal with some of the practice principles the creative tactician must consider.

ISSUES, RESOURCES, AND RELATIONSHIPS

The tactics that organizers and community groups use to effect community change depend on three related factors: (1) the substance of the issue, or goal of the effort *as perceived by the action and target systems;* (2) the resources of the parties involved in the action; and (3) the relationship of action and target systems with one another. We explore each in turn.

Issues and Modes of Intervention. The association between different modes of intervention and different responses to issues has been described by Warren.[1] The range of responses to issues which he identifies are: (a) *issue consensus,* where there is a high possibility of agreement between the action and target systems; (b) *issue difference,* where for one or another reason the parties are not in complete agreement, but the possibility for agreement exists; and (c) *issue dissensus,* where there is no agreement on the issue between the parties.

Each response is associated with a particular mode of intervention.

Thus, issue consensus yields to collaborative modes of intervention, such as problem solving and education. With issue difference, campaigns of a competitive or bargaining nature take place. Dissensus is associated with contests in which there is a high degree of conflict between the parties leading to confrontation and disruptive tactics.

What is it about issues that tends to elicit one or another response? Why do we find consensus in one

Reprinted with permission of authors and publisher from: George Brager and Harry Specht, *Community Organizing* (New York: Columbia University Press, 1973), pp. 261–82.

[1] Roland L. Warren, "Types of Purposive Social Change at the Community Level," in Ralph M. Kramer and Harry Specht, *Readings in Community Organization Practice* (Englewood Cliffs, N.J.: Prentice-Hall, 1969), pp. 205–22.

instance, difference or dissensus in another? The response to an issue, whether rational or not, indicates how the issue is *perceived* by different parties.[2] Whatever the reality, the views of the different parties regarding what the action will mean for them is crucial in determining their response. The table below combines these elements but adds violence as a fourth mode of intervention based on a perception of change which aims at "reconstruction of the entire system" to which the response is "insurrection."[3]

element changes, so too do the others. For example, the response to a rearrangement of resources may be either consensus or mild difference, in which case the mode of intervention will range from collaborative to mild campaign. Predicting change would be easier if we were able to scale and measure perceptions, responses, and modes of intervention, and could then determine the conditions under which particular responses are reversible.

Second, all of the referents of these concepts are time limited in the

WHEN THE GOAL IS PERCEIVED AS:	THE RESPONSE IS:	THE MODE OF INTERVENTION IS:
(a) Mutually enhancing adjustments; or rearrangement of resources	Consensus	Collaborative
(b) Redistribution of resources	Difference	Campaign
(c) Change in status relationships	Dissensus	Contest or disruption
(d) Reconstruction of entire system	Insurrection	Violence

There are some general remarks to be made about the typology. First, the range of responses has been simplified for the sake of clarity. In reality, there is no clear and definite cutting point for each of these sets of perceptions, responses, and modes of intervention. The typology should be conceived as consisting of several continua rather than of discrete categories. As one

2 In his development of the typology of issue situations, Warren was working with a "value-interest" dimension rather than a perception dimension which, though related, is somewhat different.

3 We hasten to note that violence is not a mode of intervention that is available to professional organizers, nor do we believe it should be. This is discussed further in Chapter 16 [of *Community Organizing*— EDs.]

sense that they are subject to on-going social and legal redefinition. What is defined as redistribution today may be redefined as a rearrangement of resources tomorrow, and what is considered conflictual at one time may be merely competitive at another. The point at which a rearrangement of resources comes to be perceived as a redistribution is not easily predicted; and what one party views as a demand for change in status may be perceived as insurrection by another. Currently rent strikes and boycotts are examples of tactics which appear to hover between contest and campaign depending on time, place, and specific application; similarly, disobedience and resistance may be responded to as insurrection or contest depending on the social climate and the specific uses made of these tactics.

We note, finally, that within this schema conflict is viewed as an element that is present to some degree in all modes of intervention when change is involved, whether the intervention is collaborative, campaign, contest, or violence. Conflict is hardly involved in collaborative tactics with integrative goals (i.e., when the effort entails mutually-enhancing adjustment of resources). In this instance, the change is ordinarily minor. In the discussion which follows, we ignore both extremes of the continuum of interventions—collaborative interventions when the goal is integrative, and violence to reconstruct the entire system—since the major work of organizers in the pursuit of community change falls among the other modes of intervention.

Perceptions, Responses, Interventions. The first mode of intervention—collaboration—is based on consensual responses to planned changes that are perceived as a rearrangement of resources. The parties to the change are in essential agreement about the coordination, or reorganization, of services. No one perceives that they stand to lose much money, power, or status by the change.

Redistribution of resources is a qualitatively different perception of a change. One or the other parties expects that he will end up with more or less of something—money, facilities, authority—but because it is perceived as remaining within the rules of the game (the institutionalized system of competition), the contending parties utilize campaign tactics to exert pressure, negotiate, and eventually compromise and agree.

Contest or disruption is generated by a challenge to existing status relationships. This view of a change creates an entirely different universe of discourse than either of the above. Contest or disruption is rooted in the competition for power in human relations. Status relationships refer to the social arrangements by which expectations, rights, and responsibilities are awarded, and these social arrangements always award more to some than to others. A threat to the system of relationships which give some people power over others is the basis for this kind of response, whether it involves parents and children, welfare workers and clients, students and teachers, or blacks and whites. When community issues are perceived by one party as eliminating or diminishing their power over others, the response may be predicted as dissensus, and contest or disruption the result.

Responses to a change effort—whether consensus, difference, or dissensus—are inevitably related to the parties' perception of the *scope* of the change attempt. In any specific instance, the greater the extent of a proposed rearrangement of resources, the more likely it is to be perceived as a redistribution. Similarly, the greater the redistribution, the more it will be perceived as status change. It might be argued, as a matter of fact, that real issues of change always involve alterations in status relationships, and that rearrangements and redistributions of resources are simply lesser degrees of status change.

Some Examples. The following examples will illustrate the interplay of the three elements—perceptions, responses, and modes of intervention.

Fluoridation, objectively, presents a good case for collaborative tactics. It is considered sensible, scientific, and it is not only inexpensive but money saving. Perhaps because health officials and community organizers themselves viewed the issue as a mutually enhancing adjustment, and in planning their strategy ignored the perceptions of other actors, they have often approached the issue from a consensus framework, relying on educational modes of intervention. Yet the issue of fluoridation has been the basis of harsh and vindictive social conflicts in hundreds of communities in the United States.[4]

There appear to be two major sets of reasons for the resistance. First, many people question the effectiveness of the proposed change and fear the possibility of fluoride being poisonous. Interestingly, this line of resistance yields to collaborative modes of intervention.[5] But the second source of resistance, which is based on the belief that fluoridation infringes on the rights of individuals, and that "compulsory medication" usurps the rights of free men, does not respond to collaborative methods. Green's research supports the conclusion that indignation over the *presumed* violation of personal freedom was more fundamental, in the minds of informants, than the danger of poisoning; that the fear of poisoning symbolized a disposition to see fluoridation as an insidious attack by a vague constellation of impersonal social forces bent on usurping the powers of the common citizen; and the root cause of this feeling of being victimized, sensed by active opponents of fluoridation, was the increasing remoteness and impersonality of the sources of power and influence affecting the daily life of the individual.[6] In short, the issue of fluoridation becomes a contest when it is perceived to be a threat to status.

The civil rights movement provides another example of a shift over time from a major focus on rearrangement and redistribution of resources to a more focused concern with change in status. Of course, throughout its history, the demands made by the movement undoubtedly *required* a change in status for success. But there was increasing recognition that it was the power of whites over blacks which was at issue. In the union organizing which preceded Martin Luther King, Jr.'s assassination in Memphis, the city was not confronting a question of redistribution of resources as they might in an ordinary labor dispute. That the striking workers perceived it as a question of status was evident in their signs which read "I Am a Man," for indeed it was their manhood that they saw at stake. That the mayor of Memphis perceived it the same way was clear in his statement that he would be damned if he would be the first southern mayor to bargain collectively with a black union.

Resources and Modes of Intervention. In our emphasis on the perceptions of the participants rather than the realities of the issues, we

[4] "Trigger for Community Conflict," entire issue of the *Journal of Social Issues,* Vol. XVII, No. 4 (December 1961).

[5] Benjamin D. Paul, "Fluoridation and the Social Scientist: A Review," *Ibid.,* p. 5.

[6] *Ibid.,* p. 7.

do not wish to leave the impression that we underestimate the importance of objective reality in shaping perception. This disclaimer is doubly necessary, since we wish now to suggest that perceptions of a change attempt are also importantly shaped by the resource requirements of action.

The Memphis strikers, alluded to above, are a case in point. The fact that a labor dispute became a symbol of racial injustice served the tactical interests of the striking union, since it greatly expanded the action system, increasing its sources of influence and the pressure it could bring to bear upon the target. In order to garner the resources for victory, the union had to redefine the effort and up the ideological ante.

Proponents also attempt to shape perceptions so that issues appear less threatening to potential targets. For example, the notion of participation by the poor in the poverty program was rationalized on the grounds of equity and as a means of developing their competence. Whether or not advocates of the program believed this to be the whole truth, the necessity for consensus and collaborative modes of intervention required that these perceptions be fostered. If the program had been perceived as promoting a change in status relationships (as happened later), it might have died aborning.

As these examples imply, our typology is not linear. That is, action efforts do not move inevitably from a particular perception (e.g., redistribution of resources) to its corresponding response (i.e., difference), and from there to the corresponding mode of intervention (i.e., campaign) as they do across the lines of

the table. They might occur in reverse order. A tactic is chosen (only one mode may be available or valued), thereby creating a particular response and perception of the effort. Or, as we shall see later, the response itself may come first, as when consensual or conflictual relations between action and target systems are defined as necessary or desired.

Apart from the requirements of the community issue itself what determines the mode of intervention? Most important are the various resources which facilitate the exercise of power. Our earlier references to the resources of board, executive, and staff of the sponsoring organization is relevant to the current discussion. There is an extensive literature which examines the resources of power. Rossi, for example, lists wealth and other physical resources, control over interaction among prestigious groups, control of communications systems, control over values (as available to the church), threats to property, and the backing of solitary interest groups.[7] Dahl adds knowledge and expertise, popularity and charisma, legality and officiality.[8] Although the inventory is not complete, it is useful nonetheless. A cursory review suggests two factors of importance for our analysis: first, some resources are more advantageous, or necessary, in using certain tactics than others and, second, these resources are differentially distrib-

[7] Peter H. Rossi, "Theory, Research and Practice in Community Organization," in Kramer and Specht, *Readings in Community Organization Practice*, pp. 51–52.

[8] Robert A. Dahl, "The Analysis of Influence in Local Communities," in Charles R. Adrian, ed., *Social Science and Community Action* (East Lansing: Michigan State University Press, 1960), p. 32.

uted among community organizations that engage in community affairs.

The need to gain the interest and commitment of the poor encourages campaign and contest modes of intervention. Coleman has demonstrated that previously nonparticipating citizens are most likely to be drawn to community action when they have objections to register,[9] and that conflict in organizations and communities closely correlates with membership participation.[10] We do not cite these observations as a standard recipe for the would-be organizer, although they are the basis of Alinsky's espousal of contest tactics. Whatever one's stance regarding the latter, it is important to understand that one of the few resources available to the poor requires perceptions of difference or dissensus—and, therefore, campaign or contest types of intervention are likely to be the tactics of choice.

The only other item on the list of resources which is readily at the disposal of the poor is the threat of disruption and threats to property. (Rossi and Dahl omit threats to life, as in guerrilla warfare which, though a resource, may be ignored for our purposes.) To threaten property is, by definition, to engage in contest or disruption. In short, two of the resources which the poor can significantly muster are resources that are bound to generate competition and conflict.

To be real, collaborative modes of intervention, such as problem solving, education, and persuasion, require that an issue entails more than a rearrangement of resources and reflect a commonality of interest. Although there are undoubtedly commonalities of interest between the poor and some target systems, this is less often the case than the widespread use of collaborative tactics would suggest. Its use might best be explained as a consequence of the unequal power of service users in relation to officials. When the reach of the poor is modest, it is, by and large, because their less potent resources require less strident behaviors. In other words, the fact that collaboration is the only mode of intervention available often determines the definitions of community issues rather than the other way around.

To collaborate because there are common interests—or because one has no other alternative—or to *appear* to collaborate for political advantage is reasonable. But to prescribe collaborative means as preferential, if not exclusive, methods, as do many professionals, is another matter. It is, we suspect, making a virtue of necessity.

Our discussion of the association between resources and tactics has, until now, assumed the poor *acting on their own*. Often this is not the case. Action systems may be composed of the poor and the nonpoor. But since the resources available to the poor and those available to influentials are different, the two tend to use tactics that are contradictory. Thus an action system which, owing to the access of its influentials, has established relations with public officials cannot easily maintain those relations, seek favors, persuade, and at the same time subject the officials to virulent public pressure. These con-

9 James S. Coleman, *Community Conflict* (Glencoe, Ill.: Free Press, 1957), p. 19.
10 *Ibid.*, p. 3.

tradictions require delicate balancing, and may require that the poor choose to go their route for a time alone.

Relationships and Modes of Intervention. The composition of action and target systems affects the perceptions of the parties regarding the action effort. By no stretch of the imagination, for example, can a breakfast program for ghetto children, an activity of the Black Panthers, be defined as, on the face of it, leading to a change in status relations. When a program is conducted by a revolutionary group such as the Black Panthers, however, it is so perceived.

There are a number of reasons why the character of the parties, rather than the issues, shape the perceptions of an action effort. Issues often serve as a means to long-range ends which are vastly different from short-range ones. Another reason is that organizations devote considerable attention to creating images of themselves and develop reputations which condition perceptions of their activities. Banfield makes this point in regard to civic associations in Chicago:

Each association created for itself a corporate personality and aura. It has made itself both the custodian and the symbol, as well as the spokesman, of certain values. . . . The association's influence with the political heads and with prospective contributors, members, and supporters depends in part upon what it "represents" or symbolizes. Projecting the right image of itself is therefore essential to its maintenance as a going concern.[11]

Perceptions of issues and the tac-

11 Edward C. Banfield, *Political Influence* (New York: Free Press, 1961), p. 273.

tics used are also shaped by past relationships between the parties. Having engaged in prior interaction leads each party to have expectations regarding the positions and behaviors of the other. As noted by Deutsch, the number and strength of cooperative bonds (e.g., superordinate goals, mutually facilitating interests, common allegiances and values, linkages to a common community) enhance present cooperation, while "experiences of failure and disillusionment in attempts to cooperate make it unlikely." [12]

The relationships of action and target systems are influenced by their respective structures.[13] Often action and target systems are the same entity. The worker trying to change an agency policy, or the community group engaged in influencing its sponsor, constitute action and target systems operating within the same structure. Even when action and target systems are separate entities, individuals or groups within each structure may overlap or have intimate connections to relevant third parties. . . .

12 Morton Deutsch, "Conflicts: Productive and Destructive," *Journal of Social Issues,* Vol. XXV, No. 1 (January 1969), p. 27.
13 For a sophisticated discussion of the connections between the structure of bureaucratic organizations and primary groups, the extent of social distance between them, and the varied ways in which this affects how they interact and influence one another, the reader is referred to the work of Eugene Litwak and his colleagues. One such discussion is Eugene Litwak and Henry J. Meyer, "A Balance Theory of Coordination Between Bureaucratic Organizations and Community Primary Group," in Edwin Thomas, ed., *Behavioral Science for Social Workers* (New York: Free Press, 1967), pp. 246–62.

By and large, these structural relationships define the modes of intervention that can be invoked, as follows:

WHEN ACTION AND TARGET SYSTEMS ARE:	THE MODE OF INTERVENTION IS:
Part of same system	Collaborative (education, persuasion) Mild campaign (political maneuver)
Overlapping systems	Collaborative Campaign (mild coercion, bargaining)
Discrete systems	Collaborative Campaign Contest and disruptive tactics.

The more intimate the relations between action and target systems (i.e., when they are the same entity) and the less powerful the action system, the more likely it will be bound by consensual means. It is easier within a single structure—and, to a lesser degree, among overlapping entities as well—for the more powerful party (the target system) to invoke sanctions than when relations with the action system are more distant. Furthermore, the closer the relationship, the more visible the action; and the greater its visibility, the more it can be controlled.

TACTICAL CREATIVITY: SOME PRACTICE CONCERNS

In this section, we discuss some of the practice principles applicable to the modes of intervention which we have identified. Each mode (collaborative, campaign, and contest) con-

stitutes a set or category of tactics, as indicated in the list below: [14]

MODE OF INTERVENTION	TACTICS
Collaborative	Problem solving Education Joint action Persuasion
Campaign	Political maneuver Bargaining Negotiation Mild coercion
Contest or disruption	Clash of position within accepted social norms Violation of legal norms

. . . *Game Plan.* An organizer and group ought to have a good idea of what they plan to do before they set out to do it. They need to identify the essential players and, as in a game, anticipate as many of the moves as possible. Some factors to be addressed in the tactical plan have already been suggested: how an issue is likely to be perceived by the various actors; the resources available to the action system; the congruence of its resources with particular tactical choices; the target's relationship with the action system. . . .

Obviously, attempts to predict the responses of another party are highly uncertain. It is possible in developing a game plan, however, to estimate possible target responses, to assess the effect of each response on one's goal, and to be ready with

[14] We have omitted violence from our list of interventions (e.g., deliberate attempts to harm, guerrilla warfare, and attempts to take over the government by force), because these tactics are unavailable to professional organizers.

alternative reactions to the response. To neglect the development of such a tactical balance sheet is to endanger not only the success of the effort but also the worker and the community group.

Researching the Target. The efficacy of a tactical game plan depends on the accuracy of the information about the target system it incorporates. Bureaucratic officials, recognizing the importance of information, tend to shield their operations from scrutiny, particularly from scrutiny by those who threaten their authority. Welfare officials, for example, have refused to allow client groups access to the regulations of their department, information which is routinely made available to social agencies.

In researching the target, the answer to three questions are almost always of major significance: Who makes the decision regarding the desired change? What rewards or punishments will impel the decision makers to make the change? What is the basis, or sanction, of the current policy? . . .

Empathizing with the Target. A related expectation of the organizer is that he empathize with the target. To observe, hear, and understand the target permits more informed tactical judgments and increased tactical options.

Unfortunately, in their anti-establishment ethos, organizers sometimes lose sight of the fact that target systems are composed of people. Indeed, some organizers may be "turned off" by the very notion of empathy for the target. The strategic usefulness of empathy for the target varies with circumstances and modes of inter-

vention. It may be most important to collaborative action, since shared understanding is required in a collaborative process. Empathy is also more necessary for workers who act from within a target system than from outside of it,[15] since sustained interaction requires that the organizer approach the other as a person rather than as an object. . . .

Image Management. However much spontaneity and free expression are prized in social interaction, it must be recognized that individuals say and do things to influence the perceptions of others toward themselves. Goffman has argued that the basic underlying theme of all interaction is the desire of each participant to guide and control the responses made by the others present.[16] The attempt to influence impressions about ourselves, and to control the definitions of situations in which we're involved, may often be unconscious and ingrained in one's "life-style." But there are many occasions when it is intentional and conscious.

Image management does not necessarily mean giving a false impression. A group may wish to replace a stereotype with a more accurate definition. For example, a professional organizer, meeting with a union official who saw social workers as well-intentioned ladies, decided to appear rough hewn to revise the false image. Sometimes, on the other hand, impression management entails pro-

---

15 It should be kept in mind that action and target systems may be subsystems of a larger entity, or may even have overlapping membership.

16 Erving Goffman, *The Presentation of Self in Everyday Life* (New York: Doubleday, Anchor Books, 1959), pp. 3–4.

jecting ambiguous images to obscure what is real. Sometimes, too, a picture may be embroidered out of whole cloth.

Unlike persons, organizations are only conceptions based on agreements and commitments among people. And, also unlike persons, the conception of an organization can only be transmitted as an *image*. No one can *see* an organization, but they can hear of its size, read its literature, meet its members, learn about its activities—all of which constitute an organization's image. In considerable measure, the success of a leader rests on his ability to manage that image. Those who overdo it appear to others as so much "sounding brass and tinkling cymbals"; those who fail to fully develop the organization's image are squandering a useful resource. . . .

Timing the Action. The order and pace of any process shape its outcome. Timing is a tactical consideration of community workers and groups, whatever the mode of intervention.

It is in the interests of those engaged in community work to effectuate an action as early in a process as possible. In the field of intergroup relations, one maneuver of this sort is known as the *fait accompli,* whereby change is initiated swiftly and unequivocally. The integration of Southern public schools proceeded most successfully, for example, in cities where officials acted quickly and firmly. Allport suggests one reason for such an outcome: "Clearcut administrative decisions that brook no further argument are accepted when such decisions are in keeping with the voice of consci-

ence." [17] Actions which reflect prevailing values are more likely to gain acceptance through the *fait accompli.* Slavin indicates another reason for its efficacy. He notes that "Where feelings run deep . . . the *fait accompli* attempts to set action . . . before opposing forces have time to mobilize their resources and develop momentum for counterattack." [18] He suggests that this point is generally recognized in such instances as armies that are committed before war is declared, political ideals that are made before legislation is proposed, and social agency policies that are implemented before they are announced. Ordinarily, of course, the *fait accompli* is more often used *against* rather than *by* community groups.

The earlier one engages in any decision-making process, the greater the impact on the decision itself. In making an early move, one usurps "the power of definition," and as a decision progresses, it becomes harder to modify. . . .

An action system that desires third-party support must appear reasonable and responsible to that party. Or it must, at the least, be able to present an effective public case to explain its unreasonableness. One means of accomplishing this is through attention to the sequence of its tactical behaviors. To justify its actions, it must avoid "jumping" the process that a third party considers

17 Gordon W. Allport, *The Nature of Prejudice* (New York: Doubleday, Anchor Books, 1958), p. 471.

18 Simon Slavin, "Concepts of Social Conflict: Use in Social Work Curriculum," *Journal of Education for Social Work,* Vol. 5, No. 1 (Fall 1969), 57.

to be correct. Protocol prescribes that certain moves must precede others, and that when actions escalate, the escalation be in response to the target's recalcitrance rather than a reflection of the action system's immoderation. An agency staff member, for example, must exhaust lower-echelon channels before he can appeal to the executive. Or if he skirts the channels, he must not appear to be doing so. A community group pressing for school change must seek to meet with school officials prior to taking to the streets— even if they believe that nothing will come of the meetings.

There are risks in this position. A major one is that the target system can deplete the community group of strength and energy through its own "moderate" response. It can dispense symbolic or token rewards in place of real ones, and it can postpone action through such a ubiquitous device as a committee to study the problem. Since community groups are inherently unstable, token satisfactions and postponements further strain their cohesiveness and staying power. The solution is to expose the target's "moderation" for what it really is when the group finds it necessary to escalate its tactics rather than to ignore the niceties of process. This is particularly important when the issue is one which makes the target publicly vulnerable. When a target system is on uncertain ground regarding the substance of a disagreement, it will inevitably decry the process which is used and challenge the tactics of its adversaries. . . .

18   Two Views on Planning Tactics: A Case Study in Model Cities

MAXIMUM FEASIBLE MANIPULATION

As told to Sherry R. Arnstein

Introduction: We, the North City Area Wide Council Inc., believe this is a unique case study. It has been put together by community people *for the benefit of other community people.* Although it will be widely read by policymakers and politicians, it is addressed only to people like ourselves who are struggling against impossible odds to make public programs relevant to poor and powerless people.

Most case studies are written by social scientists whose biases are just like those of the traditional power structure. For years they have been invading our communities and diagnosing what ails us blacks, Puerto Ricans, Chicanos, Indians, and by-passed whites. For years they have been analyzing us as apathetic, stupid, and lazy. Until now, action-oriented community groups like the Area Wide Council (AWC) have been unable to fight back. We have had neither the journals, the dollars, nor the luxury of time to put to-

Reprinted with permission of author and publisher from: Sherry R. Arnstein, "Maximum Feasible Manipulation," *Public Administration Review* 32, Special Issue (September 1972), pp. 377–390.

gether the six-syllable words and the technical jargon to tell our side of the story.

This community case study is different! It is our analysis of what happened here in North Philadelphia as we struggled to use our model cities program to create a new balance of power between ourselves and City Hall.

This study was made possible by the National Academy of Public Administration (NAPA). Mrs. Sherry Arnstein was asked to write it with the clear understanding that she would write *only what we told her to write!*

We gave her access to all our records, including newspaper clippings, minutes of meetings, and correspondence—even a daily personal diary kept by one of our staff technicians. We talked to her for many days and many nights, individually and in groups. We made appointments for her to interview other community people in Philadelphia, and established her credibility so that people would share sensitive information with her.

We did this because she and NAPA guaranteed that every word of this case study could be edited in or out by us. In putting her technical skills at our disposal, she had the right to read everything available and to argue with any of us. But we retained full veto power over every comma, word, and phrase. What Mrs. Arnstein agrees or disagrees with in this document is completely irrelevant *to us and to her* since her objective was to *help us do our thing* —not hers, not HUD's, and not the Academy's!

When we started on this unique assignment, we intended to tell what the courts call the truth, the whole truth, and nothing but the truth. As we traveled down the road, however, we discovered that it would be better to deliberately leave out some of the hangups that are internal to our community.

Such hangups are pretty well known to most community leaders. They are not so well known to the establishment types who will also be reading this document. It would be foolish to let them in on such information, because they would use it to hurt the poor and the powerless.

Our case study, therefore, emphasizes what the power structure did to us, and excludes some of those things that we now realize we did to ourselves. . . .

Month-by-month frustration: We want to tell you right off that the AWC is no longer recognized by the power structure as being in the Model Cities business. HUD and the city foreclosed on us in May, 1969, because they got uptight about the degree of power we managed to achieve over the program.

If only we had known two years ago what we now know about city and federal politics, it might have been a different story. But we were political novices, and they were experts in political chicanery. We were trying to change things, and they were trying to keep us boxed in. It's so much harder to bring about change than it is to sit there and resist it. They had the upper hand, particularly the money and the sophisticated methods for maximum feasible manipulation.

As long as we were able to centralize the community's demands for change, the city feared us, and we were able to achieve stunning victories. When they finally managed to splinter us, we lost the only real power we had— people power. Here's how it happened day-by-day, month-by-month:

Fall, 1966—Knowing nothing about the possibility of a Model Cities Program, four professional people who worked for different agencies in the community were meeting quietly to talk about the dire need for creating a new community coalition in North Philadelphia. Representing a community group, a settlement house, and a church group, these four staffers discussed how their agencies might support such a new coalition to do three things: (1) to identify issues, (2) to mobilize the community, and (3) to articulate community-defined plans.

November-December, 1966—Philadelphia officials knew about the Model Cities Program long before most other cities. Inside information from Washington, D.C., was that Philadelphia would be awarded a planning grant of $750,000. Like every city in the country we know about, Philadelphia was planning to submit its application to HUD with no input from the residents of the neighborhood, or with some last-minute public hearings engineered to result in a rubber-stamp approval from the residents.

The mayor appointed a task force to prepare the required bulky application and a policy committee to review it before it was sent to Washington in March. Sitting on that policy committee, the task force, and its several subcommittees were officials from city agencies and a few silk-stocking civic leaders. No grass roots people from the model cities neighborhood even knew about their meetings in November and December.

January, 1967—The mayor announced to his policy committee that he had named his Washington, D.C., lobbyist as development coordinator and head of the Model Cities Program. One of the first products of the new director was an administrative structure chart for the Model Cities Program. The chart confirmed that all policy decisions would be made by him, and that city officials and establishment leaders would be advisory to him. Residents like us were to have no role at all except as the passive dumping ground for the program.

At this same meeting, a few members of the city committee persuaded the mayor to invite at least one community leader from the Model Cities neighborhood to sit with them during the remaining weeks before the application was sent to Washington. Little did most of them realize that the token representative they had invited was no token man; that he really knew the historic games being run down on the community under urban renewal and the antipoverty program; that he was one of the four staff people who were already planning to create a community coalition to speak up and speak out for the people's interests. When he heard that the city's Human Relations Commission was trying to open the door for community input by holding an open meeting on those parts of the application that fell in its bailiwick, he put the word out for community volunteers to attend the meeting.

January 20, 1967—Representatives from approximately thirty community groups took time off from work to go to that afternoon meeting. At first, we listened quietly as city officials described three parts of the application: citizen participation, administrative structure, and equal opportunity in employment and housing. Then, having done our homework, we zeroed in with hard-hitting questions. Like, how come they were describing our community organizations and churches as historically ineffectual? Like, what proportion of the policy committee would be neighborhood residents? We argued that the first failure had already occurred because proposals were coming down the pipe from them with no grass roots participation.

Our temporary spokesman stated that his organization was preparing an alternate proposal for citizen participation which would see to it that policy would come up the pipe from citizens instead of down. We demanded that several mass meetings be held in the community at night so that the grass roots people could find out what was in the works and have an opportunity to suggest alternatives. It was futile because the Human Relations Commission did not have the power to agree or disagree with us. All we got was a promise to circulate minutes of the meeting around City Hall. We knew then that it was up to us to mobilize the community and get our views directly to the mayor.

January 25, 1967—When the mayor's policy committee met again, a couple of its members supported our demands for real representation on their committee. Most of them, including the mayor, put the idea down. Instead, two new task force subcommittees were created—a subcommittee on citizen participation and a subcommittee on administrative machinery. The administrative machinery group had only one community representative, but the citizen participation group had fourteen of our people including the four community staff people who had been meeting in the fall to talk about the community's powerlessness before they even knew about the Model Cities Program.

January 30, 1967—At the first meeting of the subcommittee on citizen participation, the development coordinator apologized for the lack of citizen involvement in drawing up the application. He invited us to send representatives to sit in on the remaining meetings of all the task force subcommittees. We told him that we probably could get a few people to volunteer to join these task forces. But on such short notice and at such a late date, we wanted to put our real efforts into developing a community-defined approach to citizen participation. We told him that we had called a meeting in the community for January 31, to discuss our tentative definition and mechanism.

January 31, 1967—More than seventy people attended the first meeting as representatives of block clubs, settlement house groups, civil rights groups, and church groups. We laid out our sketchy proposal for what we called an "equal partnership" with the city and talked late into the night about what structure, what ground rules, and what resources could be put together to achieve a real community definition of citizen participation. We appointed a temporary steering committee to put our ideas on paper and to present them to a still larger mass meeting of community leaders.

February 2, 1967—When the city's citizen participation subcommittee met again, we told them about our plans for a second mass meeting. Again the city invited us to send representatives to the remaining meetings of the other task force subcommittees. Again we reminded the city that while about twelve people had volunteered to attend those meetings, our real concern at this late date was not to argue over the details of 350 pages that they had already written. Instead, we wanted to focus on our partnership model for citizen participation plus a complete rewrite of their first chapter, which outlined the city's warped and paternalistic view of our neighborhood.

Late February, 1967—By late February, our temporary steering committee had worked out the details of the partnership proposal. It called for the creation of a broad-based coalition of all active community organizations that would call itself the Area Wide Council (AWC). The AWC would have partnership status at City Hall to represent the community's interests in the model cities program. To make the partnership real, the city would contract $117,000 of the HUD planning grant to the AWC. The funds would be used by the AWC to hire its own community planners, organizers, lawyers, etc., to help the community react to plans prepared by the city and to enable the community to develop plans of its own for the city's reaction. The proposal spelled out guarantees that whenever there were disagreements over plans or policies between the city and the AWC, those disagreements would be negotiated until a solution acceptable to both parties was reached. It asked for six out of fifteen seats on the policy committee of the Model Cities Program and for AWC representation on all of the city's task forces. In short, the AWC would be the legally constituted citizen structure for the program. It would have the authority, the financial resources, and the independence to bargain with the city on behalf of the community.

More than 140 representatives from community groups helped work out the details of that proposal. It was the first time that so many groups with such diverse and competing interests had gotten together. We were Black, Puerto Rican, and white organizations. We were conservatives and militants. We were from both sides of Broad Street, which had always been an organizational dividing line in the community. It was beautiful!

March, 1967—The mayor knew that we were prepared to send a delegation to Washington to protest his application, and since he desperately needed the votes from our neighborhood to get reelected, he

agreed to our partnership proposal. The application that went to Washington included our proposal almost word for word and said in plain English:

"Recognizing that the quality of citizen participation in government programs has often fallen short of the mark, even when it was sincerely sought, the MCP in Philadelphia will strive to incorporate *within its very core guarantees of citizens' authority to determine basic goals and policies for planning and implementing the program.*" (Emphasis added.)

April, 1967—Since insiders knew that Philadelphia was definitely going to be named a Model City, we moved ahead without HUD funds to develop the internal structure of the AWC. After many evening meetings, we came up with a structure which would assure that the AWC remained accountable and responsive to the total community. On April 20, more than 500 people showed up at a mass meeting and voted unanimously to "formally establish the AWC" and to adopt the recommendations of our hardworking temporary committee on structure.

The AWC structure was designed to strengthen existing community organizations and interests groups in the community. It called for the creation of sixteen "hubs" located throughout the model neighborhood. Each "hub" would build itself on whatever community groups already existed and would locate itself in offices volunteered by friendly neighborhood settlement houses, churches, or community agencies.

The AWC Board would have ninety-two members: twelve of the

fourteen original organizers who had negotiated the partnership arrangement with the city, plus the elected chairman of each of the sixteen hubs, plus the four representatives selected by each hub to serve on the four AWC standing committees. (These committees were created to correspond to the city's four task forces on physical environment, human resources, employment and manpower, and education.) The AWC structure also called for a twenty-seven-man staff which would be responsible to the AWC board. Sixteen of the AWC staff would be field workers assigned to work with the sixteen hubs.

May-July, 1967—By June, when HUD was supposed to have awarded the planning grants to the winning Model Cities, we had already begun to organize the sixteen neighborhood hubs, and had started working within each of our newly created standing committees.

In July, when HUD still had not announced the winning cities and we heard that Congress might cut some of the Model Cities appropriation, various community leaders were urged to write their Congressmen and Senators to demand full support for the program.

We also used the waiting period to support various happenings in the community. In July, for example, we organized a mass meeting to introduce the new school superintendent to the community. We begged poster paper, borrowed sound trucks, and did everything we could to get a mass turnout for him.

During that waiting period, we learned that if we were going to organize the community, we would have to respond to all kinds of community demands to deal with existing problems. We could not tell the woman whose child had just been bitten by a rat that she should join us in a year-long Model Cities planning process. We would have to begin to help people with today's problems today, or they would not believe that the Model Cities planning process would affect their lives tomorrow.

We began to digest thick reports and evaluations written by various public and private agencies—in short, to educate ourselves on what was happening and who was doing what to whom.

August, 1967—We held an emergency session to discuss the governor's announcement that the state might get the Model Cities program rolling by making state funds available immediately to each of the Pennsylvania cities waiting for federal funds. On the one hand, we were delighted. On the other, we were worried that the state might not respect the partnership we had worked out with the city. We talked about sending a delegation to Washington to find out why HUD was still holding back on its promised announcement.

Finally, we were advised that the mayor would advance the AWC $57,000 of city funds so that we would not lose the Model Cities momentum built up in the community. Finally, we could hire staff, rent office space, install telephones, and buy typewriters. Finally, we could hire an executive director. Our first move was to call a mass meeting to let the community know we were really in business. Someone figured out by then that we had already put in more than 100,000 hours of volunteer time. Calculated at the rate of

$2.50 per hour, the community had already contributed the equivalent of $250,000 to get the Model Cities Program rolling.

In August, more residents started attending AWC board meetings and raising new issues that needed immediate responses. For example, one of our Hubs pointed out that Temple University had held a hearing to expand its campus into the community, but residents had not attended because they didn't know about it and didn't understand its importance. It was agreed that the AWC would be ineffective if it limited itself to future planning and ignored immediate issues like informing and mobilizing the community to protect itself at such hearings.

Again we voted to write to our Congressmen to protest the continuing delay in launching the Model Cities Program.

November 16, 1967—HUD finally announced that out of 194 contestants, Philadelphia was indeed one of the 63 winners. However, instead of the expected $750,000 planning grant, HUD gave the city only $278,000.

November 17, 1967—More than 3,500 Black students turned out for a demonstration at the school administration building downtown. They were demanding fourteen major changes in the high schools, including recognition of the Black student movement and the right to have Black studies, Black values, and Black principals. Inside the school superintendent's office, adults from the community were discussing the legitimacy of the students' demands. All of a sudden, without provocation, police attacked the youths and turned a street demonstration into a scene of violence in which fifty-seven people were injured and twenty-nine arrested.

This incident became a major turning point in the life of the AWC when police jailed two black community leaders who had helped the students organize the demonstration. One of the jailed organizers was an AWC community organizer! From this point on, the city was bent on destroying the power of the AWC.

November 18, 1967—News headlines the following day were mixed —some blamed the police, others blamed the students. News accounts revealed that the leaflets for the demonstration had been mimeographed at AWC offices. Our executive director immediately acknowledged that the students had asked to use the AWC mimeographs. He felt it was a legitimate request from a community group (and he later argued in court that AWC's first responsibility had to be the community).

The two Black community leaders were released from jail; their bail, which had been set at $50,000, was reduced to $5,000. This action was prompted by a five-man interdenominational clergy group which petitioned the judge on the grounds that the two men weren't even present when "the police began their brutal attack on the students, nor did the defendants do anything whatsoever to incite a riot." The clergymen stated that they considered the high bail a "ransom," and one of their group wryly pointed out, "It's a strange system of justice indeed that Father————who is white and wears a collar is released on $1 bail, while————

——who is black and wears a beard is held on $50,000 bail."

November 21, 1967—The city development coordinator demanded that the AWC redefine its role and stick "simply and solely to planning." Trying to intimidate us, he sent an auditor to review our books for improper use of the $39,000 advanced to us by the city. At least two federal agencies, including the FBI, did character investigations on several AWC staff to determine what should be done about the "trouble-makers."

November 24, 1967—We refused to be intimidated and behave like a bunch of apologetic children caught stealing from the cookie jar. Instead, we reaffirmed our rights by issuing a policy statement that outlined the AWC's view of self-dignity, self-expression, and self-determination. The statement underscored the basic principle of community organization by pointing out that AWC's "acceptance in the community hinges on meaningful involvement in dealing with immediate problems while planning for longer-range solutions."

Some of our members at first objected to the proposed policy statement. There was lengthy debate on the issue. Finally, there was rousing support for the students' demonstration and the AWC's support for their demands.

December 7, 1967—Close to 600 people turned out for a special meeting called by the AWC to explain the role it had played in the students' street demonstration.

Also at the meeting was the city development coordinator. He made it clear that City Hall and HUD were planning to punish the AWC by cutting back on the city's firm

commitment to fund AWC operations at a level of $21,000 a month. He refused to see our point that when constituents who had helped to build the AWC demanded legitimate help in expressing their discontent, the AWC could not turn its back on that demand. To do so would reduce the AWC to nothing more than a tool of the power structure.

It was a noisy meeting with heated debate among community people who ranged all the way from conservative citizens to militant youth. Though some objected to the AWC's position the overwhelming number backed us all the way. They approved an AWC policy statement that residents of North Philadelphia would "determine their own capacity for participation" and endorsed a resolution "extending our support to all students who participated in the demonstration, in the struggle to get a better education."

December 10, 1967—Later in the week, the AWC's "punishment" was announced. The city used the cutback in HUD planning funds as an excuse to cut us back to $13,000 a month to force us to fire several AWC staff. Though the city was planning to accept state funds and add $187,000 from its own coffers to make up for some of the reduced HUD grant, it would not give us any of that money. The development coordinator announced that unless we agreed to the cutback, he would not sign any contract with us—even though he knew that we didn't have enough money left to meet the next AWC payroll.

December 12, 1967—We demanded a meeting with the mayor, who refused to see us. The development coordinator threatened to find another community organization in North Philadelphia to unseat the AWC if we didn't agree to a $13,000 contract. Still we insisted that we had done nothing wrong in supporting a request from the community and would not be demeaned by accepting the cutback. The city admitted that the auditors had found no discrepancies in our books and nothing which indicated dishonesty in our use of the $39,000 advanced to us by the city.

December 14 1968—Our Board announced formally that it would reject the $13,000 and try to meet our payroll by raising funds in the community. The Philadelphia Crisis Committee supported our appeal to the mayor.

January 15, 1968—The mayor appointed a new development coordinator to head the Model Cities Program. Still we were without funds!

Late January, 1968—To dramatize our stalemate with the city, and to help some of our employees get money to meet emergency food and rent problems, ten of our staff were escorted to the Welfare Department by the Welfare Rights Organization to apply for public assistance grants. By then, some of the staff had not received paychecks for more than seven weeks even though the community came to our rescue with contributions of $7,500! (Contributions the city has never repaid despite its public promise to reimburse us so that we, in turn, could offer to give the money back to the donors.)

January 22, 1968—Finally our determined campaign paid off. The city signed a contract with us for $18,000 a month. We remained committed to our position that planning and action go hand-in-hand or neither are meaningful.

February 22, 1968—One of our hubs reported that residents in the Simon Gratz High School neighborhood were furious because the planned expansion of the overcrowded school had been stalemated by the city's refusal to condemn fourteen homes occupied by white families. The hub asked the AWC to support a neighborhood demonstration at the Board of Education. In keeping with our commitment to combine planning with social action, we, of course, supported their request. We felt it was both an educational and moral crisis. More than 40,000 Black people had been kicked out of their homes in North Philadelphia for the benefit of urban renewal and Temple University. But now that fourteen white families were objecting, it looked as if the desperately needed expansion of the Gratz School might go down the drain. (The issue was ultimately settled, but unlike the thousands of dislocated Black families, the white people got paid off handsomely for their homes.)

February 26, 1968—We objected to the city's unilateral deadline of March 15 for developing a Joint Work Program for HUD. We pointed out that our AWC standing committees had to take their proposals back to the Hubs for approval before the AWC could commit itself as an organization. We proposed an alternate schedule which showed how the community's voice could be built in by adding two weeks to the schedule. Finally they agreed, but it was typical of the many incidents between us when we emphasized the AWC's interest in honest involvement as opposed to the development coordinator's interest in using the community as a rubber stamp.

March-May, 1968—Though we won our battle with the city and HUD over the November 17 incident, the battle had significant side effects. Some white liberal and conservative Negro leaders dropped away from the AWC. On the other hand, the more militant sectors of the community became more active in AWC affairs. It was a turning point: AWC became more militant, more angry, and more determined.

Meanwhile, back at City Hall, the development coordinator was violating our partnership agreement left and right. He didn't even send us copies of correspondence on his wheeling and dealing. His task forces were meeting regularly, but only the Welfare Task Force notified us of its meetings so that we could attend. He hired a man to work directly with the Hubs to try to divide and conquer the Hub structure. His Physical Planning Task Force was emphasizing lots of new public housing, while our committee endorsed strategies of subsidized homeownership for poor people. He was ramrodding plans through that would improve the city's image with HUD, while we were struggling for major constructive change in our neighborhood's quality of life.

The final blow came when we learned that instead of submitting to HUD the Joint Work Program that we had so carefully negotiated with him, he had sent in three different Work Programs: ours, his, and that of the individual city agencies. We considered the pros and cons

of demanding his resignation on the grounds that he couldn't relate to the community in even an elementary way to say nothing of an honest partnership.

May 9, 1968—Instead we asked for a meeting with HUD officials. That's how we learned that while HUD was requiring the city to submit the finished Comprehensive Demonstration Plan by January 1969, he was pushing to finish a plan within *one month* (so that Philadelphia could get Model Cities action money for pacification programs to "cool the hot summer"). That's when we realized that after all the meetings we had gone to, and all the listening we had done, and all the negotiating we had engaged in, *he was quietly moving ahead on his own to violate every one of those agreements!* How's that for a guaranteed partnership between community and City Hall!

Late May, 1968—Another major clash between the city and the community arose over the use of open space money which HUD was making available to Model Cities in order to get some quick visible results. We looked at the program and saw in it all kinds of opportunities for construction jobs for community people, planning and architectural jobs for Black and Puerto Rican professionals, plus linkages with new and exciting recreation programs planned by the youth themselves. The city, on the other hand, wanted us to concentrate solely on site selection and leave all those "minor details" to the Recreation Department.

June, 1968—Having uncovered just how dishonest our second Model Cities director was, we called a mass meeting to demand that he be replaced by a Black director screened by the Black community. But we knew by then that his dishonest dealings with us were really a reflection of the city's callousness toward the community. Our distrust of the mayor had zoomed sky high.

Though we knew the development coordinator was on his way out of his job, he did not. His next move, therefore, was to throw still another ball down the street for us to go chasing after. He gleefully reminded us that our contract with the city was again expiring on June 30, and he imposed a whole set of unreasonable conditions on its renewal. He wanted a copy of our bylaws, which he knew well that we had not yet managed to put together because of all the other balls we had been chasing. He wanted copies of all our minutes, which he knew we wouldn't entrust to him since those carefully kept minutes revealed our strategies for dealing with him. He wanted the names and addresses of our leaders, which we knew he would use to harass them since many of them held jobs in government agencies. Though he sent us late notices of official task force meetings, he demanded advance notice of all hub meetings. This he wanted so that he could try to drive wedges between us and the hubs by manipulating them.

We set up a contract negotiating committee. We instructed it to take a hard line to be sure that the community's interests were not sold down the river. We also voted to negotiate for a larger contract. We wanted more money to strengthen the hubs—to pay for their office expenses and to pay stipends of $7 per meeting to hub chairmen and other community leaders who were by then sacrificing three or four evenings almost every week for the program.

In late June, our efforts to oust the second development coordinator paid off. Though the mayor did not allow us to join him in selecting a new man, he did at least appoint a Black man as the Model Cities administrator.

July-August, 1968—This move created a temporary truce between us and the city. First we resolved the contract dispute. We came out of those negotiations with an AWC contract for $46,000 per month! Next we worked out a new structure for joint city-community planning.

We all agreed that the Model Cities executive committee which had formerly been like a secret society would now include the city's task force chairmen and city staff, the AWC's standing committee chairman and AWC staff, the Model Cities and the AWC directors. We also agreed that the executive committee would meet every two weeks to review the work of the city's task forces and the AWC standing committees.

We further agreed on the composition of a policy committee to mediate disputes which might arise between the city and AWC; and if that mediation failed, the dispute would be referred to the mayor who would decide the issue. Finally, we agreed to a new work program under which an interim report would be sent HUD by September 15 and the first-year action proposal would be ready by January 15, 1970.

September-December, 1968—What a wild period! To meet that January deadline for getting a plan to HUD, both the AWC and the city had to hire many new people, orient them to what it was all about, and let them sink or swim! By November (when the Republicans got elected) we were advised to get the plan in by December 31, because once the Republicans took over, they might hold up funding of all first-year action programs from all cities.

We worked night and day, weekends, and holidays to put together our ideas and the city's ideas. We had many differences in approach, but with our partnership arrangement, we were able to trade off so that they got some of their priorities, but so did we. At the end, it was literally a last minute cut-and-paste job which reflected our agreements on how Philadelphia would move ahead with $49 million for the first year of action.

The significance of our struggle for partnership status is best seen in the model cities administrator's page of acknowledgements: "Most rewarding was the destruction of the myth that a Model Cities community and a governmental body politic cannot enjoy a successful partnership." In addition the application said:

"This joint planning relationship between the city and the community, as could have been anticipated, has not been without its share of conflict. . . . There is every indication that with time, Philadelphia will become a model for the country of what form joint planning with citizens should assume. It must be understood, however, that this relaship will never be static or conflict-free. Rather, the basic realities of life in America today insure that some conflict will be inevitable. It is the opinion here, however, that

this residual conflict may provide the kind of dynamism that is necessary to make government truly responsive to the needs of its citizens and to further the realization of an ever-elusive democratic society."

January-February, 1969—Can you believe that after having managed to achieve this level of interaction, that right after the application went to Washington, we were again betrayed by City Hall?

What happened was that HUD decided that the $49-million plan had to be revised and scaled down to projects totalling $25 million. HUD said that the revisions and paring process, should be done during what is called a hiatus period. HUD offered the city a Letter to Proceed which meant that if HUD accepted the revised plan for $25 million, the city would be reimbursed for its operating expenses during the hiatus period.

We had known about this hiatus thing back in December, and had been assured verbally by the city and by HUD that the promised Letter to Proceed would include the AWC at its $46,000-per-month level of operations. But because our legal guard was down, we did not ask for this in writing. Well, the city arbitrarily decided in January not to renew our contract unless we would agree to slash our fifty-two-man staff down to twenty-two.

We were outraged! All of our "partners" were drawing their full pay during the damned hiatus period, but *we* were expected to fend for ourselves unless we were willing to fire more than half of our staff. It took nine weeks, a mass meeting, and two marches down to the mayor's office to turn him around.

During the nine nasty weeks, the city played real dirty pool. Trying to split the AWC staff, it offered city paychecks to the twenty-two AWC staff people whose jobs were not at stake. It even tried to buy some of them off with offers of permanent city jobs. Nevertheless, the staff stayed together. Again, the Welfare Rights Organization helped them get emergency welfare checks, and somehow they managed to survive. Finally, the mayor asked the City Council to approve city funds being advanced, and finally our whole staff got retroactive paychecks. But it was hell, and during the controversy some community factions and staff factions began to turn on each other.

March, 1969—In early March, we got our fourth Model Cities administrator, because the third one decided to seek election as a judge. Once again, the community was not consulted. We all learned about the changeover by reading the morning newspaper. This time the mayor picked a black woman from the community who knew the AWC from her personal experience with a hub.

Despite the unexpected changeover, we and the city managed to continue to work together to complete the revised $25-million plan. Strangely enough, despite all the double-dealing, our partnership was really beginning to make an impression. Some of the city and private power structure had actually learned to swing with us. Some of them really were able to appreciate what we were fighting for and to agree that our demands for drastic changes in the system were more than legitimate.

The revised Comprehensive Plan is a testimonial to that learning. It stated boldly on page one that the two basic problems in the Model Neighborhood were poverty and powerlessness. It therefore promised that Philadelphia would use the $25 million to deal with those twin problems by: "1. assisting Model Cities residents to assume some control over their own economic resources and providing effective mechanisms for participating in the policy-making system of the city, and 2. providing programs and services which are developed by, and (are) therefore more capable of meeting the needs of the . . . residents."

Page three showed the agreed-upon priorities: 50 percent for economic development, 23 percent for comprehensive community education, 21 percent for physical environment, and only 6 percent for social service delivery systems.

Later pages showed how some of these priorities would be realized by creating seven new corporations, four of which were to be community controlled in that the majority of their board of directors would be chosen by the AWC.

There it was, right out in the open for everyone to see that this was a radically different proposal from any that the politicians would have come up with if they had not been forced to bargain with the community. Among the many innovative projects proposed were:

—an economic development corporation with the power to buy land, machinery, buildings, borrow and lend money;

—a land utilization corporation or land bank to acquire needed land for community purposes;

—a housing development corporation to

construct new housing and rehabilitate old houses;

—an urban education institute to retrain and retread insensitive teachers;

—a career institute to train residents for the hundreds of model cities jobs that would be created;

—six communications centers where residents would have new educational avenues for developing communications skills, and learn how to use films, videotapes, to present their points of view and to increase their ability to make sounder decisions about public programs;

—incubator plants in which businessmen could be taught managerial skills on the job.

April, 1969—Two days before the revised plan was sent to HUD, the Nixon Administration announced new guidelines for Model Cities and stated that all applications from all the cities would be completely scrutinized to weed out "unwise and unnecessary proposals." Little did we realize that Philadelphia would be the first victim of those vague words!

May, 1969—In late May, HUD wrote to the mayor that the city's plan had "unusually heavy reliance on new corporations," had "too heavy involvement [of the AWC] in these operating corporations," and had "insufficient involvement of the city . . . and established institutions." In other words, HUD objected to the plan's fundamental strategy of power redistribution as projected in the creation of new community corporations. HUD was placing its confidence in the same old-line institutions that have traditionally betrayed the community.

June 9, 1969—Completely negating our partnership, the Model Cities administrator responded to HUD's

qualms about the AWC's power by chopping us right down to a strictly advisory role in all seven of the proposed corporations. Without consulting us, she unilaterally sent HUD a Supplementary Statement, which promised that the AWC would only be allowed to nominate one-third of the board of the new corporations; the remaining two-thirds would be chosen personally by her or by some other citizen groups chosen by her.

Late June, 1969—HUD and the city must have assumed that we would accept their outrageous conditions because they were still quite willing to sign off on the AWC's new $540,000 contract for its next year of operating expenses. In their minds, one-half million dollars must have seemed like a pretty good price for selling out a community.

As you can see, the Model Cities administrator carried out the bidding of the power structure against her own people. As we got down to the June 30 deadline when our contract would run out once again, she ignored our appeals to restore our partnership agreements (and other contract issues she was trying to force on us). Using a "take it or leave it" attitude, she insisted that if we didn't cave in by June 30, then any contract we might agree to at a later date would not be made retroactive.

We searched our souls. A few of us *were* ready to be bought off for that dollar figure. Some of us argued sincerely that it was better to accept a drastically reduced role in the program than to chuck it all after two years of blood, sweat, and tears. After much discussion, we voted overwhelmingly to refuse the unilateral contract terms. Instead, we decided to take both the city and HUD to court to demand that our right to participate meaningfully be restored.

July-August, 1969—Completely ignoring our objections, HUD announced that it would award the city $25 million for the first action year. It promised $3.3 million for immediate use to mount those few proposed projects that HUD liked. It told the city to go back to the drawing boards for the remaining $21.5 million because HUD wanted the whole community corporation strategy knocked out.

HUD allowed as how it might approve one corporation for the first year if the city could "justify not using existing institutions." But, in that event, HUD demanded two more blows against the AWC's power: that it not be allowed to nominate *any* of its own members to serve on the corporation's board, and that it not be allowed to nominate *any* of the board members after the first year of operation. In other words, even the city's drastic cut in the AWC's powers did not satisfy HUD. Incredible as it may seem, HUD demanded that the AWC be stripped of every shred of influence over any corporation that might be created.

To keep ouselves going, we again turned to the community. We launched a $10,000 drive and arranged to have our rent and telephone expenses drastically reduced. By August 15, we filed our court suit charging HUD and the city with illegally limiting our right to participate.

November, 1969—The rest of our bitter story is also a matter of history. In November, the Eastern District Court of Pennsylvania dismissed our court suit on the incredible grounds that we lacked "standing to sue." Our lawyers were just as outraged as we by the injustice of the court's decision. They and other lawyers, from as far away as California, volunteered their services to help us file a legal appeal.

Until we lost our first round with the courts, the AWC was together, and the city was restrained from organizing its own co-opted citizens group to act as representatives of the Model Neighborhood. When the district court handed down its negative decision, we were torn apart.

The five-month holdup had taken its toll and split the community into many factions. Our unpaid staff had, of course, taken other jobs. Even some of our faithful AWC supporters had given up, or they were saying that it was better to have a minor AWC role than no role at all.

December, 1969, to the present— The strongest of us refused to be beaten down. We decided to keep the AWC alive and to fight for our rights. By February, we and our lawyers had worked out the details of a legal appeal.

We are now waiting for the decision of the U.S. Court of Appeals and hoping against hope that it will make several findings on our lawsuit: (1) that the AWC, the official citizens structure of the Model Cities program, does indeed have the right to sue HUD and the city to protect our basic rights; (2) that the Secretary of HUD had no right to require the city to change the basic strategy of its Model Cities plan just because that strategy didn't fit in with his limited wisdom about power and powerlessness; (3) that the city had no right to agree to HUD's appalling requirement without even consulting the AWC which was the legally constituted citizen structure for the Model Cities program.

By January, 1970, the Model Cities administrator appointed a Citizens Advisory Committee, and we are sorry to say that even some of the AWC's top leaders agreed to serve on that plantation-type structure which (like the old days of urban renewal) can only advise, while the politicians decide. They are just names on a letterhead with no accountability to the community.

The city is now trying to turn each of the AWC hubs into neighborhood councils. It hopes to buy off each council with a lousy $10,000 or $12,000 contract if it will "participate in an advisory capacity." You won't believe us, but those stranglehold contracts actually say: that if HUD reduces or terminates its funds to the city, the councils' funds may be reduced or terminated by the city *"at its sole discretion";* that the "city may suspend or terminate payments" if the councils' required monthly reports "are incorrect or incomplete in *any* material respect"; that the city may withhold payment if the council "is *unable* or unwilling to accept *any additional* conditions that may be provided by law, by executive order, by regulations, or *by other policy* announced by HUD or (the) city"; and finally that "notwithstanding anything to the contrary contained herein, either party will have the right to terminate this contract upon thirty days written notice." (Emphasis added.)

So, temporarily, the shortsighted politicians have won. The innovative citizen-City Hall balance of power is dead here, and we have returned to an insulting plantation model under which the masters are assumed to know best and the slaves are expected to obey meekly.

They think they have beaten us down, and maybe they have cut the ground out from under what was called the Area Wide Council, but fools that they are, they forget what President John F. Kennedy once said about those who crush efforts at self-determination: "Those who make peaceful revolutions impossible make violent revolutions inevitable." . . .

Lesson Number One: No matter what HUD says, Model Cities is first and foremost a politician's game. Although the mountains of HUD guidelines and technical bulletins insist that Model Cities is a technical planning process, everyone but community people seems to know by now that it's really a political process. . . .

Philadelphia's Comprehensive Plan testifies to just how different a Model Cities plan did emerge when the politicians were required to negotiate with the community instead of just trampling all over it.

Lesson Number Two: You can't trust City Hall or HUD. That's what the Nixon administration ignores when it pronounces from on high that the goal of citizen participation is to "build trust" between City Hall and the community.

It might be beautiful if City Hall and HUD were trustworthy. But our history testifies to the fact that we'd be fools to trust the politicians. We were cheated each time we let our legal guard down. We only succeeded when we insisted that the politicians live up to their promises, and when we demonstrated that we had some power. . . .

Lesson Number Three: Community coalitions need to develop their own agendas instead of constantly reacting to the agendas of outside forces. If you allow yourself to be kept busy reacting to the government's short-term contract negotiations, unrealistic deadlines, and mountains of bureaucratic paper requirements, you get diverted from the really important task of initiating, refining, and acting on your community's agenda. You also can get diverted from keeping your own house in order. . . .

Some of us believe that if we managed to stay closer to the ground, we could have mobilized enough community support to march by the thousands on City Hall and forced the mayor to tell HUD to keep its hands off a local plan that met all of HUD's legal requirements. (Some community groups have managed to pull this off.). . .

Lesson Number Four: Community organizations must have the dollars to hire their own staff technicians, and must be able to direct that staff and to hold it accountable. We knew we started that without our own staff of technicians, we couldn't possibly keep up with all the legitimate and illegitimate agendas that they would be running on us. One of the surprising lessons we learned was that some of our own community staff could be co-opted by the power holders or be moving without us on their own agendas.

We discovered that if we were not equipped to do our own thinking,

we could easily become patsies for some of our own pros. Today, we would place more emphasis on training for ourselves as community leaders and for our staff as technicians. In saying that, however, we want to emphasize that we don't mean the kind of patronizing gobbledygook that is usually passed out by the old-line educationists. We mean honest training that is designed with us and not for us. We mean trainers selected by us for their technical knowledge, their integrity, and their ability to relate to the community.

Lesson Number Five: You can't organize a community without "deliverables." By this we mean that community people are daily struggling with basic bread-and-butter survival issues for themselves and their families. Attempts to organize them around their mutual problems for their mutual gain are doomed unless they can see tangible results of their efforts.

The Model Cities planning process, which required great personal sacrifices in hopes of uncertain payoff twelve months later, was a poor vehicle for building and maintaining a representative community coalition. For a group like the AWC to successfully organize a community, we needed to be able to deliver concrete benefits that could demonstrate the value of sticking together, struggling together, and holding each other accountable, e.g., an AWC ombudsman who could have arranged immediate help to individuals with personal problems like evictions, lack of bail money, or a child's expulsion from school. . . .

Lesson Number Six: Don't underestimate the potential support for the community's agenda from sympa-

thetic people outside the community. During AWC's four contract crises, we learned that our struggle had considerable meaning to some people outside the community.

For example, some of the staff of the city agencies and some of the HUD and OEO people were real swingers who helped us time after time. Some of them told us inside information that gave us the upper hand in negotiating with their agencies. Some of them worked with us at night and on weekends giving us great technical help on our program ideas and showing us how to use some of the laws already on the books to achieve our priority agendas.

During the first crises, some of the professionals working for the City Planning Commission were so outraged by the mayor's position that they actually contributed money from their own pockets to help us keep the AWC alive.

Some of our own AWC staff wrote checks as big as $100, $250, or $500 to help other staff deal with the payless paydays. Contributions were given by university people, Black churches, white churches, denominational offices, and the local chapter of the National Association of Intergroup Relations Officials.

Similarly, some of the press and elected officials turned out to be powerful allies. Community groups should systematically identify and encourage these political, technical, and financial allies.

Lesson Number Seven: Be prepared to fight each frustrating step

of the way when you're trying to break new ground. Here again, the establishment refuses to see what dehumanizing hoops we have to jump through every time we agree to play in their ballpark. . . .

Our experiences with unsympathetic and antagonistic officials . . . have convinced us that Model Cities is designed to deceive the community by pacifying our minds, our spirit, and our ambition.

Lesson Number Eight: Community people all over the country need to get together to create our own national power base to force "our" government to deal with us directly. We need to be able to communicate with each other, to teach each other, and to jointly pressure the government into creating honest community programs with straightforward guidelines.

We have already been in touch with community people from more than twenty other model neighborhoods and have been struggling for some time to get funds from the foundations and churches to create a National Citizens' Institute on Model Cities. Our struggles for money without strings have yet to pay off, but we'll get it somehow. In carrying out that struggle, we are mindful of what the Black abolitionist-scholar Frederick Douglass said more than 100 years ago:

"The whole history of progress of human liberty shows that all concessions yet made to her august claims have been born of earnest struggle . . . if there is no struggle, there is no progress."

POSTSCRIPT: PHILADELPHIA'S MODEL CITIES CONFLICT IN CONTEXT

MICHELLE OSBORN

When Mayor James H. J. Tate appointed Goldie Watson Model Cities Administrator in March, 1969, an intensely loyal, politically astute titan entered the fray. At a critical time.

Mrs. Watson holds her head high. When she was suspended along with twenty-five other public school teachers during a 1954 McCarthy-era investigation of Communism in the city schools, she wrote a letter to parents and friends of the Martha Washington School where she had taught for more than two decades.

"During all this time," she wrote, "I have had two aims. One, to instill a feeling of pride in their Negro heritage. . . . How often have I said, hold up your head, look the world in the eye, be proud that you are a Negro! Two, I have wanted them to know and to appreciate the duties and privileges of American citizens, and therefore, to develop a burning desire to live as first-class citizens in this great land of freedom and democracy. . . ."

In 1961, the Pennsylvania Supreme Court overturned Mrs. Watson's con-

Reprinted with permission of author from Michelle Osborn, "Postcript: Philadelphia's Model Cities Conflict in Context," *City* (October–November 1970), pp. 39–43.

viction for contempt of Congress and she was reinstated in the school system. She had refused to testify before the House Un-American Activities Committee, she said, solely on the basis of the First Amendment.

The episode speaks for Goldie Watson's character. When she believes she's right, she's immovable. A handsome woman with a commanding presence and a deep, resonant voice, she is almost invariably described as "tough." It is easy to see Mrs. Watson's strong hand in her June 9, 1969, statement, which, along with HUD's response, marked the crucial point in the controversy over the Philadelphia model cities program.

With HUD compliance, Mrs. Watson did what none of the previous three model cities administrators had been able to do: she established the city's authority over the Area Wide Council.

On May 27, HUD Assistant Secretary Floyd Hyde had written Mayor Tate: "I believe that most of the underlying technical problems which our reviewers have found in the Philadelphia application can best be approached by a major strengthening of the commitment and capacity which the city will provide for the program in the coming year."

Hyde listed three major categories of problems:

1. "Unusually heavy reliance on new corporations to carry out extraordinarily difficult assignments.
2. "Heavy involvement in these operating corporations of the same citizen group which is the major neighborhood representative for model cities planning, monitoring, evaluating, and resource allocation.
3. "Insufficient involvement of the city of Philadelphia and of established institutions, business, and voluntary agencies in most parts of the program."

"Our concern," a HUD official later said, "was how much of a program Philadelphia could actually operate."

In his June 9 reply, Mayor Tate enclosed a twelve-page statement by Goldie Watson, which, he said, represented a "critical clarification of the role to be played by the city of Philadelphia in its model cities program. This clarification is designed to insure that there can be no questions about the city's basic responsibility for that program, or about the role of government in carrying it out."

Mrs. Watson's statement said in part that while there was general agreement that AWC would serve as a delegate agency for only those programs which involve "community organization, planning, evaluation, and community advocate activities," thus resolving the question of direct control of the program, the "problem of indirect control" remained.

The key issue was the proposed nonprofit corporations: the "citizen organization is granted the right to name all or a majority of the directors of nonprofit corporations which serve as delegate agencies for . . . action programs. The administrator believes that these provisions raise serious questions related not only to the objectivity of the citizen organization, but also to the programmatic vitality and administrative feasibility of the model cities program as a whole. . . ."

Accordingly, the AWC was to nominate not more than one-third of the incorporators and one-third of the board of directors of the new nonprofit corporations, while the remaining two-thirds would be nominated by the model cities administrator or by some other citizen groups chosen by her.

Mrs. Watson had dealt established community and citywide organizations back into the game, in accordance with HUD's position, which was clearly stated June 5 by HUD Deputy Assistant Secretary Robert Baida.

Baida wrote the mayor: "In the model cities program, projects and activities should be operated by existing public and private institutions, whenever possible. In this way model cities may best achieve two of its objectives, appropriate changes in existing institutions and the improvement of delivery of services. Existing public and private institutions must be strengthened and become more responsible for, and more responsive to, the needs of the model neighborhood. . . ."

Mrs. Watson refers to this critical period as a "complete about-face." She is proud that the new neighborhood councils organized to replace the AWC's sixteen neighborhoods. Hubs chose delegates to the new citizen participation committee in an election overseen by the American

Arbitration Association. She is also proud that, unlike many of the players in the AWC drama, she lives in the model neighborhood.

But she views citizen participation as "planning, monitoring, and evaluation."

Philadelphia model cities deputy administrator William H. Will, who has been with the program from the start, took up the city's point of view from there. "We cannot fund broadly defined social action, we cannot fund self-defined social action, and we cannot fund a secret organization," he said.

The AWC made a "big point of being unaccountable to the administration. They refused to provide minutes, names and addresses of board members, and refused to subscribe to certain fiscal and accounting procedures. . . . There are no records of the Hubs. The minutes of the AWC are handwritten sheets; there is no indication who took the minutes, no indication who was at the meetings, whether or not they were duly elected, whether they represented the community. We don't know who the AWC is right now. There is literally no record of their elected officers. What limited record there is serves to raise doubts as to whether there was a quorum present when those officers were elected. To our knowledge, all but two live outside the model neighborhood. . . ."

As for the June 9 statement, Will said, "We've spent long days in court proving, we hope, two things." The AWC didn't participate in drafting the statement because they refused to do so; but "we think it's clear that they were consulted about the issues set forth in the June 9 statement. . . . I maintain, and so does Mr.

Hyde, that there was no substantial change in the federal guidelines.

"Conflict of interest was not a matter of HUD guidelines: you can't *evaluate* a project if you *operate* a project. There's one thing I plead with you to emphasize: the critical thing here is the operation of programs by a citizen participation movement. There's nothing which prevents the establishment of new nonprofit organizations or which prevents all of the board of directors from being community representatives. The only thing our statement does is to limit the influence and control of that citizen participation unit. We are looking for citizen organizations to operate programs," Will concluded, pointing out that six resident community organizations are operating model cities programs today.

Hans B. Spiegel and Stephen D. Mittenthal noted in their 1968 study of neighborhood power and control (contracted for by HUD) that HUD had until then assumed a qualified stance "implicitly sanctioning neighborhood power but rejecting neighborhood control" in model cities programs. When Goldie Watson was named administrator in March, 1969, fund cutbacks from $49 to $25 million already had been announced. In fact, the city had been notified of the reduction the previous November.

Coincident with the need to pare the program drastically, the AWC was up against its most formidable City Hall advocate to date. Soon after Mrs. Watson was appointed, she refused to release AWC monthly checks for salaries until an accounting system was established that conformed to HUD guidelines. In early March, sixty-five AWC staff members had demonstrated outside the mayor's office for seven weeks' back pay. Accommodation was reached on this issue with the aid of HUD mediation.

But HUD began to change its posture. Spiegel and Mittenthal's study had concluded with recommendations aimed at a redistribution of resources. Specifically, they recommended that HUD should "philosophically and institutionally enlarge its constituency to include target area neighborhoods."

By May 27, 1969, after five months of top-level review of all the participating cities' plans, HUD had chosen differently. City Hall authority and responsibility were to be reinforced at the expense of neighborhood power. Robert Baida, HUD Deputy Assistant Secretary, whom Will says was "key in this," put it this way in a July, 1969, speech: "The message of the [Nixon] Administration is clear: the model cities program is not to be controlled by citizen groups. Control and responsibility rest with local government. Unfortunately, this Administration inherited a philosophy in many areas of the country dedicated toward extensive citizen control."

With this shifting of the winds, what had been a continuous struggle to win power and with it legitimacy as the bargaining agent for the model neighborhood was abruptly ended. In July, the AWC's contract expired. Mrs. Watson said the doors to her office would be closed if AWC went to court. The AWC turned to the court for redress of grievances.

Judge Morgan Davis of the U.S. District Court in Philadelphia dismissed a complaint, filed by AWC August 15, 1969, charging HUD and the city had illegally limited citizen participation, on the grounds that the plaintiffs lacked standing to sue. He granted the motion to dismiss, noting "we may properly treat the motion to dismiss as one for summary judgment": on the basis of all the material facts, neither the city nor HUD Secretary Romney had violated the model cities act or HUD regulations regarding citizen participation.

On July 14, 1970, the U.S. Circuit Court of Appeals reversed the lower-court finding. The Circuit Court found that the plaintiffs did have standing to sue, that the issues could be legally reviewed, and that HUD Secretary Romney had violated the model cities act "when he accepted a proposal for major modification of the model cities program from the city which made clear on its face there had been no citizen participation in its formulation and when he imposed additional significant terms of his own without citizen participation. . . ."

The court said that "the issue is not citizen veto or even approval, but citizen participation, negotiation, and consultation. . . . While not every decision regarding a program may require full citizen participation, certainly decisions which change the basic strategy of the program do require such participation. The June 9 decision of the city and the July 3 statement of HUD made such fundamental changes in the Philadelphia program. Previously, that program had contemplated a much heavier involvement by the designated citizen participation component, AWC. The involvement was drastically reduced by the unilateral actions of the city and HUD. . . ."

When the case went back to Judge Davis "for further proceedings consistent with this opinion," AWC attorneys argued that since the defendants had stated in September, 1969, that all of the material facts were on the record, the plaintiffs were entitled to relief under the Circuit Court's decision: they asked that the AWC be reinstated.

The city and HUD argued that not all of the material facts were on record, that there were disputes as to fact, and that therefore it was proper for Judge Davis to take evidence to resolve those disputes. Judge Davis agreed and took testimony. This phase ended September 23. Judge Davis reportedly has indicated that there will be no immediate decision in the case. After the transcripts are prepared, the attorneys will submit briefs as to what his finding should be and he will hear oral argument.

In the opinion of a lawyer for the city, it's extremely remote that the AWC will be reinstated, because the Circuit Court made its decision on the basis of lack of consultation. The city's lawyer says that AWC was asked for cooperation in drafting a response to the Hyde letter and that they refused.

In the opinion of an AWC attorney, the legal procedures will involve months of delay. "The practical effect will be that the city and HUD will go ahead despite the legal shadow," he says. This attorney believes also that by then the Hubs will be so firmly entrenched that there is almost no chance AWC will regain its former role; however, he expects the case to have an impact on HUD.

William Will disagrees. The AWC was claiming co-equal decision-making, he says, which is contrary to the model cities statute. Contracts with the new citizen participation groups are written to allow either the city or the citizens to terminate within thirty days, and furthermore, Will says, the citizen participation groups will act in an advisory capacity.

From the beginning, before the existence of AWC, model cities was viewed by blacks and white activists, inside and outside city government, as an opportunity to create a vehicle for neighborhood power and control.

Urban renewal had displaced thousands to the benefit of the tax base and downtown interests. By 1967, low-income housing had become a major issue in the mayoralty campaign. In the early 1960s, a Ford Foundation "gray area" experiment in social reform became progressively paralyzed in a failure to achieve legitimacy. The poverty program's community action had opened up a can of worms. Art Shostak, Drexel University sociologist and founder of the Maximum Participation Movement, a poverty-program-inspired reform group, ascribes City Hall dominance in that program to inadequate funds, the preoccupation of the poor with getting jobs at "whatever cost to their political independence," and interest in strengthening the Democratic stronghold in the black community. Thus, the reformers were prepared for the political struggle ahead. As early as 1966, there was plenty of backstage intrigue and conflict.

In mid-January, 1967, at a meeting of the city's Commission on Human Relations, several speakers contended that the Philadelphia model cities program was already rolling along without citizen participation. Alvin E. Echols, executive director of North City Congress, a coalition of North Philadelphia block groups, said "there must be equal partnership between citizens and government." At this and two subsequent meetings, the consensus was that programs would have to come up the pipeline from the "grass roots" instead of vice versa as in the poverty program.

The city's development coordinator stressed the city's eagerness for citizen involvement. The March, 1967, application for a planning grant reflected these negotiations. It said that the Philadelphia program "will strive to incorporate within its very core guarantees of citizens' authority to determine basic goals and policies for planning and implementing the program," and that "citizen participation . . . must be a partnership of government and the community concerned. . . ."

Spiegel and Mittenthal comment on the neighborhood perception of City Hall's "divide and conquer" strategy: "Another way of looking at the style of cities like . . . Philadelphia is to view them as surprisingly sensitive and responsive political instruments. They have to cater to the needs of a multitude of constituencies with totally inadequate resources. Their practice of allocating scarcity among an abundance of varied citizen organizations and of delegating or sharing small pieces of authority with them is not untypical of the big-city politics of redistribution. The game can be played with

real finesse by these urban giants. Also, what may appear to the neighborhood as City Hall malevolence or artifice may in reality be nothing more than institutional reactions to a state of perpetual crisis. . . ."

The rising tide of black militancy, the architecture of Philadelphia's model cities operation with its citizen partnership structure and inadequate funds seemed to fate the program to perpetual crisis from the start. The AWC adversary model was constructed on the theory of the poverty cycle. Powerlessness and poverty were Siamese twins. The April 30, 1969, submission said: "As meaningful decisions (by the model neighborhood residents) are made, there already has begun the process for mitigating the condition of powerlessness."

Not only did the power struggle begin before the creation of AWC; so did the puncturing of expectations. In January, 1967, HUD guidelines mandated cutbacks in the target area, which in any case was only one (although the largest) of three impoverished areas in Philadelphia. The new boundaries now excluded about one-third of the original population, which was estimated at 300,000. By April, there were already indications that planning-grant funds would be less than one-half of the anticipated $750,000.

On November 17, 1967, two months after William Meek—black liberal integrationist, community organizer, and master of social work —was named AWC executive director, a massive Black Power student rally protesting the school board's "white mortarboard policy" outside the school administration building erupted into violence. The sequence of events leading up to police intervention is still unclear; some contended that this was an early example of a "police riot." In any case, after the police dispersed the students, some students injured passersby with aerial whips torn from parked cars. The city was instantly polarized. Overnight, the balance of power shifted to the white backlash.

Walter Palmer, a well-known community organizer and leading black militant theorist, then working for the AWC, was arrested along with CORE chief William Mathis. "Let's remove the Palmers, let's remove the Mathises," Police Commissioner Frank Rizzo said in an on-the-spot interview for the benefit of television audiences. Pressure was put on Meek to fire Palmer.

The use of AWC mimeograph machines for student leaflets became an immediate issue. Meek's position was that he had to create a planning community before there could be planning. HUD's Walter G. Farr was pushed by the press on the point of the tax money when he came to town for a luncheon December 7. He said the obvious: " 'Our money' oughtn't to be used for demonstrations."

AWC was thus publicly identified as a militant black group early in its history. In response to pressures on AWC, some white civic groups rallied to its side.

But accommodation wasn't reached until mid-1968, when Mayor Tate named Robert Williams, former special counsel to City Council President Paul D'Ortona, as model cities administrator. In August, Williams said that the model cities program was out of the "crisis stage," but that this had required more than doubling AWC's monthly budget from $18,000 to $46,000. Things seemed to simmer down until submission of the application for operating funds. By then, Mrs. Watson had been appointed administrator, and Floyd Hyde's letter expressing concern over accountability and other deficiencies in the application was soon on the way.

In their 1967 book *Dilemmas of Social Reform,* Peter Marris and Martin Rein wrote that the neighborhood does not provide a focus for community organization "except for those concerns which arise from the immediate environment—garbage collection, police protection, redevelopment plans. Community organization seems to assume that those who live near each other share a community of interests which ought to find expression in a generalized social cohesion. But unemployment, discrimination, punitive welfare regulations, even the denial of educational opportunity are not neighborhood issues, and only accidentally unite the residents of the same block. Community organization, since it provides no hierarchy of affiliation from local to national levels, trivializes major interests by its parochial bias."

The voice of a collective consciousness, as represented by the Arnstein-AWC paper, is a sign of an esthetically expressed will toward "generalized social cohesion," as well as an effort to transcend parochialism.

Mrs. Watson has another point of view: "I think the article will be used to damage the entire program," she says.

Yet the model cities strategy always was controversial. Although the solutions to poverty problems lie outside neighborhood boundaries, model cities prescribes that the solutions must be found within neighborhoods. Pitifully inadequate funds made squabbles over pie crumbs inevitable. In Philadelphia, the program did nothing to mitigate antagonisms between black and white neighborhoods. Mrs. Watson is aware of this. She stresses that the program is not a black one.

But the real question was whether model cities was the right instrument to generate new institutional responsiveness to the urban poor. The unresolved tension between government and citizens led the AWC staff—even though they were labeled militant, or radical—to spend thousands of manpower hours on a reformers' goal. At the turning point of the struggle, the clash of wills in Philadelphia was over the accountability and structure of new community-centered institutions. Mrs. Watson maintained last year that she fought long and hard in Washington to retain the community corporation idea.

Since Floyd Hyde, Republican mayor of Fresno, Calif., became HUD Assistant Secretary with authority over model cities, another kind of reform has been taking shape. Hyde has said unequivocally, "The fundamental purpose of the model cities program—and one to which I am totally committed—is strengthening the capacity of local government." Hyde told the National Journal, "How can local governments solve problems when we at the federal level fund water and sewer districts, school districts, citizen groups, hospitals, legal services, housing authorities, renewal agencies—everything but the general-purpose government, the one responsible to the electorate. . . ?"

Remolded to suit the Nixon Administration's philosophy of revenue-sharing to strengthen local government, the program's clientele shifted from citizens to mayors. In a situation such as Philadelphia's, the shift, whatever its merits, could not but lead to the kind of citizen anguish and bitterness that suffuses AWC's history of its travails.

The Spiegel-Mittenthal study remarked that "intense suspiciousness not only of public officials but of rival ethnic or racial groups, and of the white welfare/planning establishment in general, round out the angry milieu in which indigenous planning is practiced. The planning process in the neighborhood becomes as much an engine of propaganda and political agitation as it does a device for problem-solving."

The original North City Congress conception of the way in which the citizens' group might perform had been to use the technical staff as a watchdog. But Meek encouraged his planners to undertake technical planning. The result: confusion between planning and policy, or the major directions that planned change should take.

Without a political base, planning is picture-drawing. For AWC to develop political clout, it had to mobilize people-power, though the odds were overwhelmingly against success.

One observer comments that there was internal debate between the AWC planning professionals and the AWC field organizers over how "grass roots" to be, although such debate never broke down the staff's united front. Another observer comments that the staff's attitude could be characterized as "elitist" despite its populist stance, in the sense that some of them believed through their zeal, observations, empathy, and so forth, they could make decisions on behalf of the community. A third observer says Meek was constantly caught up in the "grass roots" issue. "What does it take," he asks, "for any man to participate, to have a sense of sharing knowledge and control? The attempt to develop that kind of knowledge is incredibly difficult using the framework of meetings. There's bound to be a radical discontinuity between the dream and the reality." A HUD official comments that AWC emphasis on process was at the expense of meeting deadlines and getting substantive results.

These "participation" problems expressed themselves in the lack of communications between age groups in the neighborhoods, and in reiterated feelings that central staff dominated the planning effort, and that AWC was not responsive to the neighborhood Hubs.

In March, 1968, a white field worker for AWC from the decaying Kensington section of the city was fired because of her "resentment of supervision and structure," which she termed a result of "whitey and blacky staff meeting." From her perspective, "All they talked about was Negro revolutions. But that has nothing to do with model cities as I see it."

And on June 18, 1969, the chairman of the education committee in the model cities area held a press conference to charge that the goal of the AWC staff was "to take control of the Urban Institute (one of the action programs) away from the community," and to replace community representatives with AWC puppets. She charged that Meek had fired the committee's staff and that the AWC executive board passed a resolution stating that the committee must cease and desist from meeting.

Ironically, Mrs. Watson has also spent a good deal of her staff's energies on community organizing. Some of them complain too much of their time has gone into "involving" the community, rather than getting on with the operational stage of the program.

In any case, most observers would agree that AWC's operations were "damn sloppy," in the words of one. Will turned over a six-page summary of a federal audit by Dayton Smith of HUD, dated November, 1968.

The document outlines "questionable" areas of AWC administrative practices, including "poor records of reporting for time and attendance of AWC employees," "questionable disbursements from the petty cash funds . . . ," "no records" for sick leave and compensatory time, inadequate records of leave taken, "no property records of office equipment purchased with model cities funds," "unsubstantiated" $7 payments to neighborhood committee delegates for attending weekly meetings, improperly supported travel costs.

Revision of social arrangements, as Marris and Rein point out, involves both disruption and reintegration. Totalitarian societies "ensure the power to determine how the aims of society are to be reconciled, at the cost of pre-empting all initiative of reform and so inhibiting the creative energy of its people," while democratic society "gives this energy free play at the cost of leaving it to expend itself in muddled, aborted efforts."

This "postscript" could end as Marris and Rein ended their book: "Can the process of reform we studied, however skillfully it is manipulated, ever radically improve the chances of the poor? And if it cannot, will Americans prefer to hold to their conception of the way issues must be resolved, even at the cost of ineradicable injustice? Is there a better way?"

Analytic Tasks: Perspectives on Planning as a Technomethodological Process

part IV

This section is addressed especially to those potential "Marvin the Movers" of social planning so that their meetings in which attendance is high and participation lively may also occasionally achieve substantial results.

An important intellectual orientation that guides the planner's thinking about analytic tasks is the "systems approach." To "analyze" means to break something down into its component parts. The systems approach essentially involves the analysis of phenomena in order to understand their component elements, the interaction or interdependencies among these elements, and the purposes of the activity. As Churchman explains:

Is there something essential about the concept of a system as a way of thinking? There surely is. Systems are made up of sets of components that work together for the overall objective of the whole. The systems approach is simply a way of thinking about these total systems and their components.[1]

The social welfare planner deals with social systems, the most basic components of which are people. Social systems may be conceptualized in several ways. In Reading 19, "Social System Models for Planners," Robert R. Mayer identifies five types of social systems by utilizing the concepts of *system level, structure of elements,* and the *integrative mechanisms* that unite these elements. The *system level* indicates the boundaries of the "whole" that is being examined. For example, at the micro-level the units of organization

1 C. West Churchman, *The Systems Approach* (New York: Dell Publishing Co., 1968), p. 11.

are individuals; at the macro-level the unit may be the entire organization, in which case the component elements are the organizational units, or subsystems; the macro-level may also encompass a field of related organizations within the community in which the component elements are organizations (i.e., subsystems that are themselves macrosystems) composed of units (i.e., subsystems that are microsystems). The *structure of the elements* refers to the arrangement of the system—for example, the degree of differentiation of roles and the pattern of power distribution. The *integrative mechanisms* that unite the system are its shared goals, shared values, reciprocity, and common resources. Mayer underlines the importance of understanding the types of integrative mechanisms that hold systems together.

Employing the conceptual tools of the systems approach, social welfare planners become involved in three broad analytic tasks: (a) problem analysis, (b) program design, and (c) evaluation.

a. *problem analysis*—these tasks involve research design, data collection, and assessment of social system needs and resources.
b. *program design*—the tasks here involve organizational analysis and framing policy alternatives for the bases of social allocations (who is to be served), the nature of social provisions (what they shall receive), the structure of service-delivery systems (how to actually provide the service benefit), and the modes of finance (how to pay for it).
c. *evaluation*—similar to those in the first category, evaluation tasks involve applied research skills. Evaluation differs from problem analysis in that it assesses the extent to which planning goals are being met. In a sense, evaluation may be thought of as a second order of problem analysis that identifies remaining difficulties and the new problems that have been generated after program implementation.

The precise nature of these analytic planning tasks varies considerably with circumstances and techniques. In order to provide a basic introduction to the sorts of activities in which planners engage, we will review a sample of the literature that describes theoretical and practical aspects of some fundamental planning tasks in each of these categories.

PROBLEM ANALYSIS

Much of the planner's time and effort is devoted to problem analysis. The crucial character of this phase of the planning process is underlined by Kahn (see Reading 5). It is often said in social planning that a problem well defined is a problem half solved, or at least well on the way to solution. Yet, as Rittel and Webber have pointed out (see Reading 10), the "inherent wickedness" of social planning problems is, in part, their resistance to definitive formulation.

One of the core tasks in problem analysis is assessing needs and resources. Here the limiting factors are more conceptual than technical—that is, there is no single or precise meaning to the term "need." For example, should needs be defined by normative standards (i.e., what the experts deem desirable) or by the subjective views of those whose needs are being measured? What is the "real" state of need when there is a discrepancy between subjective and normative assessments? [2] Is subjective need a "real need" if it is not expressed through some action such as seeking service? These theoretical aspects of need definition are analyzed in Reading 20 by Jonathan Bradshaw, "The Concept of Social Need." Bradshaw's taxonomy helps to clarify the different ways in which planners can measure social need.

In Reading 21, "Measuring Need in the Social Services," Richard Thayer draws upon Bradshaw's concepts to examine seven needs-assessment studies. Thayer distinguishes between "diagnostic" need assessments that measure the problem condition and "prescriptive" need assessments that address the types of resources required to alleviate a problem. The seven studies reviewed by Thayer employ various techniques to measure need such as client surveys, expert opinion, evaluation of records, and the use of census data to construct social indicators.[3] These techniques are important instruments of the planning craft, particularly for analytic tasks. The next three readings describe and analyze in detail some of these techniques for assessing needs and assigning priorities among them.

A general overview of a range of techniques for obtaining data to estimate social needs and to construct social indicators is provided in Reading 22, "Collecting Information: Basic Methods," prepared by the League of California Cities. This selection compares the costs and advantages of different methods such as questionnaire surveys, observation, interviews, meetings, and the use of existing records.

An elaborate needs assessment technique that uses the questionnaire method is described by Daniel Molnar and Marshall Kammerud in Reading 23, "Developing Priorities for Improving the Urban Social Environment: A Use of Delphi." Originally developed by the staff of the RAND Corporation, the Delphi technique quantifies intangible variables such as social needs through questionnaire surveys that tap the judgment and knowledge of expert panels. Molnar and Kammerud present a concrete example of the

---

[2] For an analysis of discrepancies between subjective and normative needs assessments and their implications for social planning, see Neil Gilbert and Joseph Eaton, "Who Speaks for the Poor?" *Journal of the American Institute of Planners,* 36:6 (November 1970), 411–16.

[3] For other approaches to needs assessment based on data obtained at a number of levels, see Harvey S. Perloff, "New Directions in Social Planning," in *Readings in Community Organization Practice,* Ralph M. Kramer and Harry Specht, Eds. (Englewood Cliffs, N.J.: Prentice-Hall, Inc., 1969), pp. 430–71; and Jiri Musil, "Goal-Setting in Urban Planning: A Case Study from Czechoslovakia," *Journal of Social Policy,* 1:3 (July 1972), 227–44.

Delphi procedure in which well-educated professionals are used as the "experts." However, Delphi panels can be composed of any group of people knowledgeable about the issue under consideration, including social welfare clients and neighborhood representatives. Molnar and Kammerud briefly note some of the advantages of the Delphi technique: anonymity, controlled feedback, and statistical group response. However, other investigators question these presumed advantages. For instance, although anonymity and statistical group response are supposed to reduce group pressures for conformity, Skutsch and Schofer observe that:

Studies in the effects of inter-round feedback in the Delphi . . . show that despite anonymity, a strong pressure to conform exists. Feedback in which the majority opinion is clearly visible causes greater movement towards the center of opinion than does feedback in which the majority is less obvious.[4]

And from a different angle, Pill raises the issue of the efficacy of specialization and individual effort versus diversity and group effort:

There is obviously the question of whether it might not be wiser to spend one's time seeking a single expert in the area of specialization one is concerned with and allowing him to thoroughly research the question to come up with a response that may be better than that of any diversified group. . . . The main point here is that Delphi is useful for "picking the brains" of a group, and it is undoubtedly true that a group has more total expertise than any of its members, but it also dilutes the opinion of the real expert on the particular question that is being considered.[5]

In some limited respects the Delphi is similar to the nominal group process technique illustrated by Andre Delbecq and Andrew Van de Ven in Reading 24, "A Group Process Model for Problem Identification and Program Planning." Both techniques rely upon the knowledge and judgment of expert panels, and both exercise strong control over interaction patterns among panel members. However, the techniques differ substantially on a number of dimensions. For example, Delbecq and Van de Ven's approach uses meetings instead of questionnaire surveys to obtain data; it does not call for anonymity of response; and it elicits in-put from three different panels that represent clients, outside specialists, and resource controllers at different phases of the process. It is interesting to note that the tasks described in Phase I and Phase II of the nominal group process technique closely resemble Thayer's distinction (Reading 21) between diagnostic and prescriptive needs assessments.

[4] Margaret Skutsch and J. L. Schofer, "Goals-Delphis for Urban Planning: Concepts in Their Design," *Socio-Economic Planning Science*, 7 (1973), 308.

[5] Juri Pill, "The Delphi Method: Substance, Context, a Critique, and an Annotated Bibliography," *Socio-Economic Planning Science*, 5 (1971), 62; for a more thorough critique of the Delphi method see Harold Sackman, *Delphi Critique* (Lexington, Mass.: Lexington Books, 1975).

PROGRAM DESIGN

The stages of the planning process cannot be divided discretely. Problem analysis and program design, for example, are not dealt with in an absolutely sequential manner—that is, a social welfare planner cannot design a program without knowing something about the problem; but the parameters of *possible* program designs (which are defined by available resources and technology) strongly influence the planner's selection of problems that can realistically be tackled. The nominal group process technique described by Delbecq and Van de Ven (Reading 24) rapidly moves from diagnosis to prescription to program development.

The major analytic tasks in program design are the articulation and elaboration of the policy choices available in selection of the target population, the form and substance of the social provision, the organizational structure for delivering the provision, and the means of financing the program.[6] Reading 25, "Assessing Service-Delivery Methods," by Neil Gilbert, examines a range of delivery-structure choices in program design. Gilbert analyzes the basic problems of service-delivery systems and offers a series of policy alternatives that address these problems. Each policy alternative is considered in light of the systematic changes required for implementation. In assessing these different policy designs for service delivery, planners are warned that any given policy may mitigate some types of service-delivery problems while intensifying others.

PROGRAM EVALUATION

There are various ways to evaluate programs depending upon the criteria of success or failure employed and the program level under examination. In Reading 26, "Program Assessment," Eleanor Bennett and Marvin Weisinger clarify the choices among evaluative criteria and describe the program levels to which these criteria can be applied. These choices represent the kinds of program information that administrators find useful. From a methodological perspective, Bennett and Weisinger review the "research approach" and the "systems approach" as two basic orientations to evaluative studies. Each of these approaches encompasses a range of techniques and research designs. The Planning, Programming, and Budgeting System (PPBS) is one of the "system approach" techniques that has stirred interest

[6] For a detailed discussion of the variables that enter into these choices, see Eveline M. Burns, *Social Security and Public Policy* (New York: McGraw-Hill, 1956); and Neil Gilbert and Harry Specht, *Dimensions of Social Welfare Policy* (Englewood Cliffs, N.J.: Prentice-Hall, Inc., 1974).

in social welfare planning circles within the last decade. Efforts to apply this technique to program evaluation on the national level are discussed in the last selection, Reading 27, "The Planning, Programming and Budgeting System in the Department of Health, Education, and Welfare: Some Lessons from Experience," by Alice Rivlin.

Despite the rather imposing title, at its core PPBS is a simple common-sensical approach to evaluation. The intellectual underpinnings of PPBS have been succinctly described by Hitch:

The second of the management techniques which comprise the PPB system is called "systems analysis" or "cost effectiveness" or "cost benefit analysis" or "operations research." It is nothing more or less than economic analysis applied to the public sector. Economic analysis is concerned with the allocation of resources. Its basic maxim is: Maximize the value of the objectives achieved minus the value of the resources used.[7]

And if PPBS now seems to be less awesome than many may have expected, the following observation makes it sound almost old-fashioned and down home:

Some of the less historically minded proponents of PPBS strongly imply that it is something brand new, providing decision-makers for the first time with a rational basis for choosing between alternative policies. Actually, cost-benefit analysis seems to have begun in the Garden of Eden. . . and the problem from the outset has been to avoid an underestimation of costs and an overestimation of benefits. Costs and gains have been compared throughout our government's history whenever a decision to spend or not to spend had to be made, and Congress explicitly called for cost-benefit studies as far back as the Rivers and Harbors Act of 1902.

PPB may for the first time identify these techniques as a "system," give them a special name, and advertise them, but the approach itself is as old as the problem of the buyer who would like to make two purchases and has money only for one.[8]

PPBS has its critics and supporters. Supporters point out that, at the very least, the technique tells the buyer how much he has spent or will spend for the goods purchased. As Rivlin suggests in recounting the HEW experiences, PPBS was useful in "facilitating some simple calculations at high levels of aggregation." This information may seem almost too obvious to be worth the costs of elaborate PPBS techniques. Yet, in the labyrinth of federal budget allocations, planners need whatever guidance they can find.

Critics grant that with PPBS the buyer obtains information in aggregate

[7] Charles J. Hitch, "Decision-Making in Large Organizations," *Planning Programming Budgeting*, Inquiry of the Subcommittee on National Security and International Operations, Committee on Government Operations, U.S. Senate (Washington, D.C.: Government Printing Office, 1970), p. 578.

[8] U.S. Senate, Subcommittee on National Security and International Operations, *Planning Programming Budgeting* (Washington, D.C.: Government Printing Office, 1970), p. 10.

terms about how much is spent for goods purchased. But, they argue, the calculations of PPBS are really inconsequential to buyers because they still do not know what they have gotten for their money or what they might have gotten if they had spent it otherwise. PPBS may be desirable in theory, but practically, Aaron Wildavsky bluntly claims, "No one can do PPBS." [9]

In part, the difficulties of implementing PPBS are similar to those encountered in more circumscribed projects of evaluative research on social programs. For example, program objectives are not usually specified in clear and measurable terms because: (a) social programs often have multiple objectives differentially valued by different groups; and (b) the broadest and most significant objectives tend to be too complex and difficult to measure. To the extent that program objectives and measurements of them are fuzzy, the evaluation of programs is reduced to descriptive assessments of effort (e.g., how many were served, how much money is being spent, and so on)—which brings us back to the buyer who knows how much is being spent but little about what is purchased. These difficulties are not insurmountable, but overcoming them requires a high degree of creativity and methodological sophistication, which those who are entering the field of social welfare planning must strive to cultivate.

[9] Aaron Wildavsky, "Rescuing Policy Analysis from PPBS," *Public Expenditures and Policy Analysis*, in Robert Haveman and Julius Margolis, eds. (Chicago: Markham Publishing, 1970), pp. 461–81.

19   Analytic Orientation

SOCIAL SYSTEM MODELS FOR PLANNERS

Robert R. Mayer

The principal business of planning, it can be argued, is to design manipulations of systems. Interest in the preservation of natural resources results in planning in relation to environmental systems. Concern for urban growth and development leads to a treatment of housing markets and urban spatial structure as systems. When we analyze problems in the provision of public services such as education or medical care, we think in terms of service delivery systems.

During the past decade planners, particularly those located in large metropolitan areas, have developed a growing awareness that social systems are vital phenomena. Public outcries in reaction to urban renewal or transportation plans have made planners much more sensitive to the social impact of changes in physical systems. In addition, the growing acceptance of governmental responsibility for the solution of social problems such as racism, poverty, and crime has made apparent the need to analyze social systems in connection with designing programs to meet the needs of urban populations.

Since recognition of the utility of social systems constructs has been quite recent, it should not be surprising that the social science literature lags behind the demands of planners in clarity and completeness. Much of the conceptualizing of social systems has occurred without regard to applications. As Gouldner points out, the classic work was done by Parsons during the Great Depression, yet there is little discernible connection between the Depression and Parson's social system (1970, pp. 167f). Indeed it was not until 1960 that a social system perspective was applied to social policy (in the work of Cloward and Ohlin in their treatment of delinquency and opportunity [1960]).

The current literature on social systems suffers from two deficiencies. First, it tends to be incomplete, that is, it does not display a range of models that corresponds to major variations in social life. Sociological thinking about social systems has

Reprinted with permission of author and publisher from: Robert R. Mayer, "Social System Models for Planners," *Journal of the American Institute of Planners*, 38: 3 (May 1972), pp. 130–39. Author's Note: The author is grateful to Professor Richard L. Simpson and Frank F. DeGiovanni of the University of North Carolina for their very helpful criticism in the preparation of this paper.

been dominated for thirty years by the views of Talcott Parsons, and only recently have sociologists begun to articulate alternative models. Second, the literature tends to be nonoperational. Partly due to its lack of concern with applications, and partly due to its preoccupation with developing a theory of society, sociology has tended to create models which are highly abstract, global, and poorly suited to the real situations which planners face. As Ramsoy has pointed out, the term "social system" is the central concept in sociology (1963, p. 17). It is generic in that it applies to any form of social interaction, whether in a national society or a small group such as a triad. This failure to relate social system concepts to social behavior below the societal level has limited the usefulness of the term for planners.

PURPOSE OF THIS INQUIRY

This paper sets forth, in simple and concise terms, five distinct models of social systems which are derived from the literature, and relates these models to actual phenomena with which planners deal. This task is essentially definitional rather than explanatory. I will not deal here with the dynamics of such systems, with planned change, or with control of social systems. My primary objective is to clarify this very complex subject. Once distinctive models have been established it will be possible to take up such issues.

I will distinguish five types of social systems: (1) a microcollectivity,

(2) a complex macrosystem, (3) an exchange system, 4) an interorganizational field (which can be characterized by two subtypes—the coalition and the federation), and (5) an ecological system.

METHOD OF ANALYSIS

Social system models will be analyzed examining the work of four principal authors: Parsons, whose central ideas revolve around social systems which are collectivities; Ramsoy, whose writings focus on complex macrosystems; Blau, whose major interest is in systems based on exchange processes; and Warren, who provides a variation on Blau at the interorganizational level. Three elements of the different models are emphasized: (1) The level of the system, that is, macro- or micro-; (2) the structure of each model, that is, how are the elements of the system arranged relative to each other; and (3) the integrative mechanisms peculiar to the model, or "the glue" which holds the system together (integrative mechanisms refer to shared goals, shared values, reciprocity, and common resources). In addition, we shall look at examples of social behavior to which these models can be applied in the real world.

Before proceeding, it is necessary to define certain basic terms which underpin this discussion.

1. *Social system.*—By social system is meant any patterned social interaction or interdependency which persists over time. This definition is very loose and incorporates a wide range of social behavior from a friendship

clique, to urban street life, to national society.[1]

2. *A microsystem.*—As defined by Blau, a microsystem is a social system in which the constituent elements are individuals or, more technically speaking, role incumbents (1964, pp. 12–32).

3. *Macrosystem.*—In contrast a macrosystem is a social system in which the constituent elements are social systems, referred to in this context as subsystems (Blau, 1964, pp. 12–32).

There is a tendency to think of macrosystems as large social systems and microsystems as small ones, in which case the only distinction rests on the question, "How big is big?" There are however some subtle and more substantive differences inherent in this dichotomous way of looking at social systems. As Blau points out, in a microsystem, composed as it is of individuals as constituent elements, personal attraction is an important integrative mechanism, whereas in a macrosystem, value consensus is necessary to provide the basis for indirect exchange. In addition, a macrosystem is characterized by an interplay between processes within subsystems and processes between subsystems. Finally, macrosystems develop enduring institutions which persist beyond the life of individual members.

---

[1] I agree with Ramsoy that "social system" is the central concept of sociology. To use more traditional criteria of boundary maintenance and value consensus ignores a considerable amount of behavior which has systemic properties (for example, urban street life), and a whole range of institutionalized conflict which has become a fact of life. To Ramsoy the single criterion of "double contingency" is sufficient.

Ramsoy refers to a similar distinction in his discussion of the problem of levels in social system analysis. Any social system can be thought of as containing smaller social systems, or as being contained by a larger social system. He calls the former an *inclusive system* and the latter a *subsystem.* These terms are useful in analyzing the relationship between different system levels. In this sense they are relational terms and not intrinsic terms. They should not be considered synonymous with macrosystem and microsystem because although all inclusive systems are necessarily macrosystems, not all subsystems are microsystems.

With these conceptual tools in hand let us now examine the various social system models.

A PARSONIAN MODEL: THE MICROCOLLECTIVITY

The first model is based on the work of Parsons and is contained in a planning model developed by Mayer (1972). Because my ultimate interest is in planning models and not basic theoretical schemes, I will focus on this translation of Parsons rather than on the model developed by Parsons himself.

The basic elements of this model are individual actors rather than groups of actors or systems. Parsons refers to the object of his analysis as the orientation of individual actors in a system of action (1951, pp. 3ff). In this sense the model is a microsystem. This assertion may puzzle many students of Parsons, since Parsons' goal is to develop a theory of society. In much of Parsons' work, however, the building blocks of the social system are social roles, and society is treated essentially as an aggregation of roles or of institutions (functional clusters of roles).[2]

One should not confuse the actor with the individual as a biopsychological being. An individual participates in many systems, but a role exists only as part of a particular system of action. The expected patterns of behavior or roles which people play in the context of a particular group are the elements of a microcollectivity. (See Figure 1.)

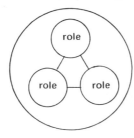

FIGURE 1. Microcollectivity

The structure of a microcollectivity is the arrangement among the particular roles and their accompanying statuses which comprise the system. Roles refer to the expected patterns of behavior which different actors perform. Statuses refer to the rights and obligations accompanying those roles. The structure, therefore, may be thought of as a division of labor and a distribution of rewards and duties among elements of the system. Such a structure can be highly differentiated or relatively undifferentiated; it can be hierar-

chical or lateral. Most systems, however, tend to some degree of hierarchy, in the sense that not everybody can be a leader.

The unique means by which this system is integrated is through shared goals and values. A collectivity exists because people have a common objective which is usually reinforced by a common set of values. The central thesis of Parsons' work is that value consensus is essential for system integration.

Examples of social behavior which conform to this model are commonplace. The classroom, friendship groups, and the nuclear family are classic examples of microcollectivities. A department or division of a bureaucracy may be treated as such a system, as may a work group in a factory, the governing board of an agency such as a planning commission, or the administration of an agency. Spatially defined units such as rooming houses or neighborhoods may become microcollectivities when inhabited by persons of common ethnicity or subculture. Client groups, as they become organized, are an increasingly important form of microcollectivity. It is interesting to note that this model, which is the oldest and most traditional of the models presented here, is currently having a revival among adherents of the New Left. The "communes" springing up around the country as precursors of a new social order are precise examples of microcollectivities (Roberts, 1971).

RAMSOY: THE COMPLEX MACROSYSTEM

Ramsoy's principal interest is in inclusive systems, which contain so-

---

2 Parsons does develop a macromodel of social systems in his analysis of the functional prerequisites of society, but this model is highly abstract and not clearly related to the one discussed here. See Lopreato (1971), and Gouldner (1970).

cial systems that can be analyzed on two levels simultaneously. Ramsoy deals with macrosystems because the constituent elements of his inclusive system are social systems which are treated as subsystems.

In discussing the nature of social systems, Ramsoy shows why Parsons' collectivity is only one of several important models of social behavior. There are a variety of situations in which shared goals are not characteristic (for example, a buyer-seller relationship), and indeed in which conflicting goals may be the essence of the relationship (for example, a football game). Thus Ramsoy introduces the notion of the noncollectivity or the nonsolidary social system.

Thus we must distinguish between two distinctly different models of macrosystems presented by Ramsoy. The first model conforms to the definitions of a collectivity in that the system is characterized by having an inclusive goal, that is, a goal shared by all subsystems, and shared values. We may call this model a macrocollectivity. In such systems, argues Ramsoy, one of the subsystems always emerges as a leadership subsystem. This position is conferred on that subsystem which most adequately reflects the inclusive goals. Presumably, the norms of such a system reinforce allegiance to inclusive goals and legitimate the power exercised by the leadership subsystem. (See Figure 2.)

Role and status define the structure of a microcollectivity, but what constitutes the structure of a macrocollectivity? Ramsoy points to several structural characteristics of the inclusive system, principally (1) the number of subsystems and degree of differentiation among them, (2) the presence of a leadership subsystem and the amount of power accruing to it, and (3) the distribution of power among subsystems. These characteristics are roughly analogous to the structural characteristics of microcollectivities. The bureaucracy, long the dominant model of organizational behavior, is the classic example of a macrocollectivity.

Ramsoy distinguishes his alternate model on the basis of integrative mechanisms. The distinction rests on what Ramsoy refers to as "the problematic relationship" between subsystems and inclusive systems. In some inclusive systems the constituent elements are collectivities which pursue conflicting goals. Such systems are held together by institutionalized means of conflict resolution. In this sense the inclusive system can not be thought of as a collectivity. Ramsoy considers this situation the extreme case of the

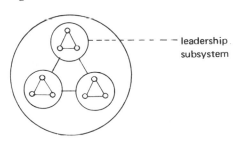

FIGURE 2.   Macrocollectivity

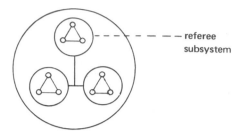

FIGURE 3.   Complex Macrosystem

complex system. Following this line of reasoning I will call this model the "complex macrosystem." (see Figure 3.)

For example, in the case of a football game, both teams, collectivities, pursue conflicting goals, namely to win. But the inclusive system has a subsystem, referees, whose function it is to control the contest. Also, the inclusive system has certain norms to which subsystems subscribe that establish the ground rules by which the contest is waged. These norms or shared values prohibit conflict, in the sense of one party seeking to destroy the other, and reinforce acceptance of the outcome of the contest on the part of all subsystems. Thus, a complex macrosystem consists of two or more collectivities which have conflicting goals, but which share limiting values that are enforced by a referee subsystem.

An example of a complex macrosystem more relevant for social policy is the unionized factory. Such a system can be thought of as including two competing subsystems, the union and the management. The union seeks to maximize wages, the management seeks to maximize profits. Yet the system hangs together and certain outcomes are achieved. Contest is built into this system by a parallel hierarchical organization representing labor and management, from the shop foreman and steward up to the plant manager and union president. There are certain mechanisms for resolving conflict, such as arbitration and the use of contracts. When none of these mechanisms work, the unionized factory breaks up into two conflicting collectivities and there is a walkout or strike.

This example is important in an era when social conflict has become a continuous fact of life. Planners need to learn how to design social systems in which conflict is a normal process and is managed without destroying inclusive goals.

It might be argued that a factory is really a macrocollectivity. It has an inclusive goal of producing certain goods, a division of labor among various departments of the plant to achieve that common goal, and norms which support management's right to make decisions about product design and marketing. This conflicting view illustrates the danger of treating social system constructs as real objects rather than as analytical tools. A factory is neither a macrocollectivity nor a complex macrosystem: sometimes it functions as the former and other times it functions as the latter. It is in the interests of management to create the atmosphere of a collectivity. It is in the interests of union leadership to "polarize" the factory and to reinforce conflicting goals.

BLAU: THE EXCHANGE SYSTEM

The work of Peter Blau contrasts clearly with previous models of social systems (1964). Blau's thesis is that models which emphasize common goals and value consensus ignore an important basis of systemic behavior, namely, exchange processes and the distribution of power.

Blau's model, by his own admission, applies primarily to systems in which the constituent elements are individuals and which are based on voluntary association. The model cannot depict systems in which interaction is coerced or controlled by forces extraneous to the individual, such as prisons or kinship groups. An exchange system consists of individuals who are mutually attracted to each other by the expectation of an exchange of rewards. In the model's simplest form the classical example is the relationship between friends.

The structure of this system is undifferentiated; it consists of actors who at the outset are equal in terms of status or power and differentiated only in the sense that each has something the other needs. Yet Blau recognizes that such systems rarely remain undifferentiated. He notes that often one party in the exchange process has a reward for which the other party cannot reciprocate. Under such circumstances, the empty-handed party has three choices: he can try to force the other party into giving up his reward; he can shop around for other sources of the reward; or he can try to live without the reward. If none of these alternatives is acceptable, the empty-handed party must give up his autonomy or subordinate himself to the wishes of the other, thereby rewarding the other with power over himself. Under these conditions a system can be said to be differentiated on the basis of power—certain parties control resources or rewards needed by other parties and are able to extract compliance in return for those rewards. (See Figure 4).

The integrative mechanisms for the exchange system is the most unique feature of this model. Mutually satisfying rewards, and not common goals or values, are the basis for holding together this system of social relationships. Even in its more differentiated state, the relationship between the person in power and those over whom he exercises power has important exchange elements. If the demands set forth by the powerholder are reasonable in the

undifferentiated

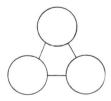

differentiated

FIGURE 4.   Exchange System

eyes of the subordinates in relation to the rewards given then subordinates attribute legitimacy to the powerholder, compliance is reinforced, and the system is held together. If, on the other hand, the powerholder's demands are considered unreasonable in relation to the rewards given, the subordinates feel exploited. If this feeling of exploitation is widely shared, it provides the basis for opposition movements which threaten the integration of the system.

In its differentiated form, Blau's model of an exchange system looks very much like a large scale organization such as a bureaucracy; that is, the model is appropriate for the same set of phenomena to which the collectivity has been applied. The significant difference, of course, is that systemic behavior has been explained without reference to common goals or value consensus. For this reason, Blau's exchange model is useful in explaining aspects of organizations left unaccounted for by the collectivity model. Value consensus and shared goals are not the only means by which systems of social relationships are held together, as anybody who has been a bureaucrat or an administrator is quick to recognize. An officeholder who consistently relies on the prerogatives of his office or on moral authority to secure the compliance of subordinates soon discovers the tenuousness of his regime. Although some degree of value consensus is necessary if exchange processes are to be sustained, the exchange model suggests that such consensus is a function of the exchange and not a prerequisite.

The exchange model is uniquely suited to the social arrangements that take place outside normative systems, or to deviant subsystems within normative inclusive systems. For example, in a study of relationships between police and criminals, Walsh discovered that some criminals negotiate a role of "stool pigeon" with the police in order to avoid arrest (1971). This arrangement is useful to the police in that it provides a source of information necessary for the surveillance of more serious crime. It is useful to the "stool pigeon" in that it guarantees him protection against arrest while carrying out his illegal activities. Thus in what may be thought of as an inclusive system structured by norms, deviant subsystems may be induced by exchange processes.

Exchange processes have much to do with the politics of planning. Most planners complain that the fruit of their labor ends up gathering dust on bureaucratic shelves. This fate results in large part because plans are usually drawn up based on goals assumed to be in the "public interest" and to have widespread commitment. These assumptions imply a collectivity which hardly exists in most American cities today. Although there may always be a need for plans which excite the imagination, action plans are made of different stuff. The exchange model suggests that in the absence of shared goals and values plans should be more in the nature of negotiated commitments to act on the part of relevant parties (contracts if you will).

The exchange model suggests a new approach in dealing with crime and deviancy: that crime and social deviancy are manifestations of the lack of value consensus among significant elements of urban populations. Rather than seeking conformity through programs of correction and rehabilitation, a more feasible approach might be to bargain with such groups around trade-offs that can be used to contain the antisocial aspects of such behavior, thus reducing the necessity for the very expensive procedures of apprehension and institutionalization. Such an approach has already been demonstrated by Shapiro (1966).

Finally, in situations of social conflict, common in much of urban life, the exchange model is the only basis for achieving solutions short of coercion. The resort to force can be detrimental to the system which practices coercion, as well as to the coerced.

WARREN: THE INTER-ORGANIZATIONAL FIELD

In his work on the interorganizational field, Warren has developed a set of system models that is particularly relevant to planning at the local community level (1967). In many respects, Warren's models are the counterpart at the macro level of Blau's exchange system.

Warren's basic interest is in explaining how "community decisions" are made, how large-scale public programs get launched and maintained over time. Warren has turned away from his earlier view of the community as a collectivity (1963), and has come to view the community as a field or environment in which a number of quasi-independent major organizations operate in pursuit of their view of the public interest. These major organizations, which Warren calls Community Decision-making Organizations (CDO's), have been legitimated through the allocation of resources, either official or voluntary, to operate within a given domain to satisfy the public interest or a public need.

The elements in the interorganizational field are formal organizations (systems); for example, the housing authority, the urban renewal authority, the board of education, the health department, the welfare department, as well as a host of voluntary health, welfare, and youth agencies. In spite of their official responsibility to local or state government or to major funding sources such as the United Fund, these organizations, according to Warren, operate largely independently of any centralized authority or control due to their discretionary power over large resources. Once the annual budgets have been approved, such agencies are active on a day to day basis in "running the community," in essence, with little accountability to some more inclusive system. Furthermore, they are not passive with respect to budget allocations—they initiate plans and lobby for expansion of domain or resources.

The basic factor which forces the elements of the interorganizational field to take cognizance of each other, and thus gives the field systemic quality, is the dependence of the elements on a common resource base, be it public monies, clientele, or legitimation. Because such elements do not necessarily interact and are not subordinate to a common authority or point of control, this system in its extreme form can be said to be an ecological system (Dunn, 1971, pp. 199f). It is the most elementary form of systemic life.

However, as Warren points out, there does emerge from time to time a degree of organization in the interorganizational field, an arrangement among elements which persists over time. Warren refers to such arrangements as "inclusive contexts." Following my analysis they can be thought of as alternative structures in the interorganizational field as a social system. Warren identifies four such possibilities. However, two of them, the *social choice* and *unitary* contexts, form the outer boundaries of the interorganizational field and actually duplicate two of the other five models discussed here. The middle two alternatives, the *coalitional* and the *federative,* are more unique to the interorganizational field. However, I will discuss all four alternatives.

Warren calls the first structure a *social choice context.* It is the most elementary form of the interorganizational field; no concerted decision-making takes place among the elements. Warren uses Banfield's lucid definition:

A *social choice* . . . is the accidental by-product of the actions of two or more actors—"interested parties," they will be called—who have no common intention and who make their selections competitively or without regard to each other. In a social choice process, each actor seeks to attain his own end; the aggregate of all action—the situation produced by all actions together—constitutes an outcome for the group, but it is an outcome which no one has planned as a "solution" to a "problem." It is a "resultant" rather than a "solution" (1961, pp. 326–327).

One may question calling such a state of affairs a social system. However, it does satisfy Ramsoy's basic criterion, that of double contingency. To the extent that resources are limited, the choices of one actor will constrain the choices of another actor in the same field. A market in which various buyers or sellers influence each other even though there is no concerted decision among either group has this nature. I prefer to call this state of affairs an ecological system because such a term is more descriptive of the phenomenon involved, and because it links the discussion to a larger body of literature which is reasonably well established. I will therefore discuss this alternative more extensively as a separate model.

The structure involving the simplest form of concerted behavior in the interorganizational field is the *coalition.* The coalition emerges when two or more parties discover that they have more to gain by collaboration on a given issue than by pursuing independent courses of action. However, as Warren points out, the decision to collaborate is confined to a specific issue, and therefore the coalition is a transitory structure—as soon as the issue is resolved the structure disappears. Furthermore, the coalition involves no centralization of power or authority. All matters taken up by the coalition must be agreed to by all participating parties. There is no area over which the coalition is given authority to act unilaterally, and it is given no resources, such as a central office or staff, with which to function independently of its members. (See Figure 5.)

The best examples of coalitions are found in the political arena. Coalitions are formed to lobby for some special legislation which en-

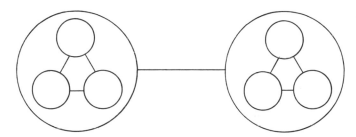

FIGURE 5. Interorganizational Field—the Coalitional Context

hances the common interest or to influence some budgetary process. For example, health agencies may coalesce to prevent legislative actions which might inhibit their freedom in fund raising. Coalitions can be thought of as incipient structures of a higher order; that is, they will either develop into a more differentiated form, the *federative* or *unitary* structure, or dissolve.

The third structure which emerges from Warren's discussion of the interorganizational field is the *federation*. This is the first differentiated structure with some hierarchical, centralized authority. The federation is a group of elements or organizations which have assigned some limited functions to a centralized body. In Ramsoy's terms, it is an inclusive system with a leadership subsystem. In more vivid terms, it is a coalition which has taken on an office, a telephone number, and an executive secretary. The distinguishing feature of a federation is its centralized authority (with accompanying resources), for it gives the federation a continuing interest in inclusive decision-making. Once such an authority is established, it is possible for the federation headquarters to initiate action, "to wheel and deal" for increased power over the constituent members. Formally, however, the federation is a consensus system in that any actions proposed by the federation must be ratified by its individual members. The federation is not a unitary system, a collectivity, because member organizations are recognized to have individual goals to pursue and the right to unilateral action in those areas not delegated to the federation. (See Figure 6.)

The integrating mechanism of the

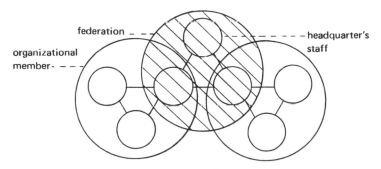

FIGURE 6. Interorganizational Field—the Federative Context

federation, therefore, is its centralized resource or leadership subsystem, which pursues inclusive goals
and tries to maximize the domain of
the federation and maintain its existence.

There are many examples of federations at the community level:
councils of churches, chambers of
commerce, united funds, or community chests. The increasing awareness that urban problems cross city
boundaries has led to the creation of
numerous councils of government or
metropolitan planning commissions.
A common complaint heard by the
staff of most such structures is that
they rarely overcome the local autonomy of constituent municipalities. This comment reflects a desire
of the leadership subsystem to convert the structure into something
beyond a federation. The metropolitan service districts, which are unitary systems, are the alternative.

The final structure offered by
Warren is the *unitary context*. A
unitary context is characterized by
leadership subsystem to which elements ascribe authority, and an orientation on the part of constituent
elements to pursue common goals in
preference to their own goals. Here
we have returned to the Parsonian
collectivity. In this sense Warren's
unitary structure is the outer limit
of the interorganizational field. It
characterizes the state of affairs when
the interorganizational field evolves
from a system of units whose only
integrating mechanism is shared resources into a collectivity. The unitary system has both the moral authority and the centralized power to
enforce concerted decisions. I will
treat Warren's unitary structure as
synonymous with the macrocollectivity discussed by Ramsoy.

THE ECOLOGICAL SYSTEM

The ecological system as a model
for social behavior is anticipated by
Warren's social choice context of the
interorganizational field. As such, its
constituent elements are organizations or systems, making the model
a macrosystem. However, it can also
be thought of as a microsystem, as in
Parsons' reference to the market as
the best example of an ecological
system.

The characteristic structure of an
ecological system assumes equality
among the individual elements; that
is, no one element has prescribed
power or authority over another.
This characteristic is referred to by
Dunn as the absence of any direct
or formal management control over
system components (1971, pp. 199f).
However, the counterpart of a stratification of elements may emerge.
Some may achieve dominance by virtue of their greater influence over
the common resources which are the
basis of the ecological system (Duncan and Schnore, 1959). (See Figure
7.)

The ecological system is characterized by interdependence among its
parts rather than by interaction. The
integrating mechanism for such a
system is a common resource base.
Without such a base, the elements
would be completely independent
and their behavior would not be
characterized as systemic. When the
sharing of this common resource
base is mutually beneficial, the interdependence is said to be symbiotic.
One should not assume, however,
that an ecological system is necessarily harmonious. Because of its dependence on common resources,
which must be assumed to be limited, the ecological system may be

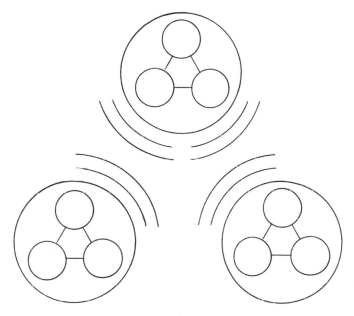

FIGURE 7.   Ecological System

characterized by partial conflict.[3]

The only way of influencing such a system, as Warren points out, is by controlling the allocation of resources or restricting the domain of activity of the elements. This process can be seen in the budgetary sessions of legislatures which review appropriations for different operating departments of government or in budget hearings for member agencies of a united fund. An aroused public opinion will often lead to legislation which restricts or expands the domain in which a CDO can legitimately operate. Consequently, budgetary decisions and public relations campaigns become important tools in dealing with such systems.

In actual practice there is no perfect ecological system. In the background there is always some latent, more inclusive system which can

[3] This point is made by Litwak and Hylton (1962) with respect to interorganizational behavior.

impose its goals and norms. For example, accepted forms of behavior between buyer and seller in a Mexican market differ markedly from those operating in an American market. At the national level, the government may set ground rules for the ecological system, as in the case of legislation governing fair trade or labor disputes. At the local community level, as Warren observes, the mayor often acts as a *deus ex machina* to resolve conflicts between competing organizations which threaten goals of the wider community (1967, p. 413). And Long notes that a newspaper often serves to arouse "the public," which then demands action (1958, pp. 259f). These interventions reflect the fact that parties external to the partial conflict of an ecological system may experience disutilities which stimulate them to act as an inclusive system and to force some collective goals on that ecological system.

Examples of such a system model are numerous. Much of urban social life is characterized by ecological relationships. At the simplest level (microsystem), Jane Jacobs has analyzed city street life in terms of the interdependency or symbiotic relationship between types of street users (1961). City planners have considerable impact on patterns of city street life through their manipulations of land use. Dense urban neighborhoods are usually good examples of ecological systems, although they have often been treated mistakenly as collectivities. Suttles describes the symbiotic relationships between ethnic groups in Chicago's Westside (1968); and Gans claims that the Bohemians and the Italians in Boston's West End constitute an ecological system—although they never mix socially, their compatible life styles allow them to share common space (1962, p. 15).

A cynic would say that most public organizations behave as though they were elements of an ecological system. The health or medical care field is a particularly good example. Specialized health serving agencies each seek legitimacy and resources to pursue their particular activities and carefully avoid any concerted action lest one agency lose public support or resources to another. Historically, the medical care system has operated as a market, a pattern which thwarts present efforts at comprehensive health planning. A similar state of affairs characterizes youth agencies; every year Boy Scout groups, Boys' Clubs, YMCA's, and similar agencies compete for youths to serve.

In summary, it should be noted that the figures depicting ecological systems and exchange systems lack any containing circles, in contrast to figures depicting models based on a collectivity. This difference reflects the fact that collectivities, unlike ecological or exchange systems, are bound together by common goals or values. This quality is expressed through boundary maintenance which determines who shall and shall not participate in the system, and through the power and authority granted the inclusive system to enforce collective interests. The exchange and ecological models take on all comers who wish to interact or who share some common resource. The system has no inherent power or authority which can hold it together. Reciprocity dictates the system's persistence.

UTILITY FOR PLANNERS

Social system models are useful to planners in two ways: they are instructive in how to achieve desired goals (the planning process), and they indicate appropriate goals around which to develop a plan (planning substance).

If planners are concerned with action, then the ability to distinguish between different types of social systems is instrumental in achieving the planner's objectives. For example, appeals to "the public interest" or to moral authority are relevant only in a collectivity. In such a system, the planner can have influence by aligning himself with the leadership set.

In an exchange system, on the other hand, exhortations of a value nature and appeals to common interests are wasted. The planner in such a system needs to be a negotiator, skillful in the art of finding trade-offs and assessing their relative values. The failure within the Model Cities Program to distinguish this difference in circumstances has been well documented by Warren (1969). The alternative is to invoke some more inclusive system which can establish ground rules that govern the exchanges or can impose solutions on the contesting parties.

In an ecological system, the planner must deal with the resource base which sustains the system if he is to have any influence. This implies that a more inclusive system exists or can be brought into existence which has some control over these resources.

Knowledge of the various social system models can also help the planner identify relevant goals or objectives. To the extent that a given condition can be identified with certain systems, the nature of the system may become an object of change. For example, the collectivity has the greatest degree of control over its members. It is also more stable and durable than exchange or ecological systems. To the extent that these qualities are desirable, the planner will strive to create conditions favorable to a collectivity. On the other hand, exchange systems are more responsive to change, and ecological systems probably foster the most individual freedom. To the extent that these conditions are goals of the planner, he will try to convert existing systems into ecological or exchange systems.

The key factor in using system models seems to be the integrative mechanisms. If a plan is to have an impact on a system, either for purposes of adaptation or change, it must deal with the mechanism which holds the system together.

In using social system models, planners should be aware of certain inherent limitations. (1) As with any theoretical construct, there is always the problem of *reification*. Social systems are not real facts, they are convenient ways of looking at real facts to identify useful relationships. (2) There is an inherent *variability* in the social behavior depicted as social systems, so that a model may fit more or less well at any given point in time. (3) There is a *restricted determinancy* about social system models in the sense that they do not completely account for social behavior. They must be melded with theories of individual systems (psychological and physiological) and physical systems (economic and natural environmental). (4) A given social system has a built-in tendency toward *equilibrium,* or more appropriately self-preservation. This is often interpreted as a tendency to preserve the status quo, to define change as internal adjustment to maintain basic system states. In any event, the study of social systems is not inherently a conservative enterprise because an understanding of the forces working for stability can be used to good advantage in planning intentional change of social systems.[4]

QUESTIONS FOR FURTHER STUDY

When distinctive systems are identified, at least two major directions for further study present themselves. One is to identify the change pro-

[4] For a further discussion of these practical limitations, see Mayer (1972).

cesses inherent in these models. The second is to identify the implications of each system for the achievement of social goals such as maximization of individual freedom or creativity, conflict resolution, or system adaptability to changing environmental conditions.

With regard to change processes, each author gives some explanation of how his system changes. Indeed in almost every case, the model's proponent anticipates the alternative models in terms of states of development in his own model. In this sense, the array of models can be thought of as a range on a continuum of states which any social system may assume. For example, small microcollectivities may combine and form a macrocollectivity. Or in Blau's terms, a system, like an amoeba, may divide into two conflicting groups, one splintering off and starting a new system. Or in Warren's terms, a social choice context may convert into a coalition, which in turn may change into a federation, which eventually may become a unitary system. Identifying these change processes and how they may be brought about intentionally will be of considerable help to planning theory.

With regard to the achievement of social goals, a given system may be more favorable to some goals than to others. For example, it can be argued that nonnormative, egalitarian systems based on exchange processes (for example, a research center), are favorable to high levels of innovation. Similarly, current proposals to give clients the resources to purchase social services in the private market presumably will make the delivery of public services more responsive to client needs.

However, as can be seen in the case of international relations, exchange systems are particularly poor at containing conflict which may adversely affect not only the parties involved but innocent bystanders as well. Unitary systems or some type of collectivity may be better suited to the achievement of social order. It is important, therefore, to understand fully each system model's implications for social goals.

REFERENCES

BANFIELD, E. C. (1961). *Political Influence.* New York: The Free Press.

BLAU, P. M. (1964). *Exchange Power in Social Life.* New York: John Wiley and Sons, Inc.

CLOWARD, R. A. and L. E. OHLIN (1960). *Delinquency and Opportunity.* New York: The Free Press.

DUNCAN, O. D. and L. F. SCHNORE (1959). "Cultural, Behavioral, and Ecological Perspectives in the Study of Social Organization." *American Journal of Sociology,* 65 (September), 132–46.

DUNN, E. S., JR. (1971). *Economic and Social Development.* Baltimore: The Johns Hopkins Press.

GANS, H. (1962). *The Urban Villagers.* New York: The Free Press.

GOULDNER, A. W. (1970). *The Coming Crisis of Western Sociology.* New York: Basic Books, Inc.

JACOBS, J. (1961). *The Death and Life of Great American Cities.* New York: Random House, Inc.

LITWAK, E. and L. F. HYLTON (1962). "Interorganizational Analysis: A Hypothesis on Coordinating Agencies." *Administrative Science Quarterly,* 6 (March), 395–420.

LONG, N. E. (1958). "The Local Community as an Ecology of Games." *American Journal of Sociology,* 64 (November), 251–61.

LOPREATO, J. (1971). "The Concept of Equilibrium: Sociological Tantalizer." Pp.

309–43 in H. Turk and R. L. Simpson, eds., *Institutions and Social Exchange: The Sociologies of Talcott Parsons and George C. Homans*. New York: Bobbs-Merrill.

MAYER, R. R. (1972). *Social Planning and Social Change*. Englewood Cliffs, N.J.: Prentice-Hall, Inc.

PARSONS, T. (1951). *The Social System*. New York: The Free Press.

RAMSOY, O. (1963). *Social Groups as Systems and Subsystems*. New York: The Free Press.

ROBERTS, R. E. (1971). *The New Communes*. Englewood Cliffs, N.J.: Prentice-Hall, Inc.

SHAPIRO, J. H. (1966). "Single-Room Occupancy: Community of the Alone." *Social Work*, 11 (October), 24–34.

SUTTLES, G. D. (1968). *The Social Order of the Slum*. Chicago: University of Chicago Press.

WALSH, J. L. (1971). "Cops and 'Stool Pigeons,' Professional Striving and Discretionary Justice in Two European Settings." Paper presented at the 66th annual meeting of the American Sociological Association, Denver, Colorado, 31 August 1971.

WARREN, R. L. (1969). "Model Cities First Round: Politics, Planning, and Participation." *Journal of the American Institute of Planners*, 35 (July), 245–52.

WARREN, R. L. (1967). "The Interorganizational Field as a Focus of Investigation." *Administrative Science Quarterly*, 12 (December), 396–419.

WARREN, R. L. (1963). *The Community in America*. Chicago: Rand McNally.

THE CONCEPT OF SOCIAL NEED

JONATHAN BRADSHAW

The concept of social need is inherent in the idea of social service. The history of the social services is the story of the recognition of social needs and the organisation of society to meet them. The Seebohm report was deeply concerned with the concept of need, though it never succeeded in defining it. It saw that "the personal social services are large-scale experiments in ways of helping those in need."

Despite this interest, it is often not clear in a particular situation what is meant by social need. When a statement is made to the effect that a person or group of persons are in need of a given service, what is the quality that differentiates them—what definition of social need is being used?

The concept of social need is of particular interest to economists. They have a clearcut measure of "effective demand": demand is "effective" when people are prepared to back it financially and ineffective or non-existent when they are not. This measure will not do for the social services, because there is nor-

Reprinted with permission of author and publisher from: Jonathan Bradshaw, "The Concept of Social Need," New Society, 30 (March 1972), pp. 640–43.

mally no link between service and payment (though some economists think there ought to be). If the social services are trying to cope with need without limiting it by the ability to pay, how is it actually assessed?

In practice, four separate definitions are used by administrators and research workers:

1. *Normative need.* This is what the expert or professional, administrator or social scientist defines as need in any given situation. A "desirable" standard is laid down and is compared with the standard that actually exists—if an individual or group falls short of the desirable standard then they are identified as being in need. Thus the British Medical Association's nutritional standard is used as a normative measure of the adequacy of a diet (see Royston Lambert's *Nutrition in Britain*). The incapacity scale developed by Peter Townsend and the measure of social isolation used by Jeremy Tunstall are also examples of normative standards used as a basis of need.

A normative definition of need is in no sense absolute. It may not correspond with need established by other definitions. It may be tainted with a charge of paternalism—ie, the use of middle class norms to assess need in a working class context—though where the aspirations are to middle class standards, this may be reasonable. A further difficulty with the normative definition of need is that there may well be different and possibly conflicting standards laid down by different experts. The decision about what is desirable is not made in a vacuum. As Ronald Walton has pointed out, the statement "x is in need" is often taken as an empirical fact. This is not so. It is a value-judgment entailing the following propositions: x is in a state y, y is incompatible with the values held in society z. Therefore y state should be changed. So the normative definition of need may be different according to the value orientation of the expert—on his judgments about the amount of resources that should be devoted to meeting the need, or whether or not the available skills can solve the problem. Normative standards change in time both as a result of developments in knowledge, and the changing values of society.

2. *Felt need.* Here need is equated with want. When assessing need for a service, people are asked whether they feel they need it. In a democracy, it could be imagined that felt need would be an important component of and definition of need, but a felt need measure seems to only be used regularly in studies of the elderly and in community development. Felt need is, by itself, an inadequate measure of "real need." It is limited by the perceptions of the individual—whether they know there is a service available, as well as a reluctance in many situations to confess a loss of independence. On the other hand, it is thought to be in-

flated by those who ask for help without really needing it.

3. *Expressed need* or demand is felt need turned into action. Under this definition, total need is defined as those people who demand a service. One does not demand a service unless one feels a need but, on the other hand, it is common for felt need not to be expressed by demand. Expressed need is commonly used in the health services where waiting lists are taken as a measure of unmet need. Waiting lists are generally accepted as a poor definition of "real need"—especially for pre-symptomatic cases.

4. *Comparative need.* By this definition, a measure of need is found by studying the characteristics of those in receipt of a service. If people with similar characteristics are not in receipt of a service, then they are in need. This definition has been used to assess needs both of individuals and areas. Bleddyn Davies has identified the community-wide factors which indicate a high incidence of pathology in one area which are not present in another. Need established by this method is the gap between what services exist in one area and what services exist in another, weighted to take account of the difference in pathology. This is an attempt to standardise provision, but provision may still not correspond with need. The question still has to be asked—supply at what level? The statement that one area, A, is in need in comparison with another area, B, does not necessarily imply that area B is still not in need.

Comparative need used to define individuals in need can be illustrated by the following statements:

"This person x is in receipt of a service because he has the characteristics A–N. This person z has also the characteristics A–N but is not receiving the service. Therefore z is in need." The difficulty in this situation is to define the significant characteristics. The method has been used by some local health authorities to compile a risk register of babies in need of special attention from the preventive services. Conditions which in the past have been associated with handicaps like forceps delivery, birth trauma, birth to older mothers, and so on, are used as indicators to babies in special need. The definition is more commonly used in an ad hoc way—a crude rule of precedence to assess eligibility for selective services provided by the personal social services.

The chart demonstrates diagrammatically the interrelation of the four definitions. Plus (+) and minus (−) denote the presence or absence of need by each of the foregoing definitions—ie, + − − + is a need that is accepted as such by the experts, but which is neither felt nor demanded by the individual, despite the fact that he has the same characteristics as those already being supplied with the service. Other examples of the twelve possible combinations are given. It will be noted that none of the squares is coterminous and the problem the policy-maker has to face is deciding exactly what part of the total is "real need" —that is, need it is appropriate to try to meet.

1. + + + +

This is the area where all definitions overlap, or (using an analogy from intelligence test studies) the "g" factor of need. An individual is in need by all definitions, so this is the least controversial part of need.

2. + + − +

Demand is limited by difficulties of access to a service. Although the individual is in need by all other definitions, he has not wanted to, or been able to, express his need. Difficulties of access may be due to a stigma attached to the receipt of a service; geographical distances that make it difficult to claim; charges which are a disincentive to take up; administrative procedures that deter claimants, or merely ignorance about the availability of the service. Demand must also vary according to how intense is the felt need. Two examples of need of this type are the non-take-up of means-tested benefits, and the underuse of fair rent machinery.

3. + + − −

Here need is accepted as such by the expert and is felt by the individual, but there is no demand as well as, and possibly because of, the absence of supply. Examples may be need for family planning facilities for unmarried girls, free nursery education, and need for chiropody services for the elderly.

4. − + + +

Here the need is not postulated by the pundits, but is felt, demanded, and supplied. The less-essential types of cosmetic surgery are examples. Also some of the work of GP, it is often thought, could come into this category—for example, the prescribing of "clinically unnecessary" drugs. The pundits may suggest that a compassionate label for this category could be "inappropriate need." On the other hand, the pundits may be exercising inappropriate value-judgments.

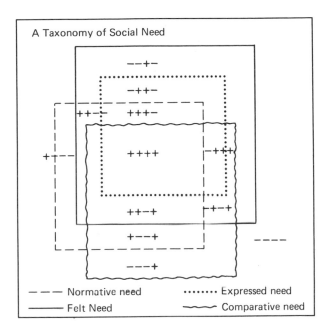

A Taxonomy of Social Need

--+-
-++-
++-- +++-
+---
+ +++-+ -++-
++-+ -+-+
+--+
---+

– – – Normative need   .... Expressed need
———— Felt Need   ⁓⁓⁓ Comparative need

5. + + + —
A need that is postulated, felt, and demanded but not supplied. These needs represent likely growth areas in the social services. An example would be the need for a fatherless families allowance or adequate wage-related pensions. Resources are usually the limiting factor in this category.

6. + — — +
Here the need is postulated by the experts and similar persons are being supplied with the service, but the need is neither felt nor demanded by the individual. Some of the work of the probation officer, or the health visitors' postnatal visits (when they are not wanted) are examples of meeting this kind of need. Another example is the unwanted supply of expensive central-heating plant in public sector housing.

7. + — — —
Here need is postulated by the pun-dits or professionals. Examples could be found in the area of preventive medicine. To the layman the need is probably obscure, technical and new. The need to provide fluoride in the water supplies was accepted as such by the public health experts long before it was felt, demanded, or supplied.

8. — — — +
Here a service is supplied despite the absence of need as assessed by the other definitions. This could be called a service-oriented service. Examples can be found in the many small and outdated charities to which the charity commissioners are striving to apply the doctrine of çy prés—for example, paying electricity bills instead of buying farthing candles for old ladies at Michaelmas.

9. — + + —
This is need which is not appreciated by the experts and is not supplied, but which is felt and de-

manded. Prescriptions for bandages requested from the GP may be an example of this. Another example is the need for improved services—the need for improved educational maintenance allowances.

10. − + − −

This represents felt needs which are not within the ambit of the social services to meet. Perhaps loneliness —or the need for love/company is an example of this. A need for wealth or fame are certainly examples.

11. − + − +

A need that is not postulated by the experts but is felt, not expressed, but supplied. People feel a need to make contributions for social benefits and the need is met by insurance stamps, but many experts feel it would be simpler to finance these benefits wholly through taxation.

12. − − − −

Absence of need by all definitions.

To illustrate how this could be used by research workers and policymakers, it might be useful to outline a hypothetical situation.

A local housing authority has become concerned about the housing position of the elderly in its area. It wishes to have assessment of the need for public sector housing for this age group. A research worker is therefore commissioned to do a study of the housing need. The first problem the research worker has to face is the question of what constitutes housing need? He can either make a decision as to what he himself believes housing need to be, or he can produce information on the amount of need under each section of the taxonomy and allow the policymakers to decide what part of the total they regard as "real need." The research worker decides to take

the latter course of action. This will provide the maximum information with the minimum number of value-judgments. In order to produce a figure for each section of the taxonomy, he must first decide on the amount of need under each of the four separate definitions.

Normative need. It has already been pointed out that there is no one definition of normative need. Let us assume that the local housing authority is laying down the norms in this situation, and that it would agree that old persons living in homes lacking any of the basic amenities, and old persons living in overcrowded accommodation, are in need by its standards. An estimate of the number of persons who are in this situation could be obtained by means of a sample survey.

Felt need. An estimate of the degree of felt need can be obtained by means of the same sample survey by asking the respondents whether they are satisfied with their present housing and, if not, whether they would like to move. Ignoring the problems inherent in exploring people's attitudes on such a delicate question and remembering that their attitudes will be affected by their knowledge of alternative housing opportunities, as well as their fears about the upheaval of the move, another measure of need is obtained.

Expressed need. The local housing authority's waiting lists provide the measure of expressed need in this context. It is, at the same time, the easiest measure of need to obtain and the most inadequate. On the one hand, the list may be inflated by persons who have resolved their housing problem since they applied for the housing and yet who have not withdrawn their application; and, on the other hand, the list may under-estimate expressed need if certain categories are excluded from the waiting list. There may be a residence qualification, applications from owner-occupiers may not be accepted unless they are overcrowded, and persons who have refused the first offer may also be excluded. All these exclusions mean that the waiting list is not an adequate measure of expressed need but, because it is the only one available, it is used as another measure of need.

Comparative need. The measure of comparative need is more difficult to obtain. It would entail investigating the characteristics of elderly persons already in public sector housing and then, through a sample survey, obtaining an estimate of the number of persons in the community (not in public sector housing) who have similar characteristics. As the local housing authority's norms have been taken for the measure of normative need, and as the local housing authority is responsible for choosing their tenants, it is likely that in this example the characteristics of tenants will be similar to those norms and thus the measure of comparative need will be very similar (though not necessarily identical) to the measure of normative need.

The research worker has now produced four separate but interrelated measures of need. By sorting, he is able to put a figure against each of the permutations of the four measures. For instance:

$+ + - +$ This will consist of persons whose houses are overcrowded or lack basic amenities, who want to move but who are not on the council waiting-list and yet who are "as deserving as" other residents in council accommodation.

$- + - -$ This will consist of persons whose housing is considered satisfactory by local authority standards, who are not on the council waiting-list, and are not in need when compared with other residents in council property and yet who want to move.

So now the policymaker is presented with a picture of total need for public sector housing in their area. He is now able to use the taxonomy to clarify his decisions. Instead of housing being allocated on the basis of either first come first served, or whether the old person is articulate, energetic, and knowledgeable enough to get on the housing waiting-list, it can now be allocated on the basis of explicit priorities. No longer is the local authority providing houses to meet need, but, rather, providing houses to meet certain specific conditions of need.

Thus the policymaker can do one of two things. Either he can decide that certain categories of the total (say, $+ + + +, + + - +, + - - +,$ $- + + +, + + + -$) constitute "real need" and plan to provide enough housing for the numbers in these groups, or secondly if it is found that need is very large and his resources are limited, he can decide that certain categories of need should be given priority. For instance, he may decide that category $+ + - +$: those in need who have not applied for help (the iceberg below the waterline) should be given priority over category $- + + +$: those in need on all bases except that they are already adequately housed on a normative measure.

The policymaker can now return to the research worker. Having made his priorities explicit, he could ask the research worker to carry out a detailed study of the "real need" categories to ascertain their aetiology so that, in future, they may be more easily identified and the services explicitly designed to get at and help them. The research worker could also use the taxonomy as a framework for monitoring the effects on need of technical advances, demographic change, changes in the standard of living, and improvements in the services.

This taxonomy may provide a way forward in an area where precise thinking is needed for both theoretical and practical reasons. Without some further classification, much social policy must remain a matter of political hunches and academic guesswork. The taxonomy provides no easy solutions either for the research worker or the policymaker. The research worker is still faced with difficult methodological problems and the policymaker has still to make complex decisions about the categories of need should be given priority. But the taxonomy may help to clarify and make explicit what is being done when those concerned with the social services are studying or planning to meet social need.

21 Problem Analysis: Alternative Measures of Needs Assessment

MEASURING NEED IN THE SOCIAL SERVICES

Richard Thayer

Social Services Departments provide services as a response to particular circumstances. The existence of a problem, or potential problem, may indicate a set of circumstances which is considered to be undesirable and thus a situation in which there is a need for help of some sort. The term "need" can be used to refer both to the identified problem and to the help which is required to alleviate it. Here, the former will be referred to as diagnostic need, and the latter as prescriptive need.

Obviously, in attempting to meet diagnostic need some forms of help will be more appropriate than others. The same presenting problem may be associated with a variety of circumstances, each creating a different prescriptive need. Thus, financial deprivation may create a need for direct financial assistance and/or a need for some form of vocational training depending on the age, sex, employability, family circumstances,

Reprinted with permission of author and publisher from: Richard Thayer, "Measuring Need in the Social Services," *Social and Economic Administration* 7 (May 1973), pp. 91–105.

place of residence and so on of the individual concerned. When a need has been diagnosed the provision of a particular form of help does not mean that the need has necessarily been met. Need can only be said to have been met when the help or service provided has brought about an intended change in the circumstances of the recipient.

This paper sets out to examine various approaches to the measurement and assessment of need and tries to relate these approaches both to each other and to the two elements of need: diagnosis and prescription.

A useful categorisation of approaches to the measurement of social need has been developed by Jonathan Bradshaw.[1] He has developed a four-fold classification of need based on the derivation of the criteria adopted for recognising need, be it diagnostic or prescriptive. The types of criteria are normative, felt, expressed and comparative and he uses these four adjectives to describe the actual assessment.

[1] J. Bradshaw, "The Concept of Social Need," *New Society*, 30/3/72.

Normative need is what the expert or professional perceives to be need in a given situation; felt need is need perceived by the subjects themselves; expressed need, or demand, is felt need turned into action in the form of a request for service; and comparative need is need, deduced by the outside observer, in circumstances where individuals not in receipt of a particular service have similar characteristics to others who do receive it.

It should be recognised that these are only categories of need or criteria. The extent of measured need within each category will vary. Normative need will vary according to the particular criteria adopted. Felt need may vary according to the observer's subjective assessment of intensity of feeling while the various channels through which demand can be expressed will give different estimates of expressed need. Comparative need will vary according to the areas which are considered and the particular social, demographic or environmental characteristics which are taken into account. Obviously, other factors may also affect the estimates but these are among the most important.

No more will be said specifically about these categories at this point but they will be used to help explain the approaches adopted in various studies which have attempted to assess and measure need.

SEVEN STUDIES OF "NEED"

1. Townsend and Wedderburn's Survey of over 4,000 old people in 1962 was part of a major cross-national survey of the relationship be-tween individual disability or incapacity of people over 65 and family and social activities, occupations, housing and levels of income. At the same time there was some specifically national research which in Britain involved an examination of the role of the health and welfare services in the care of the elderly. This is reported on in Townsend and Wedderburn: *The Aged in the Welfare State*.[2]

One aspect of this part of the study was an examination of the adequacy of existing services. Respondents were asked whether particular services were wanted or needed. In the case of home-helps they were asked whether they needed "someone to come in and help with the housework" (*Ibid.* p. 45). For chiropody the question was "do you need someone to see to your feet regularly?" (*Ibid.* p. 51, n. 3). A question was also asked about mobile meals. The replies to these questions were compared with other data, for example, whether or not the respondent was moderately or severely incapacitated, childless, living alone, or had no relatives within ten minutes' journey time. In each case those who replied that they would like help tended to be more physically handicapped and socially isolated than those who did not ask for help. Further, Townsend argues that although some who said that they did need help might not really be considered to need it there were others who said that they did not need help despite much contrary evidence. Thus 189 respondents said that they could not undertake heavy house-

2 P. Townsend and D. Wedderburn, *The Aged in the Welfare State*, 1970.

work and had no help at all but still claimed that they did not need anyone to help. The need for sheltered housing was also considered. Here the authors considered that old people who lived alone, had no children living within ten minutes' journey and were moderately or severely incapacitated were in need of sheltered housing. This was considered to be a conservative estimate as it did not include, for example, infirm married couples.

This study cannot be seen as anything more than an approximate survey of prescriptive needs of the elderly for social services. The main need which is identified is felt need, based on the perceptions of old people themselves. Nevertheless, the survey indicates a considerable excess of need over provision and it is this that Harris examines in more detail in *Social Welfare for the Elderly*.[3]

2. This survey resulted from the wide variations in provision of health and welfare services for the elderly forecast in the ten-year plans produced by local authorities at the request of the Ministry of Health. Harris outlines some of the variations in the revised plans published in 1965 (*Health and Welfare, The Development of Community Care*—revision to 1975–6), and states, rather tactfully, "The Ministry of Health had . . . had some indication that the size of the service was sometimes determined without full knowledge of the extent of local need." (*Ibid.* p. 1).

The survey examines the needs for home-helps, housing, residential

3 A. Harris, *Social Welfare for the Elderly*. 1968.

homes and other health and welfare services including meals-on-wheels, chiropody, district nursing and health visitors. Eleven local authorities were covered: two county boroughs, four non-county boroughs, and two urban districts in England, and a county of city, a large burgh and a small burgh in Scotland. It was decided to define need in terms of the criteria used by the authorities concerned. These criteria were to be identified by—

 i. asking the responsible official for a statement of the basis of these criteria,
 ii. examining the records of a sample of the population who are either on the waiting list for the service or actually receiving it,
and iii. interviewing the members of the sample in order to get details of the circumstances which lead, or were expected to lead, to them getting the service.

The criteria which are identified in this way are partly normative (those laid down explicitly) and partly comparative (those deduced from the circumstances of existing recipients). By using all three methods, Harris hoped to avoid difficulties arising from variations in the application of stated criteria and inadequacies in records and/or the memories of old people. Six random samples were drawn in each area—

a. people of retirement age
b. elderly people having home-helps
c. elderly people who had been rehoused
d. elderly people in residential homes
e. elderly people on the waiting list for rehousing (if any)

f. elderly people on the waiting list for homes (if any).

Nowhere was there a waiting list for home-helps but in fact the waiting lists which did exist often turned out to be unsatisfactory. Housing waiting lists sometimes included a high proportion of applicants who had moved or died while many people who were still on the lists no longer needed or wanted to be moved, owing to changed circumstances. It may also have been that some people had been dropped from waiting lists unknowingly, because they had not replied to Housing Department circulars.

Once the criteria of need have been established they are applied to a sample of all the elderly population. In the case of need for home-helps the total comprised all those permanently bedfast or housebound, and anyone usually able to get out who had difficulty with housework and/or shopping and/or cooking but excluding various categories within these groups such as those who only had occasional difficulty or those who could rely on other help. Felt need for service is also included so that those wishing to receive help but not eligible and those who are eligible but do not wish to receive help can be taken account of.

The difficulty of applying comparative, and some normative, criteria in estimates of prescriptive needs arises when services are highly substitutable at the margin. Thus although the characteristics of residents of old people's homes and of recipients of home-helps may differ significantly from the characteristics of most of those not receiving these services they often do not differ signi-

ficantly from each other. In these circumstances there may be a sizable number of people for whom these criteria can only indicate a diagnosed need for service of some sort and for whom a more detailed examination is necessary before specific services can be prescribed. In the case of residents of homes who express a wish to leave each individual case is outlined briefly and an assessment of prescriptive need is made normatively on the basis of this.

3. An example of a sample survey in which estimates are made of felt, expressed and normative prescriptive need is the report of the Office of Population Censuses and Surveys, *Work and Housing of Impaired Persons in Great Britain,*[4] which follows the report *Handicapped and Impaired in Great Britain.*[5]

These two reports examine the effects of impairment on various aspects of physical and social functioning and also consider certain social and environmental factors which, when associated with impairment, can cause additional handicap. One of the environmental factors studied is housing and from the survey findings four estimates of need for rehousing are made (although the survey uses the term need to describe only one).

The report considers first what it calls demands for rehousing. Respondents were asked "would you like to move from here, or do you prefer to stay?" From the answers to this question an estimate is made of demand, which comes into Brad-

[4] J. Buckle, *Work and Housing of Impaired Persons in Great Britain,* 1971.
[5] A. Harris, *Handicapped and Impaired in Great Britain,* 1971.

shaw's category of felt need. Of course a different form of question could result in a different estimate, even though it would still constitute felt need. All those who stated a desire to move were termed potential movers. A minority of these had applied to the local authority for rehousing. These were called active movers and their numbers represent the expressed need for rehousing, so far as the local authority is concerned. Since some potential movers may have "expressed" a need for rehousing in some other way (for example by making an offer for a private house) and the estimate of felt need for rehousing is not the same as felt need for rehousing by the local authority, the measures of felt and expressed need are not strictly comparable.

The report then makes an estimate of what it calls reasonable demand for rehousing, "where the impaired person's reason for wanting to move is the unsuitability of the house itself." (p. 103). Reasonable demand retains the criteria of felt need, namely that need is perceived by the individual concerned, but at the same time it introduces certain normative criteria, so that at least one of the following conditions must apply: the accommodation is being demolished; the accommodation is in bad condition or lacks amenities; the impaired person cannot manage the stairs or steps; the impaired person is unable to manage because of the house itself; or, the impaired person lives alone and is too far from relatives. The report says that "if two or more reasons are applicable priority is given in the order shown" (p. 115). In this way a further normative element can be introduced—a hierarchy

of needs based on the assessed relative importance of the criteria adopted.

Finally, the Report deals with what it calls the need for rehousing or substantial improvement. This comes into the category of normative need, being based entirely on certain observable characteristics of circumstances of impaired people irrespective of whether or not they wish to be rehoused. The four criteria adopted are: not having the use of an inside W.C.; finding having to go upstairs or downstairs to the W.C. very inconvenient; inability of persons, other than those who are bedfast, to use some rooms because of their disability; or, sometimes or always having to sleep in the living room instead of the bedroom because of disability.

It can be seen that the four normative criteria which have been adopted for estimating need for rehousing and substantial improvement differ substantially from the five criteria which are used, in conjunction with demand, to assess reasonable demand. Since the former includes the need for substantial improvement as well as for rehousing it is reasonable that there should be some differences in the criteria adopted. Nevertheless the complete omission of the two categories would seem to require some explanation. A wide range of potential criteria is usually available for estimating normative need and this would indicate some need for a fuller explanation than is given in this report of why particular criteria were chosen. Nevertheless, the various estimates of demand and need in the report do give a valuable example of the way in which the extent of estimated need can vary according to the criteria used.

One of the objects of surveys in the social services field is to ascertain the total numbers of individuals for whom it might be necessary to provide services; the overall extent of need. In the studies already discussed it was first necessary to identify numbers of the groups under consideration, the elderly and the impaired, from a sample of the general population. Estimates were then made of needs for specific services, needs being based on a mixture of normative, felt, expressed and comparative criteria.

However, even when a need which is measured is not specifically normative need it will still contain normative elements. As the Isle of Wight survey shows (see below, p. 303) respondents' perceptions of their needs tend to be constrained by their knowledge of what is available while expressed and comparative need must be stated in terms of existing services. Thus, the need for new forms of help must always be based on normative assessments derived from consideration of the problems facing particular groups who are thought to need help. Such a consideration was, in fact, the principle function of the Townsend and Wedderburn, and Harris studies. However, a group for whom services are even less well developed than they are for the elderly and the physically handicapped is the mentally handicapped.

4. A variety of studies of what were then termed the mentally subnormal are reported on by Tizard (1964).[6] This report makes estimates

[6] J. Tizard, *Community Services for the Mentally Handicapped*, 1964.

of the prevalence of mental subnormality, it looks at the problems of the families of the mental subnormal, the education and care of subnormal children, and an experimental residential unit, and then makes certain proposals and recommendations for the organisation of services. The last section includes a section on the prescriptive needs of the mentally handicapped and their families.

In Part I of the report Tizard deals with the prevalence of mental subnormality, including what he calls the administrative prevalence. This is defined as "the numbers for whom services would be required in a community which made provision for all who needed them," (p. 17) and represents total diagnosed need. The estimate of administrative prevalence is based on known prevalence in two counties, London and Middlesex, which were considered to offer fairly adequate services and to maintain up to date registers of all cases brought to notice. Obviously, such an approach contains certain dangers. It requires that a group be fairly easily identified and that most or all within that group are likely to need services of some sort. Since both these conditions apply to mentally handicapped children of school age the Tizard assumption seems reasonable and his estimates with regard to prevalence do agree closely with studies carried out elsewhere.

An advantage of being able to equate administrative prevalence with existing known cases is that it provides a very convenient sampling frame and source of information for researchers. In order to study the problems of the families of the mentally subnormal Tizard and Jaqueline Grad selected samples of various age groups from the records of the London County Council. They were then able to interview the nearest relative (usually the mother) and the ward sister or charge nurse in the case of hospital patients and examine records. An interview schedule was used and much of it was precoded but, as befits what was very much an exploratory study, the order and wording of questions was not fixed. In the words of the report: "Standard pieces of information were collected in an unstandardised way, which made effective use of the flexibility and informality of the interview," (p. 39). Information was collected on the child himself, the families and their problems, and the role played by existing services.

From the information collected the authors were able to formulate a list of the prescriptive needs both of mentally handicapped children and of their parents and outline the sorts of services necessary to meet these needs. Certain normative criteria of who could use which services were also developed. For example, the mentally handicapped of all ages are grouped into three diagnostic categories: employable; ambulant and trainable, and cot and chair and bedfast. The particular services required by each of these categories would obviously vary.

5. Sample surveys may give a picture of aggregate needs which can be used by an authority for planning the overall allocation of resources but an effective service also requires the identification of individuals with needs. Normally, identification results from a referral process but an alternative, which permits both identification and assessment of aggre-

gated need, is the 100 percent household survey. One such survey, to identify the chronically sick and disabled on the Isle of Wight, has been carried out by the Institute of Local Government Studies.[7]

Information collection was based entirely on responses to a questionnaire. Commenting on the impossibility of providing medical examination for respondents the authors state: "In all the circumstances, therefore, it seemed best to accept the statements of the respondents as being accurate. Indeed, in relation to many of the questions it could be legitimately argued that only the respondent or someone very close to him really knows the true situation." (p. 4). The needs identified in the report are partly felt needs. These are largely prescriptive but, as the authors recognize, there are limitations to the concept of felt prescriptive need, especially as manifested through the medium of a structured interview. The very existence of preset questions adds a normative element to the needs which are identified. When asked if they would like help in the form of the provision of special aids, should these be available, respondents were given examples, which included emergency alarms. In the replies the provision of special alarms was mentioned by 121 respondents whereas only 24 specifically mentioned the installation of a telephone, which was not given as an example. Since examples are an aid to understanding, the possibility

7 Institute of Local Government Studies/ Department of Social Administration, University of Birmingham, *Report on the Survey of Chronically Sick and Disabled Persons Resident on the Isle of Wight*, 1972.

of biased results must be accepted. Such biases may be desirable, for example, if it is decided to concentrate resources on (possibly less expensive) emergency alarms rather than telephones. However, it does illustrate the near impossibility of identifying felt need without the introduction of normative elements. Another limitation to such a measure of felt need is recognised in the report: "It is notable that the most well-known forms of help were most frequently requested, which suggests that ignorance of what is or might be available has limited people's requests." (p. 93). An alternative, or more probably an associated, explanation might be that respondents only request services which they think it "reasonable" to request, or hope for.

The survey also includes factual questions, for example about the respondent's ability to perform various common activities inside and outside the home. The possibility of cross checking answers to factual questions with respondents' perceptions of prescriptive needs means that estimates can be made on a combination of felt and normative needs, while the answers to the factual questions above form the basis of estimates of diagnosed needs.

6. The principal alternative to surveys as a source of data for systematic assessments and estimates of need is the population census. Bleddyn Davies . . . [8] has applied both normative and comparative criteria to census data in order to make estimates of the need for old people's and children's services. The various indices which he evolves are ex-

pressed in a form which allows comparisons to be made between different local authorities rather than estimates of need within authorities. Nevertheless, the indices can be converted into estimates of potential diagnostic need, or risk, within authorities.

The use of census data necessitates the identification of characteristics which between them will predict either need or potential need within a population. Unless the relevant characteristics are so statistically related that the extent of one will always predict the extent of the others, so that only the one measure is in fact required, it is necessary to weight the different characteristics according to their importance. In addition, if needs are to be assessed in more than one area one must either be sure that the same characteristics are relevant for all the areas or that different characteristics or different weightings are adopted as necessary.

In assessing the need for old people's services Davies acts on the assumption that these services are family care substitutes. To support this he quotes figures which show that the proportion of residents of old people's homes who are unmarried or childless is considerably higher than for old people in general. The family characteristics of recipients of local authority domestic help were in some ways strikingly similar to those in institutions. If residential and domiciliary services are highly substitutable the same indices of need will be appropriate for all services for old people. Davies does assume high substitutability at the margin although he admits that this is "a massive over-simplification" (p. 61). Absence of family care cannot

[8] B. Davies, *Social Needs and Resources in Local Services*, 1968.

be easily measured. As Davies points out, old people often prefer to live near rather than with relatives so that old people living alone is not a satisfactory measure. The Family Care Index is derived by taking the proportions of residents of homes having different sex, age, and marital characteristics and treating these as the probability that old people with these characteristics will need these services. Such an approach assumes that Welfare Departments have allocated places to those most in need and that there is no variation from area to area. If it could be shown that between different areas there were wide differences in the willingness or, more important, the ability of children to care for their elderly parents this would require a modification to the Family Care Index. However, Davies is able to demonstrate that in 1951 and 1961 the proportion of old people living in homes almost without exception gets higher as age increases, as one goes from married, through widowed or divorced to single and as one goes from females to males.

For each county borough Davies multiplies these national proportions by the numbers actually in each group and adds up the totals to give a weighted population, which stated per 1,000 of the borough's population gives its Family Care Index.

This estimate of diagnostic need (potential diagnostic need might be more accurate) is normative to the extent that it assumes that lack of family care is the principal factor determining need for services, and also to the extent that it assumes that age, marital status and sex are correlated with family care. However, the application of observed characteristics of recipients of services to the total population makes the index basically an indicator of comparative need.

Davies also introduces more specifically normative elements into his estimates however. He considers that infirmity, inadequate housing and extreme poverty are subsidiary, but nevertheless relevant, determinants of need for services. Various indices such as bronchitis mortality rate, proportion of male working population in Registrar General's Social Classes IV and V and proportion of private households with over 1½ persons per room were selected to represent poor social conditions. These were combined, using the statistical technique of Principal Component Analysis which selects that mixture of parts, or components, of each index which best explains variance in the indices as a whole. Such a mixture constitutes one way of weighting the individual indices which Davies calls a Social Conditions Index. As with the Family Care Index the intended application of the Social Conditions Index is in inter-authority comparisons but its individual elements might still be used for estimating diagnostic need within an authority.

Davies does not try to combine the two Indices. Instead he adopts the "arbitrary assumption" that only when the social conditions index differs by more than one standard error from the score predicted for it from the Family Care Index should it be considered. Thus of the eighty-three county boroughs originally considered Davies finally identifies forty-eight for which the Family Care Index is considered to be a good index of needs. In another eleven the Social

Conditions Index suggests that the Family Care Index is not a sufficient index of needs while the remainder are either too small or the Family Index is thought to be inappropriate for them.

Davies uses a similar method for assessing the need for children's services. The basic index of need is the anomie index. This is the equivalent of the Family Care Index for old people and is a measure of the presence or absence of family or community support. It was computed by principle component analysis using nine variables, three relating to immigration, two measuring population increase, two measuring the importance of boarding houses and hotels, an unemployment index and a population size index. The Social Conditions Index was based on a principle component analysis of nineteen variables.

7. Although both the Anomie and the Social Conditions Indices are derived from purely normative criteria the use of the former is justified to some extent by the comparative approach adopted by Jean Packman.[9]

Whereas Davies sets out to construct an index of need in order to compare the extent of need in different Authorities with various indices of standards of service Packman attempts to explain variations in one particular measure of extensiveness of provision—the number of children in care per 1,000 population under eighteen. As one possible explanation for this variation is varying amounts of need she examines the factors which might influence the extent of need.

A sample of approximately one

[9] J. Packman, *Child Care Needs and Numbers,* 1968.

third of counties and county boroughs in England and Wales was considered. Child care officers were asked to fill in questionnaires relating to applications for care and fit person orders over a period of six months. Approximately 4,500 were completed. The questionnaires were intended to provide "profiles" of the families concerned as well as details about the reasons for admission to care if the child or children were admitted, and the likely period of care. Various factors were found to be associated with applications for and admissions to care. Most important were factors associated with breakdown of the normal family unit; death, divorce, separation, desertion and illegitimacy. Next came ill health of parents—many forms of ill health are associated with short-term stays which account for a high proportion of total admissions but a much lower proportion of the total number in care at any one time. Mental illness, however, was particularly associated with long-term problems. The third main factor affecting long-term admissions to care was homelessness.

The extent of these factors in different areas cannot always be measured. Census figures are available for the divorced and widowed but not for the separated and deserted. There are annual returns for illegitimate births as a proportion of total live births but the possibility that many women move to another area for the actual birth means that the distribution of illegitimate births may not accurately represent the distribution of illegitimate children. There are some measures of ill health available but no direct measures of homelessness, only of general conditions.

Packman also attempted, like Davies, to identify particular social characteristics associated with families covered by the survey. In particular large families and young families were found to be particularly at risk, especially those which came from lower social classes. Unemployment and poor housing conditions were also important, and a disproportionate number of families at risk seemed to have moved to their present area within the previous two years, some from overseas.

When a large number of variables which might be thought to relate to the factors mentioned were compared with the rates of children in care in first eighty and then fifty-three county boroughs there were uniformly low or non-existent correlations. However, Packman then considered figures representing "the total child care problem." These included not only children in the care of the local authority, but also those in approved schools, in private foster homes and nurseries supervised by the local authority, maintained by the local authority in boarding schools and hotels as a result of maladjustment, awaiting adoption, and in the care of voluntary organisations. These figures tended to correlate much more highly with several of the at risk factors but not always in the expected direction. There were negative correlations with crude birth rate, infant mortality rate, proportion of population in social classes IV and V and other indices of poor social conditions but positive correlations with expectancy of life and net product of a penny rate per 1,000 population. These correlations held for the group of eighty county boroughs and one of them for the fifty-three. In both these groups there

were correlations in the expected direction and these covered indices concerned with rootlessness and mobility, the illegitimacy rate, the proportion of the population living in hotels and boarding houses and the proportion of the population born outside England and Wales.

Packman offers several possible explanations for these results. Wealthier areas probably attract the sort of "floating" and "foreign" population which is at high risk and this outweighs the effects of housing, unemployment and poverty. Coupled with this is the possibility that the older working class areas foster more family solidarity and self-help than the areas of geographical and social mobility. This seems to be borne out by wide variation in the proportion of children in care boarded out with relatives which Packman quotes—in 1963 the figures were 12.3 percent in the North-East Region but only 3.5 percent in the London South Region. She also suggests that wealthier areas might be in a better position to afford services for deprived children and also that juvenile delinquency, and poor standards of child care might stand out more in comparatively prosperous areas such as wealthy resorts and coastal towns.

Nevertheless, the main conclusions from Packman's study appear to substantiate the emphasis that Davies puts on "anomie" as the principal index of diagnostic need for child care services. This does not, of course, mean that other social conditions are unimportant but it suggests that "anomie" is probably the best index of the relative needs of different authorities while social conditions may be more suitable as an index of

variations in need within an authority.

DISCUSSION

The first main conclusion to be
drawn from these seven studies is
that Bradshaw's classification of types
of criteria is a useful way in which
different approaches may be distinguished from each other. In particular, the range of alternative approaches to estimating the need of
impaired people for rehousing demonstrates effectively the absence of
any absolute measure of need.

At the same time the four types
of criteria are closely inter-related.
All contain normative elements. In
the case of felt need it may be a reflection of questions asked or of the
respondent's perception of what it
is reasonable to expect, which will in
turn be influenced by what is available. Expressed need obviously reflects what is available and also,
often, the normative criteria controlling access to waiting lists. There
will also be a normative element in
the selection of relevant characteristics to use as comparative criteria.
Felt and expressed need are also very
closely related. Bradshaw describes
expressed need as "felt need turned
into action . . . one does not demand a service unless one feels a
need but, on the other hand, it is
common for felt need not to be expressed by demand" (*Ibid.*, p. 641).
In fact there are two possible exceptions to the rule that all expressed
need is felt need. It is not unknown
for people to be put on waiting lists
for services for which they feel no
need. In addition, there are many
examples of waiting lists which are

so out of date that they include people whose felt needs have altered
considerably. Nevertheless with these
exceptions felt need does subsume expressed need.

Which types of criteria are appropriate for assessing which concepts of need? First, one should make
the general point that where it is
possible to assess diagnostic need it
may not be possible, by the same
means to assess prescriptive need.
However, estimates of prescriptive
need should always indicate diagnostic need. This means simply that
one cannot (or should not) point out
a need for services without also dem-
onstrating the existence of circumstances which these services are intended to alter. Therefore some
approaches may be used to assess or
estimate both diagnostic and prescriptive need while others will only
be concerned with the former.

Various factors will affect the possibility of estimating prescriptive
need. These include the amount and
quality of information about the
relevant circumstances that is available and coupled with this the extent to which specific circumstances
indicate the need for a particular
form of help, or service. Where
several forms of help are close substitutes quite small differences in circumstances may affect the choice of
service. In addition, where forms of
help are not very well developed it
may be necessary to study further
their relative effectiveness (and efficiency) before definitely relating
them to diagnostic needs. Finally,
where estimates of overall, prescriptive need are required for planning
purposes it may be acceptable to assume relationships between diagnosis
and prescription which would not

be acceptable at the individual level.

Expressed need tends to be at once the most easily assessed and the least useful concept of need. It usually requires knowledge that a service exists, knowledge about the most appropriate service, a willingness to request that service and a lack of distortion caused by eligibility criteria. When it is the only measure of unmet need in a situation where resources are very limited it will obviously have some use. Coupled with carefully thought out eligibility criteria (such as point systems for council house allocation) and wide knowledge of the availability of the service it is obviously a useful mechanism for allocating existing resources but not nearly so useful for planning future provision. It also has the disadvantage that it cannot be used for assessing intensity or degree of need. However, one application of expressed diagnostic need is demonstrated by Tizard. Where a register is thought to include all or most of a group with diagnostic needs it can be used as a frame for applying other criteria, in order to assess or estimate prescriptive needs.

Felt need, as assessed through sample or 100 percent surveys, has several advantages over expressed need: it usually assumes some knowledge about appropriate services but this information can be explained beforehand, it is less dependent on the respondent's willingness to make the effort to request the service and there need be no filter in the form of eligibility criteria. It can also be more up to date than a waiting list. Respondent's perceptions would appear to be especially useful as criteria of diagnostic need. Where the receipt of a service is not obligatory the willingness of an individual to be helped will usually be a pre-condition of help being given while the use of normative criteria for cross checking, as in Townsend and Wedderburn, I.L.G.S. and Buckle is a useful way of confirming all or some of the estimates of felt need. In the case of the I.L.G.S. 100 percent household study felt need was also thought to be the best guide to individual diagnostic need. Its use as a guide to prescriptive need will vary according to the factors mentioned earlier. In the I.L.G.S. report it appears to be considered more appropriate for assessments of aggregate need for planning purposes than of individual need. What the report calls "a proper estimate of needs," that is needs as measured by the normative criteria of the Social Services Department, remains to a considerable extent the province of the social worker. The report continues: "one suspects that such an assessment would uncover a considerably greater range and depth of needs than those exposed by the survey."

Normative and comparative criteria for assessing aggregate needs have the advantage that they can be applied to both survey and census data. Comparative criteria derive their principal advantages and disadvantages from the same source. If existing provision of services goes to representatives of all groups who are potentially in need the characteristics which distinguish the recipients should also facilitate the identification of non-recipients in otherwise similar circumstances. However, if services are not being provided to certain groups, some members of which might be thought to be in need, the characteristics of the groups will not be identified and their existence will not be uncovered. Very few younger handicapped housewives receive home help so a study of existing recipients of home help would probably not elicit criteria for estimating the numbers of such women who might, on other grounds, be considered to need such help.

The Davies and Packman studies suggest that the application of comparative criteria to census data is more appropriate for identifying diagnostic needs. In particular Packman's criteria were of no use in explaining the existing allocation of one form of service (local authority residential care of children) but did explain the total range and extent of child care services. It also appears from these studies that other things being equal, census data is not sufficient for deriving comparative criteria since existing recipients (except residents of institutions) are not identified in the census.

Only Harris (1968) uses comparative criteria (in conjunction with some normative criteria) to assess prescriptive needs. Her advantage over Davies and Packman, in this respect, is that all her information, both about existing recipients and about old people in general is based on survey interviews. This enables her to collect information about characteristics of individuals in her general sample, something which census data does not permit.

Even in the case of the Harris study the existence of substitutable services, in this case residential care or a range of domiciliary services for the elderly, makes the identification of prescriptive needs difficult. Thus he circumstances of residents of

homes who expressed a desire to leave were examined on an individual basis in order to determine their prescriptive needs.

Among any group of individuals no single estimate of need, either diagnostic or prescriptive, will automatically follow the application of comparative, felt or expressed criteria. The application of each involves a certain amount of subjectivity on the part of the person carrying out the study. However, within each category the criteria are likely to be reasonably homogeneous—thus different ways of asking about felt needs can only result in a limited range of replies. However, this does not apply to normative criteria. A good illustration of the possible range of variations of normative criteria (and thus resulting estimates of need) in one study is that of need for rehousing in Buckle.

Obviously, this variation does not invalidate the use of normative criteria. Most of the studies use criteria of need with normative elements and normative criteria are often necessary to convert an estimate of diagnostic needs into one of prescriptive needs (cf. I.L.G.S.). Nevertheless, there does appear to be a special requirement that explicit explanations for the choice of particular normative criteria of need be made. It also appears desirable, where one is not considering the development of completely new services, to couple estimates based on normative criteria with the use of felt or comparative criteria as well. As the seven studies indicate, it is rarely that one single category of criteria can be used to estimate needs, while the use of various criteria may well increase the value of estimates.

22 Problem Analysis: Data Collection Techniques

COLLECTING INFORMATION: BASIC METHODS

LEAGUE OF CALIFORNIA CITIES

Obtaining data is a basic element of the needs assessment process.[1] However, since management information system activity frequently takes on a life, meaning, and purpose all its own, extreme care should be taken to ensure that data to be collected is in fact useful and usable in your needs assessment decision-making process. Careful planning should ensure that the time, expense, and energy devoted to the activity produces more than a mountain of impressive, useless information. If done well, data collection techniques can accomplish two important purposes: (1) focus upon specific data that will help pinpoint key social needs, and (2) provide a vehicle for building citizen and agency support and participation in the needs assessment process.   ⁓

Reprinted with permission of the publisher from: League of California Cities, *Assessing Human Needs* (Sacramento, Ca., League of California Cities, 1975), pp. 59–79.

1 The material in this chapter is based primarily upon Kenneth Webb and Harry P. Hatry, *Obtaining Citizen Feedback: The Application of Citizen Surveys to Local Governments.* (Washington, D.C.: The Urban Institute).

This chapter reviews several basic data collection techniques and provides a discussion of costs, applicability, practicality, and effectiveness for each. Among them are: (1) interviews, (2) questionnaires, (3) existing statistics, (4) special methodologies such as systematic field observations, and (5) meetings.[2]

INTERVIEWS

If done properly, interviews can yield data that is detailed and comprehensive, depending upon the quantity and quality of interviewer training, ability of the interviewer to establish good rapport with respondents, and the selection of interviewers who accept and believe in the purpose of the survey. If these factors are taken into account before implementation, the resulting data should be of very high quality, even on some of the more sensitive problems one is seeking to identify.

Interviews can be implemented in two ways: person-to-person and over the telephone.

1. The Person-to-Person Interview

2 Cf. Appendix D for a discussion of specific methodology cost.

Method. This method is probably the most informative and flexible because of the opportunities available to use visual aids to clearly explain the more difficult questions and issues, and to make observations of the respondent and his environment. In general, there are a few things to keep in mind when using this interview technique:

a. Care should be taken in the selection of interviewers to ensure that personal subjective bias does not affect the respondent's answers as recorded by the interviewer.
b. Ability to elicit response to more sensitive questions and questions in general might be enhanced by selecting interviewers who are of the same racial and ethnic background as the potential respondents.
c. For comparability of interview results, a well-structured and closed-end questionnaire should be used for obtaining the desired information (questionnaires will be addressed in more detail later).
d. The process of designing a questionnaire provides a good opportunity for community input. Citizens and agency personnel can be asked to review and suggest additions to questionnaire items.
e. The length of the interview should be kept as short as practical to prevent irritating the respondents. (Cost will be reduced also.)
f. The interview should be pretested to remove ambiguities and locate potential problems in response especially if a "scientific" sample is being used.

The person-to-person interview method has traditionally had the highest response rate of survey techniques in general, with the exception of a few inner-city interview studies that found residents too afraid to open their doors. Interviews of this nature do, however, provide an excellent opportunity for respondents to "sound off" about their needs and experiences to someone who is directly involved in government. This type of input serves well as a community morale builder, giving a feeling to respondents that "the government cares," particularly if government employees are used as interviewers and identify themselves as such. The drawback of this approach lies in the possibility of raising community expectations with an interview, the results of which might not be acted upon.

Finally, the costs of a person-to-person interview are unfortunately the highest of the various survey methods, both in terms of financing and agency effort. Financial costs would include staff salaries and travel, keypunching and computer processing costs (if tabulation and cross tabulation is done by machine), questionnaires, and forms creation and reproduction. Agency effort would include compiling and updating sample master lists, selecting and training interviewers, sampling respondents, interviewing and call backs, supervision and coordination of interviewers, editing, correcting, and completing questionnaire forms and tabulating and processing data. Costs in general will be directly proportional to the size of sample (adequate sample sizes are discussed below). Although costs might be higher than with other data collection procedures, a city with sufficient funds will be better served by the more complete and reliable information that this method will produce.

2. Telephone Interviews. The

telephone interview has enjoyed an increase in popularity recently due to its lower cost, ease of administration, and ability to reach a majority of the target population. This method's most immediate and obvious drawback is the lack of a telephone by some people in general and, specifically, by low-income people who also tend to have a higher concentration of social needs. Aside from this major drawback, the telephone interview can offer a substantial saving to a limited budget city for basic financial costs and agency effort. A few basic considerations should be kept in mind for the implementation of a telephone interview study:

a. The representativeness of a random telephone sample will be in question since many of the poor may not have phones.
b. The results of a telephone interview might be checked against census and local planning data for possible subgroup under-representation.
c. The use of a phone book to obtain a random sample will not account for the increasing amount of unlisted numbers. "Random dialing" (randomly choosing a sample out of a list of the last four digits of an area) might serve as an alternative.
d. Interview length should be kept under fifteen minutes to avoid irritating the respondents.
e. Personal, enthusiastic interviewers tend to receive a better response Limited study shows that women obtain better responses. In either case, a pleasant sounding voice is essential.
f. For comparability of results, a standard pre-tested set of questions should be used.
g. Interviewers should be trained for interview pace and quality, the average training time being about four hours.
h. The telephone method tends to over-represent the very young and the very old. Timing the calls around working hours will help overcome this fault.

The telephone interview has the same drawback as the person-to-person interview in that it may raise community expectations. On the other hand, it shares the same benefits in the sense that an interview can convey the notion that the government "cares."

Cost factors for the telephone interview are considerably less expensive. Although there still remain salary, response processing, training, supervision, and sample list compilation costs, there will be a savings of at least one-third due to the absence of travel and printing expenses, which can grow quite large with increased sample size. Increasing the sample size of a telephone interview will, of course, raise salary outlay but can provide, on the other hand, statistically stronger results.

The telephone interview, then, provides a medium-cost method of data collection that can generate reasonably reliable results if proper precautions are used to ensure representativeness. This method lacks some of the flexibility and visual opportunities of the person-to-person method, yet still retains a personal factor and an opportunity to make clear the content of the questions.

QUESTIONNAIRES

As a data collection method, questionnaires serve as a useful device for organizing needed information into a format that can be pre-tested and more easily processed. Questionnaires can be administered either in the form of an interview or as a self-administered mail-out. When used in conjunction with a person-to-person format, the questionnaire can provide the most reliable results in a form that can be quickly processed by hand or machine. A major consideration for questionnaires in general is proper question design. Following are some elements needed for an effective questionnaire:

a. Questions that are open-ended provide a more detailed response but are harder to process and standardize. If a questionnaire is being administered to a limited number of professional agency heads, for example, then the open-ended style will work best. If a large sample of citizens is being polled, then a "yes or no" (closed) type questionnaire will serve best.

b. Questions must be carefully phrased for their implications and effect on response—i.e., a negatively or positively phrased question on a certain issue might bias the responses in one direction or another. Questions should also be phrased so that no one can take offense. Although this seems obvious, there may be very subtle words and inferences in a question that could possibly bias the response.

c. Attention should be paid to the ordering and movement of a questionnaire so that the response to one question doesn't bias the response to another.

d. Questions should be as clear and concise as possible to avoid loss of time due to a need for explanation and directions.

e. When possible, questionnaire results should be checked against statistical records.

f. Questionnaire design should always be pre-tested. Do not print up five thousand copies until you have "debugged" it by trying it out on a small representative group.

The Mail-Out Questionnaire. There are widespread, conflicting opinions over the usefulness of the mail-out questionnaire as a data collection method. The primary argument against this method is a low response rate, which tends toward unrepresentative results. Critics of this method contend that the average rate of return (25 percent) represents a self-selected group, the answers from which cannot be inferred to the population as a whole. On the other hand, the mail questionnaire is noted for low cost, minimum staff time, and ease of result analysis. The advantages and disadvantages are as follows:

Advantages

a. It is one of the least expensive methods.

b. Some agencies have claimed good response (45 percent).

c. Its results are often more candid due to its privacy and anonymity.

d. The respondent is not subject to the stress of an interview.

e. It requires little staff time and outside help.

f. It is least disruptive of normal activity.

g. It does not require computer resources.

h. It provides for community input.

i. It shows government responsiveness.

j. It can be easily applied to rural areas without additional expense.

Disadvantages

a. There is a generally low return rate.

b. The group is self-selected and unrepresentative.

c. Interpretation and understanding of questions is not always uniform and complete.

d. It is ineffective for eliciting responses from illiterate people.

e. Its impersonal nature fails to elicit detailed responses.

Whatever its shortcomings, the mail-out questionnaire provides the city with limited resources a method of data collection that will provide for direct community input, and will generate useful statistical information at a financial and staff time cost that is not prohibitive. If time is taken to ensure that questions are simple and easy to understand, and results are double checked with census tract data for reliability, then this method can be very useful. Questionnaires can be mailed out with utility bills, welfare checks, or any regular mailing that is sure to be noticed by recipients. Mailing the questionnaire in conjunction with a bill or check will further reduce costs and produce a better response rate than when mailed separately.

PRECAUTIONS FOR ANALYZING SURVEY DATA

The interview and questionnaire methods of data collection can be called survey methods for ease of reference. In using any survey method, the data generated will be in the form of statistics which can be manipulated and interpreted in various ways. Following are some general thoughts for the use of survey methodology:

a. A survey should not ask the public to evaluate complex services or policy areas of which they know very little. Otherwise data will be suspect.
b. Survey results can be influenced by recent political events, and should be interpreted with this in mind.
c. Surveys should not be scheduled close to an election because of the possible criticism that the results might influence the ballot box.
d. If survey results are published, they should always include the details of sample size, methods of analysis, sampling methodology and data collection instruments and techniques.
e. The larger the sample size, the more reliable the results; however, if funds are limited, a reasonably good inference can be made from a sample of two or three hundred households.
f. Always be wary of immediately accepting statistical results that are supportive of what you were looking for at the outset. What other factors may have caused the results?
g. Statistics from surveys can be misleading and should be used to disprove a causal factor rather than prove one.

The question of who can and should conduct a survey is as important as properly interpreting survey results. There are several sources for staffing a survey project:

a. Outside consultants and university specialists: the method requiring the least amount of effort on the part of the government is to contract with private or university organizations. However, this method can be prohibitive in cost, and some localities will have to go far afield to obtain outside services. The advantage of using an outside firm is their lack of vested interest in the results. If the city is in need of objectivity and credibility, using an outside organization will help provide it. On the other hand, the results of a survey conducted by an outside resource are often not implemented as readily as with an internal study.
b. Government employees: using government employees to conduct a survey will be considerably less expensive provided their efforts do not

interfere with normal activity. Internal staff will normally be able to process data and conduct interviews, but a limited amount of outside consultation might be necessary for survey construction and the more technical aspects of statistical interpretation. The advantages of this method include reduced cost, higher probability of result implementation, and an opportunity for the staff to educate and be educated by the community. The disadvantages of using government employees include: possible subjective interpretive bias in handling survey results, possible suspicion on the part of the community as to the validity of a survey conducted by staff, and the possibility of disrupting normal work activity.

3. Volunteers: the use of volunteers to conduct a survey is the least expensive method, yet it is subject to some severe drawbacks. Screening and training of volunteers is required as it is with government employees, yet the knowledge stays within the organization. Volunteers tend to have high rates of dropping out of the effort before its completion and fail to complete all the assigned work (which can alter results in a random sample). Volunteers are not subject to discipline which can affect their dependability.

In general, the most effective human resource for conducting surveys is government staff with some limited technical help, if necessary. The only exception to this might arise in a situation where a controversial government program was being evaluated and outside resources are necessary to lend credibility to the results. Whatever human resource is used, it should be kept in mind that the scope of a data collection effort should be limited by, or equal to, the amount of available staffing.

The *average* survey, from the time it is requested to when the report is written on the final tabulation of survey results, will take about three months. (This applies to in-person and telephone interviews. Mailouts depend upon the respondents.) If the effort is the first for the staff and community, then the time factor will be increased. Sample size will also be a determining factor.

EXISTING STATISTICS

Depending on how the data is compiled and interpreted, the use of existing statistics can provide an economical means of collecting data for assessment and evaluation purposes. In the social realm, relevant existing statistics can be found in census data and service agency records.

Census Data. As previously discussed, the 1970 census provides data on a variety of conditions and problem indicators that can be used for identifying social needs. The cost of census data and its interpretation is dependent upon the amount obtained and the statistical interpretations that are desired. The most useful tool for analyzing statistical census data is a computer, a resource not readily available to some communities.

Service Agency Records. There is usually some data that is routinely collected on every government program and agency. This data, for example, can be found in welfare case loads or police arrest records. With a bit of imagination and statistical handiwork, previously unmeasured services or problems can be identified and evaluated through the use of a combination of existing records and statistics. For example, a Nashville program evaluation of short-term care for neglected children consisted, in part, of obtaining individual records from welfare agencies to determine intake characteristics, the Children's Home for length of stay, and Juvenile Court records for final disposition of a particular case. The combination of these statistics provided good information on the relationship between the reason for entry, effectiveness of service and the child's ultimate status. Case loads of social agencies combined with census data can provide at least a rough idea as to social need. The most difficult problem with using existing agency records, especially when combining them, is that of comparability. Differing units of measurement will make data analysis expensive and difficult, if not impossible. Nonetheless, a statistically oriented staff person may be able to accomplish a good deal with existing records with a minimum of financial outlay on the city's part. As a data resource, existing records should not be overlooked.

SPECIAL TECHNIQUES

Beyond the more widespread data collection methods such as surveys and agency records, there are special techniques for collecting data that are restricted only by the limitations of finances and imagination. One such technique has been called systematic field observations, which would include inspection ratings. For example, this method could involve a rating of housing conditions assigned by city inspector or staff on the basis of a visual comparison of the actual conditions with a series of photographs ranging from good to poor. Although this method seems unrefined and laden with subjective value judgments, it can, nonetheless, serve as an effective assessment and evaluation tool if reinforced by other types of data and collection procedures. This method's costs are primarily limited to inspector salaries and travel expenses with limited costs for data analysis and interpretation.

MEETINGS

The use of meetings, both with citizens and agency representatives, is particularly useful in the needs assessment process although it is hard to structure such experiences according to formal and standardized data collection techniques. Circumstances are not replicable, the population is self-selected and different meetings might drift in different directions. Nonetheless, if they are held out in the community or with specifically selected agency representatives they may reach individuals and elicit responses that may escape random interviews or questionnaires. In cases where formal interviewing or questionnaires may reach a broad spectrum of the community it may be advantageous to hold meetings to which specific agency personnel or community leaders are invited.

Furthermore, meetings provide for a different type of information. At a meeting, participants can react, discuss, analyze and offer feedback to city plans and perspectives. There is an opportunity for community attitudes to coalesce and for city officials to experience community feelings and to help mold a climate of opinion.

It is important that meetings be carefully planned and structured. It is probably wise for the purposes of obtaining information (rather than policy setting) to make meetings homogeneous.[3] This is particularly true in the beginning of the needs assessment process when participants may not be familiar with one another. In dealing with agency representatives, it is best to meet separately with county representatives, private sector voluntary service agencies, and community action agencies. This will allow you to focus upon the particular experiences and insights of each sector without running the risk of sparking interagency conflicts. Similarly, it is wise, if possible, to hold meetings of citizens separately and under separate format from the agency meetings. These meetings should be held on an open public basis in different sections of the city. This will provide the opportunity for citizens to offer input in their own neighborhoods and to attend alternate meetings if they miss one. These meetings should be conducted in an open style soliciting a wide variety of suggestions, comments and ideas although some effort should be made to make sure that the purposes, methods and expectations of the city are made clear. It is also possible that while *some* ethnic or neighbor-

hood leaders will be heard from through community action or service agencies, *many of them will not be.* Consequently, it may be of use to ask service agencies, neighborhood groups, and local churches to identify informed and articulate local spokesmen who could offer insights on community problems.

The most obvious advantage of this method for obtaining data is that it is cheaper than formal interviewing or questionnaire studies. It is also an integral part of the process of including the community in the decision making process. A randomly distributed questionnaire taps opinions of individuals; an open community meeting represents a public forum in which to contribute. Meetings may also be more sensitive indicators of a community mood, attitude or consensus than even the compilation of questionnaire results. At the same time, however, one of its disadvantages is the fact that public meetings may be manipulated by individuals or the emotional impact of particular issues. Other disadvantages include difficulties in quantifying results or in comparing the results of different sessions. Wherever possible, meeting results should be balanced by efforts to obtain more formal, individualized input—either from census, agency or questionnaire data. . . .

IDENTIFYING AND DEVELOPING SOCIAL INDICATORS

Why Indicators? The most significant task facing users of statistics in the social field is the identification of those measurements which best reflect overall community needs

---

[3] It should be emphasized that these suggestions are offered only for those meetings being held for purposes of information collection. They do not necessarily hold true for meetings of advisory boards, commissions or other groups charged with making decisions or resolving differences.

and conditions in health, employment, housing, or other areas. Too often new planning efforts are overwhelmed by the mountain of statistical data that may defy meaningful interpretation; or planners seek to avoid such a statistical nightmare by turning solely to citizen and provider input.

Statistical volume alone will not adequately guide policy or answer questions of need. "Soft" input from providers and clients, likewise may be biased and selective. Needed are a limited number of carefully selected numerical indicators which are as closely related to the problems under study as possible. These can serve as both guides and correctives for subjective input. The indicators themselves do not fully define needs or determine solutions; but they do show changes over time. They offer comparisons with other locations and clues for further investigation and analysis. They can provide an agreed upon figure upon which to focus attention. Even if the social indicators are not perfect, and there is not complete certainty of their validity, they at least provide a point of reference for discussion, analysis and comparison.

A set of indicators should be:

RELIABLE collected and compiled in a sufficiently formal manner that the collection could be repeated and the same results obtained.

UP TO DATE representative of current conditions. In cases where this is not possible, as in census data, it is important to identify the age of the figures. Wherever possible, yearly changes should be obtained.

VALID actually measures the characteristics they claim to measure.

It is this last characteristic that is most difficult in a social needs assessment process. The question is constantly posed: "Do demographic statistics actually measure what they claim?" A simple example is found in the criticisms of the U.S. Bureau of Census figures for number of Blacks and Chicanos. It is argued that their data collection techniques mislabel or entirely ignore members of these groups. Consequently, the categories which claim to represent them are not valid because of faulty data collection.

A more complex, yet frequent question, even when the data is not poorly collected, is: "What social problems can actually be determined with statistical data?" For example, statistical figures may suggest that a certain number of people are living on incomes below the poverty level. Can we conclude that such a number in fact represents the amount of poor people in the community? The argument can be made that income alone is not the full measure of poverty. In fact, large numbers of people who may have incomes above that figure may in fact be likely to be considered poor because of *conditions under which they live*. If they have large medical expenses, large families, exorbitant rents, they may have available to them even less funds than those with lower actual incomes. Consequently, other factors must be considered. At the same time it must also be recognized that, to some extent, income level *does* measure poverty. The problem of identifying statistical indicators, upon which meaningful conclusions about social problems may be based is a complex task.

Criteria for Establishing Social Indicators. The Community Analysis Research Project of the University of Texas at Austin suggests the following criteria for the selection of indicators:

1. The indicator set should facilitate inferences about actual conditions in the community. (They should not simply describe governmental activities.) Further, the set should be considered an introductory set capable of being improved with use.
2. The indicator set should bring together a comprehensive picture of all the most significant conditions relating to the quality of life in a community.
3. The indicator set should be simple enough so that city staff personnel can collect and present the information, and local officials will not get difficult explanations and ambiguous interpretations.
4. The indicator set should be useful to local officials in describing subcity areas of concern, in helping to set priorities, and in helping to allocate resources.
5. The indicators should require only data that is already available.

These indicators may be:

1. Compiled by census tract within the city and then compared to find the neighborhoods with the most acute problems.
2. Compiled by year and then compared

over a period of time to identify improving or deteriorating trends.
3. Compared with national, state, county indicators to identify citywide problems.
4. Compared with agreed upon community "standards" in each area.[4]

It is important to emphasize again that the statistical figures described in conjunction with the social needs assessment process are neither as detailed nor problem specific as the figures required to plan and operate an actual service program. The health indicator, for example, should reflect cases of tuberculosis, heart disease, measles, or whatever diseases are felt to best "indicate" the basic health trends of the community. To plan for the operation of a clinic, however, it would be essential to look specifically at the volume of each of these diseases, as well as the variety of other conditions, to plan equipment, staff, and facilities to adequately treat them.

---

[4] Community Analysis Research Project, *An Introductory Set of Community Indicators,* Lyndon B. Johnson School of Public Affairs, University of Texas at Houston, Spring, 1973, p. 4. The work of the Community Analysis Research Project, which includes two additional volumes, II, *A Resource Handbook for Developing Community Indicators,* and III, *Report of the Community Analysis Research Project,* should be consulted by anyone working in this field. Their materials are clear, easy to understand and particularly relevant to the problems inherent in the needs assessment and social planning process. Cf. Chart D, p. 321.

CHART D. RECOMMENDED COMMUNITY INDICATORS [1]

Economic Base	— Retail Sales: $ per 1,000 population
Education	— Number of seniors taking college board entrance exam (SAT's)
	— Average per pupil expenditures
Employment Opportunity	— Occupational Distribution: Number and % of census tract heads of households employed in various job categories
	— % of heads of households within census tract claiming no occupation.
	— Unemployment Rate: % of total work force
Health and Well Being	— Suicide Rate: Number of suicides per 100,000 population
	— Communicable Disease Index: Number of Cases of VD, TB, and hepatitis reported per 1,000 population
	— Infant Mortality Rate: Number of deaths of children under one-year per 1,000 births
Housing	— Vacancy Rate: % housing units in an area which are vacant or abandoned
	— Median assessed value of single family units
	— % total subsidized starts placed in each census tract
Land Use and Recreation	— Acres of park and recreation space available per 1,000 population
Personal Income Distribution	— Number of assistance payment welfare cases
	— Number of Income Tax Returns Claiming Adjusted Gross Income: Under $3,000; $3,000 to $5,000; $5,000 to $10,000; $10,000 to $15,000; $15,000 or more
Pollution	— % increase or decrease in concentration of particulate matter suspended in air
	— % increase or decrease in concentration of atmospheric NO_2 and SO_2
Public Safety and Justice	— Type I Crime Rate: Number of cases of murder, forcible rape, robbery, and aggravated assault reported per 100,000 population
	— Type II Crime Rate: Number of cases of burglary, larceny ($50 and over), and auto theft reported per 100,000 population
Public Service Delivery	— Number of complaints submitted to city sewer, water and garbage collection agencies per 1,000 population
	— General obligation bond rating
Sense of Community	— % voting in most recent local election compared to % voting in most recent state election
	— Household Turnover: % census tract housing units with new residents
Transportation	— % public street miles served by public transportation
	— Number of traffic accidents per 100,000 population

[1] University of Texas, *An Introductory Set of Community Indicators* (1973), p. 3.

BIBLIOGRAPHY

AMERICAN SOCIETY FOR PUBLIC ADMINISTRA-TION. *The Administration of the New Federalism: Objectives and Issues.* Leigh E. Grosenick, editor. Washington, D.C., 1973.

————. *Human Services Integration.* Washington, D.C., 1974.

BISHOP, SHARON. "One Way to Assess Needs." *The Social and Rehabilitation Record,* I, No. 1 (1973), 19–25.

BOOZ, ALLEN. *Assessing Social Services Needs and Resources—Executive Summary.* Washington, D.C., August 15, 1973. (Submitted to the Community Services Administration Social and Rehabilitation Services of HEW.)

CENTER FOR SOCIAL RESEARCH AND DEVELOP-MENT. *Analysis and Synthesis of Needs Assessment Research in the Field of Human Services.* Denver Research Institute, University of Denver, 2142 S. High, Denver, Colorado, 80201.

COMMUNITY ANALYSIS RESEARCH PROJECT. Lyndon B. Johnson School of Public Affairs. The University of Texas at Austin. "An Introductory Set of Community Indicators—Pamphlet I of the Community Analysis Research Project." Austin, Texas, 1973.

CROUCH, BOLLENS and SCOTT. *California Government and Politics.* Englewood Cliffs, N.J.: Prentice-Hall, 1972.

DEPARTMENT OF HOUSING AND COMMUNITY DEVELOPMENT, Pleasanton, California. "Human Services Element: Pleasanton General Plan." 1974.

DODGE, WILLIAM R. *Management Information Service,* Vol. 6, No. 1. "Public Involvement in Local Government in the 1970s." Washington, D.C.: International City Management Association, January, 1974.

DULUTH INSTITUTE FOR INTERDISCIPLINARY STUDIES. "Improved Coordination of Human Services." 6 vols. Minneapolis, 1972.

ERICKSON, ROSEMARY. "Social Profiles of San Diego, Vol. I: A Social Area Analysis." La Jolla, California: Western Behavioral Sciences Institute, 1973.

HATRY, HARRY P., RICHARD E. WINNIE, and DONALD M. FISK. *Practical Program Evaluation for State and Local Government Officials.* Washington, D.C., 1973. With contributions from: Louis H. Blair, Marvin R. Burt, Alfred I. Schwartz, and Alease Vaughn.

HAYWARD, CITY OF. *Social Service Directory.* Hayward, California, 1974.

HUMAN SERVICES INSTITUTE FOR CHILDREN AND FAMILIES, INC. *Alternative Approaches to Human Services Planning.* 1911 N. Ft. Myer Dr., Arlington, Virginia, 22209. 1974.

————. *Needs Assessment in a Title XX State Social Services Planning System.* 1975.

JUAREZ, RICHARD. "Socioeconomic Indicators." Management Planning Program, San Diego County. 1974.

————. "Socioeconomic Status Ranking of San Diego County Census Tracts." San Diego County. 1974.

KERR, E. BARTLETT. "A Feasibility Study for the Alameda County Board of Supervisors on the Establishment of an Alameda County Human Services Council." Oakland, California. July, 1974.

LEAGUE OF CALIFORNIA CITIES. "Action Plan for the Social Responsibilities of Cities." Claremont Hotel Building, Berkeley, California, 94705. October, 1973.

————. *Guidelines for the Preparation of a Social Element to the General Plan.* (Draft, 1974.) Berkeley, California.

————. "The New Federalism and California Cities: A Policy Review with Implications for California Cities and the League of California Cities." Sacramento, California. July, 1973.

LEAGUE OF KANSAS MUNICIPALITIES. *A Guide for Human Resources Development in Local Government.* 112 W. Seventh Street, Topeka, Kansas. May, 1973.

MULROONEY, KEITH F. "A Guide to Human Resources Development in Small Cities." *Management Information Service Report,* V, No. 10 (1973), 1–13.

NATIONAL LEAGUE OF CITIES AND U.S. CON-FERENCE OF MAYORS. "A Study of the Roles for Cities Under the Allied Services Approach of the Department of Health, Education and Welfare." Washington, D.C., 1974.

————. "The Cities, the States and the HEW System." Washington, D.C., 1972. (Office of Policy Analysis.)

NATIONAL MODEL CITIES COMMUNITY DEVEL-OPMENT DIRECTORS ASSOCIATION. *A Guide to Meeting Citizen Participation Requirements for Community Development.* 1975.

NEW ENGLAND MUNICIPAL CENTER. *Human Services Needs Assessment Study: Human Services Opinion Survey*. Pettee Brook Offices, P.O. Box L, Durham, New Hampshire, 03824. 1975.

————. *Human Services Needs Assessment Study: Socio-Economic Characteristics*. 1975.

OFFICE OF MANAGEMENT AND BUDGET, Statistical Police Division. *Social Indicators* Washington, D.C.: U.S. Government Printing Office, 1973.

PASADENA, CITY OF. *Interim Social Element*. (Draft copy.) July 12, 1974.

————. *Resource Allocation Process*. November, 1973.

PUGET SOUND GOVERNMENTAL CONFERENCE. *A Guide for Categorical Human Resources Planners*. 216 First Ave. South, Seattle, Washington, 98104. 1974.

————. *A Guide to Human Resource Planning for Elected Officials*. 216 First Ave. South, Seattle, Washington, 98104. 1974.

RIVERSIDE-SAN BERNARDINO COUNTIES. *Directory of Community Services*. 1973.

RIVLIN, ALICE M. *Systematic Thinking for Social Action*. Washington, D.C., 1971.

RUTTER, LAWRENCE. "Managing Revenue Sharing in Cities and Counties." *Management Information Service*, Vol. 5, No. 12. Washington, D.C.: International City Management Association, December, 1973.

SACRAMENTO REGIONAL AREA PLANNING COMMISSION. "Human Resources Element: Regional General Plan," 1225 Eighth Street, Suite 400, Sacramento, California, 95814. 1974.

SAN BERNARDINO, CITY OF, Community Planning and Management Program. *State of the City 1973*. San Bernardino, California. December, 1973.

SANTA BARBARA, CITY OF. *Social Services Element Planning*. (Draft) Santa Barbara, California, 1974.

SANTA BARBARA COUNTY COMMUNITY RELATIONS COMMISSION. *Directory of Social Services—Health, Education, Welfare, and Recreation*. Santa Barbara, California, 1972.

SCHRAG, HOWARD L. "The Needs Assessment Process in Idaho for Early Childhood." Idaho Human Development Institute, 1974.

SHELDON, ELEANOR BERNERT, and WILBERT E. MOORE, eds., *Indicators of Social Change: Concepts and Measurements*. New York, 1968.

SILLMAN, JERRY. *The Plan Action Process for Human Services*. Pacific Palisades, California, 1974.

SMITH, ALEX. *Developing a General Plan Social Services Element*. Inglewood Human Affairs Division. February, 1974.

————. "Human Relations—Human Resources." City of Inglewood, Civic Center, One Manchester Blvd., Inglewood, California, 90301. March, 1975.

————. "Human Relations: Toward a Definition," Inglewood, December 1974.

SUCHMAN, EDWARD A. *Evaluative Research: Principles and Practice in Public Service and Social Action Programs*. New York: Russell Sage Foundation, 1967.

SUNQUIST, JAMES L. *Making Federalism Work: A Study of Program Coordination at the Community Level*. Washington, D.C.: Brookings Institution, 1975.

UNITED WAY OF AMERICA. "123 Standards of Excellence for Local United Way Organizations." 801 N. Fairfax Street, Alexandria, Virginia, 1973.

————. *The Painful Necessity of Choice: An Analysis of Priorities and Policies in the United Way Movement*. Alexandria, Virginia, 1974.

————. Research and Systems Development Division. *Help in Using 1970 Census Data.*. New York.

————. *UWASIS: United Way of America Services Identification System*. Alexandria, Virginia, January, 1972.

BAY AREA SOCIAL PLANNING COUNCIL. *Government-Voluntary Sector Collaboration in Providing Human Care Services*. 364 14th St., Oakland, California, 94612. 1975.

UNIVERSITY OF DENVER, Center for Social Research and Development. *Socioeconomic Data Rank Order for Colorado*. Denver, 1972.

VAN MAANEN, JOHN. *The Process of Program Evaluation*. Washington, D.C., 1973.

WEBB, KENNETH, and HARRY HATRY. *Obtaining Citizen Feedback: The Application of Citizen Surveys to Local Governments*. Washington, D.C., 1973.

WEISS, CAROL. *Evaluation Research—Methods of Assessing Program Effectiveness*. San Francisco, 1972.

WESTERN FEDERAL REGIONAL COUNCIL. *C.A.A.'s and Local Government Readiness for Revenue Sharing in Six Communities*. 1974.

23 Problem Analysis: The Delphi Technique

DEVELOPING PRIORITIES FOR IMPROVING THE URBAN SOCIAL ENVIRONMENT: A USE OF DELPHI

Daniel Molnar/Marshall Kammerud

RATIONALE

For about two years, a multidisciplinary team worked on developing methodologies for studying life in the modern urban milieu.[1] The main thrust of this work was directed toward the development of methodologies and processes needed to create a new, large, free-standing city in the United States. A major part of the effort focused on developing descriptive and normative scenarios for life in a modern urban setting.

Through the use of the Delphi technique, it was possible to state explicitly those components of life about which there is dissatisfaction and also obtain some estimates of how amenable these components might be to positive change through the application of resources. This is useful information in establishing priorities for action.

DESCRIPTIVE AND NORMATIVE SCENARIOS

The first approach taken was to divide the large, multidisciplinary team into subgroups of about three or four persons and treat topics such as transportation, political structure, community services, environment, education, religion, economics, population, safety and utilities, communications, physical structure, families, recreation, and so forth. This led to scenarios that were mostly descriptive (even the normative scenarios appeared to be descriptive) based on the knowledge of three or four people and their acquaintance with some literature on the topic. In the planning sense, we needed some-

Reprinted with permission of authors and publisher from: Daniel Molnar and Marshall Kammerud, "Developing Priorities for Improving the Urban Social Environment: A Use of Delphi," *Socio-Economic Planning Science*, 9 (1975), 25–29.

[1] The team consisted of up to twenty professional researchers, professors, and planners working part-time under the auspices of the Science and Human Affairs Program of the Battelle Institute, Columbus, Ohio.

thing about priorities in treating these topics or subparts of these topics.

BASIC ASSUMPTIONS ABOUT URBAN LIVING

The use of Delphi to assist in developing the components needed for planning was based on the following assumptions:

1. That there are many things about urban living that lead to dissatisfactions on the part of urban dwellers.
2. That people think some items of dissatisfaction are more important than others.
3. That people think that some items of dissatisfaction can be alleviated, while others are difficult to correct.
4. That a panel of experts in areas such as community design, architecture, engineering, social science, planning, and related disciplines might be able to reach consensus on some items of dissatisfaction, their importance and their alterability.

With regard to the last assumption it was generally agreed that the knowledge of about thirty people, dealing with components of dissatisfaction and priorities for improvement was a realistic resource to use to approach this very complex problem.

THE DELPHI PANEL

The original panel consisted of thirty-four members; four did not participate for various reasons. Thus there were thirty members in the panel who participated in all of the Delphi rounds. Twenty-five members are researchers at the Columbus Laboratories of Battelle Memorial Institute. The remainder of the panel were each from: (i) the Battelle Seattle Research Center, Seattle, Washington; (ii) the Academy for Contemporary Problems, Columbus, Ohio; (iii) the Institute for Social Research, Ann Arbor, Michigan; (iv) the University of Delaware; (v) the University of Virginia.

The panel members are all white, 87 percent male, heavily weighted to the mid-Ohio region, predominantly researchers or administrators, and over half hold the Ph.D. Together they represent the following general disciplines: engineering, sociology, geography, psychology, economics, biology, chemistry, physics, architecture, journalism, health planning and city planning.

The above profile does not represent a random sample of urban dwellers, but this need not discredit any data generated by the panel. It is axiomatic with the Delphi method that the respondents need not be a random sample of the population. For Delphi exercises, the term "expert" means one who knows about the subject, and not necessarily a professional.

THE DELPHI TECHNIQUE

The Delphi technique is primarily a communications device, which is applied when the consensus of experts on an uncertain issue (often intangible) is desired. Its three main features are (1) anonymity, (2) controlled feedback and (3) statistical group response. The Delphi technique was originated at the Rand Corporation and is associated with such names as Norman Dalkey and

Olaf Helmer [1, 2]. Its inception was in technological forecasting and futurist opinion gathering. It has since been found appropriate for such various arenas as industrial decision making, educational planning, and studies in the quality of life.

In using the method, anonymity is effected through questionnaires or other formal communication devices. This reduces the effect on the group that might be produced by dominant individuals. Controlled feedback is used to reduce noise usually encountered in face-to-face conferences. The exercise is conducted as a sequence of rounds in which the results of the previous rounds are fed back to the participants. The statistical group response is a device to assure that the opinion of every member of the group is represented in the final response. Dalkey *et al.* [3] emphasize the advantages of the Delphi technique:

There are several properties of a Delphi exercise that should be pointed out. The procedure is, above all, a rapid and relatively efficient way to "cream the tops of the heads" of a group of knowledgeable people. In general, it involves much less effort for a participant to respond to a well-designed questionnaire than, for example, to participate in a conference or to write a paper. A Delphi exercise, properly managed, can be a highly motivating environment for respondents. The feedback, if the group of experts involved is mutually self-respecting, can be novel and interesting to all. The use of systematic procedures lends an air of objectivity to the outcomes that may or may not be spurious, but which is at least reassuring. And finally, anonymity and group response allow a sharing of responsibility that is refreshing and that releases the respondents from social inhibitions (p. 21).

The Delphi method is simple in concept and there is a great deal of latitude in the specifics of carrying it out. A typical procedure was used in this case. We used a panel of experts to give us candidate components of dissatisfaction, developed a list of labels for the components provided by the panel, asked the panel to rank and rate the descriptions in three sequential Delphi rounds, and summarized the results.

Figure 1 shows the procedure for conducting this Delphi. This is analogous to the schema used by Skutsch and Schofer in their work on goals—Delphi for urban planning [4].

THE OBJECTIVES

Two objectives were satisfied in this study: (1) to develop components for satisfaction indicators of the modern urban milieu; and (2) to determine the importance and alterability of components of dissatisfaction experienced by the urban dweller.

A "satisfaction indicator" is an explicated component of the quality of life. It is sometimes developed by studying those things that dissatisfy individuals. To phrase it positively, to satisfy an individual with respect to the satisfaction indicator for housing, for example, conditions with respect to that component must improve. Thus, the expression of dissatisfaction precipitates the articulation of a goal to improve the housing conditions. Indicators of satisfaction may serve to develop performance criteria. Variations in measures relative to the performance criteria may serve as barometers of a city's overall health.

Developing priorities for improving the urban social environment

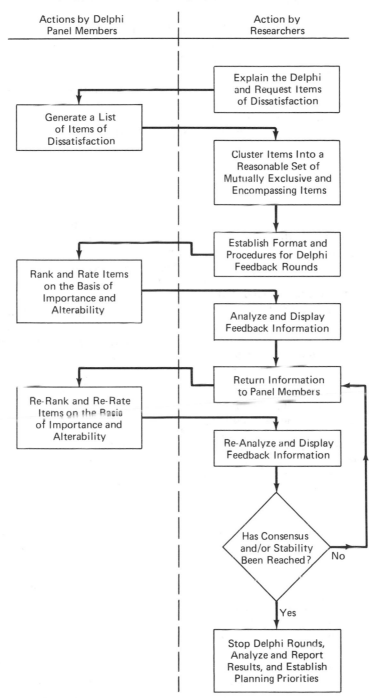

FIGURE 1. Procedure used in the Delphi exercise.

The importance and alterability of components of dissatisfaction are sometimes referred to as dynamic importance. Dynamic importance refers to the "operational consideration of which indices should be given the most attention in terms of the government effort that ought to be expended on them in order to hold the line or achieve improvements over their current levels." [5, p. 16.]

THE DELPHI EXERCISE

THE FIRST ROUND

A letter was sent to each panel member. The purpose of the letters were:

1. To invite the individual to participate in a Delphi investigation into the major sources of dissatisfaction with the urban quality of life.
2. To explain the Delphi technique.
3. To articulate the mental approach each one was to assume as an expert.
4. To illustrate the form in which responses were to be made. An open-ended questionnaire was attached to the first-round letter.

The open-ended question read as follows: "What are those components of the quality of life which most disturb the urban dweller?"

This round resulted in over 400 phrases describing those items of dissatisfaction believed to be held by the urban dweller. Each of these phrases was transcribed to cards and clustered by a three-judge group.

The items were first grouped on the basis of all two-judge categorizations. That is, if two of the three judges placed a given card in a group, that group became a candidate final group. There were some items which were grouped similarly by all three judges. Most of the items were grouped on the basis of these two- and three-judge agreements. In the case of the two-judge grouping, we checked whether the odd judge disagreed with the grouping imposed by the other two. Differences were negotiated by all three judges.

This clustering process resulted finally in nineteen clusters which were then labeled as simply as possible. These became the components of dissatisfaction. For the second round, the panel was presented a list of nineteen components of dissatisfaction and the listing of all the phrases that were grouped under each component.

SUBSEQUENT ROUNDS

Three more rounds were conducted. For these feedback rounds the following questions with an appropriate format were asked:

1. To urban dwellers in the large, what is the *relative* importance of each of the following to satisfaction with respect to the overall quality of life?
2. To urban dwellers in the large, all things being equal, how important is each of the following to satisfaction with respect to the overall quality of life?
3. In terms of planning, building and governing a new city, to what extent can each of the following be altered in a positive way?

In each case the list of items of dissatisfaction followed the question with a simple format for respond-ing.

We found that the relative rank-ing, i.e. ranking each item from 1 to 19, is difficult to do, especially when statistical feedback is included. This question was dropped after round three. A nine-point scale was used to rate each item individually both on the question of importance and al-terability. The statistical feedback was accomplished through use of a "tent" over the scale for each item, which indicated the median, and the 25th and 75th percentiles.

As mentioned previously, the Delphi consisted of four rounds, in-cluding the initial round used to ob-tain the items of dissatisfaction. Sta-tistical measures indicated a good de-gree of consensus (reduction in vari-ance on subsequent rounds) and thus the Delphi was concluded after the fourth round.

RESULTS

The first result was the nineteen items of dissatisfaction. These are the result of the clustering of over 400 items offered by the panel. They are presented here in no particular order: (a) housing; (b) cost consider-ations; (c) health care; (d) aesthetics; (e) inequality; (f) governmental re-sponsiveness; (g) leisure pursuits; (h) mass media; (i) drugs; (j) organized religion; (k) pornography; (l) safety; (m) education; (n) alienation; hu-manness, personal well-being; (o) domestic animals; (p) service func-tions; (q) transportation; (r) pollu-tion; (s) crowding.

The panel members could refer to a table of phrases from which these

labels were derived. For example, "housing" served to label the follow-ing: (a) old environment; (b) lack of adequate housing; (c) urban blight; (d) inadequate housing; (e) physical decay of cities; (f) deteriorating hous-ing and buildings; (g) areas of blight; (h) poor housing; (i) unsound and unsanitary conditions.

Some examples for the label "aes-thetics" were (a) failure to keep the city beautiful; (b) poorly planned neighborhoods; (c) lack of green space; (d) skyscrapers too close to-gether; (e) functional but unaesthetic structures (like strip development).

"Cost considerations" included: (a) cost of living; (b) property tax in-creases; (c) inflation; (d) high cost of housing; (e) higher taxes for fewer services (or lower quality).

The mean rating after round four was used to rank order the nineteen items on the basis of importance and alterability. This was a better dis-criminator of the rank ordering than the median, since several items can have the same median score.

Table 1 shows the rank order of the items based on importance. Table 2 shows the rank order based on alterability.

Figure 2 depicts the alterability of the item relative to the importance of the item. By way of explanation the nineteen items are arranged in decreasing importance based on the results of the last Delphi round of importance ratings. The mean rating was used to rank the items. The bars show the mean rating on alterability obtained from the final Delphi round.

There is no reason to expect any kind of correspondence between im-portance and alterability, and the

TABLE 1. RANK ORDER OF IMPORTANCE
BASED ON MEAN RATING, ROUND FOUR

ITEM	MEAN RATING *
Cost considerations	8.44
Housing	8.32
Safety	8.16
Health care	7.84
Alienation, humanness, personal well-being	7.52
Education	7.40
Service functions	7.00
Transportation	6.76
Inequality	6.40
Governmental responsiveness	6.04
Crowding	6.00
Pollution	5.68
Leisure pursuits	5.56
Aesthetics	5.04
Drugs	4.76
Mass media	4.32
Organized religion	3.72
Pornography	1.84
Domestic animals	1.40

* These means are based on a nine-point scale.

TABLE 2. RANK ORDER OF ALTERABILITY
BASED ON MEAN RATING, ROUND FOUR

ITEM	MEAN RATING *
Health	8.36
Housing	8.32
Transportation	8.32
Leisure pursuits	7.84
Pollution	7.68
Service functions	7.68
Education	7.64
Safety	7.40
Crowding	7.20
Aesthetics	7.00
Domestic animals	6.92
Governmental responsiveness	6.44
Cost considerations	5.84
Mass media	5.52
Inequality	5.48
Alienation, humanness, personal well-being	5.36
Pornography	5.20
Drugs	4.92
Organized religion	3.64

* These means are based on a nine-point scale.

depiction shows this to be true. Several observations are possible from an analysis of Fig. 2.

1. Housing, safety, and health care are ranked very high on importance and are judged to be highly alterable.
2. Education, service functions, and transportation are ranked quite high on importance and are judged to be highly alterable.
3. The remaining items that are considered highly alterable (seven or above) are pollution, leisure pursuits, and aesthetics, and crowding.
4. There are two items that are ranked highly important but are not considered amenable to change—cost considerations; and alienation, humanness, personal well-being.
5. There are five items that are not high on importance and are not considered very alterable. These are inequality, drugs, mass media, organized religion, and pornography.
6. Only two items are considered to be very difficult to alter (five or less)—drugs and organized religion. All the other items are deemed amenable to improvement through application of resources.
7. The items deemed most able to be altered are housing and health care —both high in importance.
8. The item rated the lowest on alterability is organized religion and it is third from last in importance.

These results, although general, should be useful to the planner. In setting priorities, the planner should be cognizant of what people think are the areas of most importance to dissatisfaction with the quality of life. In this case, six items are ranked high in importance—housing, safety, health care, education, service functions and transportation. These are also ranked high on the basis of alterability, meaning that dissatisfac-

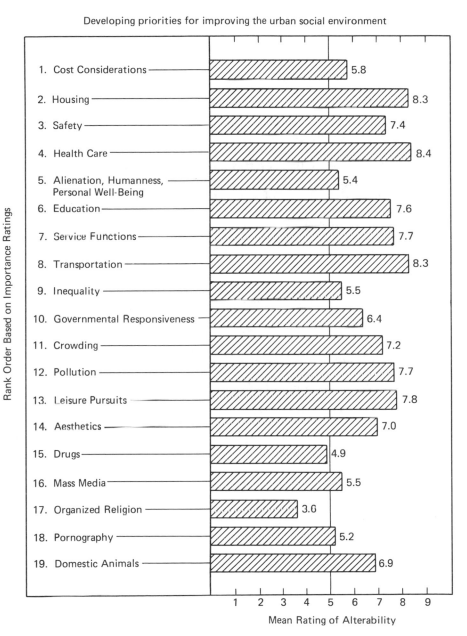

Developing priorities for improving the urban social environment

Rank Order Based on Importance Ratings

1. Cost Considerations — 5.8
2. Housing — 8.3
3. Safety — 7.4
4. Health Care — 8.4
5. Alienation, Humanness, Personal Well-Being — 5.4
6. Education — 7.6
7. Service Functions — 7.7
8. Transportation — 8.3
9. Inequality — 5.5
10. Governmental Responsiveness — 6.4
11. Crowding — 7.2
12. Pollution — 7.7
13. Leisure Pursuits — 7.8
14. Aesthetics — 7.0
15. Drugs — 4.9
16. Mass Media — 5.5
17. Organized Religion — 3.6
18. Pornography — 5.2
19. Domestic Animals — 6.9

Mean Rating of Alterability

FIGURE 2. Comparison of alterability vs. importance.

tions could be lessened through application of resources in the design of a new city. Obviously the Delphi may be used to help set priorities. These priorities are based on two measuring scales—importance and alterability. These two perspectives are a necessity in the planning sense. Obviously there may be an item of dissatisfaction that is considered very important but is not amenable to positive improvement through application of resources. In this case "alienation, humanness, personal well-being" and "inequality" are two such items. The planner must be made aware of these kinds of generalizations if he is to allocate resources in the proper way.

On the other hand, there may be some items that are considered easily alterable but not very important to the over-all quality of life. In this case aesthetics and domestic animals [2] are such items. The panel must have indicated that these are items that could be quite easily improved through applications of resources but that there are other items that are much more important.

CONTRIBUTION TO NEW CITY PLANNING EFFORT

We found that this Delphi helped solidify our thinking about both de-

[2] Domestic animals refers to dogs running loose—a very significant problem in *some* existing cities.

scriptive and normative scenarios for new city design. An extra benefit was that it helped to synthesize the thoughts of thirty people who had been working on a highly complex, ill-defined problem. It helped to integrate the knowledge of professionals with varying disciplinary backgrounds.

The next steps will be to concentrate more specifically on the items of dissatisfaction deemed most important and alterable. Likely next steps will perhaps include further Delphi exercises and cross-impact studies on these components of dissatisfaction, and to further delineate each of the components in specific operational terms.

REFERENCES

1. N. Dalkey and O. Helmer. "An Experimental Application of the Delphi Method to the Use of Experts. *Management Science*, 9, 3 (1963), 458–67.
2. O. Helmer. *Social Technology*. New York: Basic Books, 1966.
3. N. Dalkey, D. Rourke, R. Lewis, and D. Snyder. *Studies in the Quality of Life, Delphi and Decision-Making*. Lexington, Massachusetts, 1972.
4. M. Skutsch and J. L. Schofer. "Goals—Delphi for Urban Planning: Concepts in Their Design." *Socio-Economic Planning Science*, 7 (1973), 305–313.
5. O. Helmer. *On the Future State of the Union*. Menlo Park, Calif.: Institute for the Future, 1972.

24 Problem Analysis and Program Design: Nominal Group Process Technique

A GROUP PROCESS MODEL FOR PROBLEM IDENTIFICATION AND PROGRAM PLANNING

ANDRÉ L. DELBECQ/ANDREW H. VAN DE VEN

INTRODUCTION

The divisional manager of an aerospace firm is faced with the problem of designing a program to manufacture a new control system for a missile component. In order to develop the program, he will need to involve functional managers in several engineering units, obtain financial resources from top management, consult technical experts from several research institutes, and obtain cooperation of military representatives.

. . .

The executive director of a social welfare agency is faced with the need for developing services for elderly persons in a small semirural community. There is no prior history of such a program among the senior citizens. The director needs assistance from a number of other social agencies and health service institutions in working out the program.

. . .

Reprinted with permission of authors and publisher from: André L. Delbecq and Andrew H. Van de Ven, "A Group Process Model for Problem Identification and Program Planning," *Journal of Applied Behavioral Science*, 7: 4 (September 1971), 466–92.

A junior faculty member in the business school within a large state university is interested in exploring a program whereby M.B.A. candidates can provide technical assistance to small businessmen in the predominantly Negro central city area nearby. Although he is aware of other similar efforts, the exact nature of a successful program, the type of faculty involvement required, the reaction of his department chairman, and commitment of resources by the dean are all difficult to predict.

The purpose of this paper [1] is to present a group process model for situations like those cited above which planning groups can use for (a) identifying strategic problems and (b)

[1] This research was supported by funds granted to the Matrix Management Project Group in the Graduate School of Business at the University of Wisconsin by the National Aeronautics and Space Administration; and by funds granted to the Institute for Research on Poverty, University of Wisconsin, by the Office of Economic Opportunity. The authors are grateful to the following persons who directly participated in discussion of the model: Fremont A. Shull, Alan Filley, and Andrew J. Grimes.

developing appropriate and innovative programs to solve them. The model was originally developed from social-psychological studies of decision-conferences and studies of program planning in an (Office of Economic Opportunity) Community Action Agency. The model, which we abbreviate as PPM (Program Planning Model), has been used by the authors in a wide variety of organization change and task force situations—in business, industry, government, and education.

PPM is not a rationalistic econological model for system planning. It is, rather, a socio-logical model suggesting a planning sequence which seeks to provide an orderly process of structuring the decision making at different phases of planning.[2] In developing the model, we were particularly concerned with situations where a variety of groups, fragmented in terms of vested interests, rhetorical and ideological concepts, and differentiated expertise, needed to be brought together in order for a program to emerge or change to take place. Modern decision theory clearly indicated that different problem-solving phases and different types of problems called for different group processes (Delbecq, 1967). It did not, however, provide guidelines for interfacing divided groups involved in the vortex of large-scale planning situations.

These contextual differences between planning situations involving differentiated groups and rationalistic planning within an organizational function (such as capital investment planning) can be illustrated by elaborating upon the problems faced by community planners.

To begin with, the community planner faces all the realities of calcified bureaucracy. That is to say, needed physical and financial resources, technically trained personnel, and legitimating power are often locked within established business, political, and social institutions. Each of these institutions, itself, may be only moderately malleable. The character of difficulties in achieving innovation within established bureaucratized organizations is well documented in the literature (V. Thompson, 1965). The problem of community planners transcends these intraorganizational difficulties since they must coalesce resources from a number of organizations. Further, since political units crisscross the metropolitan conglomerate but seldom encompass it, problems of legitimacy are compounded.

An additional problem is that a particular public unit seldom commands sufficient technological expertise to deal with complex urban problems (Lipsky, 1968). This issue of technological expertise is, in itself, a quagmire. The combination of the "information explosion" together with increasing specialization of discipline-oriented scientists has made the term "interdisciplinary" a euphemism.

Finally, the appropriateness of technocrats' unilaterally "planning for" communities may well have passed. The involvement of citizens, clients, low-income neighborhood groups, concerned political representatives, and others makes the questions of "subsidiarity" and "Maximum Feasible Participation" most

[2] The terms "econo-logical" and "socio-logical" are taken from the decision-making studies reported in James D. Thompson and Arthur Tuden (1959).

important concerns for community planning. The contemporary planning process must include opportunities for client participation and representation in the evolution and implementation of community change programs.[3]

THE PPM PROCESS OUTLINED

PPM is directly concerned with situations like those described above. It suggests a method in which internal exchange across organizational units and extraorganizational interfaces can be sequenced, and offers an explicit process for structuring the character of participation within each phase of planning. PPM divides program planning and development into five phases. While these phases are compatible with the "scientific method," PPM suggests specific group techniques and specific roles for different interest groups at different phases in the process.[4] The entire process may be briefly summarized as follows:

Phase I: *Problem Exploration*
Involvement of client or consumer groups
Involvement of first-line supervisors

Phase II: *Knowledge Exploration*
Involvement of external scientific personnel

3 For a discussion of "Maximum Feasible Participation" in Community Action Programs, refer to CAP Management Guide 6321-1. Washington, D.C.: Office of Economic Opportunity, January 1969. Pp. 1–2. *See also* Arnstein (1969), Lipsky (1968), Mogulof (1969), and Warren (1969).

4 For a treatment of problem-solving phases in small groups, *see* Bales and Strodtbeck (1967).

Involvement of internal and external organizational specialists

Phase III: *Priority Development*
Involvement of resource controllers
Involvement of key administrators

Phase IV: *Program Development*
Involvement of line administrators
Involvement of technical specialists

Phase V: *Program Evaluation*
Involvement of client or consumer groups
Involvement of staff and administrative personnel

We can now proceed to discuss each phase in appropriate detail.

PHASE I: PROBLEM EXPLORATION

Phase I begins with the identification of a cross-section of client or consumer groups divided according to age, geography, technical applications, or whatever client or user categories are in keeping with the nature of the service or product in question. The heart of the process is a problem exploration meeting which is conducted according to the following format.

Fifty or sixty clients are brought together for a meeting to discuss their individual and common problems, which are the focal issues around which the new program will emerge. The organizational representative opens the meeting by indicating the sincere interest of his organization in understanding the character of their (the clients') problems in order that his organization might better plan its program of services. He then indicates that the purpose of the meeting is to understand the *problems,* not to explore solutions.

Further, most problems have both emotional and organizational dimensions. The emotional dimensions center around feelings such as anxiety, fear, embarrassment, and the like. The organizational dimensions often deal with authority, structure, costs, availability of resources, quality of services, and so on. He tells the client group that his organization is interested in both problem dimensions.

The organizational representative then divides clients into groups of six to nine according to common characteristics (such as age) and has these small groups sit around separate tables. Each individual is asked to write "personal feelings" on one side of a 5" x 7" card and "organizational difficulties" on the other side of the card. He then asks all present to spend the next thirty minutes listing aspects of the problem on their individual cards without speaking to anyone else at their table. The groups proceed in silence.

At the end of thirty minutes, the organizational representative provides each table with a large paper pad, felt pens, and masking tape. A junior staff member from the organization offers to serve as recorder for each table. The junior staff person asks each member of the client group, one at a time, to read aloud *one* "organizational difficulties" item from his card. He writes that item on his pad exactly as the client member reads it from his card. He then proceeds round-robin to receive one item from the next client in sequence, numbering each item. He suggests that if several members at the table have the same item on their cards, they should raise their hands so he can record it by putting check

marks next to the item. However, he avoids any debate about equivalency of items by writing all related "problems" as separate statements rather than rewording a particular one even if there is overlap. He continues writing items until all the "organizational difficulties" items are on the pad. He then tears the sheet off the pad, tapes it to the wall, and repeats the process for the "personal feelings" items.

After the group has listed all items on the two sheets of paper, members are offered a chance for a coffee break. Upon returning, they are given one-half hour to review and to discuss in a serial fashion each of the items on their two lists; clarify, elaborate, or defend any item; or add items. However, the group should avoid collapsing or condensing items into categories since a greater specificity of the problem dimensions is retained when the items are not condensed into general problem categories. At the end of thirty minutes, the group is given 3" x 5" cards. Each member is asked privately to vote (by number) on the five items he considers most crucial on the "personal" problem list and the five most crucial on the "organizational" problem list.[5] The junior organizational staff member then collects the indi-

[5] The specific voting procedure used depends upon the degree of specificity of information that is desired from the group and the nature of the topic under investigation. If the topic is very general and only preliminary information is desired, a simple *listing* of priorities is sufficient. If a more detailed understanding of priorities, in order of importance, is desired, a *ranking* of priorities is appropriate. If one desires understanding of the magnitude of difference between priorities, a *rating* or priorities is needed.

vidual votes and records the votes of the group on each of the appropriate sheets.

All the groups then come together, and the votes of each group are reported to the entire client audience. A discussion period follows: it lasts as long as the client group actively talks about the subject—usually about ten minutes.

The organizational representative then briefly explains the remaining phases of the PPM process and asks the group whether it would like to select representatives to participate in Phase II of the process. If the group wishes to proceed, members vote for their representatives. The clients are thanked and the meeting ends.

Figure 1 presents a summary of the Phase I meeting.

I. Selection of Client or Consumer Sample
(Divided according to age, geography, technical application, or other appropriate categories)

II. Meeting with Clients or Consumer Groups to explore problem dimensions

    A. Introduction (10 minutes)
      1. Welcome
      2. Expression of organization(s)' interest in clients' problems
      3. Indication that focus is on problems, not solutions
      4. Explanation of "personal" vs. "organizational" problems

    B. Directions for small group participation
      1. Assign clients to small groups of 6 to 9
      2. Instruct them in nominal group format
        a. Listing "personal" problem dimensions on 5" x 7" cards (15 minutes)
        b. Listing "organizational" problem dimensions on 5" x 7" cards (15 minutes)
      3. Provide flip chart and recorder for round-robin sharing of individually noted items
        a. Items from individual cards (first organizational, then personal)
        b. New items suggested by process

    C. Fifteen-minute break

    D. Interacting group discussion of each item on flip chart in serial fashion for clarification, elaboration, and/or defense, but not for collapsing or condensing items.

    E. Nominal group voting on 3" x 5" cards for top five priority items on both "personal" and "organizational" lists

    F. General Session—discussion of tabulated votes from each small group

    G. Explanation of PPM and election of representative(s) for Phase II

FIGURE 1. Outline of Phase I Meeting—Program Planning Model

*THEORETICAL DEFENSE OF
PHASE I*

Use of nominal groups to increase creativity. One of the objectives of PPM is to facilitate, in the greatest degree possible, innovation and creativity in program planning. The Phase I PPM format is based on research which shows that creativity can often be facilitated by following specific group processes. While research supports the desirability of involving certain types of creative individuals in later phases (Scott, 1965), Phase I emphasizes our agreement with Victor Thompson and Smithburg (1968) on the need to structure group processes. They write: "Mystical, charismatic personality qualities have been greatly overemphasized in the discussion of creativity and discovery in comparison to . . . structural rather than personality variables."

The overriding imposed process in Phase I is the use of the nominal group technique in the early part of the meetings. In recent years, a number of major research studies substantiate the superiority of *nominal groups* (groups in which individuals work in the presence of one another but do not interact) as compared with conventional "brainstorming" groups.[6] This research indicates that interacting groups produce a smaller number of problem dimensions, fewer high quality suggestions, and

[6] A complete treatment of the empirical research and the social-psychological dynamics of both nominal and interacting groups is available in Andrew H. Van de Ven and André L. Delbecq, "Nominal Versus Interacting Groups for Committee Decision-making Effectiveness," *J. Acad. of Mgmt,* June 1971, 14 (2).

a smaller number of different kinds of solutions than groups in which members were constrained from interaction during the generation of critical problem variables (Campbell, 1968; Dunnette, Campbell, and Jaastad, 1963; Leader, 1967; Taylor, Berry, and Block, 1958; Vroom, Grant, and Cotton, 1969). Since the use of nominal groups is not characteristic of most meeting formats, a word of explanation for the overriding superiority of nominal groups in the structure of PPM is in order. The following factors seem to explain the superiority of the nominal technique for the generation of problem dimensions and appropriate solutions (though in Phase I of PPM we are not concerned with solutions).

There seems to be little question that interacting groups inhibit the performance of their members (Taylor *et al.,* 1958). Despite elaborate attempts (e.g., "brainstorming") at freeing individuals to speak spontaneously and fully share their ideas, people seem comfortable in sharing only fairly well-developed ideas with the group, particularly in a newly formed group.

The second explanation relates to the tendency of interacting groups to focus on a particular train of thought. Interacting groups often "fall into a rut" by concentrating on and elaborating a single problem dimension. Individuals find it more comfortable to react to someone else's idea than to generate their own ideas. This is especially limiting since early ideas which become the focus of the group's attention often contain obvious rather than subtle problem dimensions (Dunnette, *et* al., 1963; Osborn, 1957; Taylor et al., 1958).

It is also necessary for participants to become fully and thoroughly enmeshed in the problem. The tension created by the nominal group situation, in which other members at the table are industriously writing, maximizes social facilitation-tension which is important for individuals' full involvement in the task at hand. "Creations and discovery are much more likely when there is a personal commitment to searching for a solution" (Victor Thompson and Smithburg, 1968).

The nominal group process also avoids evaluation of any particular problem dimension and the distraction of elaborating comments, while problem dimensions are being generated. This is congruent with Maier's (1963) research on creative groups.

Finally, the round-robin procedure, coupled with the separation of "personal" from "organizational" problems increases the tendency of individuals to begin sharing risky problem dimensions with other members of the group (issues that involve increasing degrees of self-disclosure). The round-robin procedure of each member's offering a single idea allows secure personality types who are greater risk-takers to engage in early self-disclosure. This modeling by the more secure members of the group makes it easier for less secure members to take their turn and suggest risky problem dimensions, particularly "personal" problems which they might hesitate to bring before the group in an interacting situation (Culbert, 1968). Experience also suggests that clients or consumers will avoid identifying "personal" dimensions dealing with social-emotional problem dimensions unless stimulated by a separate category beyond the "organizational" category.[7] . . .

SUMMARY OF THE BENEFITS OF PHASE I

Phase I, then, is a deliberate, structured process which seeks to accomplish the following objectives: (a) to facilitate problem definition by a rich input of problem dimensions through nominal group techniques; (b) to focus attention on those items which have the highest priority in the clients' or consumers' perspective; (c) to avoid reaching toward a limited few "leaders" or a single client group to create the definition of the clientèle or consumer problem, but rather to react to multiple reference groups and representative clients; (d) to force professional members to react to the realities of client perceptions rather than to their own theoretical or professional biases; (e) to create sufficient tension to assure responsiveness on the part of the professional organization to clients or consumers; (f) to provide a mechanism for the interfacing of both clients and professionals in a manner which avoids mutually frus-

[7] For example, in a meeting exploring services for elderly persons, "organizational" or "outside" problems such as cost of drugs, transportation, and so on were easily mentioned. Only when groups of elderly were asked as separate individuals to list "personal" problems did areas such as fear of death, loneliness, preoccupation with sickness, feeling disliked by younger people, and other critical social-emotional issues come out.

trating semantic hangups; and (g) to increase the legitimation of later program proposals by early involvement of client or consumer groups.

PHASE II: KNOWLEDGE EXPLORATION

Phase II begins with the identification of external scientific and organizational experts whose discipline and functional skills relate to the priority items which evolved in Phase I. Combined with internal functional experts from the principal organization(s) who will be responsible for the implementation of the planning program, this group of knowledge resource persons (hereafter referred to as "specialists") is invited to engage in a problem-solving meeting following processes somewhat similar to the Phase I format.

In preparation for the Phase II meeting, the problem items developed in Phase I are divided into major and minor categories.[8] A large visual display of these problem categories, together with an indication of the priority vote, is presented to the knowledge resource panel. Once again, the organization representative opens the meeting by stating the interest of his organization in developing an adequate program to deal with the priority problems of clients or consumers which emerged

[8] The development of this classification system is undertaken by a staff member of the sponsoring organization. If there are grey areas of dispute with respect to this taxonomy, the reclassification of items can be tested against a panel of people who were present at the earlier Phase I meeting.

in the Phase I meeting. He then discusses the character of the Phase I meeting and thoroughly reviews the display of problem items. He is careful not to interpret the items analytically but he does provide a qualitative description of problems which underlie the items by repeating the anecdotes and vignettes which client or consumer groups had mentioned in the earlier meeting. To assist in this descriptive clarification, he asks for the help of the client or consumer representatives who were elected in Phase I to be present at the Phase II meeting.

Following this review of problem dimensions, he directly defines the role of the "specialists" present. He indicates that they were invited as "idea men," not as "representatives" of their particular home organizations. He states that the purpose of the Phase II meeting is to identify alternative solution components and resources for the priority items which emerged in the Phase I meeting.[9] In this breakdown, first he asks for help in developing a list of solution components and resources *presently available* within organizations they are familiar with which can be adapted to, or which already directly relate in their present form to, the problem dimensions. Second, he asks

[9] "Component" in this case means an element or part of a solution program. "Resource" means a person, organizational unit, or funding source. For example, a problem priority identified in an OEO Phase I meeting was "lack of available medical services in geographically dispersed low-income neighborhoods in the county." In this case a solution component listed was "develop a mobile medical clinic." A resource listed was "use university medical interns."

them to recommend *new* types of solution components and resources which could be developed as partial or complete solutions to the problem dimensions.

The specialists are then divided into small groups. Each group is composed of a cross-section of age, scientific and organizational personnel, and functional expertise. Each individual in the groups receives as many 5″ x 7″ cards as there are priority items from the Phase I meeting. On one side of each card the specialist writes "Solution Components and Existing Resources which can be adopted or used." On the other side of the card he writes "Solution Components and New Resources which can and should be developed." During the next forty minutes, following a nominal group format, each specialist completes the list of existing and new Solution Components and Resources which he feels should be part of the solution program for each priority item.

Following this, the imposed group structure of the round-robin procedure described for the Phase I meeting is used again. This time a sheet divided and labeled "Existing" and "New" Solution Components and Resources is used for each of the priority categories. As before, a junior staff member records on these sheets the items read aloud from the individual cards of the specialists.

Following a break, each group engages in a discussion of the various existing and new solution components and resources which can be incorporated in the program to deal with the priority problem items. The purpose of this discussion is to de-termine the most reasonable and adequate combination of solution components and resources for each priority problem. At the conclusion of this discussion, each group of specialists presents to the total assembly the list of solution components and resources which it feels must be part of the final program.

As each group reports, two staff members record and number the components and resource items. After a short discussion, all specialists present are asked to vote (using 3″ x 5″ cards) on those components and resources which they feel are absolutely essential in constructing a minimally adequate program to solve the priority problems raised in Phase I. (Statistical techniques such as weighting and rank ordering can be employed by analyzing nominal voting.)

Once again, at the end of the meeting the organizational representative explains the remaining phases of the PPM process and asks the groups to select representatives from Phase II to participate in Phase III of the process. The groups vote for their representatives. The resource persons are thanked and the meeting ends. Figure 2 presents a summary of the Phase II meeting. . . .

SUMMARY OF THE BENEFITS OF PHASE II

Phase II, then, is a deliberate, structured process which seeks to accomplish the following objectives: (a) to reconceptualize the priority problems from Phase I in terms of essential solution components and resources through use of scientific and

I. Selection of Knowledge Resource Panel
   Involvement of external scientific personnel
   Involvement of internal and external organizational specialists

II. Meeting with Knowledge "Specialists" to explore solution components and needed resources

   A. Introduction
      1. Welcome
      2. Emphasis on the fact that the meeting's focus is upon priority problems of consumers or clients
      3. Review of Phase I
         a. Visual display of critical problems and priorities
         b. Nonanalytical elaboration of examples with assistance of client or consumer representatives from Phase I
      4. Role definition that asks specialists to be "idea" men, not "representatives" of programs or organizations

   B. Directions for small-group participation
      1. Assign specialists to small groups of 6 to 9 providing for a cross section of age, scientific and organizational affiliation, and functional expertise
      2. Instruct specalists in nominal group format on each side of the 5" x 7" cards, and ask specialists to list critical solution components and resources under "existing" and "new" headings (30-45 minutes)
      3. Provide a flip chart and person to serve as recorder for roundrobin sharing of individually noted solution components and resources (a separate sheet for each priority problem)

   C. Interacting group discussion in which each small group develops a package of solution components and resources for priority problems

   D. Report of each small group in general session. (Recorders make a master list of solution components and resources.)

   E. Nominal group voting on 3" x 5" cards on those solution components and resources absolutely essential for an effective program to solve priority items

   F. Explanation of PPM and election of representatives for Phase III

FIGURE 2.   Outline of Phase II Meeting—Program Planning Model

organizational expertise; (b) to focus on new combinations of solution components and resources, avoiding defensive discussions of existing programs; (c) to activate differentiated types of creative insight by interdisciplinary and cross-generational group composition; (d) to call attention to existing but untapped solution components and resources as well as the need for new components and resources; (e) to provide a legitimate "scientific" endorsement of essential program components and resources for an adequate solution to priority problems.

PHASE III: PRIORITY DEVELOPMENT [10]

The description of the two prior phases of PPM has emphasized the *process* appropriate for the particular meeting involved. In Phase III, the process for the meeting is not so significant as the timing of the meeting relative to the total PPM sequence.[11]

Phase III calls for a meeting—in which key resource controllers and key administrators participate, together with representatives from Phases I and II—to review the priorities and critical solution elements of the emerging program. The critical timing of the meeting can be justified as follows.

Klein (1967) describes resistance to programs as often being a function of the way change is introduced. He notes that most planners run into trouble when the agents of change have done all their planning *before* introducing their ideas to those who will be affected and who control resources. When this happens, "the innovators have usually developed a considerable investment in their plans and are often far more committed to defending them than to attempting to understand objections to them. They are not prepared to repeat with newcomers the long process of planning which finally led them to their conclusions" (Klein, 1967, p. 29). Klein goes on to note that attention to critics of an innovation plan can serve three useful functions:

First, . . . [critics] are most likely to perceive and point out any real threats to the well-being of the system which may be unanticipated consequences of the projected changes. Second, they are especially likely to react against any change that might reduce the integrity of the system. Third, they are sensitive to any indication that those seeking to produce change fail to understand or identify with core values of the system they seek to influence (Klein, 1967, p. 31).

The essential contribution of our *Phase III is that it seeks to obtain re-*

---

[10] There are several important caveats which need to be made at this point. First, PPM is not a model for protest. That is, it presumes a degree of openness to client or consumer needs on the part of resource controllers. In cases where there is extreme polarization of positions, the intermediate degree of tension which PPM generates will be inadequate. Second, we have deliberately not incorporated budgeting and financial constraints into the process. Budgeting overlays and techniques for dealing with funding issues are sufficiently complex in themselves that we are incorporating budget issues in a later paper. In addition, the later paper juxtaposes the PPM process with the structure of an organization whose primary mandate is concerned with developmental and experimental work (as often performed by a planning agency) as opposed to ongoing operating line work (as often performed by a social referral agency). *See* André L. Delbecq and Andrew H. Van de Ven, "The Generic Character of Program Management: A Theoretical Perspective." Madison, Wisconsin: University of Wisconsin, Graduate School of Business. Unpublished manuscript, March 1971.

[11] Indeed, research indicates nominal techniques are most applicable for generating information, while interacting groups are appropriate for evaluating information. In this sense, Phases I and II are the nominal preparation for Phase III. (*See* Vroom, Grant, and Cotton, 1969 for discussion of generation vs. evaluation.) To avoid rhetorical cleavage, provide focus, and create balance, therefore, greater attention to visuals (referred to below) is important.

sponses from potential critics of the program who are in a position to withhold resources or to negate appropriate involvement of functional administrative units in the implementation of the program, *while program proponents are still flexible.*

In the Phase III meeting, the outputs from the prior two phases are presented to the line administrators and resource controllers.[12] The format of the presentation is straightforward: the same list of critical problems and priorities from Phase I and the output from Phase II—the outline of agreed-upon solution components and resources—are presented to the key line administration and resource controllers. Of necessity, this represents the adumbration of a program proposal rather than the presentation of specifics. The timing of Phase III is such that by meeting date there should be sufficient content in both problem analysis and

12 The extent to which separate client or consumer representatives are invited to attend Phase III meetings is dependent on the extent to which resource control groups (often policy boards) include client or user groups in their membership. Increasingly, policy groups have so structured their board membership that proportional representation of clients is automatically assured when Phase III review before resource controllers takes place. Where this is not the case, the Phase III meeting should include proportional representation of client or consumers together with resource control board members and key administrators. Because of the difficulties of client or consumer members in holding their own during the verbal give-and-take of such meetings, the word *proportional* should be underscored. Token representation is not satisfactory. For the remainder of the discussion of Phase III, the proportional representation of client or consumer members will be assumed.

solution analysis to provide appropriate focused discussion for resource controllers and administrators. At the same time, those individuals who will be charged later with the responsibility of developing the details of the program proposal have not yet become closed-minded nor have they made decisions on all the specifics of the proposed program. As a result, program sponsors will still be in a position to respond flexibly to the type of realistic adjustments which administrators and resource controllers are likely to suggest.

It is not an unusual occurrence for meaningful programs to be vetoed by resource controllers or administrators due to rather minor implementational issues. In other words, the essence of the program may be quite acceptable, while minor matters of program implementation often may not be satisfactory. What one seeks, then, in Phase III is a review of the types of reservations or qualifications that resource controllers and key administrators may have, and the adjustments required in order for the program proposal to be fully endorsed and supported. The structure of Phases I and II is such that neither the clients nor knowledge specialists are likely to attend to system and administrative constraints which those present in Phase III will be attuned to. The juxtaposition of client or consumer representatives from the Phase I meeting, knowledge resource persons from the Phase II meeting, and administrators and resource controllers spurs bargaining and negotiation in Phase III, so that within the content of the final program proposal the essential concerns of each of these reference groups can be included. The essential process caveat is that proponents of the program elements from Phases I and II must define their roles in such a way that they are open to the inputs of resource controllers and administrators and view them as relevant new problem dimensions to be incorporated in the final program, rather than as hostile "attacks" from an audience critical of the elements which evolved in the prior two phases. A detailed process guideline for the structuring of this discussion is suggested in the elaboration of bargaining strategy by Delbecq (1967).

SUMMARY OF THE BENEFITS OF PHASE III

Phase III, then, represents an important but frequently overlooked phase of program development. It provides a step prior to "calcification" of thinking by program proponents, in which the general outline of a program plan containing both problem definition and critical solution elements is reviewed, so that administrative and resource controller concerns are incorporated in a manner that "buys insurance" relative to future endorsement and support of the program proposal. Following modifications, the output of Phase III should be a "go ahead" signal.

PHASE IV: PROGRAM DEVELOPMENT

Phase IV of the PPM model is simply a necessary step like that in conventional program evolution. In Phase IV, working from the input of the earlier three phases, technical specialists and line administrators

who are sponsors of the program develop a finalized, specific program proposal. The essential matter here is to ensure that those specialists responsible for developing the details of the program remain sensitive to critical elements developed in prior phases.

PHASE V: PROGRAM EVALUATION

Phase V brings representatives from each of the constituent groups involved in Phases I, II, and III together for a final time, to complete one cycle of the PPM process.[13] The need for this last meeting is based on several probable events: that a good deal of time will have elapsed between the initiation of Phase I and this final meeting prior to activation of the program; that some of the élan associated with involvement in the PPM process will have faded due to the extended time span; that some critical concern may have been overlooked in the technical development of the program; and finally, that a number of necessary compromises will have occurred in each phase so that cooperation, at least potentially, may be eroded by the feeling that the solution program is not "perfect." Phase V is structured to deal with the above developments in a manner which both reinvolves critical personnel and deals with honest hesitations about the technical plan in a constructive rather than destructive manner.

The Phase V meeting begins with a report from technical specialists of the details of the program to be im-

[13] In modified form the PPM cycle can be repeated, using the evaluation data prescribed in Phase V as the starting point.

plemented in the near future, but focuses this report in a specific fashion. Each critical feature of the detailed plan of action is overtly related to the input from prior phases. That is to say, it is not simply a report from technical specialists of their program plan, but rather a unified statement of program plans which seeks to operationalize the specific critical elements that emerged in earlier meetings. In this sense, the orientation of the meeting must show a clear linkage between the final plan and the problem priorities, solution and resource elements, and administrative and controller concerns raised in earlier phases. This manner of presentation (a) refreshes memories of earlier meetings and (b) directly connects planning details to prior critical elements. As such, it is an important mechanism for rekindling enthusiasm lost during the long planning cycle.

The matter of hesitations about "imperfections" remains to be considered. Since it is doubtful that any operationalization of a program will totally satisfy every representative, a portion of the Phase V process, therefore, focuses on reviewing control and evaluation measures which will test whether or not the final program proposal incorporates earlier critical dimensions. If it is felt that the final program deviates from earlier expectations, there are two types of compromises possible: (1) a change in some detail of the finalized program proposal, or (2) further evaluation to determine whether a minority objection proves to be a valid weakness in the program. Generally speaking, Type 1 changes are made when a majority of the representatives at the Phase V meeting agree.

This still leaves open the possibility that a recalcitrant minority will withdraw support. In this sense the Type 2 compromise offers a safety valve. By focusing the attention of minority members on the Type 2 compromise, individuals who retain reservations about the program against the majority judgment of the meeting still have recourse. Using a Type 2 compromise, disputation about selective details of the program can be dealt with by incorporating control and evaluation measures which test the relative effectiveness or ineffectiveness of the questioned program component.

Phase V, therefore, is a meeting designed to question whether the specialists' technical translation of the outputs of Phases I, II, and III as set forth in the final program proposal is an adequate interpretation of earlier discussions. If so, how will this adequacy be measured? Some adjustments where inadequacy is predicted may be forthcoming in the meeting. In addition, to avoid a stalemate at this late phase of program development, unresolved issues about adequacy can be handled by including in the evaluation design specific measures that will provide answers about the disputed matter for later program planning and adjustment.

SUMMARY OF THE BENEFITS OF PHASE V

Phase V, then, seeks to accomplish the following objectives: (a) to reinvolve client or consumer representatives, knowledge resource people, and resource controllers and administrators by structuring the review of the technical proposal around critical concerns developed in prior phases; (b) to examine the extent to which the technical program plan honors earlier concerns by focusing upon evaluation designs; (c) to allow an opportunity for majority-approved last-minute adjustments; (d) to provide an outlet for minority reservations in the form of careful control measures to determine whether such reservations are justified; and thus (e) through the above processes, to refocus and rekindle interest in the change program.

SOME CONCLUDING REMARKS

We feel that PPM as a group process model is an insightful conceptualization of program planning. It both highlights critical issues and provides a guideline for developing innovative solution strategies where clients or consumers, specialists, resource controllers, and administrators must be interfaced. It further suggests group processes and agenda formats which guide each phase of program evolution. Finally, the general character of the process is consistent with current research on creativity, organization change, and social planning.[14]

The authors are presently preparing a detailed description of the application of PPM in social service planning and health planning organizations in a forthcoming book.[15] From this and a number of other ap-

plications of PPM they are convinced of its practicality and power, but also convinced that considerable skill is required to activate the process. While a treatment of the requisite skills is a subject in the forthcoming book, briefly, the authors' experience suggests that practitioners often need previous training in order to (1) cognitively internalize the planning process as a discrete series of workable phases, (2) integrate the target reference groups in each phase, and (3) apply the appropriate group roles and processes necessary in each phase of the planning process.

The failure of many program planning endeavors in comprehensive health planning, urban planning, educational planning, new products development, and venture management attests that whatever approach to change is utilized, sophisticated attention to the issues which PPM seeks to cope with is required.

---

14 Once again, however, we hasten to add that PPM is a model for change, not for protest or confrontation, where groups are severely polarized.

15 See André L. Delbecq in collaboration with Andrew H. Van de Ven, *Planning for New Programs in Modern Organizations*. Chicago, Ill.: Scott, Foresman (in press).

REFERENCES

ARNSTEIN, SHERRY R. "A Ladder of Citizen Participation." *J. Amer. Inst. of Planners,* July 1969, 35 (4), 216.

BALES, R. F., and STRODTBECK, F. L. "Phases in Group Problem Solving." In M. Alexis and C. Z. Wilson, *Organizational Decision making*. Englewood Cliffs, N.J.: Prentice-Hall, 1967. Pp. 122–33.

CAMPBELL, J. P. "Individual Versus Group Problem Solving in an Industrial Sample." *J. appl. Psychol.,* 1968, 52 (3), 205–10.

CULBERT, S. A. "Trainer Self-disclosure and Member Growth in Two T Groups." *J. appl. Behav. Sci.,* 1968, 4 (1), 47–74.

DALTON, G. W. "Influence and Organizational Change." Paper presented at the Conference on Organizational Behavioral Models, College of Business Administration, Kent State University, May 16, 1969. Pp. 7–13.

DELBECQ, A. L. "Leadership Styles in Managerial Conferences." *J. Acad. of Mgmt,* December 1964, 7 (4), 225–68.

———. "The Management of Decision-making Within the Firm: Three Strategies for Three Types of Decision-making." *J. Acad. of Mgmt,* December 1967, 10 (4), 329–39.

———. "The Myth of the Indigenous Community Leader." *J. Acad. of Mgmt,* March 1968, 11 (1), 11–26.

DUNNETTE, M. D., CAMPBELL, J., and JAASTAD, KAY. "The Effect of Group Participation on Brainstorming Effectiveness for Two Industrial Samples." *J. appl. Psychol.,* 1963, 47 (1), 30–37.

GORDON, G., and MORSE, E. V. "Creative Potential and Organizational Structure." *Academy of Management Proceedings of 28th Annual Meeting,* Chicago, Illinois, December 1968.

KLEIN, D. C. "Some Notes on the Dynamics of Resistance to Change: The Defender Role." In G. Watson, ed., *Concepts for Social Change.* Washington, D.C.: Cooperative Project for Educational Development, National Training Laboratories, NEA, 1967.

LEADER, A. H. "Creativity in Management." Paper read at 10th Annual Midwest Academy of Management Conference, held at Northwestern University, Evanston, Illinois, April 7–8, 1967.

LIPSKY, M. "Radical Decentralization: A Response to American Planning Dilemmas." Reprint #28. Madison, Wis.: The Institute for Research on Poverty, University of Wisconsin, 1968.

MAIER, N. R. F. *Problem-solving Discussions and Conferences.* New York: McGraw-Hill, 1963. Pp. 247–49.

MOGULOF, M. "Coalition to Adversary—Citizen Participation in Three Federal Programs." *J. Amer. Inst. of Planners,* July 1969, 35 (4), 225–45.

MOYNIHAN, D. P. *Maximum Feasible Misunderstanding: Community Action in the War on Poverty.* New York: The Free Press, 1969.

OSBORN, A F. *Applied Imagination.* New York: Scribners, 1957.

PELZ, D. C., and ANDREWS, F. M. *Scientists in Organizations.* New York: Wiley, 1966. Chaps. 10 and 11.

SCOTT, W. E. "The Creative Individual." *J. Acad. of Mgmt,* September 1965, 8 (3).

TAYLOR, D. W., BERRY, P. C., and BLOCK, C. H. "Does Group Participation When Using Brainstorming Facilitate or Inhibit Creative Thinking?" *Admin. Sci. Q.,* 1958, 3, 23–47.

THOMPSON, JAMES D., and TUDEN, A. "Strategies, Structures, and Processes of Organizational Decision." In J. Thompson, P. Hammond, R. Hawkes, and A. Tuden, *Comparative Studies in Administration.* Pittsburgh, Pa.: University of Pittsburgh Press, 1959.

THOMPSON, VICTOR A. "Bureaucracy and Innovation." *Admin. Sci. Q.,* June 1965, 10 (1), 1–21.

———, and SMITHBURG, D. W. "A Proposal for the Study of Innovation in Organization." Unpublished paper, University of Alabama, Huntsville, 1968.

UTTERBACK, J. M. "The Process of Technological Innovation Within a Firm." *J. Acad. of Mgmt,* March 1971, 14 (1), 75–88.

VROOM, V. H., GRANT, L. D., and COTTON, T. S. "The Consequences of Social Interaction in Group Problem Solving." *Organization Behav. and Human Performance,* 1969, 4, 77–95.

WARREN, R. L. "Model Cities First Round —Politics, Planning and Participation." *J. Amer. Inst. of Planners,* July 1969, 35 (4), 24–56.

25 Problem Design: Policy Alternatives for Service Delivery

ASSESSING SERVICE DELIVERY METHODS: SOME UNSETTLED QUESTIONS

Neil Gilbert

Local social services increased considerably during the 1960s. Stimulated by national legislation to assist communities in dealing with poverty, mental illness, unemployment, delinquency, education, and the general quality of urban life, the development and growth of local services were accomplished, for the most part, with remarkable dispatch and no small amount of confusion. Attendant on this helter-skelter expansion is the increased importance of service-delivery problems. Such problems do not spring from a shortage of ideas about how to improve delivery. On the contrary, social planners and public administrators have many methods of delivering local social services to choose from. Their problems center on resolving their uncertainty about which method will best do the job.

Critical analyses of the delivery of

Reprinted with permission of author and publisher from: Neil Gilbert, "Assessing Service-Delivery Methods: Some Unsettled Questions," *Welfare in Review* 10: 3 (May/June 1972), 25–33.

social services tend to be organized around four kinds of problems: fragmentation, inaccessibility, discontinuity, and unaccountability.[1] Plans to reform the organization and delivery of social services usually concern one or more of these problems, though they rarely concern all.

For a brief operational description of these problems, consider the hypothetical case of Mr. J. After being hurt in an automobile accident, Mr. J is rushed by ambulance to ward A, where he is examined. From ward A he is taken to ward B, where he receives medical treatment. He is then taken to ward C for rest and observa-

[1] Harry G. Bredemeier, "The Socially Handicapped and the Agencies: A Market Analysis," in Frank Reissman, Jerome Cohen, and Arthur Pearl, eds., *Mental Health of the Poor* (New York: The Free Press, 1964); Alfred J. Kahn, "Do Social Services Have a Future in New York?" *City Almanac*, Feb. 1971; Richard Cloward and Frances F. Piven, "The Professional Bureaucracies Benefit Systems as Influence Systems," in Murray Silberman, ed., *The Role of Government in Promoting Social Change* (New York: Columbia University School of Social Work, 1966).

tion. If wards A, B, and C are in different parts of town, operate on different schedules, or provide overlapping services—that's *fragmentation*. If the ambulance disappears after dropping him at ward A—that's *discontinuity*. If the distance between the accident and ward A is too far for the rapidity of services needed, or if Mr. J is not admitted to ward A because of social class, ethnic background, or the like, or he is taken to a ward for mental patients—that's *inaccessibility*. And when any or all of these circumstances obtain and Mr. J has no viable course of redress —that's *unaccountability*.

These problems have many facets, are interconnected, and span a broader range of issues than I describe. Problems of *fragmentation* concern organizational characteristics and relationships, especially coordination, location, specialization, and duplication of services: Are services available in one place? Do agencies try to mesh their services? Problems of *inaccessibility* concern obstacles to a person's entering the network of local social services: Does bureaucratic selectivity based on social class, race, success potential, or other characteristics exclude certain persons from services? Problems of *discontinuity* concern a person's movement through the network of services and the gaps that appear as an agency tries to match resources to needs: Are channels of communication and referral lacking? Problems of *unaccountability* concern relationships between persons served and the decision makers in service organizations: Is the person needing help unable to influence decisions that affect his circumstances? Are the decision makers

in the service organizations he must turn to insensitive or unresponsive to his needs and interests?

SERVICE-DELIVERY METHODS

At least six methods of solving these kinds of problems can be identified. They are *coordination, citizen participation, role attachments, professional disengagement, development of new agencies,* and *purposeful duplication*. To direct the description and analyses of these methods, three questions are posed in descending order of abstraction: What global properties of the delivery system do the methods seek to alter? [2] In what specific forms are these changes manifest? What are their potential consequences?

As depicted in the table, three basic properties of the delivery system are variously affected by the proposed methods. For example, coordination and citizen participation impinge in different ways on the bureaucratic hierarchy of the system. Role attachments and professional disengagement alter the combination of roles and status characteristic of the system.[3] The development of new structures and purposeful duplication change the substantive composition of the elements in the system.

[2] A note on terminology: the designation of a social service delivery system rather than a social service system is to keep the problem focus clear—the delivery of services. The designation, social service system, would be appropriate for discussion of the adequacy and sufficiency of services.

[3] Robert R. Mayer, "Social Change or Service Delivery," in *The Social Welfare Forum* (New York: Columbia University Press, 1970), pp. 99–116.

COORDINATION

Social service workers, along with members of other professional groups, are quick to declare their faith in the generic, the whole man, and the comprehensive method of serving persons in need. They recognize the complexity of social causation and the interdependence of mental, physical, and environmental influences on people's ability to function and their chances in life. At the same time, professional workers are emphasizing specialization and the development of high-powered technical skill within narrowly defined fields of expertise. In one sense, they are advocating the coordination of services to mitigate the strains produced by the juxtaposition of specialization and the comprehensive method in the professional value structure.

Coordination is a method aimed at the development of an integrated social service system through either the centralization or the federation of service agencies.[4] These two processes are exemplified in recent changes made in the organization of local social services in England and in the United States.

In 1970 the British Parliament passed the Local Authority Social Services Act, prescribing a major reorganization of local service agencies. The reorganization entails the centralization of the staffs and functions of the children's and welfare depart-

ments, community development services, home help services, and other local agencies under the administration of newly created Local Authority Social Services Departments (LASSD). Attempts to integrate these services were made in the 1950s through the establishment of local agency coordinating committees. Titmuss[5] notes that these attempts were not successful; local services were still marked by "too much balkanized rivalry in the field of welfare," though demands for better coordination increased. In turning to LASSD as a mechanism for administrative centralization of decisions, the British use what Simon[6] recommends as among the most powerful of coordinative procedures.

However, efforts to increase coordination through administrative unification contain implications beyond merely posing a remedy for service fragmentation. For instance, administrative centralization of services usually increases the organizational distance between the persons served and decision makers. It is with this in mind that Townsend[7] sounds a note of caution about LASSD's creating a monopoly over certain services and the possible effects of such a development on social choice and accountability to service recipients. Centralization may lead to an internalization and, perhaps, heightening of what were previously interorgani-

---

4 Burton R. Clark, "Interorganizational Patterns in Education," *Administrative Science Quarterly*, Sept. 1965, pp. 224–37. He describes these forms of coordination as bureaucratic and interorganizational patterns.

5 Richard Titmuss, *Commitment to Welfare* (New York: Pantheon Books, Inc., 1968).

6 Herbert A. Simon, *Administrative Behavior*, 2d ed. (New York: The Free Press, 1965).

7 Peter Townsend *et al., The Fifth Social Service: A Critical Analysis of the Seebohm Report* (London: Fabian Society, 1970).

zational strains. The potential for intraorganizational conflict is sharpened, especially when a variety of heretofore autonomous agencies with different aims, technologies, and perceptions of the persons they serve and their problems are cast into a unitary organizational mold, as with LASSD.[8]

In addition, the consolidation of services under one administrative structure limits service accessibility to one organizational door. The "single door" access to the service network is a metaphor because the "door" may, in fact, be at a number of centers geographically dispersed throughout a community. It is a "single door" only in the sense that it functions according to the rules and regulations of one administrative authority—service network intake is concentrated in the hands of a relatively few gatekeepers bound by the same set of administrative policies. Operationally, the "single door" could prove to be a mechanism to rationalize service delivery from the standpoint of case referral and continuity or an impervious barrier to the local service network for those persons and groups of persons that, inadvertently or by design, do not fit the administrative criteria of eligibility for service.

Another major way to effect the coordination of services is through federation. This method occasionally involves the geographic centralization of different agency resources but not their administrative unification. Recent efforts along these lines

SYSTEMIC EFFECTS OF SERVICE
DELIVERY METHODS

Methods	Systemic changes
Coordination Citizen participation	Patterns of authority
Role attachments Professional disengagement	Roles and status
Development of new agencies Purposeful duplication	Substantive composition

have been made in the United States through the "neighborhood service centers" sponsored by the Community Action Programs (CAP) of the Office of Economic Opportunity. Federation encompasses a variety of more or less formal and binding arrangements. Its variability is usually reflected in the amount of time, resources, and organizational decision-making authority member organizations invest in the joint enterprise.[9] Warren [10] distinguishes between a federation and a coalition thus: the first is a continuing collaboration with a formal staff structure that has decision-making authority generally subject to ratification by component agencies; the second is formal and ad hoc and agencies do not share decision-making authority or modify their authority to accommodate the arrangement.

Federative arrangements require

[8] Townsend, *ibid.*; Peter J. Hitch, "Organizational Problems and Concepts in the Development of a Unified Social Service Department," *Applied Social Studies*, Feb. 1971, pp. 21–28.

[9] James D. Thompson, *Organizations in Action* (New York: McGraw-Hill, 1967); William Reid, "Interagency Coordination in Delinquency Prevention and Control," *Social Service Review*, Dec. 1964.
[10] Roland L. Warren, "The Interorganizational Field as a Focus for Investigation," *Administrative Science Quarterly*, Dec. 1967, pp. 396–419.

that organizations pool skill, resources, knowledge, and manpower in a cooperative endeavor. The costs to member agencies of such an undertaking frequently are higher than the organizational benefits of coordination.[11] By and large, the goals and policies of local service agencies are not like interlocking pieces of a jigsaw puzzle that given time, patience, and a constructive mentality can be fit neatly into the frame of a common cause. With some difficulty an awkward fit can be accomplished, but at a forfeit of organizational autonomy that many agencies are unwilling to endure. Thus efforts toward federation often result in loose-knit coalitions that fall considerably short of ideal. For example, one study of neighborhood service centers indicates that the component agencies are considered to be "working together" because they are situated in the same center. Though such proximity makes communication easier, it does not dictate cooperation. As the study shows, the component agencies operate as autonomous organizations, responding to their particular goals, policies, and needs, which at times are different from those of the coordination staff, the persons served, and neighborhood residents.[12]

In comparing administrative centralization and federation as means to coordinate local social services, the crucial distinction resides in each structure's control mechanisms —that is, the restrictions and inducements among the component service units. Federative structures involve a voluntary collaboration of autonomous agencies where cooperation is based primarily on reciprocity; units in these structures are not bound to a formal hierarchy of positions based on rational-legal authority, as under a centralized administration such as the LASSD. Compared to bureaucratic authority, reciprocity is a tenuous control mechanism. It is operative, as Dahl and Lindblom [13] note, "provided that the people have the same norms and conceptions of reality." The norms and reality views of the people who administer local service agencies, however, do not always fit this prescription.

CITIZEN PARTICIPATION

Unlike coordination of service methods where redistribution is geared to take place among agencies, citizen participation is aimed at the redistribution of decision-making authority and control between agencies and the persons served. The rationale as applied to delivery systems is that when service recipients choose people like themselves for positions that influence service delivery decisions, they are guaranteed access and accountability. Neither the good will of professional workers (viewed at best as paternalistic and at worst as nonexistent by the most militant advocates of citizen participation) nor bureaucratic rationality is considered sufficiently reliable to secure responsiveness to recipient needs because both professional workers and organizations have multiple objectives, their own

11 Reid, op. cit.
12 Neil Gilbert, Clients or Constituents (San Francisco: Jossey Bass, 1970).

13 Robert A. Dahl and Charles E. Lindblom, Politics, Economics, and Welfare (New York: Harper and Row, 1953).

survival in the system being fore-most.

Similar to coordination methods, the redistribution of authority through citizen participation is distinguished according to different levels or types of participation wherein authority is shared to varying degrees. There are almost as many typologies of citizen participation as there are social scientists who write on this subject; but ignoring the various nuances, three modal types usually emerge.[14] The first is nonredistributive participation or pseudoparticipation, which may involve therapy, education, or plain deception; in any case, it makes no perceptible change in the established pattern of authority. The second is nominal participation or tokenism: citizen influence on decision-making authority is clear and present though only to a degree that makes very little practical difference. The third is redistributive participation or "power to the people": here the shift in authority is such that citizen participants are able to exert substantive influence on decisions affecting the delivery system.

In citizen participation the means is valuable in itself, its value being "democracy." However, a system can be made democratic and at the same time suffer a deterioration in service delivery. If so, the method may be valid for broad political reasons but not for the objectives considered here. The basic assumption, however, is that a democratic delivery system will, indeed, be more responsive to recipient needs than a system where decision making is reserved only for professional persons.

Although participatory democracy connotes the idealized New England townhall meeting of early times where everybody had a right to vote (except, of course, women, slaves, and persons too poor to own land), in practice citizen participation invariably requires the election or appointment of representatives. People simply do not have the time or inclination to participate in the making of every decision that affects them. The point is that, rhetoric notwithstanding, this method must come to grips with the notion of representativeness and the concomitant issues of *which* citizens participate, on *whose* behalf, and *how* they are chosen.

The recent experience of social agencies suggests some of the problematic facets of this method. For instance, neighborhood elections for city councilmen and other representatives to larger governing bodies can differ from neighborhood elections for citizen representation to local service delivery systems in at least one important respect—voter turnout to elect citizen representaitves is, by comparison, usually negligible. In Pittsburgh less-than-2 percent and in Philadelphia less-than-3 percent of eligible residents participated in such elections in recent years.[15] Kramer [16] reports that the "numerous neighborhood elections in San Francisco and Santa

14 For a thorough discussion of the types of citizen participation, see Sherry Arnstein, "A Ladder of Citizen Participation," *Journal of the American Institute of Planners,* July 1969, pp. 216–24.

15 Neil Gilbert, *op. cit.;* Arthur B. Shostak, "Promoting Participation of the Poor: Philadelphia's Anti-Poverty Program," *Social Work,* Jan. 1966, pp. 73–80.
16 Ralph Kramer, *Participation of the Poor* (Englewood Cilffs: Prentice-Hall, 1969).

Clara can best be described as pseudopolitical processes." In addition to this, it is not uncommon for citizen representatives to be appointed by social service agencies or to be self-selected rather than chosen through an electoral process.[17]

Many endeavors to select citizen representatives lack formal accountability mechanisms to insure that the opinions and objectives of participants are valid expressions of local sentiment. In the absence of such accountability, citizen participation could reproduce, on a different plane, the very difficulties it seeks to ameliorate. As Weissman[18] observes, "community control tends to become control of the community by some elements to the exclusion of others and does not necessarily lead to more effective services." Under these circumstances "welfare colonialism" may be replaced by local planning and decision making in which an elite group of citizen activists monopolizes the role of neighborhood spokesman. And, in extreme cases, citizen activists may even become a generation of "political bosses" who accumulate much of the power and many of the pre-

rogatives they opposed in the "welfare colonialists."[19]

ROLE ATTACHMENTS

Social services, in the main, are performed by professional persons from the middle classes. Though services are offered to the entire community, a disproportionate segment of the people in need of services comes from the lower socioeconomic classes. Persons supporting role attachments as a better way to deliver services view the class chasm between servers and recipients as an impasse to movement into and through local delivery systems. They explain this impasse thus: the middle-class professional worker is incapable of understanding the lower-class person's outlook on life; is ignorant about the behavioral patterns and values of the people in the subculture served; doesn't speak their language and is regarded by them as "uptight." This is so partly because some professional workers are officious and partly because the norms of objectivity and impersonal treatment prescribe behavior that may be defined as unfriendly in the eyes of lower-class persons who are ignorant about the behavior and values of the professional subculture, inarticulate by middle-class standards, and are perceived as recalcitrant or even threatening in the eyes of professional persons. From this perspective problems of access and discontinuity are cast more in the shape of social stratification than

17 There is evidence that local citizen elections may improve over time. Harry Specht ("Community Organization Practice," an unpublished manuscript, 1971) indicates that voter turnout in Model Cities elections, though usually low, tends to be higher than turnouts for earlier elections sopnsored by the Economic Opportunity program. For example, nearly 30 percent of eligible voters participated in Trenton's Model Cities election in 1968.

18 Harold Weissman, *Community Councils and Community Control* (Pittsburgh: University of Pittsburgh Press, 1970), p. 174.

19 Neil Gilbert and Joseph Eaton, "Who Speaks for the Poor?" *Journal of the American Institute of Planners,* Nov. 1970, pp. 411–16.

organizational structure.[20] The case is put succinctly by Miller and Reissman.[21]

The agencies must take upon themselves the responsibility for seeing that the individual patient gets to the service, or gets from one service to another. Without the assumption of this responsibility, the concept of continuity of care or services will become a meaningless programmatic shibboleth. Nor can these problems be resolved through administrative improvements alone. *A human link is needed.* [Italics mine.]

This human link is the local nonprofessional aide, a person who, by virtue of his style and special skill, can bridge the gap between professional agencies and lower-class people, serving what Brager [22] describes as a social-class-mediating function. Certainly, there are other general economic and political values that support the employment of local nonprofessional workers, but it is only as expediters of service that their employment concerns our discussion of delivery systems.

At least three potential consequences of this method are self-defeating. First, the employment of nonprofessional workers may translate literally to mean that lower-class persons will receive services that are amateurish or of a lesser quality than are offered by professional

workers; that is, the nonprofessional worker's style and knowledge notwithstanding, the rich get professional service and the poor get participation. Second, even when nonprofessional workers are competent to perform services, efforts to integrate them into the delivery structure normally meet stiff resistance from professional workers. Pruger and Specht,[23] commenting about the source of resistance, say:

It is inevitable because it is rooted in the virtually irresistible structural forces that shape organizational behavior. . . . In the case of the organizationally based professions, the forces that insure organizational discipline complement the pressures that induce professional reliability. And because much of the professional's self-image rests on this perception of his dearly bought competence, competitors arriving on the scene through nontraditional routes must almost certainly be considered impudent upstarts, if not conscious usurpers.

Finally, even when nonprofessional workers are effective in linkage roles and are integrated into the service-delivery structure, the latter will vitiate the former and their effectiveness will wane under pressure to resolve the strains between bureaucratic conformity and the freewheeling style of local workers. After examining the integration of nonprofessional workers into agency structures, Hardcastle [24] concludes

20 Gideon Sjoberg, Richard Brymer, and Buford Farris, "Bureaucracy and the Lower Classes," *Sociology and Social Research,* Apr. 1966, pp. 325–37.

21 S. M. Miller and Frank Reissman, *Social Class and Social Policy* (New York: Basic Books, 1968), p. 207.

22 George Brager, "The Indigenous Worker: A New Approach to the Social Work Technician," *Social Work,* Apr. 1965, pp. 33–40.

23 Robert Pruger and Harry Specht, "Establishing New Careers Programs: Organizational Barriers and Strategies," *Social Work,* Oct. 1968, pp. 21–32.

24 David A. Hardcastle, "The Indigenous Nonprofessional in the Social Service Bureaucracy: A Critical Examination," *Social Work,* Apr. 1971, pp. 56–64.

that the "diminution of the non-professional's indigenous qualities—the emphasis on primary role skills, extemporaneousness, and lower-class behavior and communication patterns—appears inevitable because of the essentially bureaucratic nature of the organization."

PROFESSIONAL DISENGAGEMENT

Though the imperative of bueaucratic conformity, in the opinion of many people in social service, puts a crimp in the style of nonprofessional workers, forcing them to adopt a professional or quasi-professional way of working, it has also been observed that the same imperative seems to inhibit professional functioning. For example, Levy[25] describes a public welfare setting where the discrepancy between the needs of administrators and those of recipients poses an acute moral dilemma for many workers. He suggests that the high turnover rate of workers in this setting was related to the irreconcilability of their inner feelings with the stringent logic of welfare administration. Piliavin[26] puts the case more generally:

Social work has acquired many of the earmarks of a profession, including a professional association that has developed and promulgated standards, goals, and an ethical code for those providing social services. The members of this association and other social workers

25 Gerald Levy, "Acute Workers in a Welfare Bureaucracy," in Deborah Offenbacher and Constance Poster, eds., *Social Problems and Social Policy* (New York: Appleton-Century-Crofts, 1970).
26 Irving Piliavin, "Restructuring the Provision of Social Service," *Social Work,* Jan. 1968, pp. 34–41.

guided by its framework of values encounter a dilemma unknown to their early predecessors—they find agency policies and practices frequently in conflict with avowed professional norms.

Given these circumstances, this line of thought emerges: the way to improve the delivery of social services is not to tinker with bureaucratic structure but rather to disengage from it altogether; that is, professional workers go into private practice on a fee-for-service basis to circumvent the restrictions on service delivery posed by agency policies. In other words, they change roles from that of bureaucrat to that of entrepreneur. As many people who use social services could not afford to support a client fee system, it is further proposed that the financial base for implementing this method be furnished through government grants similar to grants for medical care to the aged.[27]

Allowing, for the sake of argument only, that government financing for private social services can be accomplished, this method has certain apparent limitations for service delivery. The private practitioner may have expertise in public welfare, child guidance, corrections, marital counseling, family service, school social work, services to the aged, and the like, but he cannot possibly be a specialist in all. In this sense he is subject to the same professional myopia as the agency-based worker, except that agencies may incorporate a variety of specialists. What is to prevent the private practitioner from imposing his particular brand of services on the re-

27 Piliavin, *ibid.*

cipient, be it education, therapy, or advocacy, rather than dealing with that person's special needs? And even for the least avaricious, the tendency to interpret recipient problems by the practitioner's field of expertise receives a dash of positive reinforcement in the fee-for-service proposition. As a means to improve the accessibility and coherence of the delivery system, the entrepreneurial model, therefore, may prove in some ways less effective than agency-based practice.

DEVELOPMENT OF NEW AGENCIES

According to this method, fragmentation, inaccessibility, and discontinuity of service, to a degree, are inherent features of delivery systems characterized by the professional - specialized - bureaucratic gestalt. Its objective is to change neither the combination of roles in various elements of the system nor the relationships between these elements through centralization or federation. Its advocates recognize that specialized-professional-bureaucratic services perform important functions despite their drawbacks as delivery mechanisms. Instead of changing roles and the like, this method involves changing the composition of the delivery system by adding a new element—one that is to function independently as a catalyst, to act on other service agencies, to pry open their entrances, and to insure that recipients make the proper service connections. In a word, *access* is to be provided as a social service.

Until recently, the provision of access generally was considered a marginal function of all agencies and professional staffs in the delivery system, rather than a core function around which to organize a distinct set of services. As a marginal function, access is unduly restricted by the narrow perspectives of agency specializations. Under these circumstances the access service relates primarily to the agency's core function instead of particular recipient problem. This phenomenon is not a byproduct of incompetence or malice. It is a normal structural reality of specialized service organizations. To make it easier for recipients to obtain services while maintaining a relatively high degree of specialization, it is proposed that a new structure be added to the delivery system—a "professionally unbiased doorway." [28] This doorway is to be created by developing special agencies offering case-advocacy, advice, information, and referral services to assist recipients in negotiating the bureaucratic maze.

Although it is in many respects a persuasive method, the consequences of access agencies may be more desired than assured: from the recipient's perspective a possible effect of this method is to further fragment and complicate service delivery. Though access services are becoming increasingly important in complex urban societies, they are nevertheless among the least tangible of social services. The recipient thus may see the access agency as merely another bureaucracy to cope with before the proper resources are matched to his needs.

This method is also likely to have

[28] Alfred J. Kahn, "Perspectives on Access to Social Service," *Social Work,* Apr. 1970, pp. 95–102.

a certain influence on the other service agencies in the delivery system. The addition of an access agency suggests that agencies providing other services will cut down on the access services they offer as a marginal function. For instance, pressure would be reduced on these agencies to make special referrals to other agencies for persons they are unable to serve; instead they would merely direct such persons to the access agency. The net effect of transferring the marginal access functions of many organizations to the core function of a single organization is presently unclear regarding the extent to which it lessens traveling time, expense, or confusion in a person's search for service. Moreover, the separation of diagnosis and treatment engendered by this action, though theoretically possible, may prove clumsy in practice.

PURPOSEFUL DUPLICATION

Here the method entails duplication of any or all the services available in the existing system, as compared to the previous method, which provides only for the development of agencies to serve special delivery functions. Purposeful duplication is advanced in two forms that have a surface resemblance but are dissimilar enough to warrant distinction: *competition* and *separatism*.

Competition involves creating duplicate agencies within the delivery system to compete with established agencies for recipients and resources. This method increases choice. More important, competition, in the belief of those who advocate this meth-

od, will invigorate agencies and professional workers, sensitizing them to recipient needs and producing greater enterprise and creative efforts at service delivery. The consequences, however, are not always so fertile as or as compatible with the motives. Instead of a healthy competition for recipients and resources, an internecine conflict may ensue between the powerfully entrenched agencies and those scraping for a foothold in the system, the outcome of which is reasonably predictable.[29]

Separatism differs from competition in both the systemic location of new structures and their purposes for being. New agencies are created and organized and kept *outside* the established delivery system. Competition is likely to be an inadvertent—and unplanned—byproduct of separatism, particularly for resources. The intention is to form an alternative network that would serve certain disadvantaged groups, those that the existing system serves poorly or not at all because of organizational and professional proclivities toward racial, ethnic, and socioeconomic characteristics. Proponents of separatism emphasize that this method contains social and political values for disadvantaged groups that transcend the improvement of service delivery.[30]

Duplicate methods in either form are very expensive. The money may be well spent if the new agencies become a dynamic force for desired

29 Martin Rein, *Social Policy: Issues of Choice and Change* (New York: Random House, 1970).

30 Richard Cloward and Frances F. Piven, "The Case Against Urban Desegregation," *Social Work*, Jan. 1967, pp. 12–21.

changes in the delivery system and reach those persons who are usually excluded from the service network. Against this are the risks of expending scarce resources to produce fruitless conflict and to create even greater fragmentation.

Six major methods of improving the delivery of local social services have been identified by the properties of the delivery system they seek to alter: patterns of authority (*coordination* and *citizen participation*), roles and status (*role attachments* and *professional disengagement*), and substantive composition (*development of new agencies* and *purposeful duplication*). They have been analyzed for their expected and unexpected consequences. And some indication has been given of how one method proposed to cope with one problem of service delivery may exacerbate difficulties in other directions.

All of these methods are plausible ways to develop more effective service delivery; they all contain different limitations and latent dysfunctions that might compromise or vitiate the advantages promised; and though a few methods may be complementary, there are obvious contradictions in using many of them simultaneously. Choices are required.

. . . Currently, policymakers concerned with selecting the right method to reform the delivery of social services operate in a realm of uncertainty. Many empirical questions about delivery methods remain to be answered.

To conclude that more research is needed (which it is), is the unblemished mark of an academician (which I am). To this advice the practitioner may nod abstractly in agreement while he continues to design and implement policy governing service delivery. That is to say in effect—policy choices regarding service delivery may eventually benefit from future investigation, but they will not await the results; choices will be made based on the knowledge we possess, imperfect as it is. Accordingly, if there is a more immediate purpose to be served by this analysis, it is to heighten our recognition of this fact: to fixate on any one method as a panacea to service-delivery problems is to prematurely foreclose the options on other methods of largely untested and untapped potential. Given the present state of knowledge about the design and consequences of service-delivery methods, efforts to exercise fully all of the available options appear to be the more practical policy course.

26 Evaluation: Alternative Models

PROGRAM ASSESSMENT

Eleanor C. Bennett/Marvin Weisinger

Today, program assessment is a key concern of management—both governmental and private. Controversy surrounds it and published contradictions are rampant. Some of the reasons for this controversy and lack of understanding is the relatively recent use of program assessment in the management processes of human services where its purpose may seem antithetical to these services. In addition, the personnel involved in assessing programs and those utilizing the results of such assessments often have conflicting philosophies and differing goals. Consequently, the information-decision-making value of program assessment can get lost or may be interpreted as a spectre capable of damaging worthy programs, productive jobs and creditable reputations.

Part of this difficulty lies in the differing backgrounds (and thus differing philosophies) of the evaluator and the practitioner-administrator. In many cases, the administrator who received his primary training

Reprinted with permission of authors and publisher from: Eleanor C. Bennett and Marvin Weisinger, *Program Evaluation: A Resource Handbook for Vocational Rehabilitation* (New York: ICD Rehabilitation and Research Center, 1975), pp. 1–27.

as a practitioner in the helping services can be quite astute in systematically analyzing the complex problems of clients and recommending appropriate actions. Yet, when he is with systematically analyzing the complex problems of a program and recommending actions, he is somewhat at a loss. In addition, the training of a practitioner emphasizes the solution of client problems with all due speed, without too much regard for economy.

On the other hand, the evaluator's background stresses precision and control. He is often at a loss to understand why the boundaries for acceptable performance for program activities are set so wide.

Communication between evaluator and administrator is often at cross purposes, even though they may be discussing the same things, they use different words. One purpose of this [discussion] is to provide an administrator with a conceptual framework which will aid him to effectively communicate with evaluation staff and to aid him in analyzing his program with the same acumen he analyzes client problems.

It must be clearly understood that the final outcome of any evaluation process is *change*. Evaluation basically is a systematic and objective method of looking at where a program presently stands and estimating how a program can do better. Change is an integral part of this examination—change to serve the clients better and change in program economy. Only through an orderly process of documented program evaluation can justifiable alternatives for action be developed for the evolution of more efficacious and economical programs.

OBJECTIVITY

What sort of information should be used to document current program activity and to justify future change? The answer that comes quickly to mind is, "objective information." Two questions can then be asked, "How objective can an assessment be?" and "How does one objectively assess a program?"

A program assessment can be conducted on one of two major levels of objectivity. The least objective, Level I, is the opinion of experts. That is, it is an assessment based upon the review of project documents or based on an onsite visit by a person recognized as "expert" in the field. The review may be superficial or in depth, but it relies on the previous experience of the reviewer for the ultimate statement of program worth. It is quite conceivable that two experts, reviewing the same program, could present two very different sets of findings. Therefore, choice of this level of objectivity should be avoided whenever possible.

The more objective approach,

Level II, is the systematic collection and analysis of hard data. If this approach is followed, it should produce findings that are reproducible no matter who undertakes the assessment.

Who administers the program assessment depends on the organization of the agency, the finances available for the assessment and the source of the request for assessment. Usually, there are three categories of people assessing programs: consultants or consulting firms, panels of knowledgeable people and departments within the organization.

Exactly who administers the appraisal many times influences the impact of the assessment. For instance, an expert visiting the program on a site visit, or an outside researcher collecting "relevant" data to generate "meaningful" comparisons can be open to attack on such dubious grounds as "lack of familiarity with local conditions" or the researcher's "Ivory Tower" approach. On the other hand, an "inhouse" assessment may be accused of a "white wash" or bias. There is no simple solution to the selection of the evaluator. However, the use of a rigorous objective approach that is replicable can usually be defended against such attacks no matter who administers the assessment.

The answer to the second question "How does one objectively assess a program?" is dependent on a number of factors: the type of information available, the precision required from the conclusions, and the funds available to undertake this assessment. There are three basic means of program assessment, that is, a program may be monitored, evaluated, or be the subject of a special study.

Monitoring is ongoing feedback of information about professional performance and program activities for the purpose of controlling those activities. This type of assessment serves as an indicator of disruption in program activities, but does not necessarily define the nature of the difficulty. No value judgement is offered concerning the "goodness" or "badness" of the program, although application of externally or internally derived standards may offer some kind of statement concerning professional activities. Examples of using monitoring methods are caseflow information and case review. In some instances, ongoing outcome measures are examined to indicate disruption of activities.

Program Evaluation usually examines annual program information and can offer a value judgement on an entire program's worth. It can identify causes of problems or reasons for success. Usually this judgement is based on program outcomes, or the outcomes of program components.

Special studies offer a judgement from the examination of one facet of a program. That facet may be universal, in that it pervades many portions of the program, or it may be highly circumscribed. The final impact of that assessment depends upon what aspect of the program has been examined. For instance, to examine "the effectiveness of counselor performance when serving the culturally disadvantaged" is a pervasive problem encompassing attitudes and program policy. On the other hand, to examine "the effectiveness of white counselor performance in dealing with aged, black alcoholics" is specific to the administration of one program and, as such, is so circumscribed as to be of doubtful utility.

Table I illustrates some of the benefits and limitations of the combinations of level of objectivity and level of assessment. Since the methods, dynamics and value of monitoring are well understood as necessary mechanisms for administrative control, our discussion of this approach is limited. . . .

It can be seen from the above discussion that objectivity is partially a matter of the degree of refinement of information from which judgements are to be made. The remainder of this [discussion] is addressed to that process which is based on the analysis of hard data and is used to evaluate programs. This technique, *program evaluation,* is just now emerging as a program-planning and decision-making tool. "*Special Studies*" may be considered as a limited or circumscribed case of the broader "Program Evaluation." Therefore, any of the following discussions which refer to Program Evaluation may be considered as perfectly applicable to the topic of Special Studies.

A PERSPECTIVE

In reviewing the program evaluation literature, several problems confront the reader. A great deal of literature is directed to extolling program evaluation's virtues as an aid in management, and an equally large collection decries the damage it can and does do, if perspective and methodology are not sound. A smaller body of representative literature discusses technique and methodology. However, these methodology articles are written from what

TABLE 1. BENEFITS AND LIMITATIONS OF PROGRAM ASSESSMENTS

| Level of Objectivity | Level of Assessment | | |
	Monitoring	Special Studies	Evaluation
	Benefits	*Benefits*	*Benefits*
I. Expert's Opinion from	Inexpensive	Inexpensive	Inexpensive
	Not time consuming	Not time consuming	Not time consuming
	May identify problems	May be perceptive	May be perceptive
	Limitations	*Limitations*	*Limitations*
A. Site Visit	Not replicable	Not replicable	Not replicable
B. Annual Report	May not identify problems	May be imprecise	May be imprecise
	May not identify cause	Lack of adequate firm data	Lack of adequate firm data
			May overemphasize minor detail
	Benefits	*Benefits*	*Benefits*
	Ongoing	Precise	Precise
II. Analysis of Hard Data	Identifies problems	Replicable	Replicable
	Replicable	Identifies cause	Identifies cause
			Broad in scope
	Limitations	*Limitations*	*Limitations*
	Does not identify cause	Expensive	Expensive
	More expensive than Level I	May be time consuming	Time consuming
		Limited in scope	

appears to be many conflicting points of view. Actually, close examination reveals only two or three points of view.

The first point of view is that of administrators who have learned to analyze their programs by using several different models. Probably the most popular model speaks of *input analysis, process evaluation* and *outcome evaluation.* A second model refers to levels of program responsibility or control and mentions *the institution* (program), *managerial functions,* and the *technical core* (service delivery) (15).

An administrator, when considering his program, may view it as a system to be controlled and regulated. He then speaks of specific parts such as inputs, process, outputs, and some sort of a "feedback loop." [1] The analyses of these parts may be defined as follows:

Input Analysis—the study of the resources (men, money and materials) used by the program to accomplish its goal.

Process Evaluation—the study of a combination of program operations and techniques used by a program to accomplish its goal. Criteria usually are addressed to questions of conformity to, and expectations of the respective professions involved. These criteria are usually called *Quality.* Many times the statistics used to monitor programs are composed of these types of data.

[1] Program monitoring and evaluation are part of the feedback loop.

Outcome Evaluation—the study of the results of a program's activities. Usually, the criterion used is the degree to which programs have attained goals. Outcome evaluation is frequently obtained through follow-up studies.

The second model relates to specific levels of program responsibility (responsibility model)—the institutional level, managerial level and technical level. This breakdown may be considered as a reduction to *program level,* that is:

Institution—(a program) is supported by a larger social system which legitimatizes the program's goals. Stated another way, we can say society expects a vocational rehabilitation program to assist the disabled to become meaningfully employed.

Technical—(service delivery) is a sub-organization or level of program. Its function is to provide the services to clients and so accomplish the program's goal.

Managerial—(program management) is another sub-organization or level of program. Its function is to mediate between services, and between services and clients. In addition, it procures resources and aids in assuring appropriate outputs.

A second point of view is that of the evaluator who usually addresses his perspective to methodology. This perspective can be divided into two camps—the researcher who speaks of comparisons and goal attainment, and the systems analyst-operations researcher who speaks of effectiveness and survival models (8). For the purposes of practical illustration, the popular goal-attainment model may be considered as an *inductive* approach, while the systems models usually are *deductive* in nature. Research constructs hypotheses about the way programs work, and the systems approach builds models describing program structure, functions and goals. Below are our definition . . . of the two approaches:

Research Approaches seek to evaluate programs through making certain comparisons between variables. The basic question is, has the program caused a change in a variable? For example, has the introduction of a PA/VR program caused more PA recipients to leave the welfare rolls? These comparisons may be: before vs. after introduction of a program, between programs operating in differing localities, between clients in a special program and clients who did not have the benefit of the special program, between client behavior before entering the program and after leaving the program, etc. Of course, certain steps must be taken to assure comparability of the data.

A special case of the research approach is the *Goal Attainment Model.* In this case, in order to determine program effectiveness, the broad objectives of the program are translated into measurable criteria and a comparison is made between these criteria and actual program performance, i.e., has the program attained its goal? *Standard Setting* or *Comparison of Planned vs. Actual Performance* are special cases of the Goal Attainment Model in which the goals are set by some formula or by professional judgement and are not necessarily one-to-one reflections of total program objectives.

Systems Approaches—seek to evaluate programs by describing the organizational structure of a program, the stated functions of the program, and the process by which that organizational structure with those functions accomplishes the program's objective. That is, the analytic process tries to build a model of the program, uses the model to simulate the program, and then offers more efficient and/or effective alternatives of action (optimization). An enormous amount of information is needed for this type of evaluation, together with a great deal of data processing effort.

A SUGGESTED MODEL

"The purpose of the evaluation process is to provide policy-makers with the basic data necessary for them to make decisions wisely. Impact evaluations of programs should provide five essential sets of information. First, they should provide all of the data necessary to determine if a particular program should be continued. Second, they should determine which of the alternative programs achieve greatest gains for a given cost. Third, evaluations should present information on the components of each program and the mixes of components which are most effective for a given expenditure so that maximum operating efficiency can be achieved. Fourth, evaluation should provide the first three types of information for persons with different characteristics so that a decision-maker may determine which individuals are best served by each program. Finally, in the course of evaluating existing programs, data should be gathered which will suggest new methods to attack problems. To date, no evaluation of programs has provided all this information" (2).

In short, the primary goal of program evaluation is to ask "Which programs are worthwhile?" or "Which programs work best?" and

then state "Why they are worthwhile" or "Why they work best." These findings may produce information for program decision-making that may result in the implementation of a change.

Suggested below is a model that approaches some of the issues for the systematic evaluation of programs.

CLASSES OF MEASURES

Basically, there are five classes of measures or criteria that are used to estimate various aspects of program worthiness. The first class of measures enumerates the resources used by the program (effort). The second class examines the results of program service in terms of broad social change (impact). The third class attempts to estimate specific client outcomes or changes (effectiveness). The purpose of the fourth class is to determine the economics of program operation in comparison with program accomplishment (efficiency). The final class of measures, *Quality,* has come to mean different things to different people. One accepted global definition is that quality is a statement of program "goodness." A second definition used equates quality with effectiveness. That is, it uses process measures . . . to represent program effectiveness. The perspective taken in this [discussion] is that Quality estimates the conformance of program activity and professional activity to accepted standards of the day. It is one reading of ongoing program process. These five measures are derived from the administrator's system breakdown of input, process, and output, where effort represents input, quality is equivalent to process, impact and effectiveness represents output, and efficiency is an input-output ratio. More specifically:

Effort is a statement of fact about the "amount and kinds of program activities used to reach program objectives." It refers to staff time, activity and commitment, and to the allocation and use of material resources (funds, space, equipment, etc.). In addition, it takes into account ancillary resources used (outside consultation, media, public relations, etc.). It answers the question "What did I do?" (14, 16).

Impact is a statement based on how the program was able to affect a broad social change together with the utility of this program technique. Usually, cost/benefit or cost/effectiveness is used for this type of evaluation.[2]

Effectiveness is a statement of fact about how well the objectives of the program were met, or a statement of fact about how well the program components functioned to meet the program objectives or the program components' objectives. Effectiveness measures answer the question "Has Vocational Rehabilitation program accomplished its objective?" or "Have clients, who are rehabilitated by Vocational Rehabilitation, gotten jobs?" In other words, "How has the program changed clients' behavior or performance?" (5, 9, 14, 16).

Efficiency is a rate that is produced when *effort* (inputs, staff time, activities, salaries, physical facilities and purchased service) expended by a program is compared to the program's *effectiveness*

2 Impact is the same as effectiveness, but on a much broader scale; that is, it can be thought of as a long-range socially pervasive change, whereas, effectiveness is usually thought of as simply attaining goals or a circumscribed change. In many cases, impact criteria are very difficult to establish and data very costly to collect Therefore, this discussion only considers effectiveness.

(output). It answers the question "Can the same program results (output) be achieved by either reducing the effort expended or by choosing other less costly alternatives of action?" 4, 11, 16).

Quality is a judgement statement made about professional competence, acceptability of services to the client and the setting of minimum performance standards by legislative and regulatory bodies. It answers the question "How well did you do what you did?" or "How well did you use the knowledge you had?" (1, 7, 16).

PROGRAM LEVEL

Having established and defined proxy measures for the system elements (input, process, outcome) the "responsibility model" (program, program management and service delivery), was selected as a suitable outline for analysis. The goals of each organizational element are defined below.

Program—goals are to meet society's expectation of a Vocational Rehabilitation organization.

Program Management—goals are to secure and organize inputs for the system (funds, staff, facilities, referrals) and then assure appropriate outputs (closures).

Service Delivery—(technical component) —goals are to perform the process of rehabilitating the disabled.

Figure 1 visually represents the conceptual outline for a program evaluation model that will include input analysis, process analysis, and outcome analysis (goal attainment) or measures of effort, effectiveness, efficiency and quality broken down by program level.

	Measure			
Program Level	Effort	Effectiveness	Efficiency	Quality
Total Program				
Program Management				
Service Delivery				

FIGURE 1.   Proposed model for program evaluation in Vocational Rehabilitation.

Using this matrix, it can be seen that any program level may be assessed by any class of measures. For example, a program evaluation may measure the effectiveness and efficiency of the entire program and the efficiency of program management, service delivery, etc. It is this procedure of measuring the program levels with multiple measures which will provide the most powerful (therefore the most defensible) program evaluation.

Many of the other terms which are so frequently discussed when referring to program evaluation, are specific methodologies or mathematical techniques used in estimating program effectiveness or efficiency. For instance, cost benefit is a measure of impact, while case review is a way to judge the quality of coun-

selor performance, but more importantly, it is a way to gather data for studying program effectiveness.

A WORD ON INDICES

Indices are counts, rates, ratios, or scales used to represent a class of measures. For example, a popular index is "the number of clients who gained jobs." This is used as an indication of program effectiveness. The relatedness of job placement to vocational training may be used to indicate the quality of counselor performance. There are many similar administrative yardsticks that are currently maintained and comprise a compendium of program evaluation measures. Table 2 is an illustration matching some of these popular indices with the specific measures and program levels.

Indices also provide elements necessary for the development of standards. For instance, a ratio made between annual accepted cases and cases closed (Status 26) may be used as a standard for monitoring programs. However, a second element necessary in the development of a standard is a judgment of the usefulness of that ratio as a standard. This judgment is usually arrived at by one of several different methods: the use of expert opinion, normative standards, the use of empirical evidence from outstanding research efforts, or the use of ratios from outstanding state programs.

SOME ADDITIONAL CONSIDERATIONS

Development of Evaluation Criteria from Program Objectives. A program may be considered worthwhile when it meets two basic requirements; the objective (i.e., goal or purpose) of the program is reasonable, and the program reaches this goal.

In most cases, consideration is not given to the *reasonableness* of program objectives. Therefore, no consideration is given to the reasonableness of the criteria developed from program objectives to measure program effectiveness. That is, if a program objective is to move the handicapped into gainful employment, one possible effectiveness criterion is the number of clients that are employed some time after completion of the program. In many instances, however, program objectives cannot

be so easily translated into evaluation criteria because these objectives are not really reasonable. Some avowed program objectives may consist more of rhetoric than potential, because they may have been established only in response to political considerations. In other cases, the statement of program purpose is so vague and diffuse that development of measurable criteria that reflect these objectives becomes exceedingly difficult if not impossible. Further, to try to use evaluation criteria that attempt to reflect overstated or vague program objectives may result in an evaluation that "proves" the program a failure. It is only with ingenuity that the evaluator can come up with reasonable criteria against which the program can be measured. In addition, he must use his abilities to convince decision makers that these criteria truly reflect program objectives, and that the resultant findings truly reflect program accomplishment.

The second factor which should be taken into consideration is the *time frame* of the program and the *environmental pressures* that impinge upon the program during the period being considered. For instance, a day care program was established in a district to assist AFDC mothers to work. Some time after the initiation of the program, this district's job market became depressed. The objectives of the program were, of course, not met—not because day care does not work, but because the objective is presently not reasonable. It might be noted in passing, that there are instances when a program objective is not reasonable at the time a program is planned. In the above example, if

TABLE 2. EXAMPLES OF INDICES USED IN PROGRAM EVALUATION

Program Level	Measures			
	Effort	Effectiveness	Efficiency	Quality
1. Program	Annual No. of Clients	Annual No. of Status 26* / Annual No. Status 08, 26, 28, 30*	Annual VR Budget / Annual No. Status 26 : Average Weighted Closure Status	Adherence to Regulations
2. Service Delivery	Annual Cost per Service	Annual No. Status 26s	Total Service Cost / Annual No. Status 26	Adherence to Regulations
a. Counselor Performance	No. of Contract Hours per Client	Annual No. Status 26 / No. of Counselors	No. Contract Hours per Counselor / Annual No. Status 26	Rehabilitation Counselor Rating Scale
3. Program Management	Program Management Budget	Profile of Organizational Characteristics	Management Budget / Annual VR Budget	
a. Administrative Function	Procurement of Satisfactory Sources for Input and Output from the Program			
b. Community Relations	Cost of Community Relations Functions	Annual No. Acceptances / Annual No. Referrals	Annual No. Acceptances / Annual No. Referrals : Cost of Community Relations	Nature of Interagency Agreements
c. Staffing	Annual $ Spent on Recruiting	No. of Staff Hired in Job Description	$ Spent on Recruitment / No. of Special Staff Hired	Experience of Staff
d. Inservice Training	No. of New Techniques Presented to Staff	No. Who Use Techniques / No. of Staff Who Could Use Techniques	$ Spent on Training : No. 26 Closures After Training / No. 26 Closures Before Training	Experience of Training Staff
e. Fiscal Administration	Knowledge of No. of Sources of Funds Available	No. of Sources of Funds Received / No. of Available Sources	Annual VR Budget / Total Cost of Fiscal Administration	Adherence to Regulations

Status 08—Closed from Referral, Applicant, or Extended Evaluation Statuses. This status has been provided to furnish a means for identifying all persons not accepted for vocational rehabilitation services, whether closed from referral status (00), applicant status (02), or extended evaluation (06). All persons processed through referral, applicant, and/or extended evaluation, and not accepted into the active caseload for vocational rehabilitation services, will be closed in this status.

Status 26—Closed Rehabilitation. Cases closed as rehabilitated must as a minimum: (1) have been declared eligible, (2) have received appropriate diagnostic and related services, (3) have had a program for vocational rehabilitation services formulated, (4) have completed the program insofar as possible, (5) have been provided counseling as an essential rehabilitation service, and (6) have been determined to be suitably employed *for a minimum of 60 days.*

Status 28—Closed Other Reasons Before Individualized Written Rehabilitation Program Initiated. Cases closed in this category are those cases which, although accepted for rehabilitation services, did not progress to the point that rehabilitation services were actually initiated under a rehabilitation plan. Included here are cases which are transferred to another state rehabilitation agency, either within the state, or in some other state.

Status 30—Closed Other Reasons Before Individualized Written Rehabilitation Program Initiated. Cases closed in this category are those cases which, although accepted for rehabilitation services, did not progress to the point that rehabilitation services were actually initiated under a rehabilitation plan.

f. *Upper Performance Level.* The upper performance level for a data element is defined as the average value (of all agency averages) for the data element, plus one standard deviation. (The average and the standard deviation are computed over the population of individual agency averages.)

g. *Lower Performance Level.* The lower performance level for a data element is defined as the average value (of all agency averages) for the data element, minus one standard deviation.

the day care program was planned when the job market was already depressed, the objective is unreasonable and the program is doomed to failure in advance.

The Environment. In too many cases, programs are evaluated as if they were operating in a vacuum. In the illustration above, it was a depressed job market that was unexpected at the time the program was planned that caused the ultimate "failure" of the program. This is only one environmental influence that can impinge on a program and alter measures of final outcome. It is the astute evaluator who will look at the environment in which a program operates for such variables as other programs competing for clients, job market, social acceptance of the program by the public and decision-makers, etc. No program functions outside of its environment, and careful consideration of these environmental factors is important in any program evaluation.

Goal and Time Frames. Many times the evaluation literature speaks of immediate, intermediate and long-term evaluating goals. Usually, these time-frame types of goals are used in discussions concerning evaluations of innovative or demonstration programs. In most instances, immediate goals are effort measures and question whether the program has invested the necessary resources to make a program work. Intermediate goals are usually quality measures, and they question whether the program staff have followed the clinical techniques set forth. Long-term goals are usually effectiveness measures and they question whether the program outcome was satisfactory, given

that the necessary resources were accumulated and the prescribed techniques were used.

The "Follow up" Study. An entire program may be evaluated by following up clients, with given variables or indices (had job at closure), showing a client's behavior change. These follow-up measures always show outcome and therefore are effectiveness measures. In this discussion we will speak of "Effectiveness Studies" which refer to the type of measures used, rather than follow-up studies which speak of a point in time in a client's case history. In short, . . . both Effectiveness Studies, Outcome Studies, and Follow-up studies are one and the same thing!

Evaluation of Sequential Activities. It is not appropriate to evaluate the effectiveness of any single step when that step is part of a sequential set of activities. That is, it is not feasible to evaluate "placement" effectiveness when the index used is dependent on the performance of the client "evaluation" and "training" steps. For instance, if the evaluation staff knows the training department wants to maintain classes of twenty clients and it recommends fifteen suitable clients and five less suitable clients, training may then "train" all twenty, but placement still may only be able to place the fifteen "best" clients. Is placement then ineffective? The exception to this rule is the referral step and the final outcome step. Referral is not proceeded by any program activity and outcome reflects the total program accomplishment. . . .

The purpose of program evaluation is to:

—determine which are the best programs and why;
—suggest ways to strengthen existing programs;
—suggest new ways to solve problems.

This is best achieved by the analysis of hard data, using measures of effort, effectiveness, efficiency and quality. Hard data measures are rates, ratios and index numbers which have been extracted from counts, costs, time, rating scales, psychological test results, etc. The most powerful evaluations are those in which both the entire program and program components are examined.

Because of their ability to evaluate all aspects of a program, the most appropriate approaches are the Research Approach, which examines program objectives, and the Systems Approach, which examines the program structure and functions used to reach program objectives.

Further, follow-up studies which refer to a point-in-time in a client's case history are actually measuring program effectiveness. Therefore, follow-up studies and effectiveness studies are one and the same thing. The term describing the measure (effectiveness) is preferred over the term describing the point in time (follow-up). . . .

APPROACHES TO EVALUATION

. . . There are two basic evaluation approaches: the research approach and the systems approach. Both have many variations with varying degrees of accuracy and cost. They represent two different ways of thinking about problems, goals and programs. Briefly, the research approach utilizes an inductive way of thinking. This means, specific facts, combined in some way, will show a relationship from which a general theory can be drawn. The systems approach is deductive in that it takes a general overview of a program, breaks it into specific units and then draws conclusions.

RESEARCH APPROACH

In many cases the research approach uses two different population groups to compare the effects of one type of service or program against another type of service or program, or one type of service against no service. The population group that receives no service or the non-experimental type of service is called a *control group*. Hatry (9) has suggested five evaluation designs that provide reasonable comparisons. These are:

Before vs. after program comparison. "Compares program results from the same jurisdiction measured at two points in time: immediately before the program was implemented and at some appropriate time after implementation. . . . This design often is the only type which is practical when available time and personnel are limited. It is also appropriate when the program's duration is short, of narrow scope, and when the conditions measured have been fairly stable over time."

Time trend projection of pre-program data vs. actual post-program data. "Compares actual post-program data to estimated data projected from a number of time periods prior to the program." "This design is useful where there appears to be an underlying trend (upward or downward) over a period of time that would seem likely to have continued if the new program had not been introduced." Careful consideration must be given to any other changes that might be altering this trend or will alter this trend.

Comparisons with similar jurisdictions or population segments not served by this program. "Compares data from the jurisdiction where the program is operating with data from other jurisdiction where the program is not operating. . . . This design protects somewhat against attributing change to a specific program when in reality external factors that affect many local governments are responsible for bringing about the change."

Controlled Experimentation. "Compares pre-selected, similar groups, some of whom are served and some of whom are not (or are served in different ways). The critical [aspect] in this design is that the comparison groups are pre-assigned before program implementation so that groups are as similar as possible except for the program treatment." Traditionally, this design has been used when change in client behavior is anticipated.

Comparisons of planned vs. actual performance. "Compares actual, post-program data targets set in prior years—either before program implementation or at any period since implementation." This design establishes goals or target numbers of clients to be rehabilitated, or costs per rehabilitation to be expended within a given period of time and then examines actual performance relative to these goals. . . .

The major difficulty with this last approach is the determination of goals. If the number of clients to be rehabilitated is set too low, then the program will surely reach the goal and be "successful" as far as "effectiveness" measures are concerned. (It might not be as successful if efficiency is examined.) If, on the other hand, the numbers are set too high, the program will be a failure or only the very "best" cases will be selected for service so that the number of Status 26's can be maximized. Some effort must be made to insure that the planned performance is a realistic estimate of what the program can expect to accomplish.

Minimally, how the projected goals were established should be explained in enough detail so that the reader understands the reasons and justifications for using a specific number for a program goal.

In Standard Setting or Expectancy Setting, formulas are sometimes derived from previous program performance so that present program activity can be quantified and compared. Thus, means may be computed for several variables for previous time periods and then weights are assigned to these means. A global picture of performance is then developed from these means and weights.

Clearly, the major function of the above evaluation designs is to measure the changes in performance of the program clients by identifying those changes that can be reasonably attributed to the program's services. . . . In order to evaluate efficiency and quality, the same types of comparison designs would be used, but different measures would be employed. . . . In choosing an evaluation design, three additional factors must be considered: timing (retrospective or prospective), the funds available, and the accuracy desired. "The first four designs discussed above are progressively more expensive, with the fourth usually considerably more expensive than the others. The first three and the fifth can often be accomplished with but a very few man-months of analytical effort, the amount depending heavily on the amount of special data collection required. The fourth design will likely take many calendar months and possibly years. . . . The designs [other than the last] are also progressively more effective in providing, by far, the most reliable results. The designs presented above are not either/or choices. Some or all of the first three [and the fifth] are in fact, often used together . . ." (9).

Using comparative points of time, evaluation may concomitantly examine technological change and/or a program process.

Technological change or change in program philosophy, or changes in therapeutic technique may have an impact on agency operation or clinical services. Following the introduction of these changes, the obvious question becomes, "Did this technological change make the program more effective, more efficient, or were higher quality services provided?" The purpose of such an evaluation is to determine, first, whether the new procedure is actually being followed and second, that changes in program effectiveness can be attributed to this new procedure (all other factors being held constant). This type of evaluation answers the question, "Is procedure X in fact being done and, in fact, is this change making a better program?" or "We have just started to use screen-in, screen-out procedures this year. Now we have a higher rate of Status 26's. Did the counselors really use the screen-in—screen-out procedures and is this contributing to the higher closure rate?" (12) This approach represents a combination of process and outcome evaluation.

SYSTEM APPROACH

The systems approach has developed rapidly because of the advent of computers. Prior to this, the processing and analyzing of the large volume of data required in this approach was not realistic. There are several popular analytic techniques used today. These include operations research, cost-benefit analysis, systems analysis, and systems engineering.

Operations research is the application of scientific methods, techniques and tools to problems involving the operation of a system so as to provide those in control of the system with optimum solutions to problems. In other words, operations research is the application of scientific method to the problems inherent in programs for the purpose of finding solutions to these problems. The problems, because they center on operational aspects of programs, will consistently involve costs. The methodology used in operations research follows the scientific method. One of the most popular applications of the operations research approach is cost/benefit.

Cost-Benefit/Cost-Effectiveness Analyses are becoming increasingly popular as evaluative tools in various fields. They started as analytical tools in the decision-making process of defense strategies and policies, and have now extended into human service areas such as rehabilitation program evaluation, health services effectiveness and the like.

"Both cost-benefit and cost-effectiveness analyses have their foundations in the operations research approach. Cost-benefit analysis can be applied wherever program inputs (costs) and outputs (benefits) are both measurable in money terms. The cost effectiveness approach is applicable whenever both the program inputs are measurable in monetary terms but program outputs are not.

"Broadly defined, the cost-benefit approach is an analytical study designed to assist a decision maker in identifying a preferred choice among possible alternatives. The cost effectiveness approach may be defined as an . . . 'attempt to minimize dollar cost, subject to some mission requirement (which may not be measurable in dollar terms) or conversely to maximize some physical measure of output subject to a budget constraint.'

"CB/CE, as approaches to decision making, have their own share of limitations and virtues, like all other analytical tools. Their limitations are those inherent in all analyses of choice. While CB/CE are readily applicable in evaluating projects which give rise to a stream of purely private benefits and private costs, they become increasingly tenuous for projects which generate significant externalities. The greater the magnitude and range of exter-

nalities generated by a project the more difficult it is to apply CB/CE analysis.

"While some sort of social discount rate may be used in the evaluation of such projects, it is the choice of the discount rate figure that is problematic. The choice of a social discount rate is arbitrary and by sufficiently lowering this discount rate, any investment can be made to look profitable." (13).

The above problem of defining *costs, benefits* and *externalities* (spill-over effects) must be clarified. In order to define what money represents *cost,* an illustration will be given. If General Motors produces a car, the cost of producing that car includes expenditures for central management staff, sales, promotion, depreciation of capital investments, and those unsold cars that are rejected and cannot be sold. Applying this concept to vocational rehabilitation, costs should include program costs (services, administration, purchased services and overhead) services free to V.R., cost of recycling clients, and client earnings forgone (3). *Benefits,* on the other hand are more difficult to estimate. The problem involves the question of how to estimate the future income of rehabilitated clients. Questions surrounding salary increases and therefore, increased tax returns must be asked. Other questions surrounding the *externalities* generated in the rehabilitation process must also be considered. These include such things as the handicapped father who cannot work, but following rehabilitation, can stay at home and supervise the running of the household, thus allowing his wife to support the family. "In addition to this major limitation in the application of CB/CE to social programs, other issues involve the necessity of (1) specifying meaningful objectives or measurement goals; (2) predetermining adequate measures of performance; (3) developing viable policy and program alternatives against which to measure the cost benefit and/or cost effectiveness of any given policy or program" (13).

"Despite the limitations and difficulties inherent in the CB/CE approaches, both have the potential for contributing to more systematic and efficient decisions relative to social program planning and implementation. They are one type of tool to help the decision maker to understand relevant policy and program alternatives, estimates of risks, and estimates of possible pay-offs associated with varying courses of action" (13).

This brief presentation points out the most important strengths and weakness of cost/benefits and cost/effectiveness studies. . . .

Systems Analysis describes a program (or system) in terms of the structure of the system and sub-systems, and the processes by which the function of that system and sub-system are accomplished. (1) *Structure* is the organizational breakdown of a program by levels and components. For instance, it may be broken down into levels of responsibility—commissioner, middle management, and the counselors who render services; or it may mean the system divided by programs, such as physically disabled, mentally ill, PA/VR, etc. Also included in Systems Analysis is a description of the community's expectation of the program and the program's expectations of the community. The analysis of this relationship is usually examined through communication, financial support, committee attendance, etc. (2) *Function* means the activities performed by that structural unit to accomplish program objectives. For example, the commissioner might be responsible for policy formulation, goal setting and the over-all program responsibility. Baumheier developed a structural systems analysis based on responsibility and then identified five functions for each structural unit. These five functions were: problem identification, policy formulation and goal setting, planning, program operation, and evaluation. (3) *Process* describes how the structural unit operates to perform its function.

In order to define the structure, function, and process of a system, consistent use of certain analytic techniques has been made. These include space and layout analysis, analysis of records, forms and reports, methods and procedures analysis, organization studies, and analysis of communication channels. The specific tools employed usually include flow charting, model building, definition of the basic resources of staff, their level of knowledge and information, money available, and the identification of what data or information is needed to reach the program's objective or goal.

Systems Analysis may range from description, to analysis, to forecasting or prediction of the feasibility of alternatives. The major difference between systems analysis and operations research is the scale of the project and the time projection. Operations research provides more immediate solutions to problems.

"One factor to be kept in mind, is that comprehensive quantitative systems analysis to evaluate programs requires large scale commitment of financial resources, a high degree of research sophistication, and a total program commitment to evaluate goals. The reality is that the most rigorous type of systems evaluation is not feasible in many, or most, applied social program situations. This is not to say that evaluation methodology should not be defined and carried out as rigorously as possible, or that power is not lost when standards are less rigorous. However, it is to suggest that some comprehensive systems approaches are the only feasible approaches in many situations and that with care they can provide meaningful information to serve as a valuable planning and evaluation tool" (6).

Systems Engineering is a broad term usually associated with the design of new systems and the redesign of old systems. Historically, systems engineering implied the arrangement of physical components of some system, such as the arrangement of computers in an information system. Presently, the term has been broadened to include the design of any system. The purpose of systems engineering is to design all program components to interrelate with one another and for the program to interrelate with the total system. For instance, if a new PA/VR project was being initiated, the systems engineer would want to coordinate the new program with all existing programs. The method employed to design a plan would be flow charting of clients, information, and staff effort, and the establishment of an information-decision system. (10).

REFERENCES

1. AMERICAN PUBLIC HEALTH ASSN. *A Guide to Medical Care: Vol. I.* Washington, D.C., 1965.
2. BORUS, M. E., and W. R. TASH. *Measuring the Impact of Social Action Programs: A Primer.* Ann Arbor: University of Michigan and Wayne State University, Institute for Labor and Industrial Relations, 1970.
3. CONLEY, R. W. "A Benefit-Cost Analysis of the Vocational Rehabilitation Program." *Journal of Human Resources,* 4:2 (Spring 1969).
4. DENISTON, O. L., I. M. ROSENSTOCK, W. WELCH, and V. A. GETTING. . . . "Evaluation of Program Efficiency." *Public Health Reports,* 83:7 (July 1968).
5. DENISTON, O. L., I. M. ROSENSTOCK, and V. A. GETTING. "Evaluation of Program Effectiveness." *Public Health Reports,* 83:4 (April 1968).
6. DERR, J. M., and E. S. BAUMHEIER. *Systems Approach to the Evaluation of Social Intervention Programs.* Denver: University of Denver, Social Welfare Research Institute, May, 1973.
7. DONABEDIAN, A. "Evaluating the Quality of Medical Care." *Milbank Memorial Quarterly,* 44:3 (Part 2) (July 1966).
8. *Florida Difficulty Index in Achieving Rehabilitation.* Tallahassee: Division of Vocational Rehabilitation, 1973.
9. HATRY, H., R. E. WINNIE, and D. FISK. *Practical Program Evaluation for State and Local Government.* Washington, D.C.: Urban Institute, 1973.
10. INSTITUTE OF REHABILITATION SERVICES. *Training Guide in Caseload Management for Vocational Rehabilitation Staff.* Washington, D.C.: Dept. of HEW, Vocational Rehabilitation Admin., 1965.
11. JAMES, G. "Planning and Evaluation of Health Programs." In E. Confrey, ed., *Administration of Community Health Services.* Chicago: International City Managers Assn., 1961.
12. MACMAHON, B., T. F. PUGH, and G. B.

HUTCHINSON. "Principles in Evaluating Community Mental Health Programs." *American Journal of Public Health,* 51 (1961).

13. RAICHUR, L., and E. C. BAUMHEIER. *Overall Comments of the Cost-Benefit/ Cost-Effectiveness Approach.* Denver: University of Denver, Social Welfare Research Institute, May, 1973.

14. SUCHMAN, E. *Evaluative Research:* *Principles and Practices in Public Service and Social Action Programs.* New York: Russell Sage Foundation, 1967.

15. THOMPSON, J. D. *Organizations in Action.* New York: McGraw-Hill, 1967.

16. TRIPODI, T., P. FELLIN, and I. EPSTEIN. *Social Program Evaluation: Guidelines for Health, Education, and Welfare Administration.* Itasca, Ill.: F. E. Peacock, 1971.

27 Evaluation: Potentials of PPBS

THE PLANNING, PROGRAMMING, AND BUDGETING SYSTEM IN THE DEPARTMENT OF HEALTH, EDUCATION, AND WELFARE: SOME LESSONS FROM EXPERIENCE

Alice M. Rivlin

INTRODUCTION

In this paper, I take the opportunity to look back on an operation in which I have been, until recently, deeply immersed. I have just left the Department of Health, Education, and Welfare after three years of working to implement the planning, programming, budgeting system. This is a good chance to set down briefly my own thoughts on what was accomplished, what the difficulties were, and what could be done better or differently in the future.

To implement the PPB system, Secretary John W. Gardner established a new office under an assistant secretary for program coordination (later and more aptly called planning and evaluation). I suspect he

Reprinted with permission of author and publisher from: Alice M. Rivlin, "The Planning, Programming, and Budgeting System in the Department of Health, Education, and Welfare: Some Lessons from Experience," in Robert Haveman and Julius Margolis, eds., *Public Expenditure and Policy Analysis* (Chicago: Rand McNally College Publishing Company, 1970), pp. 502–17.

would have done this even without the impetus of the president's directive on PPBS. A new secretary trying to understand and manage the vast, sprawling Department of Health, Education, and Welfare clearly needed a staff of his own to analyze where the department's resources were going, what was being accomplished, and how the job could be done better.

We conceived of our mission as that of helping the secretary make better—or at least more informed—decisions about the allocation of resources among the many programs and possible programs of the department. These decisions would be reflected primarily in the department's budget and legislative program.

We proceeded on six assumptions:

1. Decisions will be better if you know what you are trying to do—if objectives are stated and resources devoted to the accomplishment of a particular objective are grouped together.
2. Decisions will be better if information is available on how resources are presently being used—by major objectives, ways in which objectives are being carried out, types of people being served, and so forth.

3. Decisions will be better if the effectiveness of present programs is evaluated.
4. Decisions will be better if alternative ways of accomplishing objectives are considered and analyzed.
5. It makes sense to plan ahead—to decide first what the department should be doing several years in the future, and then what immediate legislative and budgetary changes are needed to move in the desired direction.
6. It is good to be systematic about decision making—to follow an explicit procedure for reviewing long-range plans periodically in the light of new information, evaluation and analysis, and translating changes of plans into budgetary and legislative consequences.

We worked on all six of these premises at once. What follows is a brief attempt to describe what we did and what we learned from the experience.

PROGRAM BUDGET AND INFORMATION SYSTEM

The secretary of HEW now has some new tools which he did not have three years ago. He has a program budget and information system which enable him to get a better grasp of what HEW does and where the money goes than he could get from the budget in appropriations terms.

Making up a program budget involves identifying the major objectives and subobjectives of the department to which resources are devoted. In a complex operation like HEW, where many programs have multiple objectives, there is certainly no unique way of organizing a program budget. We tried several ways

and did not find an ideal one. Our first attempt at a program budget was organized under three major objectives of department activity: (1) "human investment"—improving the earning capacity and ability to function of individuals and families, (2) providing income and other benefits to individuals and families, and (3) institutional and community development. These three categories cut across the organizational lines of the department. Manpower training programs managed in various parts of the department, for example, were grouped together in category (1) while construction programs of various sorts were put together in category (3). This crosscutting was useful for some purposes, but not for others. It made it difficult, for example, to look at education as a whole and see the relationship between department programs to provide services for children and those for training the teachers needed to provide those services. To facilitate looking at these questions, we moved in the next program budget to the more conventional major objectives of (1) improving health, (2) improving education, (3) income maintenance, and (4) social and rehabilitative services.

The program information system sorts out department funds not only by program objectives, but also by population group served, type of activity, method of finance, and so forth. Using the information system, the secretary can see, for example, what portion of the department's resources go for health; within health, how much is for the development of health resources; and within health resources, how much is for the training of physicians. He can see who is helped by HEW programs—how much goes to the old, the young, the poor. He can see what means are used to further objectives —how much for construction, how much for research. He can see how much goes to the states in formula grants, and how much in the form of project grants. He can also see how all these proportions have changed over the last several years.

These are important questions, and the answers do not leap out of the appropriations budget. Some of these questions had, of course, been asked before by secretaries or by members of Congress, and estimates of the answers had been painstakingly put together, but now the secretary has ready access to this kind of information on a regular basis.

In my opinion, the greatest impact of the program information system has been in facilitating some simple calculations at high levels of aggregation. My favorite example is Secretary Cohen's astonishment at a table showing that most of the department's recent budget increases had been devoted to older people and relatively little to children. Why the father of Medicare should have been surprised at this, I do not know, but he was; and he immediately began talking about a new emphasis on programs for children.

Granted that a program budget can provide useful information to decision makers and new ways of looking at programs, how useful is a program budget as a decision tool? Our HEW experience indicates, I think, that a program budget is a useful *planning* tool, but at the moment of budget decision making the

program budget cannot be substituted for the appropriations budget. Both are necessary. Let me explain this.

HEW operates under several hundred legislative authorities and separate appropriations categories. Sensible planning necessitates organizing these activities in terms of major objectives and subobjectives of the department and deciding on the relative emphasis to be given to these various objectives and subobjectives. For example, planning for health has to involve such questions as these: What should the department be doing to improve the access of individuals to medical care by providing them the means of paying for such care? How much effort should the department be making to increase the supply of medical services by training doctors or building hospitals, or other means? To what extent should the department be investing in future medical discoveries rather than present provision of services? On the education side, planning for the department must involve questions such as these: Should the department expand its aid to elementary and secondary education at a more rapid rate than its aid to higher education? Should it increase the proportion of resources devoted to improving the education of the poor rather than that of the whole population? How much emphasis should be put on finding new methods and approaches to education as opposed to increasing resources going into the present system?

Obviously a program budget cannot answer these questions, but it is a useful framework for laying out the choices so that decisions can be made about them. Once these major decisions are made, however, they cannot automatically be translated into a budget to be sent to the president and the Congress. Each of the several hundred programs operated by HEW has unique characteristics. It has a legislative history and an authorization level. It is handled by a particular committee or subcommittee whose chairman may have definite views. It may have a strong lobby supporting it or gunning for it. It may be administered by states or localities or other non-federal institutions. All of these particular characteristics or programs are relevant to a decision to translate a program budget decision into budgetary and legislative terms. For example, a secretary of HEW may decide to increase the resources devoted to experimenting with new methods in education. Once he has decided that, however, he is confronted with where to put the money. Should he use Title III of the Elementary and Secondary Education Act, which is largely controlled by the states? Should he use the regional laboratories under Title IV of the same act which are administered in an entirely different way and have different strengths and weaknesses? Should he ask for a new authorization and run the risk that a committee which has shown itself reluctant to fund new programs will deny him the funds? No matter how useful the program budget proves, as a way of organizing information and as a planning tool, the final decisions on the budget must be made in appropriations terms and in the light of all of these complicated

considerations which, though they may not be desirable, are facts of life for a secretary of Health, Education, and Welfare.

The answer to the question "Have decisions been made in program budget terms in HEW?" is both "Yes" and "No." Since the advent of PPB, major decisions have been made in program budget terms—decisions to emphasize health services for the poor, family planning, education research and innovation, efforts to help welfare recipients become self-supporting, etc. The process of translating these major decisions into appropriations terms, however, necessitates continuous walking back and forth between the two sets of budget categories. At some points in the decision process the program budget formulation was extremely helpful to the decision makers, especially, I think, in the health area where it facilitated joint consideration of health programs administered in several different agencies. At other points the program budget seemed to make decisions more complicated because a particular appropriation was either buried in a larger total or split among several program categories. For example, Title I of the Elementary and Secondary Education Act is primarily an education program, but provides some funds for health services for disadvantaged children. An estimate of the health expenditures from Title I showed up in the program budget under "health." At the moment of decision on "how much for Title I?" it was necessary to add the two pieces together and make a decision on Title I as an entity.

I see no simple solution to this

problem, although simplification of the HEW appropriations structure would help. Both kinds of budgets are necessary to good decision-making, and HEW executives simply have to be adroit at considering decisions both in program and in appropriations terms, and translating back and forth frequently.

EVALUATION: MEASUREMENT OF PROGRAM ACCOMPLISHMENT

The second result of PPB in HEW has been a new emphasis on evaluation of what programs actually do. The first step was to collect information on a regular basis about the "outputs" of programs. The secretary now has available in the program information system a continuing series of measures of the "outputs" of individual programs—hospital beds constructed, teachers trained, patients served, persons participating in basic literacy programs, etc. In some cases it was almost impossible to find a meaningful output measure for a program. "Number of research projects supported," for example, is not an interesting statistic. Yet, it is the only readily available measure of output of a research program. At best, these output measures are rough guides to what the program is buying, and can be useful in showing the secretary what he would give up if he shifted money from one program to another. For example, how many nurses does one give up to train a psychiatrist, or how many teachers could be trained for the price of a hospital bed? These statistics are better than no information on what the program is buying, but they do not throw much light on what is actually being accomplished. They do not tell the secretary what the program is contributing to the health or education or welfare of the nation.

Evaluating the effectiveness of most HEW programs is difficult—not because the people who run them are incompetent or falsify the information, but for at least three more basic reasons. First, it is usually far from obvious what one would *like* to have happen—what the measure of success of the program should be. For example, Title I of the Elementary and Secondary Education Act gives money to school districts to improve the education of disadvantaged children. Should we look for a measure of success of this program in the test scores of these children, in their dropout rates, in their future ability to hold a job, or in some measure of their attitude toward themselves and their environment? Second, most HEW programs are designed to help individuals function better. Their success can only be gauged by following the individuals over some considerable period of time to find out what actually happened to them. Followup is expensive even if done on a sample basis. Third, it is difficult to disentangle the effects of HEW programs from all the other things which affect the health, education, and welfare of individuals. If infant mortality drops in a particular locality, it may be the result of a prenatal care program, or better nutrition, or higher incomes, or a lower birth rate, or a combination of all of these things. In some cases, control groups and sophisticated statistical techniques can help sort out these various factors; in some cases, they cannot.

Can a government agency be expected to evaluate its own programs? In particular, should program managers be expected to participate in evaluation? Can they be objective about their own programs?

Before trying to answer these questions, I think it is important to distinguish two kinds of evaluation. The first (and the one in which Congress seems to be most interested) is overall evaluation of the accomplishment of a program. It is the attempt to answer the question: To what extent is a program meeting its objectives? It amounts to giving a grade—often a pass or a fail grade—to a program as a whole. For example, one might want to know how many additional doctors have been trained as a result of a program of aid to medical schools, how many welfare recipients have become self-supporting as a result of training and day-care programs, or what has happened to the incidence of measles as a result of the measles vaccine program.

While program managers must cooperate in providing the information necessary for these overall evaluations, it is too much to expect them to carry out the evaluation themselves. No one wants to admit failure. In order to insure objectivity, it is necessary to have the information analyzed and judgments made by someone not directly responsible for the execution of the program—perhaps someone outside the government altogether.

For many important HEW programs, however, I think this kind of overall pass-or-fail evaluation is next to impossible. For example, it is not really possible to answer the question, What is Title I of the Elementary and Secondary Education Act accomplishing? Title I provides only a small part of the resources used to educate disadvantaged children, and school itself is only one of the influences (and probably not the most important one) on the performance of these children. If a national testing program showed an increase in the test scores of disadvantaged children, everyone would be happy, but it certainly would not be clear what proportion of this increase, if any, should be attributed to Title I. A negative finding—no change in the tested performance of poor children—might suggest that Title I money was being wasted, but would not prove that nothing could be done through the schools to help these children. Title I funds (as well as other education resources) are spent in many different ways in different localities presumably with varying degrees of effectiveness. The really interesting problem for the evaluator is not to figure out what the average effectiveness of the program is, but to identify the kinds of education projects which are successful with low income children so they can be replicated and expanded.

This second kind of evaluation—that designed to identify successful ways of spending money for a particular objective and to improve the average effectiveness of a program—should be of tremendous importance to a program manager who wants to do a good job. It should have his full support and participation. The manager of a manpower training program should have a strong interest in discovering which types of training projects are most successful. The manager of a family planning program should have a strong interest in discovering which ways of delivering family planning services are the most effective. In the long run, I think this kind of evaluation is of more importance to the wise use of government resources than is the overall pass-or-fail type.

Evaluation—of both types—is still in its infancy in HEW. The planning and evaluation staff has succeeded in getting some funds authorized for evaluation in various legislation and in some cases in getting the funds appropriated. We worked with the staffs of several of the HEW agencies—most notably with the Office of Education—to design evaluation plans, and we funded a number of pilot evaluations. But designing sound evaluation techniques and collecting, processing, and interpreting the information takes time and expert staff resources. These resources are not presently available in HEW, nor is it easy to find them outside the government. To do a good job on evaluation, it will be necessary to recruit a staff of competent people who can work closely with managers of major programs to define what kinds of information are needed, to design a system for collecting this information, and make sure that it does get collected and analyzed.

ANALYSIS OF ALTERNATIVE COURSES OF ACTION

Systematic analysis of alternative ways of reaching objectives is the heart and soul of PPB. A good analysis specifies an agreed-on objective or set of objectives, outlines alternative ways of reaching these objectives, and brings together as much

information as possible about the costs, benefits, advantages, and disadvantages of each. The analyst uses the results of program evaluation and goes beyond them to try to estimate the effectiveness of new programs. In a sense he is an evaluator of programs which do not exist yet.

Analysis of alternatives is, of course, not a new idea. Studies of program alternatives of various sorts have been done in different parts of HEW for years. What was new in the last three years was the existence of a staff of economists and other analysts in the Office of the Secretary which was specifically devoted to studying the major options open to the secretary with respect to budget and legislation. Perhaps even more important was the presence of an assistant secretary in budgetary and legislative decision meetings whose job it was to see that relevant analysis was considered at the decision moment. By way of illustration, let me describe briefly two recent analyses carried out by the planning and evaluation staff at HEW which should be of considerable interest to the Congress and the general public as well as to the executive branch.

The first is a study of higher education undertaken at the request of President Johnson, and released by Secretary Cohen just before he left office.[1] In this study we made an attempt to specify the various objectives which the federal government has in supporting higher education

[1] U.S. Department of Health, Education, and Welfare, *Toward a Long-Range Plan for Federal Financial Support for Higher Education* (Washington, D.C., 1969). Estimates are for the 1960 high school graduating class.

—objectives such as improving access to higher education on the part of all students, improving the quality of higher education by increasing the resources available to institutions, and preserving diversity and autonomy in American higher education. The study examines the available information on the degree of equality of access to higher education on the part of students from different income levels, documenting the fact that students from low-income families have relatively low chances of going to college even if they have high ability. A student of good college potential, scoring in the top two-fifths on high school achievement tests, is more than twice as likely to enter college if he comes from a family in the top quarter of the income distribution than if he comes from one in the bottom quarter.[2] The study also examines available information on the financial health of higher education and the relative strength of public and private institutions. One interesting and somewhat surprising finding of this part of the study was the widening gap in resources per student available in public and private institutions, with *private* institutions enjoying a more rapid increase. Between 1959–60 and 1965–66 the study found:

There was a marked disparity in the rates of increase in revenues per student in public and private institutions, with public institutions' revenues per student increasing 4.0 percent annually while the comparable rate of increase for private institutions was 8.1 percent.[3]

An attempt was made to lay out the major options available to the federal government in support of higher education—the student-aid through loans, grants, the work study-program, and institutional aid of a variety of types—and to evaluate the advantages and disadvantages of these various alternatives as ways of furthering the particular federal objectives. The report contained a set of recommendations, but these may well be of less importance than the analysis itself.

A second analysis which I would like to discuss briefly concerns major alternatives to the present welfare system.[4] Estimates were made of the number of people who would probably still be in poverty five years from now if present welfare programs were continued, and of the cost of such continuation. It was estimated that the cost of present welfare programs would rise from about $3.7 billion in 1969 to perhaps $6.2 billion by 1974, but that poverty would not disappear in this period:

. . . poor households will still number some 8.8 million by 1974, compared to 10.8 million in 1966, even if we are successful in maintaining a high rate of employment and economic growth.[5]

An attempt was made to analyze major alternatives to continuation of the present welfare system. The

---

2 *Ibid.*, p. 5.
3 *Ibid.*, p. 11.

4 U.S. Department of Health, Education, and Welfare, Office of the Assistant Secretary (Planning and Evaluation), *Program Memorandum on Income Maintenance and Social and Rehabilitation Services Programs of DHEW* (November 1968), pp. III.1–III.20.
5 *Ibid.*, p. III.1.

alternatives considered included a children's allowance and a negative income tax-type program which would give aid to the working poor as well as those aided by present welfare programs. The various alternatives were evaluated with respect to cost, coverage, contribution to closing the poverty gap, savings to the states, and their effects on incentives to work, incentives to establish separate households, incentives to move from low to high income states, and other factors.

Analytical effort in HEW has been hampered by two main factors —lack of staff and lack of information. Studies of the sort just described take many man-months of effort. The present staff of analysts under the assistant secretary for planning and evaluation can handle only a small number of studies a year, and must choose the three or four issues which seem likely to be of importance in upcoming budgetary or legislative decisions, perhaps leaving aside issues of more basic long-run importance. Better use could be made of analysts in universities, foundations, and elsewhere if funds were available to finance more outside studies.

The second difficulty (that of lack of information) is more basic. Indeed, it may be that the most important result of the PPB effort in HEW so far has been the discovery of how little is really known, either about the status of the nation's health, education, and welfare, or about what to do to change it. A recent report of the department prepared in the Office of Planning and Evaluation, attempted to measure the nation's progress toward certain widely accepted social goals.[6] The study was an attempt to see what could be said about such questions as: What is the state of the nation's health? Are we getting healthier? Are we better educated? Are we winning the war on poverty? If nothing else, the volume served to illustrate the thinness of social statistics and how little is really known about the state of the nation even with respect to such apparently measurable factors as physical health and intellectual capacity.

The child health study, which has been discussed by Dr. Wholey, is a good example of an analysis which uncovered more questions than it answered.[7] I remember being astonished when we first started the study that doctors could produce no evidence that children who saw doctors regularly were healthier than children who did not. They all believed it (and I do, too), but they did not have any statistics to prove it. I was equally astonished to find that educators have little or no evidence that children who get more expensive education (newer buildings, higher paid teachers, more teachers, etc.) learn more than children who get less expensive education. They believe it (and so do I), but the available statistics do not prove it, nor does presently available information

[6] U.S. Department of Health, Education, and Welfare, *Toward a Social Report* (Washington, D.C., January 1969).

[7] See Joseph Wholey, "The Absence of Program Evaluation as an Obstacle to Effective Public Expenditure Policy: A Case Study of Child Health Care Programs," in U.S. Congress, Joint Economic Committee, *The Analysis and Evaluation of Public Expenditure: The PPB System, op. cit.,* vol. 1, pp. 451–72.

give any solid clues about what kinds of schools are best, or whether particular educational methods are more effective than others.

Analysis, experimentation, and evaluation must proceed together if we are to make progress in providing decisionmakers with good bases for decisions in health, education, and welfare. Serious effort on the evaluation of federal programs would give the analyst more data. Additional analyses will also provide a better idea of where the gaps in information are and what kind of statistics should be collected.

SOME CONCLUSIONS FROM EXPERIENCE

Anyone who thought that PPBS was a magic formula to make the allocation of federal resources easy had better think again. There is no magic formula because these decisions are inherently difficult. They are difficult, first, because they are made in the face of great uncertainty and, second, because the outcomes affect different groups of people importantly and differently. Far from making the decisions easier, the PPB system has undoubtedly made decision makers more aware than ever before of how hard the decisions they have to make really are.

In the defense area, uncertainty is the dominant difficulty. Good analysis of the costs and effectiveness of alternative U.S. actions is highly useful, but it can only reduce the uncertainties by a small percentage. A tremendous amount of guesswork about enemy motivations and inten-

sions is still necessary. There is little room for experiment. Decisions are not made in small, discrete steps but tend to be of the all-or-nothing variety, and the cost of making a mistake is great.

In the domestic area, the uncertainty surrounding decisions *need* not be so great, although at present it probably is. It would be possible to run domestic programs as a continuous series of experiments—to try different things, to evaluate the results, to expand those that work well, and cut back on those that do not. Good evaluation systems will certainly not be quick or easy, but they can be used to make programs far more effective than they are now, not just at the federal level but at all levels of government. The potentiality of PPBS for reducing the uncertainty surrounding decisions seems to me far greater in the domestic than in the defense area.

The other difficulty—the differential impact of decisions on people—is, however, far more obvious and troublesome in the domestic than in foreign area. Defense decisions result in some people being better protected or bearing a heavier burden than others, but these differential effects are not nearly so obvious as in domestic programs. In domestic programs of direct service to particular types of people, everyone knows who the immediate beneficiaries are. A good PBB system can illuminate these distributional decisions, but cannot make them any easier. Indeed, assembling and publicizing information on who is helped by particular government programs may intensify political conflict.

I view PPBS as a commonsense

approach to decision making. The terminology may well change—and probably should—but I fail to see how a secretary of Health, Education, and Welfare who wants to do a good job can get along without planning ahead, evaluating the effectiveness of programs, analyzing alternatives carefully, and making decisions in an orderly way in the light of maximum information. It does not matter what he chooses to call it, but he badly needs the basic tools of PPBS.

The progress made in the department in the last three years is clearly a start toward improved decision making, but it is only a start. More attention needs to be paid to evaluation, and more resources need to be devoted to building up a con-tinuous flow of useful information on the effectiveness of programs. Far more resources need to be devoted to good analysis, especially to understanding the complicated interactions between federal programs and what happens in the state, local, and private sectors. Better ways need to be found within the department for focusing attention on major long-run decisions, and considering budgetary and legislative options at the same time. Above all, the secretary himself has to use the system. If he wants good analysis, he will get it. If he wants good information, he will get it. If he wants to make decisions in an orderly way, considering all important options carefully and systematically, he will, with patience, be able to do so.

Index

Ackoff, R. L., 100
Addams, Jane, 6
Adrian, Charles R., 230
Ahearn, Frederick L., Jr., 14
Aiken, Michael, 16, 147, 148, 153ff, 156, 157, 159, 162, 163
Alba, Victor, 121, 132
Alexis, M., 347
Alford, Robert R., 16, 147, 148, 153ff, 156, 162
Alinsky, Saul D., 7, 12, 66, 231
Allport, Gordon W., 235
Alonso, William, 4
Altshuler, Alan, 52, 178
Andrews, F. M., 348
Argyris, C., 164, 178
Armstrong, David A., 50
Arnoff, E. L., 100
Arnstein, Sherry R., 16, 150, 151, 237ff, 261, 335, 354
Arrow, Kenneth J., 88
Austin, George A., 88

Bachrach, Peter, 64
Backstrom, Charles H., 213ff
Baida, Robert, 256, 258
Baker, Elizabeth, 153
Bales, R. F., 164, 178, 335, 347
Banfield, Edward C., 15, 21, 44ff, 101, 121, 132, 163, 170, 178, 194, 288
Barnard, Chester, 166, 178, 186
Barnett, H. G., 162
Bauer, Raymond, 131, 132
Baumheier, E. S., 378, 379
Bavelas, A., 171, 178
Beckman, Norman, 52
Bell, R., 170, 178
Bellush, Jewel, 162, 185
Bennett, Eleanor C., 15, 269, 311ff
Bennis, Warren, 129, 132
Bentham, Jeremy, 45

Bentley, Arthur F., 213, 214
Berelson, B., 166, 178
Berger, P., 164, 178
Berry, P. C., 338, 348
Bishop, Sharon, 320
Blank, David, 53
Blau, Peter M., 182, 206, 274, 275, 279, 280, 281, 288
Block, C. H., 338, 348
Bolan, Richard S., 14, 15, 148, 164ff, 172, 178, 179
Borus, M. E., 378
Boulding, Kenneth E., 90, 120, 132
Bradshaw, Jonathan, 267, 290ff, 297, 300, 308
Brager, George, 16, 151, 226ff, 356
Braybrooke, David, 87, 90, 129, 132
Bredemeier, Harry G., 349
Broom, Leonard, 183
Brown, Charlane, 147
Bruner, Jerome S., 87, 128, 132
Brymer, Richard, 356
Buckle, J., 300, 309, 310
Burke, Edmund M., 14, 21, 47, 164, 179
Burns, Eveline M., 269
Burton, Ian, 131

Callahan, James J., Jr., 204
Campbell, J. P., 328, 347, 348
Cartwright, D., 164, 168, 179
Cartwright, Timothy J., 76, 77, 119ff, 130
Chapin, F. Stuart, Jr., 163
Chevalier, Michel, 125, 130, 132
Churchill, Winston, 40
Churchman, C. West, 100, 265
Clark, Burton R., 351
Clark, Terry N., 147, 153, 157, 162, 164, 179